The Book of Revelation

2nd Edition

by Larry R. Helyer and Richard Wagner

for dummies®

A Wiley Brand

The Book of Revelation For Dummies®, 2nd Edition

Published by: **John Wiley & Sons, Inc.**, 111 River Street, Hoboken, NJ 07030-5774, www.wiley.com

For general information on our other products and services, please contact our Customer Care Department within the U.S. at 877-762-2974, outside the U.S. at 317-572-3993, or fax 317-572-4002. For technical support, please visit https://hub.wiley.com/community/support/dummies.

Wiley publishes in a variety of print and electronic formats and by print-on-demand. Some material included with standard print versions of this book may not be included in e-books or in print-on-demand. If this book refers to media such as a CD or DVD that is not included in the version you purchased, you may download this material at http://booksupport.wiley.com. For more information about Wiley products, visit www.wiley.com.

Library of Congress Control Number is available from the publisher.

ISBN 978-1-394-37082-5 (pbk); ISBN 978-1-394-37083-2 (ebk); ISBN 978-1-394-37084-9 (ebk)

Contents at a Glance

Table of Contents

Introduction

A common cartoon theme involves a person wearing a sandwich sign or carrying a poster that proclaims, "Repent! The end is near!" What's implied is that some sudden, violent event is just around the corner and that people need to brace themselves for whatever's coming. And usually, the end that's near involves something terrifying.

The idea of a dramatic and destructive end to the earth has been around for ages. It's the stuff of some great sci-fi movies, and a lot of the elements that go into these stories come right out of the Bible. In fact, terms such as *repent* and *antichrist* and *Armageddon* are direct references to messages, characters, and events that make up the book of Revelation. When you examine these themes and images in the context of religion, faith, and biblical history, things get even more interesting.

The book of Revelation is not an easy read. Some people, after slogging through Revelation, seem to suffer from PTRRD: Post-Traumatic Revelation Reading Disorder. Maybe you've had this experience. You start reading with a rush of enthusiasm, and all goes well through the first three chapters and their letters to the seven churches. Then things start to get hairy: visions from heaven, creatures with eyes covering their bodies, plagues, horses of different colors, angels everywhere. Seven seals are opened, seven trumpets are sounded, seven bowls are poured out, and things get really confusing. Throw in grapes of wrath, red dragons, giant hail, and something called the rapture, and, well, you get the idea. *Lost* becomes more than just the name of a television series — it's the perfect descriptor of your mental state.

My intent is to help you avoid PTRRD. I act as your tour guide to help you navigate the amazing book of Revelation. Even if you can't figure out every single detail, clues that open large chunks of the text abound. I promise you'll come away with a better understanding of what Revelation is about, as well as a ton of cool information that you can sprinkle into conversations and impress your friends!

About This Book

The first thing you may discover is that there's no consensus on how to interpret the book of Revelation. About the only thing all serious students of Revelation can agree on is that in the end, good wins over evil. Theological views about what happens, when it happens, and to whom it happens vary widely. In *The Book of Revelation For Dummies*, 2nd Edition, I introduce the leading views and point you to some of the most likely meanings.

Revelation is arguably the most perplexing book in all the Bible, so my goal is to be clear and concise. Therefore, I aim for an easy-to-understand, approachable discussion, without trying to bombard you with a lot of theological gobbledygook.

The topics in the book are logically ordered, so you can read from start to finish if you want to. But this is a reference book, so don't feel you have to read it from cover to cover. You may prefer to browse the Table of Contents, flip through the pages, or thumb through the index to locate a topic that you find particularly engaging.

To make sure you get the most out of this book, keep the following conventions and definitions in mind.

>> **Apocalypse:** The word *apocalypse* has become associated with a devastating event, including the end of the world. But the primary meaning is "an unveiling or revealing." The book of Revelation reveals how the world ends and so is called an apocalypse. Scholars refer to any literature that addresses the end of the world as *apocalyptic.*

>> **Bible references:** The Bible verses I quote are from the New Revised Standard Version translation, unless otherwise noted. I cite passages using the standard convention, *Book chapter: verse.* For example, John 3:16 refers to *John* as a book of the Bible, 3 as a chapter of the book, and 16 as a verse in the chapter. If you don't see a colon in a Bible reference, the number refers to an entire chapter; in other words, Rev. 4–5 means chapters 4 through 5 of the book of Revelation.

When I refer to the *Old Testament,* I'm talking about the sacred Scriptures that Christianity shares with Judaism. Jews refer to them as the *Tanak,* or Hebrew Bible. For Protestants and Jews, they consist of the same 39 books; Catholics include several additional books, collectively called the *Apocrypha.*

I occasionally refer to Jewish works that aren't part of the Bible, such as *1 Enoch.* If you're really interested in reading the book of *1 Enoch,* check out the English translation with introduction and notes by E. Isaac in James H. Charlesworth, ed., *Volume 1. The Old Testament Pseudepigrapha: Apocalyptic Literature & Testaments* (Doubleday). See also Larry R. Helyer, *Exploring Jewish Literature of the Second Temple Period: A Guide for New Testament Students* (InterVarsity).

>> **Christianity:** For the purposes of this book, *historic Christianity, biblical Christianity,* and *orthodox Christianity* are interchangeable terms. Each speaks

of beliefs that the church has historically held for some 2,000 years. Simply put, Christianity is Trinitarian (believing in one God existing in three persons, Father, Son, and Holy Spirit), based on the life, death, and resurrection Jesus Christ and his teachings, and embraces the entire Bible as authoritative and reliable.

>> **Dates:** When I refer to dates, I use the newer designations BCE (before common era) and CE (common era) rather than the more traditional BC (before Christ) and AD (*Anno Domini,* in the year of the Lord). If you're unfamiliar with the newer terms, no sweat. The year 34 BCE is the same as 34 BC, and 1050 CE is equivalent to AD 1050.

>> **Names of God:** Although God has many names, I generally use *God* and *Lord* in this book. Also, in accordance with historical usage, I use the traditional masculine pronoun *he* to refer to God.

>> **Prophecy and prophesying:** People often think of prophecy as being limited to future events. But from a biblical perspective, *prophecy* is a noun that refers to something more general: the act of speaking the mind and counsel of God. Biblical prophets were, in a sense, the mouthpiece of God, delivering important information to God's people. Biblical prophecy, among other things, addressed current events, offered guidance on behavior, revealed elements of the character of God, reassured God's people, and often predicted future events. Sometimes, prophecy about the future was conditional: If bad behavior continued, bad things would happen; if behavior was brought back in line with God's will, bad things would be averted. The point is that biblically speaking, prophecy is more about forthtelling (preaching) than foretelling.

Note that *prophesy* is a verb describing what prophets do: Prophets prophesy prophecy!

>> **Cross-references:** Cross-references to another chapter within this book are capitalized by the word *Chapter* before the chapter number; when referring to a book of the Bible, the word *chapter* is lowercased.

Foolish Assumptions

In writing this book, I don't assume any religious commitment for the reader. Regardless of your faith background, you're probably curious about biblical prophecy and the book of Revelation. If so, this book's for you!

Although I don't assume you have previous knowledge of the Christian Bible, you probably have access to one — either in print or online — so you can check out references to specific Bible passages.

Icons Used in This Book

The icons in this book help you quickly identify specific kinds of information that may be of use to you:

REMEMBER

The Remember icon highlights important ideas for you to keep in mind to deepen your understanding of Revelation.

TIP

This icon draws attention to important points that help you make sense of Revelation's prophecy.

WARNING

Steer clear of the pitfalls flagged in the Warning paragraphs.

TECHNICAL STUFF

The Technical Stuff icon indicates more advanced or scholarly information about the topic being discussed. It's useful but not essential for an overall understanding of the discussion.

Beyond the Book

If you're looking for a handy reference to quickly access key information, consider visiting the Dummies website to find the Cheat Sheet created for this book. Just head to www.dummies.com and search for "Revelation For Dummies" to get concise summaries and tips.

The Cheat Sheet gives you a brief overview of the book's content, providing both a structured outline of Revelation and clear explanations of key terms to help you understand the different ways it can be interpreted. Important reading strategies are emphasized, and you'll also find a chart that summarizes the main perspectives on the Millennium, allowing you to quickly compare each viewpoint and see how it influences other themes throughout Revelation.

Where to Go from Here

Revelation For Dummies, 2nd Edition, is organized into four sections:

>> Part 1 serves as a guide to the book's structure; delves into questions about the author's identity, era, and context; and highlights key Old Testament connections that enrich your understanding of Revelation.

>> Part 2 examines the four principal interpretive frameworks used to approach Revelation, ultimately favoring a blended or eclectic perspective.

>> Part 3, the most extensive section, offers an in-depth exploration of the book's intricate storyline, leading you from the historical context of the first century CE all the way to the grand finale — redemptive history's conclusion in the New Jerusalem.

>> Part 4 offers great tips and insights for studying and reading Revelation and prophecy.

Now that you're at the end of the introduction, you have your boarding pass and are ready to begin your journey into the apocalyptic world of Revelation. You have several routes to choose from as you begin your trip:

>> If you're interested in reading the book from cover to cover, turn the page and proceed to Chapter 1.

>> If you'd like to know who this guy called John is (who wrote the book), go to Chapter 2.

>> To get a perspective on the major ways people interpret Revelation, check out Chapter 4.

>> If you'd like to use this book as a companion guide as you're simultaneously reading your Bible, turn directly to Part 3.

>> If you like to read the last page of a novel first, then read Chapters 14 and 15. They tell you how it all turns out in the end!

1
Revealing the End of the Biblical Story

Get a bird's eye view of Revelation's structure, leading themes, and symbolism.

Explore the book's author, the recipients, and the probable date of composition.

Examine the background of Revelation in Old Testament prophecy, especially the 70 weeks of Daniel 9.

Delve into apocalyptic literature and its pervasive influence on the mood, themes, and imagery of Revelation.

Chapter **1**

One Man's Visions, All Mankind's Destiny

Many people love fantasy stories populated with strange apparitions. Others love a good mystery. And still others love an adventure story full of action and battle scenes. If you fall into one of those camps, you're in luck. The book of Revelation is all these and more.

But a word of caution: Revelation is also a challenging book. It's full of grotesque creatures like a red dragon, two beasts, and demonic locusts. And rather than following a straight, chronological storyline, it's punctuated by backtracks, delays, and interludes. Further adding to the degree of difficulty, the whole package comes as a series of prophetic visions, each requiring decoding and unpacking — no small task!

This chapter doesn't try to explore the symbolism behind the events that are chronicled throughout Revelation (I save that for Chapter 5). It also doesn't pore over the details of these events, personalities, and issues (that's what Part 3 is all about). Rather, I get you started in the right direction by painting in broad strokes the structure and content of the final book of the Bible. Along the way, I point you to parts of this book where you can find more details on each specific subject.

Why Read Revelation, Anyway?

Humans have always had an insatiable curiosity to know their future and what's going to happen in the "last days." That's at least part of the reason the *Left Behind* series was popular and why new Nostradamus documentaries and end-of-the-world sci-fi movies show up almost every year. For many, the appeal in reading and understanding Revelation is, quite frankly, not altogether different from the desire to peek into a fortune teller's crystal ball. Doomsday cults and survivalists thrive on supposed insider information about the End Times, some of it drawn from the book of Revelation!

Making sense of Revelation can be tough going because of its structure, symbolism, and divergent interpretations. You can easily become discouraged and wonder why you should even bother to read it. Here are several reasons why I consider Revelation essential reading:

>> **It provides a fitting conclusion to the entire Bible.** No one likes a cliffhanger, and each part of the Bible offers an episode or theme in a larger, connected story. The story is one of redemption that begins with Adam and Eve's expulsion from the Garden (Gen 3) and culminates in a joyous return of the redeemed to a New Garden (Rev 22). In short, the book of Revelation offers the ultimate conclusion!

>> **It helps explain the biblical view of God and his relationship with humans.** Many people turn to Revelation in search of definitive answers about what will happen. Revelation does that, but it provides so much more. Above all else, God's majestic sovereignty, his impartial justice, and his amazing grace shine forth. The book of Revelation is good news because nothing in all creation "will be able to separate [God's people] from the love of God in Christ Jesus our Lord" (Rom 8:19).

>> **It gives readers a glimpse of heaven.** The Bible offers few specifics on what heaven will be like. The Old Testament gives only a few glimmers of what is popularly referred to as "heaven." Jesus and his apostles provide a few more details in the New Testament. But saving the best for last, the final chapters of Revelation offer a grand unveiling of the new earth God has prepared for his people. John's vision pictures that blessed state as a new city (the New Jerusalem) and a new garden (the Garden of Eden) both of which are pristine and perfect (see Chapter 14).

>> **It offers a message of hope.** It's easy to be a little freaked out by the gloom and doom warnings of the book. But despite all the battles, beasts, and bad things depicted, Revelation is really all about hope. It portrays, in vivid detail, the biblical view of good triumphing over evil and suffering.

Gaining a Bird's Eye View of Revelation

A major challenge in reading Revelation is sorting out and identifying the leading themes and primary storyline while a kaleidoscope of images leaps off the page. But if you take a step back and get a solid understanding of the big picture, you can begin to dive into the details and make sense of how they all fit together. It's somewhat like tackling a large puzzle. First you sort the pieces by color and pattern and then work on the borders. After that you're ready to assemble the centerpieces.

Although Revelation contains a lot of confusing symbolism and has many interpretations (see Chapter 4 for a discussion of these interpretations), the book falls into six sections, and I offer an overview of each of these parts in the following sections.

Prologue and inaugural vision (1)

The first chapter of Revelation functions as a prologue (introduction) to the entire book. It provides the context for understanding what follows (see Chapter 6), reveals the central character, the Son of Man (Jesus Christ), identifies the author, and states the purpose of the book. Within the first several verses, you discover that

>> Jesus Christ reveals "what must soon take place" (1:1 and 3).

>> The author is John, a servant of Christ and fellow sufferer with his readers (1:1, 4, and 9).

>> The initial audience are members of seven churches in the province of Asia (1:4).

>> John wrote his book on the island of Patmos (1:9 and 11).

>> The purpose of the book is to encourage readers by what they hear (1:3).

The prologue indicates how the book came to be written: God gave the revelation to Jesus, who communicated it to John through an angel sent for this specific purpose. John apparently received the content through a series of visions. After pondering these visions and their relationship to redemptive history in the Hebrew Bible, Jewish traditions, and early Christian traditions, he composed the present document. As you will see, however, many aspects of this document also reflect the Greco-Roman culture in which John lived. Finally, he dispatched a trusted messenger (or messengers) to hand-deliver it to seven churches of the Roman province called Asia (Rev. 2–3). See Chapter 7 for details.

Today's readers constitute a secondary audience for this book thanks to the original readers who copied and forwarded John's letter to contemporary churches. This process was repeated many times throughout church history up until the 15th century CE. Figure 1-1 shows the chain of transmission.

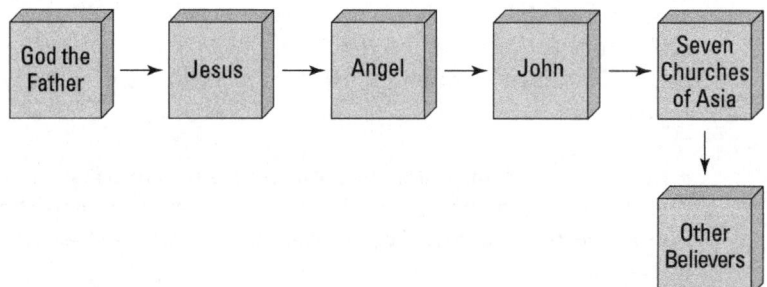

FIGURE 1-1:
Passing on the book of Revelation.

REMEMBER

One of the keys to understanding the basic structure of Revelation is in 1:19. In this passage, Jesus instructs John, "Write, therefore, what you have seen, what is now, and what will take place later." Although scholars offer various interpretations of the verb tenses of this verse, the grammar and structure of the book point to a threefold timing of events: past, present, and future. In other words, Jesus tells John to write about

>> The vision of the risen Christ he *has already seen* (Rev. 1)

>> The *current* condition of the seven churches (Rev. 2–3)

>> The events that *will take place* at some unspecified time ("after this") in the future (Rev. 4–22)

TECHNICAL STUFF

Some scholars hold that the first phrase in 1:19 ("what you have seen") refers to the totality of what John sees as described in the entire book. The next phrase ("what is") refers to the messages to the seven churches. The third phrase ("what is to take place after this") refers to the series of visions in chapters 4–22.

Figure 1-2 shows how Revelation 1:19 provides a broad chronology for looking at the entire book.

The importance of the inaugural vision can hardly be overstated. The risen Christ assures John that death no longer holds believers in fear (1:17–18). That is precisely the message Christians in the seven churches needed to hear, a message of hope that has sustained Christians for nearly two thousand years.

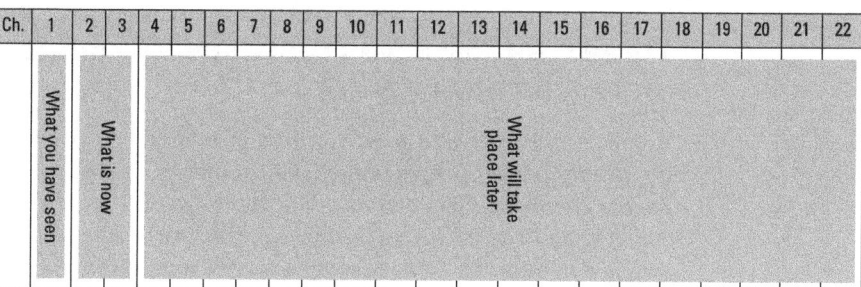

FIGURE 1-2:
Revelation
1:19 provides a
broad overview
of the book.

The figure shows a chart with "Ch." and chapters numbered 1 through 22. The sections labeled: "What you have seen" (Ch. 1), "What is now" (Ch. 2–3), and "What will take place later" (Ch. 4–22).

Messages to seven churches (2–3)

Revelation 2–3 contains individual messages that Jesus dictates for the seven churches in Asia (see Chapter 7). Each of these churches is in a different spiritual state. For the faithful churches in Smyrna and Philadelphia, Jesus offers only encouragement for their steadfast faith. For the churches in Sardis, Ephesus, Pergamum, and Thyatira, he commends them for some aspects of their faith but also rebukes them for specific areas of failure. Finally, for the church in Laodicea, there is no commendation, only rebuke. The church is urgently summoned to repent.

Ascent to the throne room (4–5)

John's rapture to the throne room has immense significance for the rest of the book of Revelation. This awesome glimpse into the heavenly control room around which the entire universe revolves assures readers then and now that the sovereign God is in complete control of all things. John's vision conveys visually and aurally what the Apostle Paul writes in Romans 8:28: "We know that all things work together for good for those who love God, who are called according to his purpose."

End of everything old (6–19)

The old order doesn't depart without a fight. The Dark Lord pulls out all stops to maintain his grip on planet Earth and the humans who inhabit it. Satan's kingdom of darkness, however, is no match for the kingdom of light ruled over by the rightful King. The Lion of the tribe of Judah, who is also the Lamb of God (Rev 5:5–6), unleashes a series of judgments that bring it crashing down and prepare the way for a brand-new world.

Three heptads: Seven seals, seven trumpets, and seven bowls (6–16)

Revelation chapters 6–16 move through a series of progressively severe judgments consisting of three *heptads*, which means a set of seven. The three sets are tiered: The seals affect one fourth of the earth; the trumpets are more extensive (one third of the earth) and intensive; the bowls are global in extent and catastrophic in intensity. I describe these heptads in the following list:

>> **Seals:** Judgments begin in Revelation 6 when the Lamb (Jesus) breaks seven seals of a heavenly scroll. As each seal is opened, a judgment occurs (see Chapter 9).

>> **Trumpets:** After the Lamb opens the seventh seal, there is a period of silence for half an hour. Then seven angels blow seven trumpets in succession. As each is sounded, a more severe judgment occurs (Chapter 10).

>> **Bowls:** The last judgments are unleashed when seven angels pour out seven bowls of God's wrath on the earth (Chapter 12). There is no escape and no shelter.

There is no consensus on how the seals, trumpets, and bowls are interrelated. Some scholars argue that the events are sequential, while others believe they occur simultaneously or overlap. Additionally, some interpret them in purely symbolic terms. In Chapter 9 of this book, I offer my take on the relationship between the heptads.

TIP

As you read Revelation 6–20, don't expect a single, linear storyline. The narrative includes a series of interludes that pause the action and zoom in on certain aspects of the main story.

Judgment on Babylon the Great (17–18)

Revelation 17–18 graphically portray the destruction of Babylon the Great. Unpacking the meaning of the city and the woman symbolically associated with it requires a broad-ranging synthesis of many biblical texts, as well as explorations into the trappings of Imperial Rome during the late first century CE. I reserve for Chapter 11 a discussion of the identity and catastrophic end of this mysterious city and the prostitute who ruthlessly rules over it.

Revelation 19–20 take up the counterpoint city and the woman who reigns there, namely, the New Jerusalem and the spotless Bride of Christ (see Chapter 14 for further explanation).

Triumph of the Crucified (19)

The three heptads and the fall of Babylon the Great set the stage for the grand finale, the second coming of Jesus (the first coming was his earthly life), and the battle of Armageddon, in which Jesus leads his angelic army to victory over Satan's forces (see Chapter 12). Satan is bound for 1,000 years, commonly known as the *Millennium* (see Chapter 13). During this time, Jesus and his faithful followers reign on earth. At the end of this period, Satan is loosed one final time to deceive the nations of the world. Jesus, however, decisively defeats the Satanic hordes and consigns Satan to the lake of fire forever (Rev. 20:10).

Beginning of everything new (20:1–22:5)

What a contrast for the church after King Jesus returns and installs his kingdom on earth! No longer buffeted by Satan's attacks, infiltrated by false teachers or weakened by lax and indifferent believers, the church reigns alongside her victorious king. It is at long last the fulfillment of the Lord's Prayer, "Your kingdom come. Your will be done, on earth as it is in heaven" (Matthew 6:10).

REMEMBER

A controversial aspect of this victorious kingdom on earth revolves around the meaning of the Millennium — is it literal or figurative? I take up this contentious issue in Chapter 13 explaining the options and allowing you to draw your own conclusion.

In Revelation 20:11–15 all stand before a great white throne. God judges each person impartially in accordance with two books: a book of deeds and a book of life. Believers in Jesus — those whose names are found in the book of life — are welcomed into the holy city (see Chapter 13). Those whose names don't make the guest list are thrown into the lake of fire (Rev. 20:15).

Revelation 21:1–22:7 takes you on a guided tour of the New Jerusalem, the permanent home of all God's redeemed people. The holy city is situated in a new heaven and a new earth. This new world is more than just an improved version of the current one; it's a perfect world in which God himself dwells with his people (Rev. 21:3–5). See Chapter 14 for details.

Epilogue and concluding vision (Rev. 22:6–21)

Mirroring the inaugural vision, this brief section features encouragement, exhortation, and a warning. The story has been told. Redemptive history has arrived at its destination. Not all, however, will enjoy the blessing and bliss of the New Jerusalem. You read about those outside the city. They may not enter. That is all John says about it. Chapter 15 explains more about this difficult topic.

John closes out Revelation with an epilogue that marks the end of his prophecy (see Chapter 15). The major refrain in this final section of the book is Jesus's three fold reminder, "Behold, I am coming soon!" (Rev. 22:7, 22:12, 22:20).

Each of these announcements precedes a call:

>> **Obedience:** A call to "keep the words contained in this book" (22:7)

>> **Action:** A call to act because he will "give to everyone according to what he has done" (22:12)

>> **Faith:** A call to believe Jesus when he says he is coming and to be able to testify to that claim to the rest of the world (22:20)

Delays and interludes

Inserted into the narrative flow of Revelation is a series of delays and interludes that amplify and augment the primary storyline. These interludes include the following:

>> **Interlude 1:** After the sixth seal, there is an interlude in which 144,000 believers from the twelve tribes of Israel are sealed and sanctified. These are joined by an innumerable multitude that come "out of the great ordeal" (see Chapter 9). At Revelation 8:1, after the seventh seal is broken, you expect the end. Instead, there's a slight delay of half an hour. Much more about John's masterful use of delay later.

>> **Interlude 2:** After sounding the sixth trumpet, an angel appears with a little scroll which John eats. Then two witnesses prophesy for 3.5 years after which they are martyred (Chapter 10).

>> **Interlude 3:** After the seventh trumpet sounds accompanied by an angelic anthem, God's Temple opens, and you expect the grand finale. Instead, John gives a rather lengthy interlude consisting of five zoom-in episodes. These episodes include:

- A woman, a child, and a red dragon (Rev. 12)

- Two bad-boy beasts of the Dark Lord (Rev. 13)

- On Mount Zion with the Lamb (Rev. 14:1–5)

- Three angelic announcements (Rev. 14:6–13)

- End-time harvest and vintage (Rev 14:14–20)

>> **Interlude 4:** After the seven bowls of God's wrath are poured out, you once again expect the end. But John pauses the action and zooms in on five episodes before revealing God's end game. These episodes include:

- Vision of Babylon the Great and the prostitute (Rev. 17)

- Lament over the fall of Babylon (Rev. 18)

- Hallelujah chorus over the fall of Babylon (Rev. 19:1–8)

- Invitation to the marriage supper of the Lamb (Rev. 19:9–10)

- Return of the King (Rev. 19:11–21)

GETTING IN THE SPIRIT

As you read through Revelation, the curious phrase "in the Spirit" may jump out at you. John uses *in the Spirit* to mark the specific visions he has when writing Revelation. The Apostle Paul uses that same phrase in his epistles (Romans 8:9), but the way in which John uses the term is altogether different. John is referring to the mysterious state that he's in as he experiences these visions. In John's view, God somehow frees him from his normal human limitations and enables him to tangibly experience these visions in his mind and spirit.

In the Spirit appears four times in Revelation: 1:10, 4:2, 17:3, and 21:10. Every time John uses this phrase, he is documenting the details of one of these four visions (see the table). Each of these visions "transports" John to a new geographical location — the island of Patmos, heaven, a desert, and a mountaintop. John never clarifies whether these locations are part of the vision he has on the island of Patmos or whether he is somehow supernaturally beamed to these locales.

You can think of John's in-the-Spirit experiences as something like a four-part miniseries. Each experience is a separate installment, but together, they form a cohesive storyline.

Verse	John's Location	Vision	Theme
1:10	Patmos	Hears a loud voice	Messages to the churches
4:2	Heaven	Sees a throne with someone sitting on it	Judgments on a sinful world
17:3	Desert wilderness	Sees a woman on a beast	Final victory over evil
21:10	Mountain	Sees the New Jerusalem coming down from heaven	A new world order

Monitoring the Book's Timeline

One of the biggest problems most people have with the book of Revelation is that they expect a traditional, linear model of storytelling. A *linear story* begins at a particular point in time and then uses progressive scenes to move the characters to some sort of destination. Other stories start out with the characters looking back at something, tell what happened in the form of a flashback, and return to the present. For most films out of Hollywood, these two tried-and-true formulas are almost always used, primarily because they're a natural way to tell a story and are easy for audiences to understand.

However, once in a while, a story comes along that — like the book of Revelation — doesn't fit into this storytelling model. *Snow Falling on Cedars* and *The English Patient* are two prime examples. Both have multiple storylines with flashback sequences involving different characters. If you don't want a mental workout, stories like these can be quite frustrating. But if you persevere and stick with them, you can find the increased texture worthwhile, adding to the overall experience.

TIP

As you read through Revelation, prepare yourself: The book of Revelation may start out linear for several chapters, but various vignettes or interludes interrupt the main story. When you equip yourself for that reality, you'll be in a much better position to deal with the timing of events.

As you consider how various pieces of the book fit together, keep in mind the following two topics: transitional phrases and parallel events.

And then some: Interpreting transitional phrases

REMEMBER

Revelation is filled with scores of transitional phrases, such as "then I saw," "and I saw," "after this," and "after these things." But not all these transitions refer to a chronological sequence of prophetic events. For example, of the 53 instances of the word "then," some refer to the temporal order in which John himself experienced visions. Others refer to a temporal sequence between events within a vision. In other words, one must distinguish between two aspects:

>> John's personal experience while receiving visions

>> The content of the visions — horsemen ride, beasts arise, angels fight, and so on

For example, suppose I were to tell you, "I saw the season finale of *Andor*. Then I saw reruns of all the episodes over the summer." In this example, "then" refers to the timing in which I saw the episodes, not what happened in the episodes.

Although some transitions may be open to interpretation, you shouldn't just dismiss all transitions, either. In particular, the phrases "after this" and "after these things" are noteworthy. Combined, these two phrases appear just six times and don't always seem to relate to the order in which John received the visions. For example, its usage in Revelation 4:1, 15:5, 18:1, and 19:1 implies a temporal sequence of events. However, its usage in 7:1 (which introduces the 144,000 believers of Israel) answers the question raised at the end of chapter 6: Who can withstand the wrath of God? (6:17). John uses the term again in 7:9; in this context, the phrase refers to the order in which he received the visions rather than a sequential flow of events.

As you will see, the four major interpretations of Revelation and the different perspectives on the Millennium have a significant bearing on how one interprets the meaning and timing of various events narrated in the book. I'll discuss these matters more fully in Chapters 4 and 13.

Parallelism: Watching things go down at the same time

Revelation has a flow of events, but how each section fits into the timeline isn't always apparent. Although commentators disagree on the particulars, most agree that at least a few of the portions of the book parallel each other. Perhaps the most obvious example is Revelation 12's story of the woman in the desert, which is told in two ways in different places in the chapter (12:6 and 12:13–17). A second example, though more contested, is the 3.5-year period mentioned several times throughout the book (11:3, 12:6, 12:14, and 13:5). Some hold that these references indicate that the associated sections parallel each other.

Many futurists (who believe Revelation 6–22 describe future events — see Chapter 4) downplay parallelism. They think that, by and large, the book progresses in a linear fashion from beginning to end, except for the vignettes (see the earlier "Judgments and vignettes" section). Other futurists view Revelation 6–11 and 12–19 as parallel accounts of the Great Tribulation. Offering a different take, people who embrace a symbolic interpretation of the prophecy (once again, see Chapter 4) see up to seven parallel sections in the book.

The issue of parallelism is also a key factor in the interpretation of the Millennium, which appears in Revelation 20:

» Premillennialists hold that all the events from Revelation 6–19 happen before the Millennium.

» Amillennialists view the Millennium as a recapitulation of or a parallel to the entire church age.

Chapter 13 takes up the vigorously debated interpretation of the Millennium.

IN THIS CHAPTER

» Searching for the author of Revelation

» Understanding the author's world

» Discerning the author's purpose for writing the book

» Determining the date of the book

» Appreciating the book's genre

Chapter **2**

Setting the Stage: The Author and the World in Which He Lived

B ooks — perhaps with the exception of dictionaries, phone books, and instructional manuals for gas grills — reflect the personality of the author. What's inside a book has a lot to do with who the author is, the times in which they lived, the places where they lived, and the experiences that shaped their life. So usually, the more you know about the author, the better you understand and appreciate what you read in the book itself.

Just like any other literary work, the books of the Bible reflect the character, writing style, and life experiences of their authors. Christians have long believed that the Bible is God's word communicated through human words, crafted by real people with unique perspectives. These writers were not just taking dictation; they were fully engaged as authors. Therefore, the more you learn about the individual behind a biblical book — such as John, and the world he inhabited — the better you can appreciate and interpret his writing.

In this chapter, you are introduced to John, the author of Revelation. You also gain a basic understanding of the Greco-Roman world in which he lived, his purpose for writing the book, and when he wrote it. You also discover the unique genre of this final book of the New Testament.

ID-ing John Doe, Author of Revelation

When you walk into your local bookstore and scan the bestsellers display, you see the author's name spread out in large letters on each book. The more successful the author is, the larger the font. In fact, for super-selling authors like John Grisham and Tom Clancy, their names appear so large that you often must search for the title. But regardless of whether you're dealing with a bestselling author or a first-time writer, you can usually pick up a book and find a brief biography providing at least a snippet of the author's credentials. Even if the author is using a pseudonym (writing under an assumed name), someone somewhere knows the author's identity — after all, the publisher needs to know where to send the royalty checks!

Biblical authors, of course, wrote long before the invention of printing presses and large publishing companies. Modern readers wish biblical authors had provided more biographical details about themselves. (Had they done so, it would have headed off some of the fierce debates about the authorship of certain biblical books!)

At the time of the writing, many people personally knew the author of a biblical book, even if no name was provided (as in the case of Hebrews). As it turns out, many of the books in the New Testament were written as letters. When you write a letter to a friend, do you add a detailed biographical note at the end? Of course not! The recipient knows you even if you merely sign off with your initials.

The authors of the books of the Bible sometimes included their names, but often-times didn't. The author of Revelation identifies himself four times (Rev. 1:1; 1:4; 1:9; 22:8) simply referring to himself as *John*. No last name. No title. No biographical data. Because John was a popular name of the day, he could be any old John. So, who is he?

The consensus of the church since the second century CE identifies the author as the Apostle John. Yes, *this John*. He and his brother James were two of the original twelve disciples of Jesus, and John was viewed as Jesus's best friend. He's the author of the Gospel of John and the three letters bearing his name (referred to as the *Johannine epistles*). In fact, the list of church fathers who credit the Apostle John as the author of Revelation reads like a virtual who's who of the early church, including Justin Martyr, Irenaeus, Hippolytus, Clement of Alexandria, Tertullian, and Origen.

WARNING

Be mindful not to fall into the trap of assuming that people in the past were less intelligent or insightful than those today when considering the question of authorship.

Doubting the apostle's authorship

Not everyone through the centuries has agreed that the Apostle John, son of Zebedee, is the author. Dionysius, who was the pope of the influential Alexandrian church (Egypt) in the mid-third century, said the author was an obscure first-century church leader named John the presbyter (the elder). He based his argument on *internal evidence*, evidence in the text itself that pointed to someone other than the celebrated Apostle John. Dionysius claimed that the vocabulary and style of Revelation were so different from the Gospel of John and the Johannine epistles that the same author couldn't have written it. According to Dionysius, there are discrepancies:

>> **The author of Revelation identifies himself by name.** This is not the Apostle John's custom in the other writings attributed to him. For example, in the Gospel of John he doesn't explicitly identify himself by name (he is probably the "disciple whom Jesus loved" [John 13:23, 21:7, 21:20]), and in two of his three epistles (1 John is anonymous), he calls himself the "elder" (2 John 1:1; 3 John 1:1).

>> **Revelation is composed in a less refined Greek than the other works linked to the Apostle John.** The author demonstrates a good grasp of Old Testament Scripture, being familiar with both the original Hebrew and the Greek Septuagint. But his Greek in Revelation lacks the polished style found in the Gospel and the letters attributed to John.

>> **The vocabulary and writing style (the author's *voice*) of the acknowledged Johannine writings contrast with Revelation.** Most authors fall into similar writing patterns. If you have favorite authors, you can often discern their tone and voice, even if the topics they're writing about vary. The sentence structure, style, and vocabulary are similar from article to article and book to book. The Gospel of John and the epistles have this common feel to them. For example, the Gospel of John begins with, "In the beginning was the Word" (John 1:1), and 1 John opens with a similar affirmation: "We declare to you what was from the beginning" (1 John 1:1). This type of similarity and familiarity doesn't carry over to Revelation.

Dionysius's position gained a few followers over the centuries, including Martin Luther. Not until recent times, however, did his view gain momentum. Today, a majority of modern scholars have jumped on the Dionysius bandwagon and added additional arguments against apostolic authorship.

Defending the apostle's authorship

Many conservative scholars, however, continue to defend the traditional view. As detailed in this section, supporters of Johannine authorship present both internal and external evidence to substantiate their position, including:

>> **John's purpose in identifying himself in Revelation.** Even though the Apostle John never names himself directly in his other writings, the fact that the author of Revelation does so doesn't necessarily rule him out. In fact, a good reason exists for doing so. Keep in mind that Revelation is explicitly called a prophecy (Rev. 1:3; 22:7, 9). Since according to 1 John 4:1, "many false prophets have gone out into the world" (see also 2 John 17), John may have felt it necessary to name himself lest there be any doubt about the book's authenticity and trustworthiness.

>> **John doesn't feel compelled to appeal to his status.** When the author does give his name, he doesn't attach a title. He's simply *John.* Because the Apostle John held such a prominent place in the early church, simply mentioning his personal name carried sufficient weight, requiring no further identification.

>> **Revelation stresses eyewitness testimony.** The Gospel and 1 John stress eyewitness testimony. Revelation carries over this emphasis in Revelation 1:1–2 ("He made it known by sending his angel to his servant John, who testified to the word of God and to the testimony of Jesus Christ, even to all that he saw") and in Revelation 22:8 ("I, John, am the one who heard and saw these things [. . .]"). Compare this to a similar emphasis in the Gospel of John (John 19:35 and 21:24) and the first epistle of John (1 John 1:1–3).

>> **Details are consistent with what scholars know of the Apostle John's ministry.** The writer speaks of the churches in western Asia Minor in a manner implying familiarity with their circumstances, location, and spiritual condition. Credible second-century historical records state that the Apostle John lived in Ephesus from 70–100 CE. While there, he had a thriving ministry that spread throughout the region. The details dovetail nicely with the date.

>> **The texts share some words and phrases.** Despite stylistic differences between Revelation, the Gospel, and epistles, common words and phrases do appear. For example, the Gospel of John refers to Jesus as *Logos* ("Word") in John 1:1. The only other reference to Jesus as *Logos* in all the Bible is in Revelation 19:13. In addition, only John 1:29 and Revelation 5:6 refer to Jesus

as a "Lamb." Moreover, both the Gospel of John (19:37) and Revelation (1:7) quote the same Old Testament verse, Zechariah 12:10.

>> **Passages in Revelation recall the Gospel of John and Johannine epistles.** Although much of Revelation is obviously focused on the prophetic visions of John, the book also contains a few sections resembling pastoral messages addressed to Christian communities (Rev. 1:1–8; 1:17–3:22; 22:18–21). It is precisely in these portions that similarities to the Johannine epistles and Gospel of John appear. The major differences, therefore, lie in the apocalyptic portions of the book of Revelation. Even here, however, Johannine echoes may be heard (see Rev. 5:6; John 1:29; 1 John 2:2).

>> **Revelation's less polished style has an explanation.** Although proponents of apostolic authorship agree that the book isn't as well-written as his other works, they suggest three explanations:

- The Book of Acts describes John as an "uneducated," "ordinary" man (Acts 4:13). But when he wrote his Gospel and epistles in Ephesus, the fifth largest city in the empire, he may have employed a trained secretary (called an *amanuensis*). That option wasn't available when he wrote Revelation since he was exiled on the isolated island of Patmos. Furthermore, the Greek of Revelation betrays a significant Semitic (Aramaic-Hebrew) influence, which fits John's profile as a Galilean Jewish expatriate.

- Because of the way John received prophetic visions, he may have hurriedly scribbled down the content — what literary critics call a stream-of-consciousness style. Perhaps, to ensure that the original vision remained unchanged (see Rev. 22:18–19) he didn't enlist the assistance of an amanuensis to smooth out his rough Greek even after returning to the mainland, which, according to the church historian Eusebius, he did.

- Some scholars propose that John wrote Revelation as early as 65 CE. If an early date is correct, it would have been his first written work — almost 30 years before he wrote his Gospel and epistles. During that time, having ministered in a Greek-speaking environment, his writing skills significantly improved.

Certainty on the question of authorship is problematic because both sides appeal to supporting internal evidence. But if debate over internal evidence results in a draw, perhaps the external evidence (testimony and tradition) tips the scales.

Except for Dionysius, all the other church fathers in the second and third centuries who spoke to the issue claimed apostolic authorship. Adding more weight to their collective testimony, some of the original readers of Revelation (members of the churches to whom the book was addressed) were still living in the days of

Justin Martyr and Irenaeus. In short, objectors can't simply sweep the testimony of the early church under the rug and ignore it.

REMEMBER

Bottom line: Conservative scholarship presents a persuasive case for apostolic authorship. In this book, when I refer to *John*, I mean the Apostle John, son of Zebedee and brother of the Apostle James.

Understanding the Troubled Times in Which John Lived

As the longest living apostle, John participated in a spiritual revolution that spread from Roman-occupied Palestine across the entire Mediterranean world (see Figure 2-1). Remarkably, John's spiritual journey began as a Galilean fisherman and early follower of Jesus. Called to be one of Jesus's twelve apostles, he soon became a leading figure in the rapidly growing Jesus movement. Widely recognized by his peers as "the disciple whom Jesus loved," he became a central figure in spreading the Gospel throughout the Roman province of Asia (modern-day western Turkey).

In the mid-fifties CE, the Roman government could be counted on to maintain justice (see Romans 13), but by the nineties that changed. No longer a protector of law-abiding Christians, the empire turned persecutor. In the following sections, I explore the challenging new circumstances facing the Christian community.

Increasing Roman domination: Rise of the Imperial Cult

By the end of John's life, Rome neared its greatest territorial expansion, spanning three continents. No rivals challenged Rome's domination in military, political, and economic spheres. The Mediterranean was a Roman sea. As the empire grew increasingly rich, wealth filtered down from the emperor and the aristocratic patrician class to a burgeoning middle class of freed persons and skilled artisans. The Pax Romana — Rome's era of relative peace — ushered in unmatched stability, economic power, and standard of living. In this cultural climate, pursuit of material wealth and sensual pleasure preoccupied daily life.

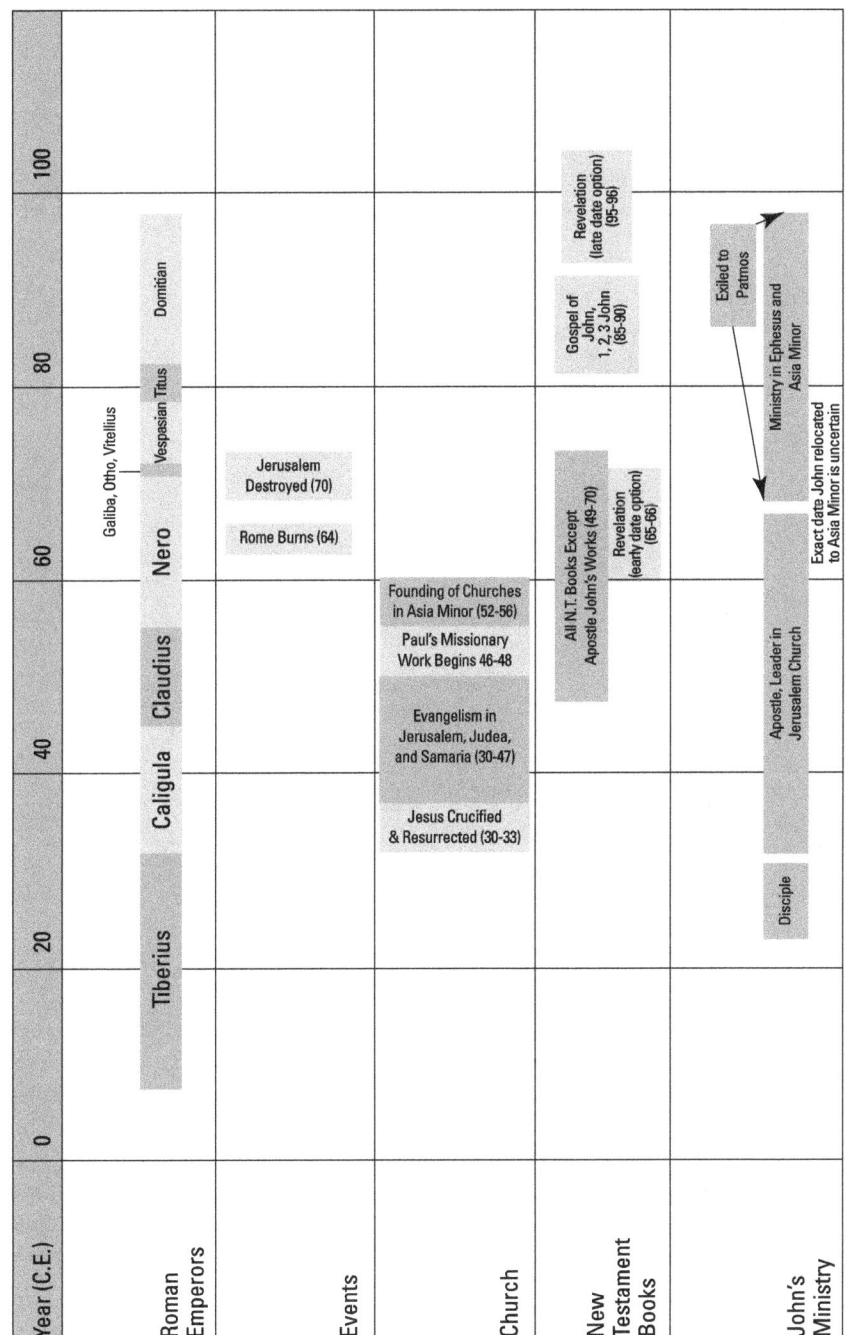

FIGURE 2-1: Historical events during the Apostle's lifetime.

Year (C.E.)	0	20	40	60	80	100
Roman Emperors		Tiberius	Caligula / Claudius	Nero	Vespasian / Titus / Domitian	
				Galiba, Otho, Vitellius		
Events			Jesus Crucified & Resurrected (30-33)	Rome Burns (64) / Jerusalem Destroyed (70)		
Church			Evangelism in Jerusalem, Judea, and Samaria (30-47) / Paul's Missionary Work Begins 46-48 / Founding of Churches in Asia Minor (52-56)			
New Testament Books				All N.T. Books Except Apostle John's Works (49-70) / Revelation (early date option) (65-66)	Gospel of John, 1, 2, 3 John (85-90) / Revelation (late date option) (95-96)	
John's Ministry		Disciple	Apostle, Leader in Jerusalem Church	Exact date John relocated to Asia Minor is uncertain	Ministry in Ephesus and Asia Minor / Exiled to Patmos	

Imperial Rome's influence spilled over into religion. Abandoning the traditional Greek and Roman gods as outdated, most turned to a state religion in which loyal citizens venerated the emperor as divine and regarded him as the guarantor of peace and prosperity for the empire. State-sponsored veneration of Roman emperors was self-serving because it bolstered political unity and loyalty across a diverse empire. Table 2-1 lists the Roman emperors of the first century CE.

TABLE 2-1

First-Century Roman Emperors

Emperor	Years of Reign
Augustus	27 BCE–14 CE
Tiberius	14–37
Caligula	37–41
Claudius	41–54
Nero	54–68
Galba	68–69
Otho	69
Vitellius	69
Vespasian	69–79
Titus	79–81
Domitian	81–96
Nerva	96–98

Deification — elevating a person to the status of a god — usually required approval from the Roman Senate following the death of an emperor as was the case with Julius Caesar and Augustus Caesar. However, when Caligula, Nero, and Domitian demanded that they be deified and worshiped during their lifetime, the senate refused because of their arrogance. The three coastal cities Ephesus, Smyrna, and Pergamum competed for the honor of building and maintaining a temple dedicated to Caesar Augustus. Pergamum won out and proudly boasted of being "the First City in Asia." During John's lifetime, Ephesus erected a temple to the divine Domitian.

The Imperial Cult created a crisis for Christians. During Domitian's reign (AD 81–96), he demanded veneration as "Lord" and "God." For Christians, this was a bridge too far; there was only one God, the Father, and one Lord, the Lord Jesus

Christ (see 1 Cor 8:5–6). As you will see in the study of the seven churches (see Chapter 7), failure to participate in the Imperial Cult entailed grave consequences.

Jewish population forced into exile

The Jewish population living in its ancestral homeland experienced a major catastrophe and disruption during John's lifetime.

Before 70 CE, a majority of Jews lived in a small, backwater Roman province on the eastern edge of the Empire. Though subjects of Rome, Jews were granted several privileges. For example, they were free to practice their religious customs, rituals, and temple worship without interference and were not compelled to participate in the Imperial Cult.

The Jewish War against Rome and the fall of Jerusalem in 70 CE changed everything. With a semi-autonomous Jewish state a relic of the past and Jerusalem with its magnificent Temple reduced to rubble, surviving Jews were scattered across the empire as refugees or slaves (this scattering is known as the *Diaspora*). Gradually, however, they reacquired the privilege of observing their ancestral religion and exemption from participation in the Imperial Cult.

TECHNICAL STUFF

A majority of Jews lived in the Diaspora from the Babylonian exile in 586 BCE until the 21st century CE when a majority were residents of the State of Israel. Currently, the Jewish population of Israel has surpassed 10 million.

A widening gap between Jews and Christians

The war against Rome and its disastrous outcome contributed to a growing gap between Jews and Christians. The explosive growth of the Christian church was now owing primarily to an influx of Gentile converts rather than Jews. As a result, the shared heritage of Jews and Christians was, unfortunately, either forgotten or repudiated.

The book of Revelation expresses this new reality but also reflects its indebtedness to Hebraic roots. The target audience for Revelation was primarily Gentiles, and the book (like all other New Testament books) was written in Greek, not Hebrew. Despite this, Revelation remains rooted in Jewish thought. Allusions, echoes, imagery, and symbolism from Old Testament books like Daniel, Ezekiel, Isaiah, Joel, and Zechariah appear throughout, in fact, more often than in any other New Testament writing! What's more, the Jewish people figure prominently in the narrative storyline, reminding readers that the future of the church and Israel are intertwined (see Rev. 2:9, 14; 3:9; 5:5; 7:4–8; 11:1–2; 21:12).

Growing persecution of Christians

As previously mentioned, Diaspora Jews regained some of their former privileges and exemptions after the Jewish War. Established and recognized non-Roman religions had been permitted and practiced in the empire without interference or penalty. Initially, Christians were viewed as a sect of Judaism and thus not branded as *illicitas* (prohibited). As tension between synagogue and church escalated, Jewish communities across the empire began complaining to the authorities that Christians were not Jews but members of a new (and forbidden) sect. The threat staring Christians in the face was the prospect of losing their protected status under the umbrella of Judaism.

During John's lifetime, the hostility between Christians and Jews finally led to a parting of the ways. Jewish Christians were no longer welcome in synagogues and Christian leaders began denouncing Jews and preaching harsh anti-Jewish sentiments. Echoes of this emerging rhetoric and tension may already be overheard in the messages to the seven churches.

Becoming a Roman target

State-sponsored persecution, imprisonment, and even death were becoming a distinct possibility. In fact, you learn that Antipas suffered martyrdom for his Christian faith in Pergamum (Rev. 2:13). John, too, experienced persecution firsthand. He wrote the book of Revelation while exiled on Patmos (see Figure 2-2), a rocky island in the Aegean Sea where the government maintained a penal mining colony. John says he was on Patmos "because of the word of God and testimony of Jesus" (Rev. 1:9). Like Paul and Peter before him, he was arrested for preaching the Gospel. The provincial governor probably banished John to Patmos to hinder the rapid growth of the church (although others suggest that John's wording may leave room for his being there as an evangelist instead). One thing is certain: he wasn't there on vacation!

Refusal to worship the emperor resulted in harsh punishment (see the earlier section "Increasing Roman domination: Rise of the Imperial Cult"). In the aftermath of the great fire in Rome (64 CE), Nero blamed the Christians and launched a massive roundup and sadistic execution of thousands of Christians. This outbreak of violence, however, was mostly confined to Rome and limited in duration. This began to change during the reign of Domitian. Demanding that he be worshiped as "Lord" and "God," Christians who refused were starting to experience sporadic persecution throughout the empire. Some evidence suggests that Domitian ordered an empire-wide crackdown on Christians, but most scholars think the persecution was local in nature.

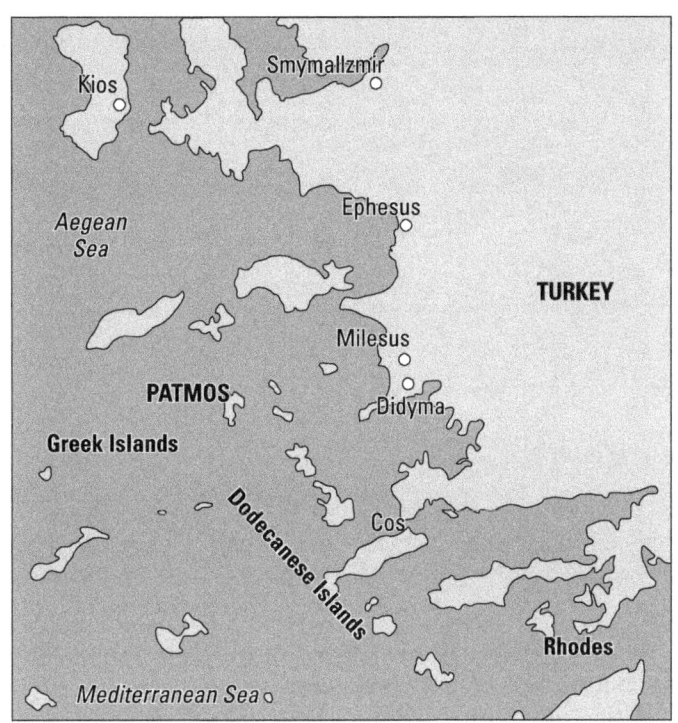

FIGURE 2-2:
Map showing the
location of the
Island of Patmos.

The evidence from the book of Revelation suggests that John was addressing churches faltering under increasing persecution from hostile fellow citizens, Jews, and provincial officials. Popular participation in and support of emperor worship resulted in increasing levels of persecution for dissenters such as the Christians. But not until the second century CE did state-sponsored persecution of Christians become an empire-wide phenomenon.

Encouraging the suffering church through Revelation

John wasn't the only Apostle who ministered to churches in the province of Asia (see Figure 2-3); the other leading apostles, Paul and Peter (these three constituted a kind of "Big Three" in apostolic circles) either visited or wrote to congregations there. Paul addressed three of his letters — Ephesians, Colossians, and 1 Timothy — to believers and associates in this region, and Peter wrote two (see 1 Peter 1:1 and 2 Peter 3:1). Irenaeus and Ignatius, influential leaders in the second century CE, spent their formative years there before taking on prominent roles as bishops in France and Syria, respectively.

Christian congregations stood on the cusp of the age of martyrdom in which the state launched an all-out assault against Christians (2nd–4th centuries CE). The situation recalls the plot of the movie *The Empire Strikes Back*. Could the Federation prevail against the evil Emperor Palpatine and his powerful lackey Darth Vader? The question for beleaguered Christians was, could the church withstand an all-out attack by the Roman Empire?

Not to worry. Christ's embattled church possesses vastly more resources to resist the "dark side" than an apprentice Jedi knight, Luke Skywalker; his mysterious teacher, Yoda; a powerful princess, Leia; and a swashbuckling smuggler, Han Solo. Believers are indwelt with the abiding presence of the risen Lord who promised, "I will build my church, and the gates of Hades will not prevail against it" (Matthew 16:19). Christ's gift of the all-powerful Holy Spirit has no equal. The book of Revelation leaves no doubt about the outcome: the Lion of the tribe of Judah will vanquish the Dark Lord and his minions.

The central message of Revelation is unmistakable: Jesus Christ calls on his followers to remain steadfast — even if it means death. The book shows that the early church was struggling with a Satanic threat to its very existence (as seen in Revelation chapter 13), yet John makes it clear that God will never leave nor forsake his people; *the church will survive.* He assures believers that justice will ultimately triumph, urging them to stay committed in their faith through every trial until Christ returns. Through Revelation, John exhorts the early Christians to hold firm, reminding them that their faith is being tested not simply by flesh and blood but by demonic powers allied with Satan.

Although John addressed his prophetic message to the seven churches of western Asia Minor, his words continue to resonate whenever and wherever believers have faced similar circumstances. Like the first listeners, they are inspired to be faithful to "Jesus Christ, the faithful witness" (Rev. 1:5).

Debating the Date of Revelation

Debate over when John wrote Revelation continues unabated — if only he had included a "Written in the year . . ." note at the book's start, much confusion would have been avoided. But alas, no such timestamp exists, leaving scholars to argue over its dating.

TALKING IN NEW TESTAMENT TERMS

The opening and closing of Revelation, written in the style of a letter (more on that below), contains expressions similar to those in Paul's epistles to the Colossians (ca. 60–62 CE) and Thessalonians (ca. 50–51 CE). This is close in time to the early date for Revelation.

- Revelation 1:4 ("Grace and peace to you from him who is, and who was, and who is to come") closely mirrors Colossians 1:2 ("Grace and peace to you from God our Father").

- Revelation 1:5 ("Jesus Christ, who is the faithful witness, the firstborn from the dead") echoes Colossians 1:18 ("And he is the head of the body, the church; he is the beginning and the firstborn from among the dead").

- Revelation 22:21 ("The grace of the Lord Jesus be with all the saints") is close in wording to 1 Thessalonians 5:28 and 2 Thessalonians 3:18.

Locating Revelation in the 60s CE

The 1960s in America was a time of discontent and social upheaval, marked by a sexual revolution and violent anti–Vietnam War protests. I was a college student at the time wondering when my draft number would come up. I mention this because there are similarities to the era of emperor Nero's reign in the 60s CE. That decade was also marked by widespread discontent, turmoil, and violent protests by Jews in Palestine against Roman rule, leading to outright revolt in 66 CE. In response, Nero dispatched five Roman legions, plus several auxiliary legions, to put down the rebellion. Vespasian, Nero's most capable general, systematically crushed all Jewish resistance. His son Titus finished the job by destroying Jerusalem and its Temple in 70 CE. Some scholars point to this turbulent decade as the likely time of composition for Revelation, around 65 CE. Leading arguments for the early date include the following:

>> **A still-standing Temple in Jerusalem:** Revelation 11:1 refers to the Temple in Jerusalem: "Come and measure the temple of God and the altar and those who worship there." In this passage, it sounds like the Temple is still standing. However, as mentioned above, the Romans destroyed it, along with everything else in the city in 70 CE. Therefore, Revelation was written sometime before the Temple was destroyed, ca. 65 CE.

>> **A clue in Revelation 17:9–10:** Some scholars interpret this passage to be referencing Nero as the sixth Roman emperor, ". . .they are seven kings; five have fallen, one is, the other has not yet come; and when he does come, he must remain only a little while." After Nero's suicide in 68 CE, rumors began to circulate — and eventually turned into legend — that he had not truly died but was instead lying in wait in Parthia, plotting his return to Rome with an army to exact revenge on his enemies, including many prominent citizens and officials. Revelation 13:3–4 is often read by these scholars as a nod to this enduring Nero myth.

>> **Another supposed clue occurs in Revelation 13:18:** "Let anyone with understanding calculate the number of the beast, for it is the number of a person. Its number is six hundred sixty-six." Using a technique called *gematria* in which letters of the alphabet are assigned numerical value, hidden meanings are then discovered in texts (more on this in Chapter 11). In this case, if you tweak the spelling of Nero's name to Neron Caesar in Hebrew, it comes out to 666. Thus, Nero is the beast.

>> **Coarse Greek, indicating Revelation is John's first writing:** Revelation is written in a less polished Greek than the Gospel of John and the epistles. The book of Revelation may be John's first effort at writing in koine (common) Greek (as spoken in the empire). Thirty years later, when he wrote the Gospel and epistles, his writing skills in Greek had improved.

As Chapter 4 explains, the early-date theory is crucial for the preterist interpretation of Revelation because preterists contend that many of the prophecies John gives in the book were fulfilled in the first century.

Placing Revelation in the 90s

Most Bible scholars date Revelation to around 95–96 CE during Domitian's reign (81–96 CE). Its position as the last book in the biblical canon appropriately reflects both its subject matter (End Times) and its date of composition, approximately 5 to 20 years after the others. Arguments for this later date include:

>> **Church tradition:** The consensus of early church leadership held that Revelation was written in the 90s. Irenaeus stated that Revelation was written during Domitian's reign. Other early church fathers — including Clement of Alexandria, Origen, Victorinus (who wrote perhaps the first-ever commentary on the book), Eusebius, and Jerome — agreed.

>> **The state of the seven churches:** The depressing state of many of the seven churches in Revelation 3 sounds altogether different from what was going on during Paul's ministry to this same region in the 60s. During Paul's day, the churches did, of course, have their struggles, but there is no mention of actual *apostasy* (falling away from faith in Christ) to the extent that John depicts in Revelation 3.

>> **The timing of John's ministry to Asia:** Scholars know John left Palestine before the fall of Jerusalem in 70 CE. However, they question the likelihood of his immediately assuming the major leadership position in the churches in Asia Minor. After all, during this timeframe, Paul's influence on the churches in the region would still have been strong.

>> **Earthquake in Laodicea:** Historical evidence indicates that an earthquake destroyed the city of Laodicea in the early 60s. Therefore, the physical presence of the city, let alone an established church in Laodicea during the 60s, seems doubtful.

Moreover, Jesus's criticism of the Laodicean church centers on their spiritual apathy: "So, because you are lukewarm, and neither hot nor cold, I am about to spit you out of my mouth" (Rev. 3:16). Apathy in the aftermath of a major disaster like an earthquake seems contrary to typical human behavior. People who have lived through such traumatic events are rarely indifferent about their faith; instead, they tend to feel either anger toward God or a deep longing for comfort. If the earthquake occurred in the early 60s, a new generation would be of age in Laodicea by the 90s with no firsthand experience of the earthquake. Lukewarmness in this environment would be more likely.

CHURCHES IN START-UP MODE?

One of the most compelling arguments for the later date of Revelation is the deteriorating state of the seven churches in Revelation 3 — too little love, moral compromise, lukewarm faith, and so on. When you read the letters that John addressed to each, the churches don't sound like they're in "start-up mode" as they would've been back in the 60s. Instead, some time seems to have passed since the start of the church.

When you compare these churches to the Israelites in the Old Testament or even modern-day churches, seeing faith deteriorate over a generation isn't unusual — but having such problems within a few scant years is. The typical scenario occurs when a generation fails to pass its faith on to the next generation, causing the up-and-comers to forget the faith of the earlier generation. If that's what happened to the Asian churches, then a later date seems more likely.

>> **Emperor worship:** Some commentators believe that Revelation 13 alludes to the Roman practice of emperor worship. Worship of emperors while they were still living didn't gain prominence until the reign of Domitian (81–96 CE).

>> **Christian persecution outside of Rome:** Although Nero is well-known for his persecution of Christians, his focus was limited to the city of Rome itself, not the entire Roman Empire. Some scholars argue that persecution was more widespread throughout the empire, including western Asia Minor, during Domitian's reign.

Later-date proponents also find two notable flaws in the early-date justifications:

>> The Temple in Revelation 11 is either an eschatological (End Times) or symbolic temple, not the pre-70 historical one.

>> The idea that 666 stands for *Nero* in Hebrew is a stretch. After all, the target audience for the book wasn't Jewish but Gentile, so John's intention to convert a name in Hebrew to a number doesn't seem realistic. What's more, you must change the common spelling of Nero in Hebrew to get the 666. Finally, and this carries considerable weight, early church father Irenaeus denied it referred to Nero or any other Roman dictator.

Unveiling Revelation's Unique Character

The book of Revelation stands unique among books in Scripture, not only because of its subject matter but also because it combines three distinctive genres or types of writing:

>> **Epistle:** In its opening and closing, it resembles an epistle (or letter) in the New Testament.

>> **Prophecy:** Revelation shares characteristics of prophetic books such as Isaiah, Ezekiel, and Daniel. Prophecy is a message from God, communicated through a messenger (prophet) who proclaims God's will and occasionally predicts God's purpose. Revelation is in fact called a prophecy (Rev. 1:3, 22:7).

>> **Apocalypse:** Apocalypse means "an unveiling or revealing." Revelation, like the Old Testament book of Daniel, unveils God's grand plan for all creation. This divine plan, revealed through angelic messengers, describes the End Times when good overcomes evil. The message is conveyed through vivid images and symbols.

In this section, you take a closer look at these three types of writing and how John wove them together to create his unique book.

Revelation as epistle

When most people think of Revelation, the elements of prophecy and apocalyptic symbolism come to mind first. But the overall framework of the book is that of an epistle because it shares the characteristics of an epistle superimposed on an apocalyptic writing (the later section, "Revelation as apocalyptic literature," explains more about that genre).

An *epistle* is the letter-style writing of all the New Testament books except the Gospels and Acts of the Apostles. These letters (which became books of the Bible) circulated among the various churches at the time and were read aloud. An epistle followed the Greek model of letter-writing, which normally included the following:

>> An introduction that lists the writer and the recipients and provides a formal greeting and thanksgiving

>> The body of the letter

>> A conclusion that includes a farewell, which was typically written by the sender to show the credibility and authenticity of the letter

Revelation follows this epistle model. Although the apocalyptic content that makes up the body of the letter isn't something you find elsewhere in the New Testament, the opening and closing of the letter are surprisingly common. At the start of the book, John writes in Revelation 1:4, "John to the seven churches that are in Asia," an opening line that's similar to other epistle openings, as is his identification of the recipients in Revelation 1:11. The closing benediction "The grace of the Lord Jesus be with all the saints. Amen" (Rev. 22:21) is similar to that of the Letter to the Hebrews and several epistles by the Apostle Paul.

TIP

John had a specific target audience for the book; therefore, as you read through Revelation (as well as the Old Testament prophetic works), ask yourself how the original readers would understand John's words and how to apply the lessons. After that, you can consider how to best apply the teachings in your own context.

Revelation as apocalyptic literature

Revelation is popularly known for its apocalyptic style. *Apocalyptic literature* is a specific genre of writing that's characteristic of what Jews wrote between 300 BCE and 200 CE and of the early Christian church. The apocalyptic style had several unique characteristics, including the following:

>> **It was written during times of hardship and persecution and longing.** Apocalyptic literature was popular in ancient Israel during some of its most difficult days. Biblical apocalyptic writing tells readers to prepare for suffering but to also have hope and confidence that God has ordained the events that are going to transpire. For example, Zechariah wrote his book to a defeated people of Israel who had just returned from exile and felt powerless to change their circumstances.

>> **It uses vivid imagery and symbolism to represent real-world counterparts.** The most obvious quality of apocalyptic literature is its use of seemingly bizarre imagery. Although you tend to see fantastic imagery today only in sci-fi and horror films, the biblical apocalyptic style isn't considered fantasy fare or fiction. Instead, symbolism adds drama and deepens the meaning of the message. Apocalyptic writing often represents people and countries as animals, such as a lamb, dragon, or strange beast. Take, for example, Daniel 8:21, which refers to a male goat as the king of Greece and a large horn between its eyes as the first king.

Similarly, real cities and nations receive symbolic names, such as Babylon, Sodom, Egypt, and Jerusalem; these names are usually the great powers or cities of the era in which the book was written. What's more, political and social problems are often shown as natural disasters involving the sun, moon, or stars.

>> **It often features angels as guides.** Angels are often the guides for the author during the visions. For example, as recorded in Daniel 7–12, Daniel has visions in the night, which an angel then explains to him.

>> **It uses numbers to convey meaning.** In apocalyptic literature, numbers (such as seven) usually carry significance beyond their arithmetic purposes. Given that, be wary of assuming literal 24-hour, 7-day-a-week time periods when you come across a measurement of time. The "ten days" in Revelation 2:10 and "one hour" in Revelation 17:12 may simply refer to short periods of time. So, too, the 1,000 years in Revelation 20 may not necessarily mean 365,242 days but may instead refer to a more generic "very long time," much like Peter writes in 2 Peter 3:8: "But do not ignore this one fact, beloved, that with the Lord one day is like a thousand years, and a thousand years are like one day."

Besides Revelation, the only other apocalyptic book in the Bible is Daniel, although Ezekiel and Zechariah have sections sharing this literary style. However, many apocalyptic works were written before and during the early church period but were not considered *Scripture* (coming directly from God). Nonetheless, the book of Revelation wasn't just the lucky one that made it to the big leagues of canon. It's altogether distinct from the "pretenders." Unlike the extra-biblical writings, in Revelation, John identifies himself as the writer, declares the book to be inspired by Jesus, and specifically states that the book is a prophecy.

Revelation as prophecy

The book of Revelation is not merely a book that contains prophecy; rather, as John states, it *is* a prophecy (Rev. 1:3; 22:7; 22:10; 22:18–19). In the Bible, *prophecy* is a message from God mediated by means of a divinely called messenger.

Most Old Testament prophecy is preaching designed to bring about repentance and recommitment to the *Old Covenant*, the promise between Moses and God on Mount Sinai (see Exodus 31–34 in the Bible). New Testament prophecy is similar, except believers are called to a renewed commitment to the New Covenant, the agreement between God and humanity made possible by the sacrificial death of Jesus.

Prediction, though not the predominant feature, is still an important part of prophecy in both the Old and New Testaments. Christians believe that in some cases, the predictions have already been completed in history. Most Christians, for instance, think that numerous Old Testament prophecies predicted the coming of Jesus as Messiah, as well as his death and resurrection. In other cases, future events have yet to happen (such as passages in Daniel that deal with End Times).

In most cases, prophets who wrote down the message focused on the details of the event but avoided specifics concerning exactly when that event was going to occur in history. They did so because the point of the prophecy was to warn people to be faithful and expectant, not simply to provide a play-by-play guide to how history was going to play out.

Many people find biblical prophecy confusing and sometimes wonder whether it's God's way of teasing or confusing people for some reason. But that's not the case. The Bible is clear that prophecy is designed to

>> Encourage and comfort believers (1 Corinthians 14:3)

>> Give hope (Rev. 1:3)

>> Refocus believers on God's character and promises (Rev. 1:3)

At its heart, Revelation is intended to accomplish each of these.

Revelation as inspired Scripture

Historic Christianity believes that all Scripture originated from God but was written down by human authors. In 2 Timothy 3:16, Paul describes Scripture as *inspired by God* (literally meaning *God-breathed*). But how the mechanics of this process worked is an age-old mystery. The closest you come to an explanation is in the words of Peter: ". . . men and women *moved by the Holy Spirit spoke from God*" (2 Peter 1:21). That still leaves a lot of unanswered questions. You do know, however, what didn't happen: God didn't temporarily take over the minds of the biblical writers and turn them into zombie scribes, nor did he just rubber-stamp the ideas of the human authors. Instead, Christians believe that the Holy Spirit superintended the writers without overriding their personality or personal expression during the process.

Not all the books of the Bible were written in the same manner, even though they're all considered to be inspired. Matthew and John wrote personal accounts about the life and ministry of Jesus (John 14:26). Mark and Luke, both trusted associates of Peter and Paul respectively, relied on the Holy Spirit to write down eyewitness accounts. The New Testament epistles were personal letters written "in words not taught by human wisdom but taught by the Spirit" (1 Corinthians 2:13).

The way in which John received the content of Revelation was extraordinary, involving visions, dreams, and direct communication with angelic messengers. According to Revelation 1:1, God the Father gave the revelation to his son Jesus. Jesus then shared the vision with John through an angel. While John was "in the Spirit" (1:10), he received a series of visions, the details of which he faithfully wrote down (1:2), creating the book of Revelation. Countless numbers of Christians continue to hear God's word in its pages.

IN THIS CHAPTER

» Exploring prophecy in the
Old Testament

» Discovering Old Testament
symbolism in Revelation

» Exploring the meaning of the
70 weeks in Daniel 9

» Deciphering the Olivet Discourse
in Matthew 24–25

Chapter **3**

The Prequels: Prophecies throughout the Bible

Toss out the term *prophecy*, and your friends may start talking about Nostradamus or any number of mystics and seers who claim to have seen the future. But say *biblical prophecy*, and anyone familiar with the Bible is likely to turn the conversation to the book of Revelation and the End Times. However, prophetic (and apocalyptic) writings in the Bible run throughout both the Old and New Testaments, not just in Revelation. In fact, approximately one-third of the Bible is devoted to prophecy. According to Christians, some have already been fulfilled, and some are still in the works.

In this chapter, you peek into some of the biblical prophecies outside the book of Revelation. You explore some of the prophetic works of the Old Testament that are often associated with End Times prophecies. You also explore the Olivet Discourse (a sermon delivered on the Mount of Olives), a key New Testament prophecy spoken by Jesus himself. As you examine these prophecies, you discover their interrelationships and the influence these prophetic teachings have on the book of Revelation.

Understanding the Old Testament Backdrop to Revelation

Like most devout Jews of the time, John was familiar with the writings that now make up the Old Testament. These writings highly influenced the book of Revelation, more than they influenced any other New Testament book.

Although Revelation doesn't directly quote the Old Testament, it contains around 250 references to it, drawing from books such as Isaiah, Daniel, Ezekiel, Psalms, Exodus, Jeremiah, Zechariah, Amos, and Joel.

REMEMBER

These references are far more than mere trivia — they enrich the narrative John unfolds by rooting his visionary account in the longstanding traditions of biblical history. By artfully weaving these connections into the overarching story of redemption, John underscores the deep unity of Scripture and the trustworthiness of its prophetic messages. Consider these links as invitations to delve more deeply into the treasures of the Old Testament.

Here are just some of the more significant allusions to the Old Testament. This first set is from Genesis, the first book in the Bible:

>> Revelation mentions the "tree of life" (from Genesis 3:22) four times — 2:7; 22:2; 22:14; and 22:19.

>> The judgment against God's enemies described in Revelation 19:20 and 20:10 — where they are cast into a lake of fire burning with sulfur — echoes the fate of Sodom and Gomorrah, which were destroyed by a downpour of burning sulfur in Genesis 19:24.

>> The symbol of the woman clothed with the sun, having the moon under her feet and wearing a crown of 12 stars on her head (Rev. 12:1) recalls the imagery of Joseph's dream in Genesis 37:9.

>> Several times in Revelation, John loosely alludes to Exodus 3:14 ("I AM WHO I AM") when he refers to God as "he who is and who was and who is to come" (Rev. 1:4, 1:8, 11:17, 16:5).

>> The plagues of hail (Rev. 8:7), locusts (Rev. 9:3), sores (Rev. 16:2), water changed to blood (Rev. 16:3–4), darkness (Rev. 16:10), and unclean spirits that look like frogs (Rev. 16:12–14) relate closely to six of the ten plagues that befall Egypt in Exodus 8–11.

GOING META WITH THE STORY OF STORIES

Scholars sometimes use the term *metanarrative* for a comprehensive story that explains many other stories. The Bible, considered as a whole, is a metanarrative, a story of redemption (salvation) that provides the framework and context for the many stories within its pages.

In the book of Exodus, the Lord delivers the Hebrew people from Egypt (Exodus 8–12). A prominent feature of that deliverance is a series of devastating plagues, reducing Egypt to shambles. Yet during these plagues, the Hebrews are spared and, in the tenth and final plague, passed over. (The term *Passover* comes from this miraculous rescue.)

The historical books of the Old Testament (Judges, 1 and 2 Samuel, 1 and 2 Kings) also recount God's repeated interventions on behalf of his oppressed people. In every case, the Lord comes to their rescue. He wields his "strong right hand" (Exodus 15:6) — a biblical idiom denoting God's power and authority.

The New Testament employs the imagery of the Hebrew Passover to describe the salvation that Jesus, the "Passover Lamb," provides (John 1:19; 1 Corinthians 5:6–8; Colossians 1:13–14). The following examples show how the book of Revelation functions as the capstone of the grand metanarrative unfolding in the pages of the Bible.

>> Revelation 11:8 uses Egypt as a symbol of evil power. Egypt was an oppressor and enemy of Israel during the days of Moses (Exodus 1:8–22).

>> In Revelation 1:5, John says that believers gain freedom from sin at the cost of Jesus's blood, which symbolizes the Passover in Exodus 12.

>> John says in Revelation 15:3 that the redeemed people sing the "song of Moses," which recalls the song Israel sang after crossing the Red Sea (Exodus 15:1).

>> The woman who flees into the wilderness to escape the dragon in Revelation 12:14 is reminiscent of Israel's escape from Pharaoh into the wilderness.

>> The symbolism of the Temple and the Ark of the Covenant in heaven in Revelation 11:19 recalls the prominent role played by the Temple and Ark of the Covenant throughout the Old Testament.

>> The use of trumpets in Revelation 8 resembles the way people use trumpets in the Old Testament — for worship, battle, and symbol of the Lord's presence (for example, Numbers 10:9; Judges 7; 2 Samuel 6:15).

Many of Revelation's other references to the Old Testament borrow imagery from books named for the prophets:

>> Jesus is described as the "first and last" in Revelation 1:17 and 2:8 and the "alpha and omega" in Revelation 22:13. Isaiah depicts God in the same way in Isaiah 44:6 and 48:12.

>> The winepress of the wrath of God in Revelation 14:9 echoes the winepresses in Joel 3:13 and Isaiah 63:3.

>> The scroll that John eats in Revelation 10:8–11 resembles God's commissioning of Ezekiel as a prophet in Ezekiel 2–3.

>> The beast depicted in Revelation 11–20 recalls imagery from Daniel 7.

>> Revelation 12:14 uses the phrase "time, times, and half a time," which is the same phrase as in Daniel 7:25 and 12:7.

>> The sealed scroll in Revelation 5 is like the sealed book in Daniel 12:4.

>> The angel standing on the sea and on the land in Revelation 10:5 resembles the angel over the waters of the river in Daniel 12:7.

>> The four horses from Revelation 6 parallel the chariots with horses in Zechariah 1:8–11 and 6:1–8.

>> The olive trees in Revelation 11:4 are reminiscent of the olive trees in Zechariah 4.

>> The seven lampstands in Revelation 1:12 are like the lampstands in Zechariah 4:2 and 4:10.

Clearly, John was well-versed in the Hebrew Scriptures; much of the symbolism and phraseology in Revelation have their roots in the Old Testament. One Bible scholar (Austin Farrer) even referred to Revelation as a "rebirth of images," a term that emphasizes the extent to which the book borrows imagery.

In his classic *Commentary on the Apocalypse*, H.B. Swete says that 278 of the 404 verses in Revelation refer to the Old Testament.

TECHNICAL STUFF

Peeking into Old Testament Prophecy

Israel's history as a nation begins when God delivers them from slavery in Egypt, using some motivational plagues and the parting of a sea. After forty years — they take the scenic route through the wilderness — God helps the Israelites establish a home in Canaan, which they call the *Promised Land.* However, both during their sojourn in the desert and their settlement in the land, they continually break their agreement with God and lapse into idol worship and immorality.

As a result, God called individuals to be his spokespersons to the nation, summoning them to return to their "first love," the only true and living God. These prophets — such as Isaiah, Jeremiah, Ezekiel, Daniel, Joel, and Zechariah — proclaimed their messages from God orally and then later wrote them down for posterity.

Here are a few reasons for writing down these messages:

>> To document the sovereignty and power of God as demonstrated through historical events

>> To reveal God's plans for his people

>> To provide advance warning to those rejecting God's commands

>> To give comfort to God's faithful people

Prophecy in the Old Testament centers primarily on preaching: warning the disobedient and encouraging the faithful. Occasionally, however, there are predictions concerning the *Messiah* (the *Anointed One*, whom Christians identify as Jesus) and his coming kingdom. Many conservative scholars hold that the Old Testament, particularly Daniel, contains a considerable amount of End Times prophecy.

Interpreting Old Testament prophecy is especially challenging because the timing of its fulfillment is often unclear or not specified within the text. For example, two prophecies may appear in close textual proximity, but their fulfillments occur in widely separated times. One helpful analogy is to envision the prophets standing on a mountain range (like the Smokies) and viewing the peaks in the distance but unable to glimpse the intervening valleys. In other words, their prophecies are high points, not all points.

Another challenge scholars face in interpreting prophecy is whether a single prophecy has more than one fulfillment — whether it has a historical fulfillment as well as an eschatological (concerning the End Times) fulfillment. For example, most scholars hold that Isaiah 17 was fulfilled in the Assyrian invasion in Hezekiah's time, which eventually led to the destruction of the Assyrians (Isaiah 17:14). But some interpreters believe this prophecy also foretells the battle of Armageddon (see Rev. 16:12–16).

Here are some Old Testament prophets who addressed the End Times.

Isaiah

The prophet Isaiah, whose ministry took place between 740 and 687 BCE, wrote the book of Isaiah. He prophesied during the reigns of Uzziah, Jotham, Ahaz, and Hezekiah. The book of Isaiah contains many *messianic prophecies,* or prophecies about the future Messiah, the deliverer of the Jews. Here is a sampling of passages often tied to End Times prophecy:

>> Isaiah 2:1–5 gives a peaceful vision of the End Times in which people will "beat their swords into plowshares."

>> Isaiah 11:11–16 points to a regathering and restoration of the Jewish people in their ancestral homeland.

>> Isaiah 13–14 talks about the destruction of Babylon. Scholars have different views on whether this is a literal or figurative reference to Babylon, especially as it relates to the destruction of Babylon in Revelation 18 (see Chapter 12). Some hold that this section of Revelation indicates that Babylon will be rebuilt as a city in the End Times; others maintain that it's a figurative Babylon, headed up by the antichrist.

>> People often call Isaiah 24–27 the *Little Apocalypse* because it seems to parallel what Revelation depicts in the last days. Isaiah 24 talks about the devastation that awaits the earth because of the sinfulness of its inhabitants. Isaiah 25 explains how God will overcome the evil in the world and protect those who are faithful to him. Isaiah 25:7 may allude to the end of the antichrist's deception (Rev. 13). The salvation of God's people is in Isaiah 25:8–9 (Isaiah 25:8 seems to parallel Rev. 21:4). Finally, many see Isaiah 27's reference to the Leviathan as parallel to the dragon in Revelation 20:2.

>> Isaiah 65:17 talks about God's establishing a "new heavens and new earth." Some scholars contend that this chapter describes the Millennium (the period depicted in Revelation 20 in which Jesus reigns on earth for 1,000 years). Most, however, think Isaiah's imagery best fits Revelation 21:1 after the Millennium.

>> Some scholars who hold to the futurist perspective (see Chapter 4) point to the establishment of the state of Israel in 1948 as the fulfillment of Isaiah 66:8 ("Shall a land be born in one day?").

Ezekiel

Ezekiel was a prophet to the Jewish exiles from 593–563 BCE, during their Babylonian captivity. He prophesied about the destruction of Jerusalem and its eventual restoration. The book of Ezekiel is nearly all in first-person narrative and uses apocalyptic imagery that's like John's writing in Revelation.

The following passages are often tied to End Times prophecy:

>> Ezekiel 34, 36, and 37 talk about a restored, reunited Israel. Some argue that 36:24 indicates that this gathering is not just the return from Babylon in the 6th century BCE but a future return from all over the world.

>> In Ezekiel 38–39, Ezekiel prophesies a great battle that will take place. The nations of Gog, Persia, Ethiopia, Put, Gomer, and Beth-togarmah will attack Israel from the north. The rich imagery of Ezekiel 39:17–20 sounds like that of Revelation 19:17–21.

Interpreters differ on whether this battle takes place before, in the middle, or at the end of the Tribulation (the seven-year period of unprecedented evil that futurists believe will occur prior to the second coming of Jesus). Some commentators consider it to be the final battle at the end of the Millennium (Rev. 20:7–10).

>> Ezekiel 40–48 describes in detail a new Temple, a new sacrificial system, and a new division of land among the Jewish tribes. Some commentators see this as fulfilled during the Millennium. Note that the description of the river in Ezekiel 47:1–12 is like that of Revelation 22:1–2, which is after the Millennium.

Daniel

Daniel was a Jew taken captive to Babylon. Amazingly, he was elevated to the role of an advisor to the king within the Babylonian court and later the Persian court. The first six chapters of the book of Daniel narrate Daniel's various crises and exploits while serving in government (scholars label this section a court history). The remaining chapters recount four apocalyptic visions of future events.

The following passages from Daniel are often associated with End Times prophecy:

>> In Daniel 7, Daniel prophesies about four beasts from the sea. The first is like a lion with eagle's wings. The second is a bear. The third beast is a leopard with four heads and wings — it has authority to rule. The final terrifying beast has two rows of iron teeth and ten horns. Later in the chapter (Daniel 7:17), Daniel says that these beasts represent four kings who will come to power. Some scholars believe this section parallels Revelation 17:7–13. Daniel 7 concludes with the removal of the last king and the establishment of God's reign.

>> Daniel 8 describes the vision of Daniel in Susa, the capital of Persia. He depicts a two-horned ram (kings of Media and Persia) and a goat (Greece). Many commentators see Daniel 8:5–8 as referring to Alexander the Great and Daniel 8:9–12 as a reference to Antiochus Epiphanes, who desecrated the

Jewish Temple in Jerusalem. Others think the antichrist is the "little horn" in Daniel 8.

>> Daniel 11 provides a rather detailed account of the conflicts between the Ptolemies and Seleucids (successors of Alexander the Great). In Daniel 11:21–45, however, many futurist commentators (see Chapter 4) believe the narrative shifts from the historical to the eschatological (End Times) and prophesies events pertaining to the future antichrist ("a despicable person").

>> Many scholars see Daniel 12 as a description of suffering during the Great Tribulation (Rev. 6–19).

Daniel 9 is one of the most discussed and debated chapters of Old Testament prophecy. I will discuss it in more detail in the section titled "Examining the 70 Weeks of Daniel 9."

Zechariah

Zechariah was a prophet who ministered from 520 to 518 BCE to the many Jews returning from exile to Jerusalem; he called for rebuilding the city and Temple. Zechariah's apocalyptic prophecies clearly point to the coming Messiah and look far into the future to a time in which the people of Israel would be removed from their homeland and forced into exile. Some of Zechariah's prophecies that are associated with End Times include the following:

>> Zechariah 1–2 describes the reestablishment of Jerusalem, and it prophesies that the four nations who scattered Judah will be cast out.

>> In Zechariah 4, Zechariah describes a lampstand (menorah) and lamps, which parallels the imagery in Revelation 1. Futurist commentators (see Chapter 4) often interpret the two olive trees in Zechariah 4:11–13 as being the two witnesses from Revelation 11:3–4.

>> Zechariah 6 describes four chariots and horses that are reminiscent of the four horses in Revelation 6.

>> Zechariah 11 describes the destruction of Israel by evil shepherds, the last of which may refer to the antichrist.

>> Zechariah 12 talks about Jerusalem threatened by her enemies but eventually protected by God. The same theme carries over to Revelation.

>> Zechariah 13 predicts that two-thirds of Israel will perish, but a remaining third will be purified and saved — a vision that mirrors the judgment scenes depicted in Revelation.

> ⟫ Zechariah 14 talks about God's coming to the rescue of a Jerusalem under serious attack. In the end, the Lord will rule over all nations. Once again, John voices this message in Revelation.

Jeremiah

Jeremiah served as a prophet roughly a century after Isaiah, beginning his ministry around 628 BCE and continuing until 586 BCE. Throughout this period, he warned the people of Judah of impending calamity, urging them to return to God. Jeremiah foretold that Babylon would conquer Judah, leading to the exile of its survivors to Babylon (in present-day Iraq), where they would remain under the rule of Nebuchadnezzar for 70 years — a prophecy realized during Jeremiah's own lifetime. The book of Revelation later echoes this prophecy.

Joel

The book of Joel is divided into two main sections. The first part describes an actual plague of locusts that decimated the land of Israel. In the second part, however, the locusts morph into apocalyptic demonic beings who wreak havoc on the nations of the world. This terrifying imagery reappears in Revelation 9.

Examining the 70 Weeks of Daniel 9

As you look at prophecy throughout the Bible, one of the most significant yet perplexing passages you're likely to come across is Daniel 9:20–27. Daniel was an old man at the time he wrote the book and had been in Babylon most of his life. Pondering Jeremiah's prophecy that Israel would be in captivity for 70 years (Daniel 9:2), Daniel realized this period was coming to a close.

After Daniel prays to God for mercy on behalf of his people, the angel Gabriel appears and announces that another 70 weeks are decreed to accomplish several things:

> ⟫ To remove and atone for Israel's sins once and for all
> ⟫ To establish everlasting righteousness
> ⟫ To seal (fulfill) all prophecy
> ⟫ To anoint a new Temple

Disagreement over this passage centers on the meaning and significance of those 70 weeks. Here's how the angel Gabriel breaks them down:

>> **7 weeks:** "Know therefore and understand: from the time that the word went out to restore and rebuild Jerusalem until the time of an anointed prince, there shall be seven weeks" (Daniel 9:25).

>> **62 weeks:** "And for sixty-two weeks it shall be built again with streets and moat, but in a troubled time" (Daniel 9:25).

>> **1 week:** "After the sixty-two weeks, an anointed one shall be cut off and shall have nothing, and the troops of the prince who is to come shall destroy the city and the sanctuary. Its end shall come with a flood, and to the end there shall be war. Desolations are decreed. He shall make a strong covenant with many for one week, and for half of the week he shall make sacrifice and offering cease; and in their place shall be an abomination that desolates, until the decreed end is poured out upon the desolator" (Daniel 9:26–27).

Commentators have championed various views concerning this passage, but you can boil them down to three main interpretations: dispensationalist, traditional, and critical.

Having a long week: The dispensationalist view

Dispensationalism is a theological system of biblical interpretation that divides history into seven distinct periods or "dispensations." In this system, Daniel's prophecy of the 70 weeks is crucial for interpreting Revelation 6–19 because these chapters describe what happens in Daniel's 70th week.

Let's unpack this a bit more. The dispensationalist view holds that the 70 weeks are not ordinary weeks but weeks of years (as in, 1 week equals 7 years). That means Daniel's prophecy of 70 weeks equals 490 years.

Breaking down the timetable

According to dispensationalists, the first 69 weeks took place prior to the crucifixion of Jesus, and the final, 70th week, is still future. Therefore, the entire church age, which began at Pentecost (ca. 30 CE), falls in a gap or parenthesis period between the 69th and 70th week. It is precisely this alleged "gap" that opponents find unconvincing.

Dispensationalists usually place the starting point of Daniel's 70 weeks at 445 BCE, when King Artaxerxes permitted Nehemiah to rebuild Jerusalem (Nehemiah 2). The first 7 weeks end around the time of the completion of the rebuilding effort in Jerusalem (approximately 400 BCE — see the "A year isn't always a year" sidebar). The next 62 weeks end in approximately 30 CE with Jesus's triumphant entry into Jerusalem just days before his crucifixion. Some dispensationalists have differing timetables, such as the first seven weeks lasting from 587–538 BCE and then the 62 weeks starting in 440 BCE and ending at the birth of Jesus in 6 BCE or at his crucifixion.

Though following differing dating schemes, dispensationalists all agree on two things:

» An extended gap — now lasting nearly 2,000 years! — comes after the 69th week and before the 70th week. Jesus's crucifixion, the destruction of the city and Temple of Jerusalem in 70 CE, and the entire church age fit into this gap.

» The 70th week refers to the Great Tribulation, the same period depicted in Revelation 6–19. At the beginning of the seventieth week in Daniel 9:27, another "prince" from a great empire will enter a covenant with Israel. But midway through the week (3.5 years), he'll break the covenant, stop the sacrifices in the Temple, and substitute "an abomination that desolates" (Daniel 9:27).

Naming the cast of characters

According to this view, Daniel 9:25–27 refers to both Jesus and the antichrist. The "anointed prince" and "Anointed One" in Daniel 9:25–26 are Jesus, but the "prince who is to come" in the last part of verse 26 and the "he" in verse 27 refer to the antichrist.

Reading the End Times

Dispensationalists believe Daniel 9:27, Revelation 6–19, and Jesus's teaching in Matthew 24 refer to the same time period (see "Exploring the Olivet Discourse" section later in this chapter). They hold that Jesus explicitly refers to "the abomination of desolation" from Daniel 9:27 in Matthew 24:15. Moreover, the description of the beast in Revelation 13 echoes Daniel 9:27. In short, Daniel and Jesus are describing the same evil person. Note these striking similarities:

>> Blasphemes in the Temple

>> Makes an idol

>> Introduces a reign of terror

>> Reigns for 3.5 years

>> Persecutes God's people

Seeing time as relative: The traditional view

Traditionalists generally believe that Daniel's 70 weeks aren't so much a precise calendar of eschatological events as a witness to the work of Jesus the Messiah. In other words, God gave Daniel the prophecy so that the Jewish people would recognize the arrival of their Messiah.

Unlike dispensationalists, traditionalists don't equate a week with a 7-year period. Instead, they see Daniel's 70 weeks as symbolizing an unspecified period. It's the events that matter, not the timing.

Checking out the schedule

Many traditionalists believe the starting point of the 70 weeks is when King Darius (Cyrus) of Persia decided in 538 BCE to permit the Israelites to return to Jerusalem after 70 years of captivity and to rebuild the Temple and the city (2 Chronicles 36:23; Ezra 1). The next 62 weeks begin around 400 BCE and end with the birth of Jesus (around 4 BCE).

There's disagreement among holders of the traditional view, but the final 70th week is usually broken into two parts. The first half of the week ends in 70 CE with the destruction of Jerusalem, and the second half ends sometime in the future with the second coming of Jesus. Therefore, the entire church age (from the 30s CE to the present day) is within that second half of the 70th week.

ID-ing the prince and the Anointed One

Traditionalists don't believe that Daniel refers to antichrist at all in this passage. According to this view, the "prince" and "Anointed One" in Daniel 9:25–27 refer to Jesus. They also view Daniel 9:26 and 9:27 as parallel verses, referring to the same events. What's more, traditionalists maintain that the "desolation" in Daniel 9:26 refers to the crucifixion of Jesus. The Roman destruction of Jerusalem in 70 CE serves as Jesus's judgment on Israel.

Avoiding the future: The historical-critical view

TECHNICAL
STUFF

The historical-critical approach to biblical studies seeks to understand the Bible in its historical, literary, and social settings. Though many adopt this approach without any faith commitments, one can employ it within a framework of Christian faith. I have learned much from the results of historical-critical scholarship, but I also recognize its spiritual poverty when untethered to faith. Anselm of Canterbury described his quest to understand truth as "faith seeking understanding." I'm trying to follow his example.

In general, critical scholars deny any predictive prophecy in Scripture. Thus, Daniel 9 is really narrating historical events as if they were yet future. Such after-the-fact prophecy is not genuine prophecy at all.

Laying out the timeline

According to the critical view, the first 7 "weeks of years" (49 years) point to the period 587–538 BCE. However, before the 8th week starts, many proponents push the timeline back 67 years to 605 BCE, when Jeremiah received the prophecy that Israel would go into captivity for 70 years. The last week of the 70 weeks, according to this view, refers to 171–164 BCE, a chaotic period in the history of Israel that saw the murder of Onias III (the high priest) in 171 BCE, the desecration of the Jewish Temple in 167 BCE, and the rededication of the Temple in 164 BCE by Judas Maccabaeus.

Such a timeline raises acute problems. Although the events noted are significant in Jewish history, saying that sin ended and everlasting righteousness was introduced stretches credulity to a breaking point. What's more, Jerusalem and the Temple were damaged but not destroyed in 167 BCE.

Associating characters with historical figures

The critical view tries to match references to the "Anointed One" and "prince" to historical figures. "The Anointed One" could be either of two Jewish high priests,

Joshua (9:25) or Onias III (9:26). The "prince" in 9:26–27 refers to Greek king Antiochus Epiphanes, who desecrated the Temple.

Abandoning predictive prophecy undermines the truthfulness of the Gospel. That's a high price to pay for academic respectability.

Exploring the Olivet Discourse: Jesus's Prophecy

Perhaps no other text in the New Testament is more important for understanding Revelation than Jesus's discourse on the Mount of Olives in Matthew 24:1–25:46 (see also Mark 13:1–37; Luke 21:5–36). This discourse covers

>> The future destruction of the Temple in Jerusalem

>> A future period of great turmoil and tribulation

>> Signs of Jesus's return to earth

REMEMBER

There are two opposing interpretations of the Olivet Discourse:

>> **Preterist:** Preterists hold that the prophecies about signs of the end, the destruction of the Temple, and the coming of the Son of Man in Matthew 24 were all fulfilled when the Romans destroyed Jerusalem in 70 CE. *Full preterists* claim that all the prophecies in the New Testament are already fulfilled; *partial preterists* hold that many of the events were fulfilled in 70 CE but not those about the return of Jesus.

>> **Futurist:** The futurist view agrees that Jesus's prophecy about the Temple's destruction was literally fulfilled in 70 CE. But the prophecies concerning the End Times and the second coming of Jesus remain unfulfilled. A major objection to the preterist position is that the historical details about the Roman siege of Jerusalem and destruction of the Temple (as recounted by the Jewish historian Flavius Josephus) differ significantly from Jesus's statements in the Olivet Discourse.

This section explains the two main interpretations of Jesus's message and how they relate to Revelation.

Noting the signs of the times

As Matthew 24 begins, Jesus tells his disciples that the Temple will be destroyed. The stunned disciples then ask Jesus, "Tell us, when will this be, and what will be the sign of your coming and of the end of the age?"

At the outset, Jesus cautions that the end of the age won't take place immediately. Before the end of the age even begins, false prophets will claim to be the Messiah, and wars and rumors of wars will arise (Matthew 24:4–8). However, he goes on to say that the beginning of the end ("birth pangs") will be marked by wars between nations and kingdoms, along with famines and earthquakes. Many futurists believe this passage refers to the first 3.5-year period of the 7-year Tribulation and that it parallels the seal judgments of Revelation 6. As you will see, I take a slightly different view (see Chapter 9).

Next, in Matthew 24:9–14, Jesus describes a time of great spiritual conflict. On the one hand, Christian followers will be persecuted, martyred, and despised. False prophets will rise to mislead people. On the other hand, God's people who persevere to the end will proclaim the Gospel of Jesus around the world. When the whole world has heard the good news, the end will come. Futurists claim this section describes the events of the second half of the Tribulation (Rev. 13:1–18).

Jesus then alerts his disciples about a future crisis, specifically referring to the book of Daniel (likely 9:27 and 11:31): "So when you see the desolating sacrilege standing in the holy place, as was spoken of by the prophet Daniel [. . .]" (Matthew 24:15). The *desolating sacrilege* may refer to the man of sin sitting on his own throne in God's Temple and claiming to be God (see 2 Thessalonians 2:4). Preterists connect this passage to the events surrounding the Roman destruction of the Temple in 70 CE; futurists believe it refers to the sacrilege of the antichrist who exercises worldwide power during the second half of the Tribulation (Rev. 13).

Jesus then counsels believers to run for the hills (okay, *mountains*) because it will be a time of unprecedented suffering. He again warns against being led astray by false prophets.

Witnessing Jesus's (second) big entrance

In Matthew 24:29–31, Jesus describes his second coming by painting a vivid picture of the events:

>> The sun and moon become dark, and the stars fall from the sky. (Jesus may be alluding to Isaiah 13:10 or Joel 2:30–31. Some preterists see these references to the Old Testament prophets as Jesus's way of comparing the Romans' future destruction of Jerusalem with the Babylonian captivity of ancient Israel.)

>> The people see "the sign of the Son of Man" and begin to mourn.

>> The Son of Man comes "'on the clouds of heaven' with power and great glory."

>> He sends angels to gather up God's people.

Full preterists claim that these last few points refer to the spreading of Christianity in the Roman world in the early centuries. Partial preterists and futurists counter, saying that a plain reading of the text indicates the literal return of Jesus to the earth.

Futurists also debate the timing of the *rapture* (when God's people are taken up into heaven) in relation to the second coming of Jesus. Some futuristic commentators believe Jesus doesn't discuss the rapture at all in Matthew 24:29–31. Others, however, insist that the rapture is indicated in 24:30–31 as well as later in the chapter in 24:40–42 (see Chapter 4 for more discussion of the various views).

Keeping your guard up

As if answering the question, "So what do we do in the meantime?" Jesus uses the second half of Matthew 24 and part of Matthew 25 to share several parables aimed at getting his followers to apply a central lesson of his teaching — and of Revelation: *Be ready!* These stories include the following:

>> The parable of the fig tree (Matthew 24:32–35)

>> The example of Noah (Matthew 24:36–39)

>> The lesson of people taken away (Matthew 24:40–41)

>> The parable of the faithful house owner (Matthew 24:42–44)

>> The lesson of the wise servant (Matthew 24:45–51)

>> The parable of the ten virgins (Matthew 25:1–13)

>> The parable of the talents (money) (Matthew 25:14–30)

Finally, in Matthew 25:31–46, Jesus tells the story of the judgment of all nations after his return — a time in which he'll separate sheep and goats. In the same way, John warns his readers of the importance of always being ready and watchful.

Considering the "generation" gap

Perhaps the verse that sparks the greatest debate in the Olivet Discourse is Matthew 24:34: "Truly I tell you, this generation will not pass away until all these things have taken place." The problem centers on how to define the word *generation*.

Preterists argue that a straightforward reading of this passage implies Jesus was addressing his contemporaries. That means the prophecies would come to pass during the lifetime of at least some of his listeners.

Futurists counter by saying "this generation" doesn't mean the generation of the disciples:

>> Some argue that you can translate the original Greek word as "race" or "a common type of people." If so, then Jesus was simply saying that the Jewish people won't pass away before these prophecies are fulfilled.

>> Others hold that "this generation" refers to the generation that witnesses the end-time events Jesus describes. In other words, those living during the "birth pangs" (Matthew 24:8) won't pass away before the second coming of Jesus.

>> Still others point to the fact some biblical prophecy has both a partial (near) and a complete (future) fulfillment. For example, consider the prophecy of Moses in Deuteronomy 18:15: "The Lord your God will raise up for you a prophet like me from among your own people; you shall heed such a prophet." This prophecy was partially fulfilled in the succession of prophets who followed Moses. But early Christians believed the "you" (singular) was Jesus (see Acts 3:22–23 and 7:37). This perspective is compatible with the previous option.

2

Interpreting the Book of Revelation

Gain an overview of the four major approaches adopted to interpret the book of Revelation.

Compare and evaluate the strengths and weaknesses of the differing perspectives.

Understand why symbolism plays such a central role in Revelation.

Sort out the meaning of key images and symbols used in Revelation.

Chapter **4**

Choosing a Perspective for Understanding Revelation

I t's a curious phenomenon: Sincere individuals can observe the very same incident yet walk away with completely different interpretations of what occurred. Take, for example, a car accident. Ask several witnesses to recount what happened, and you're likely to hear several distinct and even conflict-ing stories.

Just as honest people can witness the same event yet draw very different conclu-sions, this phenomenon is clearly seen in how Revelation has been interpreted. Since early Christianity, leading viewpoints on decoding John's vision have emerged — yet even the most devoted, Scripture-focused interpreters rarely agree. For some, Revelation's vivid images are seen as spiritual metaphors rele-vant to all eras, while others contend these symbols point to real events destined to unfold in a specific period.

Throughout the history of the church, four main approaches to interpreting the book of Revelation have developed. Generations of Christians have grappled with the challenging symbolism found in Revelation, leading to a rich diversity of interpretations that persist to this day.

In this chapter, I guide you through each of these perspectives, beginning with a brief overview of how early Christians understood John's vision. Then, I unpack the details of all four interpretive methods, considering what each perspective brings to the table, along with their respective strengths and challenges.

Solving the Revelation Puzzle: Four Solutions throughout History

The debate over the real meaning of Revelation is nothing new. Throughout church history, various perspectives on how best to read, understand, and interpret the apocalyptic letter of John have competed for acceptance. And although there are more variations and spinoffs than you can shake a stick at, they generally fall into four general approaches: the futurist, historicist, preterist, and idealist.

Here are basic definitions of how each perspective views the events of Revelation:

>> **Futurist:** Everything in chapters 4–22 is going to happen in the future.

>> **Historicist:** Some has happened, is happening, and is going to happen.

>> **Preterist:** Everything already happened in the past.

>> **Idealist:** Nothing literal happens; everything is symbolic.

Okay, I admit these definitions are a bit simplistic since each view falls into a range along the literal-allegorical continuum (Figure 4-1). What this means is that futurists read Revelation more literally than everyone else and idealists view the book's message in more allegorical and metaphoric terms than everyone else. The other two positions fall somewhere in between.

Early church views

The early church in the second and third centuries usually (though not exclusively) interpreted Revelation in a literal manner, tying John's words to actual events that would take place soon, perhaps within their lifetime. Some of the best-known church fathers during this period — such as Papias, Justin Martyr, Irenaeus, Tertullian, and Victorinus — were outspoken in their beliefs, which today's scholars identify with the premillennial and futurist approaches.

(*Premillennial* simply means the belief that all the events from Revelation 4–19 will happen before the Millennium begins — see Chapter 13.)

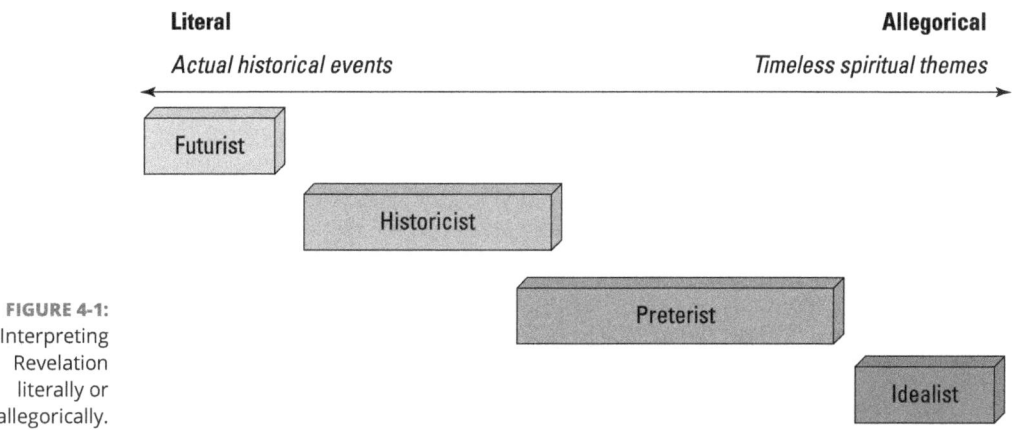

Literal **Allegorical**

Actual historical events *Timeless spiritual themes*

Futurist

Historicist

Preterist

Idealist

FIGURE 4-1: Interpreting Revelation literally or allegorically.

However, the influential Alexandrian church rejected the literal approach. Led initially by Origen in the early third century, they developed a more figurative, allegorical method for interpreting the Scriptures. Tyconius (around 390 CE) articulated an idealist approach, which, with the backing of Augustine — arguably the most influential theologian between the time of the Apostles and the Protestant Reformers — became the standard view of the church for nearly 1,000 years.

The Middle Ages and Renaissance

The idealist approach had a virtual monopoly on prophetic interpretation until the historicist method was developed, most concretely by Joachim of Fiore (theologian and founder of the monastic order of San Giovanni in Fiore, Italy) in the twelfth century. He claimed a vision from God led him to look at Revelation considering actual history. Joachim argued that many of the judgments prophesied in Revelation were fulfilled in historical events after the time of John.

By the thirteenth and fourteenth centuries, the historicist view gained more prominence, particularly among the Franciscan religious order, as an alternative to the still-dominant idealist approach. However, the Protestant Reformation was what really jump-started the historicist approach. Many reformers, including Martin Luther, came to believe that Revelation 4–22 was a prophetic snapshot of church history and identified the first beast in Revelation 14 as a symbol of the Roman papacy. This historicist approach became the dominant view in the newly emerging Protestant church over the next 300 years, until the mid-nineteenth century.

Into the modern era

During the Reformation era, Spanish Jesuits developed the preterist and futurist approaches, which helped counter the anti-papal (anti-pope) leanings of the historicist approach:

» Luis de Alcazar (1614 CE) articulated the preterist method, claiming that John's work wasn't talking about current or future events at all but instead was oriented to the early church's battle against Judaism (Rev. 1–12) and Roman paganism (Rev. 13–19). During the nineteenth and twentieth centuries, the preterist view had periodic surges of interest and has recently gained more prominence.

» Francisco Ribera developed the futurist approach in the late sixteenth century. Some in the Roman Catholic Church held his views over the next two centuries, but Protestants rejected futurism until the nineteenth century. However, during the 1830s, J. N. Darby, the founder of dispensationalism, incorporated Ribera's ideas into his framework. (*Dispensationalism* holds that human history is divided into seven "dispensations," or eras, represented by the seven churches in Revelation 2–3 — see Chapters 3 and 13 and the upcoming section "Meaning of the letters to the seven churches.") This futurist approach would soon spread among other groups as well, gaining momentum into the twentieth century, particularly in the Protestant evangelical church.

Throughout the nineteenth and twentieth centuries, the idealist approach to Revelation remained popular in other parts of the church, especially among Roman Catholics and those who embraced a more theologically liberal view of Christianity.

Today, in the twenty-first century, the historicist method has faded significantly in popularity, while futurism, preterism, and idealism all have strong followings. Of these three, the futurist method has emerged over the past half-century as the most widely championed interpretation. It's often portrayed in the media and the arts, as you can see in the bestselling *Left Behind* book and movie series.

Figure 4-2 shows how these four methods of interpretation have grown and weakened in popularity within the church over the years.

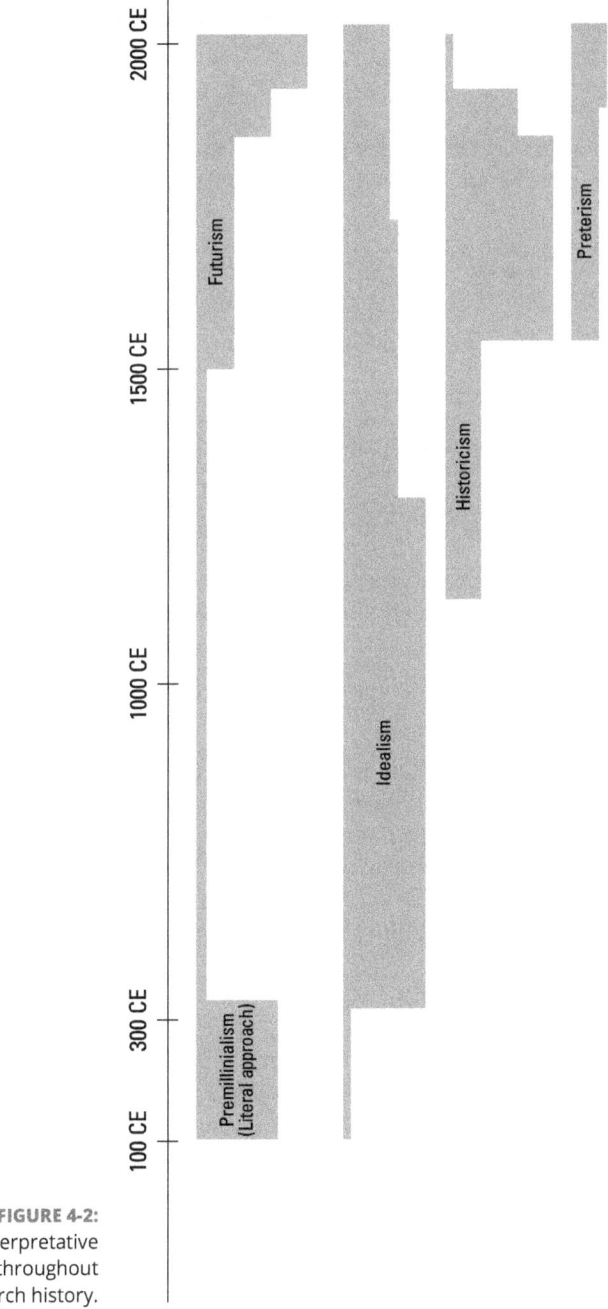

FIGURE 4-2:
Interpretative
views throughout
church history.

Futurist: Real Events Will Take Place

Futurists believe that much of John's prophecy, starting with Revelation 4:1, chronicles real events that will take place on this earth sometime in the future. According to this view, the bulk of the book reveals a calendar of events including:

>> A 7-year period of judgment called the Tribulation (Rev. 6–18)

>> The second coming of Jesus, which immediately follows the Tribulation (Rev. 19)

>> A literal 1,000-year reign of Jesus on the earth (Rev. 20)

>> A final judgment of the world (Rev. 20)

>> The creation of a new heaven and earth (Rev. 21)

Figure 4-3 shows the futurist's timeline of Revelation.

This viewpoint has gained popularity over the past 150 years, especially in Protestant evangelical churches, where it is the leading voice when it comes to biblical teaching on End Times.

Of the four positions, the futurist method is the most literal in interpretation. While acknowledging symbolism in John's work, futurists believe these symbols are handmaids to literal interpretation, unless the text specifically states otherwise. Therefore, according to most futurists, the numbers used in the book — such as the 144,000 in Revelation 7 or the 1,000-year reign of Jesus in Revelation 20 — should be taken literally, not symbolically. Likewise, the cosmic disturbances and disasters foretold in the seals, trumpets, and bowls are real cataclysmic events not symbols portraying political and social upheavals.

On the other hand, futurists aren't completely tone deaf to symbolism in Revelation. At the very least, "Sodom and Egypt" in Revelation 11:8 is symbolic because the text clearly says so, "Their dead bodies will lie in the street of the great city that is prophetically [or NRSV footnote, *allegorically*] called Sodom and Egypt, where also their Lord was crucified." Futurists recognize many other passages as symbolic as well.

REMEMBER

Futurists don't believe that Revelation's vivid symbolism warrants a fundamental shift in interpretation. They're not likely to look for hidden meanings in the text and instead argue that Revelation tends to be straightforward in its interpretation.

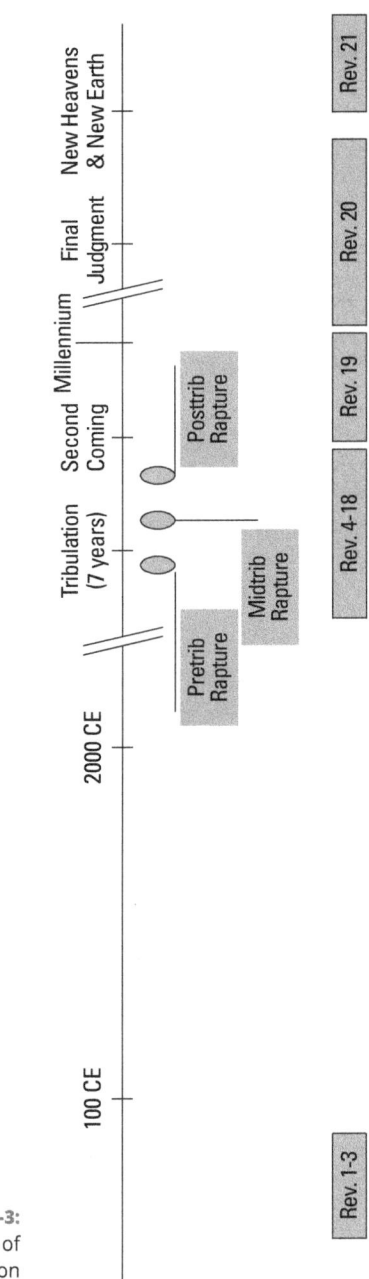

FIGURE 4-3:
Futurism's view of
how Revelation
will play out.

Various futurist perspectives

Not all futurists agree on the details of interpretation. In fact, several strands of futurism branch off based on a variety of issues. In this section, I discuss four noteworthy areas of difference.

Meaning of the letters to the seven churches

Futurists differ on how to interpret the letters to the seven churches in Revelation 2–3. Most believe these letters are just what they appear to be: letters from John to the seven first-century churches in Asia Minor.

Older dispensational futurists argue that each church represents a period of church history (see Table 4-1 for one interpretation). This approach to Revelation 2–3 is somewhat related to the historicist approach, deviating from a plain reading of John's book for these two chapters (see the upcoming "Historicist: Covering the Gamut of Church History" section).

TABLE 4-1   **Seven Churches Representing the Church Age**

Church Receiving a Letter	Period Represented (CE)	Description of Time Period
Ephesus	Apostolic church (30–99)	Early New Testament church
Smyrna	Martyred church (100–313)	Roman persecution of Christians
Pergamum	Imperial church (313–590)	Constantine makes Christianity the official state religion
Thyatira	Papal church (590–517)	Leadership of the Roman Catholic Church
Sardis	Church of the Reformation (1517–1700)	Protestant Reformation
Philadelphia	Missionary church (1700–present)	Missionaries spanning the globe sharing the gospel
Laodicea	Theologically "liberal" church (1800–present)	Modern church holding less value in Scripture as God's authoritative word

Timing of the rapture

The *rapture* is the point in time when Christians who are still alive on earth will be taken up to heaven to be with Jesus (see Chapter 8). Futurists differ on whether the rapture occurs before, during, or after the Tribulation judgments discussed in Revelation:

- » *Pretribulationists* (*pre-tribs*) believe that John's rapture to heaven symbolizes the rapture of believers (Rev. 4:1–2). This parallels the rapture accounts in 1 Corinthians 15:52–54 and 1 Thessalonians 4:13–18. In addition, they also point out that the word *church* is conspicuously absent from John's book after the close of Revelation 3.

- » *Midtribulationists* (*mid-tribs*) hold that the rapture will take place midway through the Tribulation period.

- » *Posttribulationalists* (*post-tribs*) say it'll happen at the end of the Tribulation, as part of the second coming of Jesus.

Chronology of Revelation

Most futurists believe that, starting at Revelation 4:1, there is a sequence of events that take place during the End Times and culminate in the New Creation. Others argue that Revelation contains parallel sections (Rev. 4–11 and Rev. 12–19), providing complementary descriptions of the Tribulation preceding the second coming.

Timing of judgments

Most people who subscribe to the futurist approach hold that the seal, trumpet, and bowl judgments described in Revelation 6–19 have yet to take place. They represent judgments that are far more severe than the world has ever experienced.

A minority futurist perspective sees the six seal judgments as already taking place during the church age. The trumpet and bowl judgments are still waiting in the wings.

INTERNET EXEGESIS: THE END IS NEAR!

One of the criticisms that non-futurists have concerning the futurist approach is its tendency to promote sensationalism and what might be called *Internet exegesis* — interpreting Scripture based on current events. Suppose an article on new facial recognition or eye-scanning technology pops up on one's news feed, Facebook, YouTube, or Instagram. Almost certainly a media-savvy futurist will latch on to it as a precursor to the mark of the beast (see Chapter 11 for details). Decades ago, the European Union was already labeled the modern-day Babylon, and the euro a forerunner of antichrist's worldwide cryptocurrency economy. And of course, the antichrist is whomever happens to be the most notorious villain at the moment!

(continued)

(continued)

The important point isn't speculating on whether these theories are true or false but rather recognizing that they are, in fact, *theories*. If the futurist view is correct, John's prophecy must be fulfilled in actual events. But because Christians believe only God knows the details, people can only play guessing games regarding world events. People in every generation have declared world events and leaders or specific dates as definite fulfillments of specific prophecy in Revelation, only to be proven wrong once again.

Examining the futurist approach

Futurists hold up several arguments to support their position. They say that futurism is consistent with the following:

>> **The history of fulfilled prophecy:** Futurists contend that a literal perspective closely parallels the way in which God fulfilled Old Testament prophecy (see the "Fulfilled Prophecy: Literal or Symbolic?" section in this chapter). Therefore, they argue it's reasonable to assume the same principles apply to Revelation as well.

>> **A plain reading of the judgments of Revelation:** The futurist approach argues that, even if you don't understand the specifics of the End Times judgments, a plain reading of Revelation tells you that they're going to be unspeakably bad. Therefore, according to futurists, because events of such scope and magnitude have never occurred in human history, the preterist and historicist views can't be true.

>> **Traditional scriptural interpretation:** The futurist approach maintains that an accurate reading of Revelation 4–22 shouldn't be much different from the way you approach Revelation 1–3 and the rest of the Bible. Therefore, futurists argue that by following the grammatical-historical method of interpretation, you arrive at a futurist understanding of the prophecy. (See Chapter 17 for some practical guidelines that are part of the grammatical-historical method of interpretation.)

>> **Early church leanings:** Though developed in the Middle Ages as a Catholic response to the Protestants' historicist approach, the roots of the futurist view go back to the early second-century church.

However, critics note some challenges to futurism:

>> **Futurism requires more tweaking of the text than the other viewpoints.** In Revelation 1 and 22, John clearly says that the events he is writing about will "soon" transpire. Critics charge that futurists depart from the literal meaning

of "soon" to sustain their claims. (See the "Are we there yet? or, how soon is 'soon'?" section in this chapter for more on this issue.)

>> **Much of Revelation loses relevance for the historic seven churches.** If everything after Revelation 4:1 happens in the future, how much applies to the original readers? It would seem very little. (For details on this issue and the futurist response to it, see the later "Who is John really writing to?" section in this chapter.)

Historicist: Covering the Gamut of Church History

REMEMBER

The *historicist* interpretation of Revelation sees John's book as revealing the entire course of history during the church age. In other words, the book's prophecy started in the early church and, because there aren't clearly defined starting and ending points, the prophecy is being continuously fulfilled in "real time." The historicist, therefore, sees Revelation as history in the making.

The basic approach

Because prophecy in Revelation is an ongoing process, historicists look at major historical events after the first century and then attempt to map them back to specific prophecies in Revelation (see Figure 4-4). For example, some believe that the opening of the seals in Revelation 6–7 symbolizes the barbarian invasions against the Western Roman Empire, while the locusts of Revelation 9:1 represent the Arabs who attacked the Eastern Roman Empire. Other prophetic events in history range from the Protestant Reformation to the French Revolution, to such modern issues as the United Nations or U.S. race riots. Although the view is less common today, classic historicists embraced the idea that the papacy (the office of the Roman Catholic pope) was the antichrist (beast) discussed in Revelation 13:1.

FIGURE 4-4:
A timeline of the historicist view of Revelation.

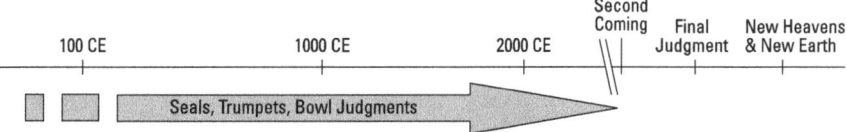

Under the historicist approach, prophecy is fulfilled through real events, but Revelation is also dripping with symbolic significance. Historicists look at the dating discussed in Revelation as key. Specifically, they hold to a *year-day* principle, meaning that one day in Revelation symbolizes one year in actual history (paralleling the year-day relationship in Ezekiel 4:4–6).

The historicist interpretation has an impressive list of proponents from the past, including Martin Luther, John Wycliffe, John Knox, William Tyndale, Sir Isaac Newton, John Wesley, and C.H. Spurgeon. However, like disco music and tapered jeans, the historicist approach is out of style today. Few people in the twenty-first century subscribe to this perspective.

Examining the historicist approach

As evidence for the validity of their interpretation, historicists hold up some rather compelling mappings of real historical events to the lens of prophetic judgments in Revelation.

Critics, however, insist that the matchmaking attempts of the historicist are much like an Internet dating service: Odds are you'll get an occasional hit, but more often misses or forced fits. Critics also note these challenges:

>> **No consensus among historicists:** Although historicists may agree on a general interpretative model, this group shows little agreement on the specifics of fulfilled prophecy. That raises a pressing problem: How useful is the prophetic message of Revelation if no one can be sure about its fulfillment?

>> **Most historicist models reach too much for a solution:** Non-historicists argue that trying to map history over the past 2,000 years into Revelation's judgments is like trying to fit a round peg into a square hole.

>> **Fulfillments are too Euro-centric:** Most historicist accounts base much of the fulfilled prophecy on events that impact the European church and overlook the worldwide church.

>> **Not all timing easily fits into the year-day principle:** Non-historicists point to various parts of Revelation in which the stated timeframes are inconsistent with the year-day model — in particular, Revelation 11:2, 12:6, 12:14, and 13:5.

WARNING

One potential danger that historicists (and futurists, too) should recognize is a tendency to become preoccupied with the nitty-gritty details of prophetic fulfillment. When this happens, readers risk turning Revelation into little more than a math problem to be solved rather than the word of God. Therefore, it's important not to lose sight of the overarching message John was delivering — to be faithful and obedient to Jesus regardless of circumstances.

Preterist: Explaining Historical Events from the First Century

REMEMBER

Preterists believe that the prophecies discussed in Revelation correspond not to future events but to events that *already* took place back in the early centuries CE. In other words, Revelation is fulfilled prophecy (or at least largely so).

According to the preterist approach, John wrote the entire book of Revelation as a promise of deliverance for the seven churches in the Roman province of Asia that were suffering intense persecution from Jewish authorities and local governmental officials. The seal, trumpet, and bowl judgments were thus directed at the Jews and the Roman Empire (see Figure 4-5).

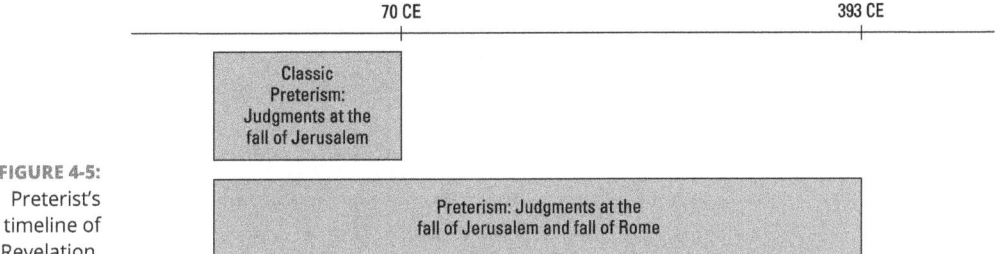

FIGURE 4-5:
Preterist's timeline of Revelation.

Classic preterists hold that John's prophecies were fulfilled in the destruction of Jerusalem in 70 CE, though a smaller group of preterists extends this window to include the fall of the Roman Empire in 393 CE. Not surprising, the classic preterist position largely depends on an early dating of John's writing (in the 60s, prior to the fall of Jerusalem in 70 CE). See Chapter 2 for more on the date of Revelation.

The preterist view formally developed in the Middle Ages and served as a minority opinion for centuries. However, it's recently become a popular model within some scholarly circles in the Reformed tradition. What's more, the preterist approach has a definite appeal to readers who find the futurist's End Times talk too sensational or downright wacky. Preterists see their view as a far more down-to-earth solution, while still holding true to the reliability and divine inspiration of the Bible.

Although preterists argue that the prophecies were fulfilled in actual historic events, they interpret many of the judgments more symbolically than futurists do. Therefore, the classic preterist holds that the return of Jesus (Rev. 19) is the execution of his judgments, not a physical return of Jesus to the earth (because that obviously didn't occur in 70 CE).

Preterists often consider Matthew 24 (also Mark 13 and Luke 17, 21) as a mini-version of Revelation because Jesus discusses many of the same themes (see Chapter 3). Because the Olivet Discourse appears in the first three Gospels but not the Gospel of John, preterists suggest that Revelation may be John's elaboration on Jesus's discourse. (The Gospel of John was written about thirty years after the Synoptics.) They point out that, in context, Jesus's discussion about judgment in the Gospels seems to be related to the destruction of the Temple in Jerusalem. If so, John is following suit in his book of Revelation. (For more on the Olivet Discourse, see Chapter 3.)

Various preterist perspectives

Not all preterists agree on particulars. Here are two notable points of difference:

>> Timing and nature of Jesus's second coming

- *Full (classic) preterists* claim that the prophecies of the entire book — including Jesus's symbolic second coming — were already fulfilled back in the first century.

- *Partial preterists* believe that the judgments were fulfilled in the first century but there will be a literal second coming of Jesus in the future, along with a final judgment of all people.

>> View of Revelation as prediction versus description

- Many classic preterists affirm the predictive nature of John's writing, believing that these prophecies were fulfilled within years of John's writing.

- Some who call themselves preterists believe John was simply *describing* current events rather than predicting events that would take place in the future. From this perspective, Revelation was the persecuted Christian church's response to the powers that were attacking the church.

Examining the preterist approach

Preterists see several strengths to their interpretative view, including the following:

>> **Relevance to the original readers:** If John is prophesying about events that will transpire within a handful of years after his writing, then he functions very much like an Old Testament prophet preparing his contemporaries for what to expect shortly. Practically, Revelation also is very similar to other epistles. (See the "Who is John really writing to?" section later in this chapter.)

>> **Consistency with a plain reading of the timing:** John repeatedly says that the events in the prophecy will happen "soon" (1:1; 22:7, 12, 20). A preterist can take that word at face value. (See the "Are we there yet? or, how soon is 'soon'?" section.)

>> **Consistency with the Olivet Discourse:** Preterists hold that the Olivet Discourse (Matthew 24, Mark 13, and Luke 17, 21 — see Chapter 3) tells of the coming destruction of Jerusalem. Given the parallels between Jesus's teaching on the Mount of Olives and Revelation, they believe the two prophecies point to the same events.

Critics identify several challenges to this viewpoint:

>> **Dependency on early dating of Revelation:** The classic preterist relies on the early dating of Revelation (before 70 CE). However, as Chapter 2 discusses, the certainty of an early date is no slam dunk.

>> **Difficulty in seeing all the prophecies fulfilled:** When you compare the fall of Jerusalem (and/or the later destruction of Rome) with the details provided in Revelation, preterists identify remarkable parallels. Specifically, they hold up nonbiblical historical accounts (such as those of the well-known Jewish historian Josephus) that depict stories of suffering and disaster. However, critics argue that even taking those accounts at face value, it remains a stretch to see John's prophecy fulfilled to the extent that Revelation requires.

>> **Mixture of figurative and literal interpretations:** Critics charge that preterists are selective about what is literal, symbolic, or both. Preterists insist on a plain reading of some of the text, such as the "I am coming soon" wording in Revelation 22, literal references to the Temple in Jerusalem (Rev. 11), and allusions to Nero (Rev. 17). Yet non-preterists argue that preterists run away from a plain reading of the text in other passages. Although futurists and historicists view the white rider in Revelation 19 as Jesus, preterists believe the image symbolizes the preaching of God's word.

>> **Differences between ancient history and John's prophecy:** Critics insist that if the preterist approach is valid, then church history would've been much different. Instead of continued suffering and prolonged persecution, early Christians would've received total victory over the Jews and Romans. What's more, because the final judgment and destruction of evil have yet to occur, then at least some of Revelation is incomplete.

>> **Origins in a reactionary period of history:** The original proponent of the preterist approach did so in part as a response to papal attacks against the Protestant reformers' historicism (see the earlier section "Solving the Revelation Puzzle: Four Solutions throughout History"). By itself this doesn't invalidate the view, but critics argue it reflects theological bias and lack of objectivity.

Idealist: Identifying Themes, Not Literal Events

REMEMBER

The *idealist* position (also known as the *spiritual*, *allegorical*, or *symbolic* approach) looks at Revelation as a figurative description of the constant, cyclical battle between good and evil that exists throughout human history (see Figure 4-6). The idealist, therefore, doesn't look for prophecy to be fulfilled in actual, literal events. You may think of idealists as viewing Revelation as a fictional story elaborating great spiritual truths.

FIGURE 4-6: The idealist view of Revelation.

Idealists interpret the book of Revelation as a message from John to encourage believers of his time, emphasizing God's ultimate triumph over evil and urging perseverance during difficult periods. The battles described are seen as spiritual struggles, like those mentioned by the Apostle Paul in Ephesians 6:12: "For our struggle is not against enemies of blood and flesh, but against the rulers, against the authorities, against the cosmic powers of this present darkness, against the spiritual forces of evil in the heavenly places." The prophesied judgments are viewed as symbolic of the recurring natural disasters and socio-political issues that humanity has always faced. This idealist perspective highlights the vivid symbolism in Revelation while downplaying its predictive aspects.

Various idealist perspectives

Within the idealist camp, you find a variety of perspectives. Here's the basic tour:

» **Conservative versus liberal idealists:** Most theologically conservative idealists affirm the idea of Jesus's eventually returning to earth, defeating Satan once and for all, and establishing his permanent kingdom. More-liberal idealists maintain that all the talk of a second coming in the Scriptures is allegorical not an actual, personal return to the earth for a second time.

» **Hybrid idealists:** Some commentators tend to combine the idealist approach with the preterist, forming a hybrid idealist-preterist position (see the earlier section titled "Preterist: Explaining Historical Events from the First Century"). From this perspective, prophecy was fulfilled figuratively within the first century but without any ties to historical events. Other commentators blend the idealist approach with the historicist and even the futurist interpretations.

Examining the idealist approach

Proponents of the idealist approach point to the following strengths of their interpretation:

» **Consistency with the apocalyptic nature of Revelation:** Idealists put all their interpretative eggs in the apocalyptic basket, so to speak. They hold that apocalyptic literature wasn't meant to be taken as a codebook to actual events. Instead, just as artistic expressions like poetry and opera deal with broad moral themes, so, too, does John's Revelation.

» **Relevance in any age:** Because this approach deals with the prophetic messages on a higher, more abstract level, you don't need to try to match up each passage of Scripture with a historical event, as the other approaches do. Therefore, from the perspective of the idealist, all the Scriptures are relevant to every generation of the church, not just a minority of believers facing those events in a specific place and time.

Critics of the idealist approach note several shortcomings, including the following:

» **Idealism stops short.** Futurists, historicists, and preterists are quick to point out that they can agree with many of the broad symbolic themes that the idealist espouses such as good will triumph and justice will be served. However, they argue that idealists dismiss the historical context and the numerous predictions concerning future events.

» **An allegorical interpretation waters down Scripture.** A literalist argues that when you interpret the Scriptures allegorically, you reduce their authority because the meaning resides in the interpreter, not the text.

» **It's less consistent with Old Testament prophecy.** Critics hold that the nonliteral nature of this approach is far less consistent with the normal patterns of Old Testament prophecy. (See the "Prophecy fulfillment: literal or symbolic?" section in this chapter.)

» **Symbolism must turn literal — at some point, anyway.** Christians generally believe that God will ultimately conquer evil and establish a lasting kingdom with Jesus as sovereign. If so, then the battle between good and evil must be realized through real events in space-time history. That means the concluding chapters of Revelation are more than glittering generalities; they involve actual occurrences.

Evaluating the Four Approaches

As you examine each of the basic interpretations of Revelation, you can identify several key questions:

>> How consistent are these approaches with the way in which Old Testament prophecy was fulfilled?

>> How relevant was Revelation to the original readers?

>> How consistent are these approaches with John's statements about the timing of fulfillment?

>> Was the persecution of the early Christians serious enough to justify the position that the judgments have already been fulfilled?

I discuss these questions in this section. But first, Table 4-2 summarizes the views that each approach has on the major sections of Revelation.

TABLE 4-2

Four Major Interpretations

Interpretation	Chapters 1–3	Chapters 4–19	Chapters 20–22
Futurist	Actual letters to actual churches (or representatives)	Describes a 7-year Tribulation that is to come	Millennium; final Judgment; new heaven and new earth
Historicist	Actual letters to first-century churches in Asia	Represents events throughout history	Millennium; final Judgment; new heaven and new earth
Preterist	Actual letters to first-century churches in Asia	Represents conditions in the first century (particularly the fall of Jerusalem)	Represents heaven and God's final victory
Idealist	Actual letters to first-century churches in Asia	Presents a symbolic conflict of good and evil	Symbolizes victory of good over evil

Prophecy fulfillment: Literal or symbolic?

One of the key debates about Revelation is the degree to which its prophecies are meant literally. In other words, do the prophecies translate into actual historical events? Or do they symbolize key themes that are taking place throughout history?

The way in which the Bible addresses fulfillment of past prophecy can be a valuable guide in determining how best to interpret Revelation. Scholars generally use four ways to describe how prophecy was fulfilled in biblical history:

>> **Real event, as told through a literal description:** The prophecy describes a real event that was literally fulfilled. Take, for example, several Old Testament prophecies that were literally fulfilled in Jesus's life and death: his birth in Bethlehem (Micah 5:2; Matthew 2:1–6), his triumphal entry into Jerusalem riding a donkey (Zechariah 9:9; Matthew 21:1–11), his betrayal for thirty pieces of silver (Zechariah 11:12–13; Matthew 27:6–9), and dividing of his garments at his crucifixion (Psalm 22:18; John 19:23–25).

>> **Real event, as told through a plainly obvious figure of speech:** The prophecy gives a figurative description of a real event fulfilled in history. For example, Isaiah 53:5 prophesies the death of the servant of the Lord: "But he was wounded [pierced] for our transgressions, crushed for our iniquities." Although Isaiah doesn't identify the servant nor the mode of his death, the New Testament provides the answer to both: Jesus of Nazareth and crucifixion.

>> **Real event, as told through a symbolic description:** A prophecy may foretell a real event using symbolic language. For example, consider Jesus's statement in John 2:19: "Destroy this temple, and in three days I will raise it up." Jesus was referring not to the literal Temple in Jerusalem but to himself. In hindsight, the symbolism becomes clear (John 19:22). Or take Psalm 118:22: "The stone that the builders rejected has become the chief cornerstone." The disciples of Jesus later realized this was a messianic prophecy (Matthew 21:42; Acts 4:11; 1 Peter 2:7). Finally, the prophet Ezekiel wrote of angels scattering coals over Jerusalem (Ezekiel 10:1–22), prophesying the destruction of Jerusalem that took place shortly after that (2 Chronicles 36:11–15).

>> **Prophecy fulfilled in general terms:** Prophecy may be couched in broad general terms rather than in specific events, places, or people. For example, the Lord promised blessing on Abraham and his descendants forever (as in Genesis 12:3).

REMEMBER

In general, predictive prophecy in the Old and New Testaments foretold events that transpired in our space-time world. Sometimes, the prophecy is literal (Micah 5:2) and other times, figurative (Ezekiel 10:1–22).

For more information on whether an interpretation is more literal or figurative, please see Figure 4-1 and the earlier sections on the individual theories.

Are we there yet? or how soon is "soon"?

In Revelation, John seems to highlight the immediacy of the events that he's prophesying. John kicks off his book telling readers that these events "must soon take place" (Rev. 1:1) and that "the time is near" (Rev. 1:3). John then closes out the book in chapter 22 with not one, not two, but three statements from Jesus saying, "I am coming soon" (Rev. 22:7, 12, 20).

These statements are like sweet music to the preterist ear. After all, a plain reading of these verses is consistent with this interpretative approach, which insists Revelation has already been fulfilled. The preterist is also eager to jump on Revelation 22:10–11, where Jesus specifically instructs John that he *must not* "seal up" the words of the prophecy, because "the time is near." Preterists contrast this passage to Daniel 12:9, in which God tells Daniel that he *must* "seal up" his prophetic message because it wasn't a message for his lifetime. The preterist then reasons that if John's message were for the church thousands of years later, then Jesus would've told John to seal up his prophetic words as well.

Although a preterist, historicist, and idealist can take those words of imminence at face value, the futurist can't.

>> Futurists argue that *soon* is best translated in context as *suddenly.* In other words, whenever Jesus does return, the event will happen suddenly.

>> They point out that in apocalyptic literature and biblical prophecy, time is sometimes non-linear: The future is talked about in the present tense and sometimes even in the past.

>> They suggest that God's concept of "soon" is quite different from ours. The Apostle Peter makes this point in 2 Peter 3:8–9: "With the Lord one day is like a thousand years, and a thousand years are like one day. The Lord is not slow about his promise, as some think of slowness."

Who is John really writing to?

John identifies the audience of his letter as the seven churches in Asia. However, depending on the approach you take, the actual relevance of the prophecy for the first readers/listeners varies.

The preterist approach holds that Revelation was entirely written for believers represented by the seven churches of Asia. Relevance for later readers derives from general truths inferred from the text.

On a strictly futurist or historicist approach, the bulk of Revelation (4–22) is largely irrelevant for the original audience because it is written, either partially or completely, for a wider and later audience. For example, consider John F. Kennedy's famous speech at Rice University in 1962. In this address, Kennedy uttered the famous words, "We choose to go to the moon in this decade," in front of a crowd of thousands in Texas. But the speech was clearly intended for the entire nation.

In addition, critics of *the pre-trib rapture* theory (believers are caught up to heaven in Rev. 4:1) say such a timeline calls into question the very purpose of the book in the first place. If the church is indeed raptured at the start of Revelation 4, then the prophetic details of the entire Tribulation period would be meaningful only to the unbelieving people "left behind." Pretribulationists (who believe that the rapture will occur before the 7-year Tribulation) counter by saying that God will use the Tribulation period to bring nonbelievers to faith. They add that the events of Revelation 19–22 (second coming, Millennium, the Last Judgment, and new heavens and new earth) are relevant to all Christians of any era, regardless of whether they're on the earth at the time that these events transpire.

Was first-century persecution really that bad?

One of the linchpin issues for the preterist position is the extent of persecution that the Christians in the Roman province of Asia were experiencing in the 60s CE. If there was considerable persecution, then this fact helps preterists in their claim that John, in his prophetic judgments, is speaking of the fall of Jerusalem as a judgment on the Jewish people. However, if the persecution of believers was limited, then the preterist has a harder case to prove.

Evidence for the extent of Jewish persecution of Christians is inconclusive. Although the book of Acts records frequent persecution of Christians by the Jewish leadership in Jerusalem and Judea, the extent to which that persecution spread beyond the home base of Judaism, particularly into western Asia Minor, is unclear. Acts mentions Jewish teachers following Paul around and making life difficult for him. It also talks about Jewish attempts to incite persecution by the Gentile community. Preterists are quick to point out that the word used in Revelation to refer to the Tribulation (*thlipsis*) is the same word used in Acts (11:19, 14:22) and in 2 Thessalonians 1:4, 1:6.

On the other hand, the kind of persecution described in Revelation appears far more intense than what Acts records. It's also important to note that on his missionary journeys Paul often attended synagogue worship and was occasionally invited to speak. That's a different situation than you read about in Revelation 2–3. Revelation presupposes that a parting of the ways has occurred between Christians and Jews and that argues against the dating assumed by the preterist view.

Finding common ground

When history eventually plays out, one of the four main approaches for interpreting Revelation will prove to have been more on target. But until that time, do your best to interpret the text responsibly. More important than having the right approach for interpreting Scripture is having the right conduct based on the plain meaning of Scripture.

Fortunately, the inspiration, authority, and trustworthy nature of the Bible can remain intact while people identify with any of these four views. In other words, Christians can agree to disagree. Justin Martyr offers a fitting example of the right attitude regarding how one views Revelation. Though this second-century church father held a premillennialist (futurist) view, he acknowledged that genuine Christians thought differently.

These four approaches differ considerably in their interpretation of the book of Revelation. However, futurists, preterists, historicists, and idealists can all affirm that Revelation was written, primarily, to encourage Christians to persevere during difficult times and to remind them that the Dark Lord will not prevail against them.

Chapter 5

Deciphering Symbols with Your Secret Decoder Ring

The modern mindset is practical. Most people prefer straightforward access to information rather than symbolism, abstract concepts, and vague imagery. So people living in the twenty-first century often have difficulty getting a handle on the symbolic nature of Revelation. The first five books of the New Testament are narratives describing the ministry of Jesus and the early church. The next set of books — pastoral letters by Paul, Peter, and other apostles — are relatively straightforward and accessible to the general reader. But when you get to Revelation, it's a whole new ball game.

In this chapter, I'll give you a brief introduction to the fascinating world of symbolism and imagery found in the book of Revelation. First, I'll suggest reasons why John relied on apocalyptic symbols — spoiler: It wasn't just to be eccentric or elusive! Then, you'll take a closer look at some of the key symbols appearing in the book.

Giving John's Readers a Heads-Up

Much like the modern world, where warnings and disclaimers preface even the most routine experiences — think of coffee cups cautioning that contents are hot or movies alerting viewers that the format has been adjusted — the Book of Revelation opens with its own heads-up. Before delving into John's visionary message, readers are informed that what follows will not be straightforward prose, but a tapestry woven with symbols and imagery (Revelation 1:12–20).

Why Use Symbols?

Most readers would probably prefer John to be Captain Obvious, laying out the Revelation of Jesus in as clear a prose as possible. Understanding the point of the book would be so much easier if specifics such as these were used:

>> Jesus will be coming back on March 3, 2027. Be there or be square.

>> Beware, the antichrist will be named Thragg and his right-hand man is General Kregg.

>> The Millennium is not to be confused with millennials or Gen Y.

Obviously, that's not the approach John adopts in Revelation. What I want to show you is that, by understanding how to read his book within its historical context and intended purpose, you can appreciate and apply its enduring message.

What prompted John to write Revelation with so much symbolism? Let's explore some of the key reasons behind his choice in this section.

Following biblical tradition

REMEMBER

Although Revelation may be best known for its use of symbolism, the reality is that symbolism is present in many parts of the Old and New Testaments. In the Old Testament, God often speaks through the prophets using symbolic actions and symbolic objects. The books of Daniel, Ezekiel, and Zechariah make heavy use of *apocalyptic imagery,* a literary device that employs images and symbols to represent historical events, nations, and persons.

Although Jesus didn't typically employ apocalyptic imagery in his teaching, he often taught through parables — brief, simple, true-to-life stories crafted to reveal deeper truths about the kingdom of God. For instance, in Luke 8:10, he says,

"The knowledge of the secrets of the kingdom of God has been given to you, but to others I speak in parables, so that, 'though seeing, they may not see; though hearing, they may not understand.'"

Several times Jesus says, "He who has ears to hear, let him hear" (Matthew 11:15; 13:9; Mark 4:9). In essence, those truly seeking to understand his message will discover its meaning, while those who are disinterested observers will fail to grasp its true intent — precisely the point Jesus makes at the conclusion of each message to the seven churches in Revelation 2–3: "Let anyone who has an ear listen to what the Spirit is saying to the churches."

Adding a fuller meaning to the plain text

REMEMBER

You know the old saying, "A picture is worth a thousand words." Well, in the same way, symbolism and imagery can often provide greater clarity and illumination than plain words alone. Consider, for example, John's use of the name "Babylon" to describe a great, evil world power in Revelation (Rev. 17–18). To any Jew, the mere mention of Babylon would have an emotional impact given what ancient Babylon did to the Jewish people and their temple (586 BCE). The echo of Babylon the Great in Revelation was now heard as Imperial Rome who also destroyed the Jewish state and its temple (70 CE). John's imagery had more impact on his readers than if he had simply mentioned an unnamed demonic force.

From a modern, Western perspective, symbolism is typically viewed as a tool for illustration. In this mindset, people start with a truth or fact and then use a symbol to help clarify or explain it. But in John's Middle Eastern perspective, the process works differently. Stories and symbols do more than clarify ideas — they are the medium of choice for expressing truth. Instead of beginning with a concept and using a story to illustrate it, the richness and details within the story itself reveal its meaning and truth when thoughtfully pondered.

Getting people's attention

Jesus frequently employed symbolism and parables to capture the attention of his listeners. Even now, stories are far more engaging than plain explanations. This is evident every Sunday during sermons, when congregations become noticeably more attentive as soon as the pastor or priest shares an illustration or tells a story, rather than expositing a text.

Symbolism actively engages both the mind and the emotions of a reader. It requires individuals to interpret images based on their own life experience, prompting deeper reflection. This process naturally leads to more meaningful connections, making the imagery — and its message — more impactful and lasting.

John's use of vivid imagery delivers a jolt meant to awaken the churches from complacency. For instance, portraying Babylon as a harlot in Revelation 17 is far more attention grabbing than simply stating, "Babylon is evil."

Reinforcing unity

Symbolism works only if readers have the prerequisite tools and experience to interpret it. When they do, symbols establish a bond between author and reader and serve as a sort of passkey into the author's world — in literary terms, the universe of discourse.

Connecting the original readers

TIP

For many modern readers, John's use of symbolism presents a stumbling block. A helpful way to approach the problem is to liken the symbolism in Revelation to political cartoons — if you know something about the figures and imagery used to portray them, you get it. Otherwise, it goes right over your head.

Believers in the churches of Asia Minor understood John's imagery and symbolism because they shared the same universe of discourse including the Old Testament Scriptures and the many facets of Greco-Roman society. To the original readers, the symbolism was not a special "Bible code" for which you needed technical assistance.

Tying the Old and New Testaments together

Chapter 3 demonstrates that most of the symbols John uses in Revelation are drawn from the Old Testament prophets Daniel and Ezekiel. When you study symbols in the context of the entire Bible, you gain new insights into God's master plan for the ages. To put it another way, prophetic symbolism links the testaments by vividly illustrating truths that are part and parcel of one grand overarching (or meta) story, the story of redemption.

Keeping some secrets

The book may be called Revelation, an unveiling, but symbols provide enough ambiguity to keep it from being a tell-all. Some level of mystery protected the original readers from hostile neighbors and potential persecution by zealous supporters of the Imperial Cult.

The Book of Revelation communicates through a rich tapestry of symbols. Broadly speaking, these symbols can be sorted into three main categories:

- **Fully explained symbols:** John explains some of the symbols. For example, the seven stars are angels, and the seven lampstands are the seven churches (Revelation 1:20). The red dragon in Revelation 12:3 is clearly decoded as Satan in Revelation 12:9 and 20:2.

- **Indirectly explained symbols:** Other symbols aren't explicitly defined in Revelation, but John relies on a reader's Old Testament knowledge to understand their meaning.

- **Unexplained symbolism:** A final group doesn't have any parallels in Scripture, and John never explains the meaning.

Protecting the underlying message

When you look at the political and social context of apocalyptic literature, you see that its authors wrote in times of turmoil and distress. Regardless of whether John composed Revelation during the 60s or 90s CE (see Chapter 2), he certainly wrote during a time of intense trouble and persecution. John's use of symbolism avoids direct mention of Imperial Rome and thus shields believers from the serious charge of state treason.

Encouraging continued reliance on God

Though commentators often fall into the trap of trying to ignore this fact, the ambiguity of symbolism hinders certainty from pinning God down on the exact details concerning the last days. After all, consider the major interpretations of the book (see Chapter 4). Preterists read Revelation and see its fulfillment in first century. Futurists look at the way the world is heading and see its fulfillment soon (or even already beginning). Idealists point to cycles of evil throughout history as evidence of continuous fulfillment. At the very least, this diversity of opinion calls for a dose of humility on the part of interpreters.

Understanding Common Interpretations

Deciphering the imagery in Revelation can feel as challenging as learning Kanji (a Japanese writing system)! While some symbols are opaque and open to different interpretations (see Chapter 4), readers intuitively decrypt the meaning of most. This chapter serves as your springboard for diving deeper into the symbolism (see Part 3 for more details).

Discovering the meaning of the major symbols

John's use of symbolism in Revelation is a major focus in *The Book of Revelation For Dummies*, 2nd Edition. Nearly every page in Chapters 6 to 15 explores these provocative images in some depth. To help you get started, here is a quick guide to some of the most significant symbols you'll encounter in Revelation. For a fuller explanation of each, refer to Table 5-1, which points you to where each symbol is discussed in detail.

TABLE 5-1   Major Symbols in Revelation

Symbol	Reference	For Dummies Chapter
"One like the Son of Man"	Rev. 1:13–16	6
24 elders	Rev. 4	8
Scroll	Rev. 5:1	8
Seals	Rev. 6	9
Four horsemen of the Apocalypse	Rev. 6:2–8	9
Martyrs	Rev. 6:9–11	9
Day of the Lord	Rev. 6:12–17	9
144,000	Rev. 7:4	9
Silence in heaven	Rev. 8:1–2	9
Trumpets	Rev. 8:2–12	10
Mighty angel	Rev. 10	10
Two witnesses	Rev. 11:3–11	10
Pregnant woman	Rev. 12	11
Red dragon	Rev. 12	11
Wings of a great eagle	Rev. 12:14	11
Mark of the beast	Rev. 13	11
Babylon	Rev. 14	11
Bowls	Rev. 16	12
Millennium	Rev. 20	13

SUPER SEVENS AND SADISTIC SIXES

Within the Bible, the number seven shows up nearly 400 times to symbolize completeness and perfection. Already in the first two chapters of Genesis God creates the world
in six days and then rests on the seventh. Genesis 2:3 says, "So God blessed the seventh
day and hallowed it, because on it God rested from all the work that he had done in creation." The number seven appears over 50 times in Revelation alone, referring to seven
spirits, churches, trumpets, bowls, seals, persons, horns, eyes, thunders, plagues,
and signs.

If the number seven is God's number, then the number six symbolizes both humanity
and human fallenness. The number six represents incompleteness and imperfection —
falling short of God's perfect number seven.

The scroll

The opening verse of Revelation 5 begins by talking about a scroll: "Then I saw in
the right hand of the one seated on the throne a scroll written on the inside and
on the back, sealed with seven seals." The scroll proves to be anything but an
ordinary document. It's something like a last will and testament because the
information revealed in the contents enumerates the heirs and describes their
inheritance. But it's also a book of destiny outlining key moments that bring salvation history to a grand conclusion. Because of that, it's a message for all people
and for all times.

The seals

In Revelation 6, the seven seals on the scroll are opened one at a time. Therefore,
the breaking of each seal is an event — a judgment — that takes place *before* the
reading of the scroll's "last will and testament."

Four horsemen of the Apocalypse

The breaking of the first four seals in Revelation 6 reveals four horses, known collectively as the *four horsemen of the Apocalypse*; they're differentiated in part by
their colors — white, red, black, and pale green:

>> **White horse:** The rider on the white horse, equipped with a bow and adorned
with a crown, comes out to kick some booty. Some take this rider to be Jesus
himself, symbolizing the spread of the Christian gospel across the world.
Others contend the rider is the exact opposite — the antichrist, wearing the
disguise of white but bent on destruction.

- >> **Red horse:** The rider on a red horse is clearly a bad dude, spreading violence and war wherever he goes.

- >> **Black horse:** The rider on the black horse symbolizes the famine and starvation that occurs because of the economic inequality that exists between the haves and the have-nots.

- >> **Pale horse:** The rider on the pale horse is none other than Clint Eastwood. Couldn't resist that one! The pale rider, like the Grim Reaper, symbolizes death that follows in the wake of war and famine.

The Day of the Lord

The phrase "Day of the Lord" is essential for understanding both Revelation and the writings of the Old Testament prophets. It points to a future moment when God will hold court and deliver judgment upon the world, marking the time when God's ultimate purpose for humanity is fulfilled. This expression shows up nineteen times in the Old Testament and four times elsewhere in the New Testament. In Revelation, the Day of the Lord is linked to passages like Revelation 6:14 and 6:17. (For more details, see Chapter 9 about the Day of the Lord.)

Silence in heaven

When the seventh seal is opened in Revelation 8, there's an ominous silence in heaven for about half an hour. The silence is noteworthy because it signifies the point of no return for the existing world — the old order is passing away and the new order is beginning. John reveals the full details of that new world in Revelation 21.

So why 30 minutes? Perhaps it functions like an intermission during a theater performance. At any rate, the break in the action is relatively short. Get back in your seat and prepare for some real fireworks in the next act!

The trumpets

In Revelation 8, John describes seven angels sounding seven trumpets. Throughout the history of God's people, the trumpet has been a powerful symbol — used not only to signal the Israelites during their journey through the wilderness and in times of war, but also to remind them that God was guiding and fighting for them. The trumpet blasts served both as a call to action and a sign of divine direction.

The trumpets in Revelation 8 signify an amplification of judgments in the last days leading up to the second coming of Jesus. They also serve as God's loudspeaker to remind listeners that he is the supreme commander directing the battle from his throne room.

Babylon

Babylon, known as a major military and political force in Old Testament times, makes a striking return in Revelation 14:8 and chapters 17–18. Some interpret these passages literally, expecting ancient Babylon to rise once more in the Middle East as a world power and the stronghold of the antichrist. More likely Babylon functions as a code word for first-century Imperial Rome and typifies the future capital of the antichrist's empire (wherever that might be).

The bowls

Like the seals and trumpets, the seven bowls in Revelation 16 symbolize a set of judgments on humankind during the last days. The seven bowls represent the final outpouring of God's wrath just before the second coming of Jesus.

The Millennium

In Revelation 20 John describes a 1,000-year reign of Jesus, a timeframe commonly referred to as the *Millennium.* Here are the traditional interpretations:

>> *Premillennialists* believe that this is a literal 1,000-year period that will take place following the second coming of Jesus. Many premillennialists are also *dispensationalists,* who believe that human history is divided into seven dispensations (eras), the Millennium being the seventh.

>> *Amillennialists* believe the Millennium is purely figurative, referring to the current church age or the reign of deceased saints with Jesus in heaven (or perhaps both).

>> *Postmillennialists* believe the Millennium occurs prior to the second coming of Jesus; it's an age in which the world will be Christianized and transformed by the gospel.

For details on these views, please see Chapter 13.

Assembling the cast of characters

The book of Revelation features an all-star cast of characters. Here's a thumbnail sketch of the leading actors and actresses.

The mystery man ("One like the Son of Man")

Early on in Revelation 1, John talks of a vision he had in which a mysterious person stands amid seven lampstands. John describes him in vivid detail:

"[He was] clothed with a long robe and with a golden sash across his chest. His head and his hair were white as white wool, white as snow; his eyes were like a flame of fire, his feet were like burnished bronze, refined as in a furnace, and his voice was like the sound of many waters. In his right hand he held seven stars, and from his mouth came a sharp, two-edged sword, and his face was like the sun shining with full force." (Rev. 1:13–16)

In this passage, John is speaking of Jesus. The description seems like a rather scary picture of Jesus until you understand the symbolism:

» The robe and sash refer to the attire worn by Jewish high priests.

» The whiteness of his head and hair symbolizes either Jesus's purity and holiness or his wisdom and dignity.

» His fiery eyes depict divine omniscience (complete knowledge) and judgment.

» His bronze-like feet contrast with the soiled feet of fallen humankind and the pagan gods' feet of clay.

» His mighty voice symbolizes his sovereignty and power.

» The seven stars represent the angels of the seven churches (Rev. 1:11), which are the chief focus of Revelation 2–3.

» The two-edged sword from his mouth symbolizes the word of God in its power, authority, and revelation of truth.

» The radiance of his face conveys his divine nature.

The twenty-four elders

Scholars have several theories about the twenty-four elders in Revelation 5. Some see them as glorified believers who represent either the entire people of God (Jews and Gentiles) or else just the New Testament church (Christians). Others believe they're an angelic choir who sing praises around the throne of God. A few contend that John adapts a 24-point star god from ancient Babylonian mythology.

The mighty angel

The mighty angel in Revelation 10 is a source of disagreement. Some think this is Jesus because he's described in terms usually associated with God. Others object saying nowhere else is Jesus depicted as an angel. Instead, they suggest it's an archangel, perhaps Gabriel or Michael.

The two witnesses

Revelation 11 introduces readers to "two witnesses" who prophesy in Jerusalem for 1,260 days while wearing sackcloth. John then refers to these two individuals as "two olive trees" and "two lampstands."

Interpretations of the two witnesses vary widely. Some believe they symbolize the enduring testimony of the church, while others take a more literal approach, viewing them as two specific individuals who will preach to the Jewish people in Jerusalem. The identities of these figures have sparked much speculation — possibilities include Zerubbabel and Joshua the high priest, Peter and Paul, Israel and the church, Enoch and Elijah, or Moses and Elijah. The description in Revelation 11 best matches Moses and Elijah, the dynamic duo of Old Testament history.

The 144,000

Interpretations of the 144,000 mentioned in Revelation 7 are varied. Some view them as representing all Christians, while others believe they refer specifically to Jewish Christians, especially given the reference to the twelve tribes of Israel. There is also an opinion that the 144,000 are a select group of Christian martyrs who hold a special place due to their unwavering faithfulness (as held by Jehovah's Witnesses).

Pregnant woman

In Revelation 12, John portrays a pregnant woman "clothed with the sun, with the moon under her feet, and a crown of twelve stars on her head." There are several identifications for this mystery woman. Some believe she symbolizes the people of God throughout history, including both ancient Israel and the church. Others suggest her depiction draws from a Christian re-interpretation of pre-Christian mythology. Another theory identifies her as Domitia, the wife of Domitian and mother of Domitian's son — Domitian even proclaimed her the "mother of God." In Catholic, Eastern Orthodox, and many Protestant traditions, the woman is the Virgin Mary, the mother of Jesus. A variant of this view considers her as both the Virgin Mary and a symbol of all God's people.

Red dragon

There's little debate over the red dragon who menaces the woman, since the symbol is decoded for us in Revelation 12:9. The red dragon, adorned with seven heads and ten horns, is Satan himself.

The wings of a great eagle

The mention of "the wings of a great eagle" in Revelation 12 recalls images of powerful rescue and protection. Some see a connection to the eagle described earlier in Revelation 8:13, interpreting this figure as an angel sent to shield faithful believers during times of trouble. Others — mostly American evangelicals — point out that the bald eagle is the national symbol of the United States of America! More likely, the symbol conveys the idea of divine shelter and refuge amid tribulation.

The beast and his mark

In Revelation 13, John portrays two of the most intriguing symbols in all the book: the beast and his mark. According to Revelation 13:16–18, the beast requires his followers to receive a number stamped on their right hands or foreheads; the mark is required to buy or sell in the beast's controlled world economy. That mark, says John in Revelation 13:18, is 666.

Many have long speculated on whether 666 is a literal number or a symbol for something else. Some futurists have speculated that Social Security numbers, bar codes, microchip implants, or some other identification technology is the mark of the beast. Others see 666 as pointing to an address, area code, or the numeric value of a person's name.

Throughout history, countless speculations about the identity of the beast have appeared in print. Suggestions include figures such as Nero Caesar, the Pope, Napoleon Bonaparte, Adolf Hitler, Joseph Stalin, and even more recent leaders like Mikhail Gorbachev who had a prominent birthmark on his forehead! Most evangelical scholars hold that the beast is an actual person and the number 666 is a symbol of his wickedness, but we're still waiting for his appearance in the final acts of world history.

3

Taking a Grand Tour of the Book of Revelation

IN THIS PART . . .

Read the prologue and opening vision to orient yourself.

Identify the main figure and his titles.

Follow human history to its conclusion.

Note the author's use of delay and interludes.

IN THIS CHAPTER

» Looking at features of apocalyptic writing

» Understanding John's prologue

» Considering the letter format and themes

» Reliving John's vision of Jesus

» Previewing coming attractions

Chapter **6**

Setting Up the Scope of the Book (1:1–20)

I f you suffer a plane crash in the ocean and somehow survive to find yourself stranded on a deserted island, the first thing you must do is get your bearings — that is, determine your situation. Remember the movie *Cast Away*? If you're a first-time reader of the book of Revelation (or even an infrequent visitor), the task at hand is essentially the same: How do you make sense of this strange book?

This chapter gives you the lay of the land: what apocalyptic literature is, who wrote the book of Revelation, to whom it was written, why it was written, and basically what it says. These are all important questions; otherwise, most of the book may fly right over your head and you will find it difficult to survive on a strange island called *The Apocalypse of John*!

Declassified! Releasing God's Secrets in the Apocalyptic Press

John wrote the book of Revelation during the heyday of *apocalypticism*. This rather obscure term speaks more of a mindset than of a specific literary genre, though certain works in the period 200 BCE to 200 CE do share some common literary traits.

Apocalypticism is primarily a view of reality. The Greek word *apocalypsis* (which the word *apocalypse* is derived from) denotes action: uncovering, unveiling, disclosing, or revealing something previously hidden or secret. In short, an *apocalypse* is a public disclosure of previously classified information. This section covers its essential features.

Touring God's headquarters and giving away the ending

Apocalypses often include esoteric (secret) information about the workings of the heavenly realms and how this influences the earthly realm. In biblical literature, this information is conveyed to a well-known figure of Jewish tradition — or in the book of Revelation, a Christian — who is transported to heaven and given a heavenly tour. This person then writes down what's revealed and makes it accessible to a larger audience. An angelic guide often explains the meaning of these visions. The Old Testament books of Ezekiel, Daniel, and Zechariah also include apocalyptic sections involving angelic informants (Ezekiel 40:3–4, 43:6–27; Daniel 7:15–28, 8:15–27, 10:10–21; Zechariah 1:9–2:13, 4:1–6:15); in fact, the book of Revelation is indebted to these Old Testament passages.

So, what's God's big news? Apocalyptic works claim to inform the reader about an unfolding eschatological drama. *Eschatology* is just a big word for the study of the End Times or last days. The grand climax of this drama is imminent — that is, it can happen at any moment. As the prologue of Revelation explains, "The time is near" (1:3).

Choosing sides: Dualism

Apocalypticism takes seriously the notion that reality consists of two distinct elements or principles that operate in the universe. Such a view is called *dualism*, and it can exist on several levels:

>> **Ethical (or moral):** In this case, a fundamental opposition exists between good and evil. In the book of Revelation, God himself is the ultimate source of all that's good; Satan and free moral agents who refuse to submit to God are the ultimate source of evil. This kind of personal, ethical dualism underlies the basic conflict in the book of Revelation.

>> **Visible and invisible:** This kind of dualism acknowledges that there are two realities. The first is the realm that you can see, touch, and handle — that is, the material world of creation, which is good. But behind the visible is the realm of the invisible, where spiritual beings like God, Satan, and angels of various ranks and orders, both good and bad, exist. Obviously, the book of Revelation assumes this kind of dualism as true, as does historical Christianity.

>> **Matter and spirit:** In this kind of dualism, matter is associated with evil, and spirit relates to the good. A religious-philosophical movement called *Gnosticism* advocated such a divide. This system, emerging during the second half of the first century and appearing full blown in the second, offered salvation and escape from the realm of the material, which included the human body, and return to the realm of pure spirit through secret knowledge (hence the name Gnosticism, deriving from the Greek word *gnosis*, meaning "knowledge"). The book of Revelation clearly doesn't share this view.

TECHNICAL STUFF

Christian Gnostics even denied that Jesus, as the Son of God, truly assumed human flesh. In his first epistle, John the Apostle vehemently denounces this idea (see 1 John 2:18–29; 4:1–6). And in Revelation, John may be attacking an early form of Gnosticism in the messages to Pergamum (2:14–15) and Thyatira (2:20–23), where false teachers are encouraging compromise with Christian moral values. The connection with Gnosticism is this: Many Gnostics held that what one did in the body didn't affect the spirit; consequently, they reveled in licentiousness while believing themselves to be the elect people of God.

In short, the book of Revelation embraces two kinds of dualism: the ethical and the visible/invisible.

Christian apocalyptic works assume a struggle for supremacy between Jesus and Satan. Human beings are caught right in the middle of this struggle involving both visible and invisible powers. In other words, behind the imperial power of Rome lurk demonic forces opposed to the kingdom of God. Followers of Jesus (later identified as the Lamb) must make a choice; divided loyalties and sitting on the fence aren't options.

Note that the conflict is truly cosmic in scope. According to the Bible, no one and nothing is exempt or excluded. This struggle is cast in the form of a drama consisting of several acts. Second Esdras and 2 Baruch, Jewish apocalyptic works contemporary with the book of Revelation, have a similar drama that unfolds in stages or acts (2 Esdras 5:21–6:34; 2 Baruch 53:1–74:4).

Being encouraged to stick with it

Apocalyptic writing generally has an exhortatory purpose. *Exhortatory* derives from *exhort,* which essentially means "to encourage." Biblical apocalyptic literature is directed first and foremost to those who make a profession of faith in God.

REMEMBER

Christian apocalypses are distinguished from their Jewish counterparts by their insistence that Jesus is the Messiah (the *Anointed One*) and that only he can redeem and restore a fallen world. Thus, the primary purpose of Revelation is practical: to encourage the faithful to hold fast their commitment to Jesus.

Despite its gloomy assessment and deep pessimism about the present world, under the malevolent influence of Satan, Revelation does offer hope: Jesus will ultimately triumph. Therefore, Christian believers are encouraged to cling tenaciously to their faith in Jesus and not defect to Satan and the dark side.

GETTING THE ESSENTIAL MESSAGE

Every profession has its own lingo. If you've ever hung out with computer geeks, you know that when they get focused on some narrow technical subject, they almost sound like they're speaking a foreign language. They understand each other because they're insiders who know the technical terminology. If you want to understand what they're talking about, you must have one of them translate the technical terms into layman's terms — more familiar concepts that you can understand.

Much of the book of Revelation is "insider stuff" directed specifically to those who are Christians and who understand the language of faith that's unique to Christian experience. But given the complexity of the metaphors and images, even insiders have trouble fully understanding John's visionary book.

Still, anyone can grasp the basic message: Jesus is going to return to earth, overthrow Satan's evil empire, reward his faithful followers, punish those who reject his lordship, and create a new heaven and new earth. Or as many put it, *Jesus wins.*

Probing the Prologue (1:1–3)

The prologue (the opening section of a literary work) provides essential information for understanding the meaning and structure of the book of Revelation. The prologue wastes no time informing you what the book is all about:

"The revelation of Jesus Christ, which God gave him to show his servants what must soon take place; he made it known by sending his angel to his servant John, who testified to the word of God and to the testimony of Jesus Christ, even to all that he saw." (Rev. 1:1–2)

In this section, I briefly examine the essential information the Apostle John conveys to his first-century readers.

Unveiling the good guy

Revelation is more than mere information: It's a revelation of a person, Jesus. It's somewhat like the unveiling of an official portrait of the President of the United States or a comparable world figure. Typically, there's a ceremony in which a select audience is invited to view the finished portrait for the first time.

The book of Revelation is a literary portrait of the risen and glorified Jesus Christ. It's a magnificent portrait consisting of narrative and descriptive brush strokes depicting a person very much alive, in complete control, and full of compassion. In a sense, you, the reader, are invited to view a newly commissioned portrait of Jesus. You watch as the drape shrouding the canvas falls to the floor, and suddenly an imposing figure, larger than life, directs his gaze right at you.

Checking out John's sources

"Deep Throat" was the informant who brought down the Nixon administration during the Watergate fiasco. For decades, only two reporters from *The Washington Post* knew who Deep Throat was. (In 2005, W. Mark Felt, associate director of the FBI, revealed that he was the source.) But no such mystery surrounds Revelation; according to Revelation's writer, John, God himself is the source of the greatest scoop ever. That's a bold claim!

In Revelation, John doesn't get a face-to-face interview with God the Father, but the message comes through some reliable channels. John makes the following assertions:

>> This unveiling is authorized by God and comes from Jesus Christ himself.

>> An unnamed angel serves as the mediating or revealing agent who oversees the delivery of the message (vision).

>> John is the recipient and the recorder (writer) of the message (prophecy).

>> John receives this revelation (message) through a series of visions.

>> John testifies that what is in the book is what he has seen. This implies that John is charged with making the contents known to a wider audience. It's not about a private religious experience having only individual significance.

The prologue explicitly claims that what follows in the book is a trustworthy, divine communication. Unless you have prior grounds for accepting this book at face value (that is, you're already a committed Christian), you'll have to suspend judgment on the question of the trustworthiness of the message until you've examined the book in more detail and reflected on its implications. My task, as your guide, is to help you assess what it says; you can then decide whether you believe it's true.

Receiving blessings

Revelation promises a special blessing to those who read the prophecy aloud (likely during Christian worship services) and to those who listen and put the lessons of its warnings and encouragements into practice (1:3). Reading sacred texts aloud was the prevailing custom in the Ancient Near East as well as during the Greco-Roman period.

TECHNICAL STUFF

Those who read texts silently were sometimes thought to be under the influence of an evil spirit — their lips moved but there was no sound!

The blessing or benediction in Revelation 1:3 is the first of seven scattered throughout the book (14:13; 16:15; 19:9; 20:6; 22:7, 14). Each offers encouragement and consolation for Christians who find themselves locked in the struggle with evil. Of course, the number of benedictions is significant: Seven in the Bible represents completeness and perfection. By the time you come to the seventh benediction, the End Times drama has run its course.

Saluting the Saints in Asia (1:4–6)

The opening (Rev. 1:4–6) conforms to the conventional letter format of the first century with but slight modification. Salutations typically consisted of four pieces of information:

>> The name(s) of the writer or writers

>> The name(s) of the recipients

>> The greeting

>> A prayer of thanksgiving

I run through all four elements in this section.

From John with love: Revelation's writer

Conservative scholars make a good case that John, author of Revelation, is the Apostle John, one of the original twelve apostles of Jesus (see Chapter 2). According to church tradition, this John was a highly respected church leader whom the Roman provincial government exiled to the rocky island of Patmos "because of the word of God and the testimony of Jesus" (Rev. 1:9).

THE CHANGING TIDE OF PERSECUTION

The Romans viewed the early Jesus movement as one of the sects of Judaism (Pharisees, Sadducees, Essenes). Because imperial Rome recognized Judaism as a sanctioned religion, Jews and Christians were free to practice their religion so long as they were loyal to the empire. Some eastern religious sects were not recognized and even repressed. What changed for early Christians were two seismic events:

- **The fire in Rome in 64 CE:** To counter accusations that he ordered the burning (probably true), Nero accused Christians of setting the fire. Needing a scapegoat, he unleashed a brief but violent campaign against Christians in Rome, killing hundreds.

- **The Jewish revolt against Rome in 66–74 CE:** Because Christianity had Jewish roots, was considered a sect of Judaism, and featured leading figures who were Jewish (Jesus himself), the Jewish revolt against Rome brought Christians again under suspicion. After the revolt, Rome viewed Christianity as a religion distinct from Judaism.

However, not until Domitian's reign (81–96 CE), when loyal citizens were expected to participate in emperor worship (especially in the province of Asia), did a more hostile attitude toward Christians begin to appear.

REMEMBER

John was a victim of government-sponsored religious persecution. This circumstance is important for understanding the message of the book of Revelation. The Roman Empire was just beginning to manifest overt hostility toward this rapidly growing phenomenon called Christianity. Prior to this, the Romans had maintained a tolerant attitude.

To whom it may concern: The recipients

Revelation 1:4 reveals that the initial readers were members of Christian house churches in the Roman province of Asia (in southwestern Turkey today — see Chapter 2 for a map). A messenger whom they knew and trusted, a fellow believer named John, wrote the scroll containing what's now called the book of Revelation (Rev. 1:9). Both John and the readers shared commitments to Jesus Christ and his teachings.

Heaven says hello: Passing on the greeting

The greeting "grace to you and peace" reflects a standard Christian greeting. What's unusual about this greeting is that it comes not from John but from three heavenly beings I explain in the following sections.

God

Revelation's greeting first comes from "him who is and who was and who is to come." This is a title for God, stressing his eternal and self-existent nature. This is how God describes himself to Moses in the book of Exodus. When Moses encounters God through a burning bush in the Sinai desert, God reveals his special name: "I AM WHO I AM" (Exodus 3:14).

Seven spirits

Revelation's greeting also comes from "the seven spirits who are before the throne of God." Later in chapters 4 and 5, the throne room scene, these seven spirits function as worshipers around the throne and as messengers sent out into the world to do God's bidding.

So, who are the seven spirits? Some suggest they are the seven archangels of Jewish tradition (1 *Enoch* 20:1–8; Tobit 12:15; 2 Esdras 4:1; and Daniel 10:13; for a further discussion of these beings, see Chapter 8). Others think the expression refers to the Holy Spirit because the number seven in apocalyptic literature often conveys the idea of fulness and perfection. Still others suggest it's a symbolic reference to the perfections of God. I leave it as an open question but lean toward the archangel view.

Jesus

Finally, the greeting comes from "Jesus, the faithful witness, the firstborn of the dead, and the ruler of the kings of the earth." Each title for Jesus is a window into the message of this book and resonates with hope for the Christians of Asia Minor:

>> **Faithful witness:** The Greek word rendered "witness" is *martys*, from which is where the English word *martyr* is derived. John's Gospel emphasizes the role of Jesus as a witness to God's saving intentions. Through Jesus, God intends that all should have an opportunity to become children of God (John 1:12–13).

   John is noting that in Jesus's earthly ministry, he demonstrated his unflinching commitment at the cross, and he now serves as a role model for the Asian Christians. They, too, must render their witness to Jesus's sacrifice on the cross, even if it means dying on one themselves. Christians must be clear about this: They can't compromise with Rome's religious system that venerates the divine Caesar.

>> **Firstborn of the dead:** According to the Bible, here lies the hope of all who commit to the cross of Christ: Beyond death awaits a glorious resurrection body, just like the one in which Jesus triumphantly rose from the dead. Throughout Revelation, John repeatedly reminds his readers about this hope, a hope that provides backbone for the perilous days ahead.

>> **Ruler of the kings of the earth:** Talk about being countercultural! This title flies directly in the face of the Roman Imperial Cult with its false claims about the divine Caesar and *Roma* (the Latin name for Rome). Revelation proclaims a subversive message: all glory and dominion belong to the rightful King of kings and Lord of lords — even more reason for the faithful to remain steadfast in their commitment to King Jesus.

Singing Jesus's praises: Doxology

In place of a prayer of thanksgiving or a prayer for the welfare of his readers, John substitutes a *doxology* (a hymn or prayer of praise) offering up praise to the central character in the book of Revelation: "To him who loves us and freed us from our sins by his blood, and made us to be a kingdom, priests serving his God and Father, to him be glory and dominion forever and ever. Amen" (Rev. 1:5–6).

This doxology focuses on the biblical claim of Jesus's unique, saving work in the divine plan of salvation: He is the redeemer. As the redeemer, he accomplishes two essential actions:

>> **Jesus overcomes sin.** This idea presupposes that apart from Jesus's intervention, no one can overcome the deadly effects of sin. The New Testament views

sin as a master having complete control over the life of a person outside of Jesus (John 8:34; Romans 6:5–14).

>> **Jesus ordains believers as priests.** As priests, Christians serve God in worship. A *priest* in biblical thought is one who mediates the blessings of God to others and who intercedes for the needs of the believing community. According to the New Testament, all believers are considered priests and have the privilege of exercising priestly ministry — consisting of prayers of praise, thanksgiving, and intercession (Ephesians 1:3–14; Hebrews 13:15; 1 Peter 2:5–9). Christian liturgy, then, is an indispensable part of what it means to be in the kingdom of God.

TECHNICAL STUFF

The word *liturgy* derives from two Greek words, *laos* ("people") and *ergon* ("work"). Thus, *liturgy* is the work that the people of God perform in his presence. Central to Christian liturgy is *Communion,* also known as the *Eucharist* or *Lord's Supper,* in which Jesus's death on behalf of his people is tangibly remembered and made present. The sacrifice of Jesus on the cross is the very heart of Christian worship.

Don't miss the two things attributed to Jesus in this doxology: glory and dominion. This is an implied rebuttal of the claims of imperial Rome through its elaborate symbolism, rituals, and pageantry.

Sounding the Theme (1:7–8)

In Revelation 1:7, John suddenly departs from the typical first-century letter-writing style (see "Saluting the Saints in Asia [1:4–6]") and blurts out with a startling pronouncement: "Look! He is coming with the clouds; every eye will see him, even those who pierced him; and on his account all the tribes of the earth will wail. So it is to be. Amen."

John's exuberant utterance is both the theme and the conclusion of Revelation, and it combines two Old Testament passages, Daniel 7:13 and Zechariah 12:10–12. Both texts, in their respective contexts, describe the dramatic appearance of a figure whose sudden arrival on earth not only alters history but completes history. John views the "one like a human being coming with the clouds of heaven" in Daniel 7:13 and the "one whom they have pierced" of Zechariah 12:10 as references to Jesus.

John's announcement affirms or implies the following:

>> Jesus's return to earth is a highly visible, public event that will be seen worldwide. Revelation 19 adds more details to this unprecedented event.

>> Jesus's return to earth has relevance and importance for all people living at that time.

>> Jesus's return to earth is, according to the Bible, certain. John adds his *Amen* — "may it be so" — to this confident pronouncement. This announcement that Jesus is coming back frames the entire book: Three times in chapter 22, Jesus himself proclaims, "I am coming soon!" (Rev. 22:7, 12, 20).

As if to further underscore the certainty of Jesus's return, God now adds his *imprimatur* (approval): "'I am the Alpha and the Omega,' says the Lord God, who is and who was and who is to come, the Almighty" (Rev. 1:8).

REMEMBER

Only two times in the book of Revelation does God speak: in Revelation 1:8 and in 21:5–6. In both instances, the point is clear: He is the end-all and be-all; everything unfolds under his all-wise and holy counsel. This idea recurs throughout the entire book.

Initiating the Visions (1:9–11)

In typical letters of the first century, after the salutation, greeting, and thanksgiving, the author transitions to the body of the letter. In a way, that's how Revelation 1:9–11 functions: It introduces the main subjects of the rest of the letter; however, the letter format falls away and the document assumes the shape of a typical apocalyptic writing, in which John recounts a series of visions, unpacking the central theme of Jesus's return to earth. (For more on apocalyptic writing, see the earlier section titled "Declassified! Releasing God's Secrets in the Apocalyptic Press.")

John briefly recounts the circumstances and occasion on which he received the first of several (perhaps a total of seven) visions. The vision in chapter 1 is called the *inaugural vision.* Here are the salient features of John's first visionary experience.

John's location

John receives his vision on Patmos, an isolated, rocky island about 35 miles offshore from Miletus, on the mainland of Asia Minor (southwestern Turkey — see Chapter 2 for a map). The island itself is approximately 6 miles wide and 10 miles long. More importantly, it was not, in the first century, a luxurious resort or vacation paradise! It served as a place of banishment for political prisoners and agitators.

The significance of John's self-ID

John's self-identification carries special meaning for his readers. He's a Christian brother who shares with them three realities:

>> He shares the persecution that goes with being a follower of Jesus.

>> He shares what it means to be in the kingdom. The *kingdom* refers to the present, invisible, spiritual reign of Jesus over his church. Christians believe it'll be succeeded by Jesus's future, visible reign in glory over all creation at his second coming.

>> John shares the patient endurance of Jesus. Disciples of Jesus must be prepared to endure suffering for the sake of the gospel. John serves as a positive role model in this regard.

Persecution comes with the territory for those who decide to follow Jesus. Jesus was aware of this and repeatedly warned disciples to count the cost carefully. In John's Gospel, Jesus issues this warning: "If they persecuted me, they will persecute you" (John 15:20; see also Matthew 5:10–12). The Apostle Paul likewise warns the new converts at Thessalonica: "In fact, when we were with you, we told you beforehand that we were to suffer persecution; so it turned out, as you know" (1 Thessalonians 3:4).

Occasion

John simply states, "I was in the spirit on the Lord's Day [. . .]" (Rev. 1:10). The expression *in the spirit* refers to a state of religious exaltation and ecstasy, somewhat like being in a trance. The individual experiences what psychologists would label a heightened or altered state of consciousness.

This condition has a long history, with notable examples occurring among the Old Testament prophets. Exceptional in this regard was the sixth-century prophet Ezekiel. Several times in his book, he narrates extraordinary, spiritual experiences that involve clairvoyance and levitation (see Ezekiel 1–11). The Apocalypse of John shows many instances of indebtedness to Ezekiel for imagery, symbols, and concepts.

John says the vision occurred on "the Lord's Day." This is the earliest documented instance of this expression being used for Sunday, the day set aside by Christians for worship and rest. The Gospels explain that Jesus rose from the dead on a Sunday following the Jewish Passover (Mark 16:2; Matthew 28:1; Luke 24:1). Not surprisingly, this day of the week held special significance for Christians and was the occasion for their coming together to celebrate the Lord's Supper and the resurrection (Acts 20:7, 20:11; 1 Corinthians 16:2).

Angelic orders

After announcing he was "in the spirit," John explains what really got his attention that day: "[. . .] and I heard behind me a loud voice like a trumpet saying, 'Write in a book what you see and send it to the seven churches, to Ephesus, to Smyrna, to Pergamum, to Thyatira, to Sardis, to Philadelphia, and to Laodicea'" (Rev. 1:10b–11).

John gets a jolt! Like a trumpet, a heavenly voice blares out a commission, and he needs to write down what he's about to see. The book must go to seven churches; all located in the Roman province of Asia.

Such a scenario seems surreal to most people in the modern world, but it wouldn't have seemed so to John. He viewed himself in a succession of prophets for whom divine revelation was a reality. The God of Israel has a long track record of bursting into people's lives — whether they're ready or not — and commissioning them to serve as his ambassadors. Several such commissioning scenes occur in the Old Testament (see Jeremiah 1:4–19; Isaiah 6:1–13).

Just when John's ministry seems to be over, owing to circumstances beyond his control, the Lord intervenes and commissions him for another assignment. And although he probably didn't realize it at the time, the book of Revelation turns out to be the culmination of God's self-revelation in Scripture; it concludes the *canon* (the inspired and authoritative collection of books making up the Bible). Not bad for a ninety-year-old man!

Seeing the First and the Last (1:12–18)

The second half of Revelation 1 falls into two sections: In verses 12–16, you discover what John saw when he turned around to look in the direction from which the voice came; in verses 17–20, you read about John's reaction to what he saw and his consequent commission by the risen Jesus.

These two moments contain the main outline of the book, and they structure the visions that follow in chapters 2–22. This first vision is like a table of contents. It also provides some essential information enabling readers to decode the symbols that occur in the visions of chapters 2–3. In short, John hands you a master key that unlocks the coded apocalyptic language.

Standing among seven menorahs

When John turns around in Revelation 1:12, the first thing catching his eye are seven golden lampstands. These are not candlesticks, as the King James Version of the Bible has it, but seven-branched lampstands, called *menorahs* in later Jewish tradition, like those used in the tabernacle and temple (Exodus 37:17–24; 1 Kings 7:49). Each menorah consists of seven branches capped with a small bowl containing olive oil for fuel. The center bowl is the reservoir for the other six, and a wick rests in each bowl, providing illumination when lit.

However, John's attention is quickly riveted to a much more imposing presence — a person.

The human-like figure — Son of God, Son of Man

Standing among the seven lampstands is "one like the Son of Man" (Rev. 1:13). The description echoes Daniel's vision of a human-like figure arriving on the clouds of heaven and assuming dominion over an everlasting kingdom (Daniel 7:13–14); this "one like a human being" accepts worship and directly approaches the throne of God. But although he possesses the attributes and rights of God, he also appears very human.

Mystery surrounds this person because he remains unnamed in the book of Daniel. Some Jews in the first century identified this figure as the promised Messiah; you can see this, for example, in a work called the *Similitudes of Enoch*, which probably predates the writing of Revelation (see *1 Enoch* 37–71).

In Revelation, using descriptive language clearly evocative of Daniel, John identifies this mysterious person as Jesus. Similarly, in John's Gospel, Jesus calls himself the Son of Man: He tells an audience in Jerusalem, "For just as the Father has life in himself, so he has granted the Son also to have life in himself; and he has given him authority to execute judgment, because he is the Son of Man" (John 5:26–27). The title *Son of Man* becomes almost synonymous with *Son of God* in this context.

Understanding the Son's appearance

The Old Testament prophets Ezekiel, Daniel, Isaiah, and Zechariah provide essential background material for Revelation. John frequently borrows and reworks ideas and themes from these books. Each feature of the wardrobe and appearance of the "one like the Son of Man" (see Rev. 1:13–16) calls for comment:

>> **"Clothed with a long robe and with a golden sash across his chest":** High priests in the Jewish Tabernacle and Temple wear this item (Exodus 28:4;

29:5). As John has already stated (Rev. 1:5) and makes abundantly clear throughout the book, Jesus offers up his own blood as a sacrifice for sins. He is both priest and sacrifice.

>> **"His head and his hair were white as white wool, white as snow":** The color white is often symbolic of purity and holiness. White hair and a white beard often represent wisdom and dignity. In Daniel 7:9, these characteristics describe the "Ancient of Days," or God. By applying this description to Jesus, John affirms that Jesus is part of the Godhead (which also includes God the Father and the Holy Spirit).

>> **"His eyes were like a flame of fire":** This is a symbol of divine omniscience and judgment. Jesus knows the hearts and minds of all; his gaze penetrates the deepest darkness. Human beings are an open book before this judge.

>> **"His feet were like burnished bronze":** The high priests of ancient Israel served barefoot in the Tabernacle and Temple. Jesus's feet shine like highly polished bronze, contrasting with the soiled feet of mere human priests; this probably points to the divine and sinless character of Jesus (see Hebrews 7:26–28). The imagery may also imply strength.

>> **"His voice was like the sound of many waters":** This feature emphasizes the sovereignty and power of Jesus. Like the waves crashing against the rocky cliffs of Patmos, Jesus's voice booms out across the universe.

>> **"In his right hand he held seven stars":** John unpacks this symbol in 1:20, so I postpone comment until the section "Decoding the mystery of the stars," later in this chapter.

>> **"From his mouth came a sharp, two-edged sword":** This image makes a statement about the power and penetration of Jesus's words. The double-edged sword was well-known to John's audience as the *gladius*, a short sword only a couple feet in length and standard issue for Roman legionnaires. It was especially lethal in close, hand-to-hand fighting. Jesus's words, then, effectively accomplish his purposes (Isaiah 49:2, 55:11; Hebrews 4:12).

>> **"His face was like the sun shining with full force":** John couldn't fail to recognize who this Son of Man was. He had seen him before. The synoptic Gospels (Matthew, Mark, and Luke) all narrate an extraordinary moment called the Transfiguration, when three disciples, including John, see the earthly Jesus begin to radiate with glory. It happens on an unnamed "high mountain" in Galilee (Matthew 17:1). For a moment, Peter, James, and John see the divine nature of Jesus of Nazareth unveiled:

"And he was transfigured before them, and his face shone like the sun, and his clothes became dazzling white. Suddenly there appeared to them Moses and Elijah, talking with him. [. . .] suddenly a bright cloud overshadowed them, and from the cloud a voice said, 'This is my Son, the Beloved; with him I am well pleased; listen to him!'" (Matthew 17:2–4, 7)

The similarities between the Transfiguration and what John now sees are apparent.

Meeting Jesus face to face

Have you ever met someone famous whom you admired a great deal? Did you stutter a bit when trying to talk? Did your palms sweat? Did you feel mildly faint? Did your brain shut down overwhelmed by the emotion of the event? Well, just imagine meeting the Man Upstairs face to face! The Bible records several instances of human encounters with God:

>> Abraham, on the night the Lord makes a covenant with him (Genesis 15:12)

>> Moses, when the glory of the Lord passes before him on Mount Sinai (Exodus 34:8)

>> Joshua, before the captain of the Lord's army at Jericho (Joshua 5:14–15)

>> Isaiah, when he sees "the King, the Lord of hosts" on his throne (Isaiah 6:5)

>> Ezekiel, when he sees the mobile throne chariot of God (Ezekiel 1:28)

>> The three Apostles Peter, James, and John on the mount of Transfiguration (Mark 9:6)

John's reaction to the presence of Jesus is typical of all who experience a personal *theophany*, or appearance of God: John falls before the feet of Jesus "as though dead" (Rev. 1:17).

Reassuring Jesus's servant

Jesus's reaction to John's collapse is reassuring. He places his right hand on him, probably his shoulder. The right hand in biblical thought is a symbol and sign of power. By placing his right hand on John, Jesus assures him of acceptance and favor.

The gesture is followed by verbal assurance: "Do not be afraid" (Rev. 1:17). Several times, when John the Apostle was a young man, he heard Jesus say these words. The last time was shortly before the crucifixion. Jesus had just informed his disciples that he was leaving them and returning to his Father. In response to their anxiety, Jesus twice reassured and consoled them: "Do not let your hearts be troubled. Believe in God, believe also in me. [. . .] Do not let your hearts be troubled, and do not let them be afraid" (John 14:1, 14:27). And now in his old age, John once again hears these soothing words spoken by a familiar voice.

Seeing who holds the keys

After telling John not to be afraid, Jesus identifies himself as "the first and last, and the living one. I was dead, and see, I am alive forever and ever; and I have the keys of Death and Hades" (Rev. 1:17–18). The titles Jesus uses for himself are divine titles, the very things that define God: the self-existent one, the one who is the source of life itself.

The risen Jesus of the book of Revelation is Lord of life and death, holding all the keys that matter, "the keys of Death and Hades" (Rev. 1:18). This is incredibly good news for believers because Jesus promises to raise up (resurrect) all who believe in him at the last day (John 5:24–29).

TIP

The message of Jesus's triumph over death is a theme that recurs throughout the book of Revelation — a timely message then and now.

Charting the Course (1:19–20)

The brief section in Revelation 1:19–20 is valuable because it lays out the main sections of the book of Revelation. This occurs within a commissioning scene reminiscent of the Old Testament prophets (Isaiah 8:1; Jeremiah 30:2; 36:2; Ezekiel 43:11; Habakkuk 2:2). Jesus also gives John an interpretive key for understanding the next major section of the book (chapters 2–3). Read on.

Getting a commission to write

The one like the Son of Man tells John, "Now write what you have seen, what is, and what is to take place after this" (1:19). This sentence serves as a table of contents for the rest of the book of Revelation. Notice how it falls into the following three sections:

» **What you have seen:** This sums up the inaugural vision of Jesus granted to John on the island of Patmos, now viewed as a past event (1:9–18).

» **What is:** The next two chapters consist of seven prophetic messages directed to seven house churches located in the Roman province of Asia (2:1–3:22).

>> **What is to take place after this:** *This* refers to what was happening in the seven house churches. Beginning at chapter 4, however, John describes his visions of what happens "after this." He is caught up to the heavenly throne room, where he sees Jesus enthroned at the right hand of God the Father. From the throne, Jesus directs the course of history to its grand finale. Everything unfolds in accordance with God's will, symbolized by a scroll of destiny. Revelation 4–19, therefore, by means of a series of visionary experiences, carries the action forward from the time of John at the end of the first century until the triumphant return of Jesus at some unspecified time in the future (19:11–16).

Decoding the mystery of the stars

In Revelation 1:20, Jesus explains to John the mystery of the seven stars in his hand: They are "the angels of the seven churches." As for the seven lampstands, they represent the seven churches of Ephesus, Smyrna, Pergamum, Thyatira, Sardis, Philadelphia, and Laodicea, already mentioned in 1:11. The equation of the lampstands as churches seems straightforward. The seven angels are most likely literal angelic beings in God's service on behalf of the churches (see more in Chapter 8).

Chapter **7**

Reading the Seven Letters to Conflicted Churches (1:19–3:22)

G etting mail has always been popular — even in the first century. In fact, one of the notable achievements of the Roman Empire was the establishment of safe roads over which imperial couriers delivered official letters. Because FedEx and UPS didn't exist yet, travelers and messengers hand-carried personal mail.

After John finished writing the book of Revelation, he sent it to seven churches in the Roman province of Asia, located in what's now western Turkey. As soon as they began reading, these churches would've immediately understood the unusual nature of their mail: It contained seven heavenly messages from Jesus himself, delivered through John.

Jesus addresses these congregations in a stern but compassionate manner. Much is expected of them, but much is promised for those who persevere. They're under enormous pressure to abandon their exclusive commitment to Jesus as Lord and to compromise his high moral standards. In many respects, these seven messages embody the primary purpose of the entire book: to exhort believers to be faithful till the end, even at the cost of their lives.

In this chapter, you explore the content of the seven letters in Revelation 2–3 and gain an increased awareness of the difficulties facing early Christians living in the Greco-Roman world. You also appreciate how each letter is specifically tailored for the congregation it addresses, while at the same time addressing all the churches. Readers also get occasional glimpses into the historical background of the cities in which these house churches were located. Finally, you discover some of the foundational beliefs and behaviors of early Christians.

The Symmetry of the Messages

Peeking into Revelation 2–3, one question that immediately comes up is whether these individual messages are really letters. After all, they don't follow the typical letter format as seen in Paul's New Testament letters and other letters of that era. The closest parallel seems to be prophetic letters and *oracles* (divine messages delivered by prophets), such as those in the Old Testament (2 Chronicles 21:12–15 and Jeremiah 29). In fact, Amos 1–2, with its seven stereotyped judgment oracles, provides the most striking comparison — underscoring the prophetic nature of the book of Revelation. As a result, the best label for these seven letters may be *messages*.

Before diving into the content of the messages, you need to be aware of their structure and pattern. Here's why the organization is significant:

>> Most members of these house churches couldn't read — some authorities estimate that only about 15 percent of the members of a given congregation were capable of doing so. The arrangement of each message falls into a stereotyped pattern consisting of the same basic components, serving as a memory aid to listeners.

>> Carefully structured messages reflect a characteristic of prophetic speech. This confirms John's claim that his work is "prophecy" (1:3).

>> Structuring and patterning also occur regularly in the teaching of Jesus in the Gospels. A quick reading of the Sermon on the Mount displays this feature as well (Matthew 5–7).

In the following sections, I draw attention to this structure.

Surveying the structure of each letter

The basic structure of each message is as follows:

>> **Charge to write:** "To the angel of the church in [. . .] write"

>> **Identification of sender:** "These are the words of [. . .]"

>> **Commendation or condemnation:** "I know [. . .]"

>> **Pastoral admonition:** "Remember [. . .], Do not fear [. . .], Repent [. . . and so on]"

>> **Pastoral exhortation:** "Let everyone who has an ear listen [. . .]"

>> **Promise:** "To everyone who conquers [. . .]"

The only deviation from this outline occurs with the last two items; in the last four messages, the positions of the exhortation and promise are reversed. This minor variation is probably not significant and only reflects John's desire for some artistic variation!

Yet despite the similar structure, each message is tailor-made for a given church. Here are three features of the messages that call for special comment:

>> All the messages identify and describe Jesus as the sender, but their descriptions, though based on the initiating vision of Jesus (1:12–16 — see Chapter 6), vary for each individual church. For example, the message to the church at

Smyrna identifies Jesus as "the first and the last, who was dead and came to life" (2:8). Given that the believers at Smyrna were about to undergo severe persecution (2:10), they needed a special reminder of Jesus's power over death.

>> The pastoral admonitions in the messages are specific and unique to each church. As the chief shepherd of his sheep (see 1 Peter 5:4), Jesus offers just the right balance of encouragement and rebuke.

>> The promise to each individual church varies, but all the promises point to the same reality: everlasting life. In Smyrna, for example, Jesus promises that the "second death" will not harm them, which is highly appropriate for their circumstances (2:11).

REMEMBER

Although each message is personalized for a specific church, the implied audience isn't limited to that church. On the contrary, the messages are clearly intended for all seven churches because each letter concludes with a summons to hear what Jesus is saying to the *churches* (2:7, 2:11, 2:17, 2:29, 3:6, 3:13, 3:22).

Considering the overall pattern of the messages

In addition to the basic structure, you should take note of the relative spiritual health of each congregation:

>> Churches 1 and 7 (Ephesus and Laodicea) are in grave peril.

>> Churches 2 and 6 (Smyrna and Philadelphia) are the only ones not censured for some shortcoming.

>> Churches 3, 4, and 5 (Pergamum, Thyatira, and Sardis) are okay but not great.

This pattern forms a *chiasm*, a literary device in which parallel ideas or lines of text conform to a pattern: A–B–C–B'–A':

    A Ephesus (2:1–7)

        B Smyrna (2:8–11)

                C Pergamum (2:12–17)

                C Thyatira (2:18–29)

                C Sardis (3:1–6)

        B' Philadelphia (3:7–13)

    A' Laodicea (3:14–22)

Ephesus and Laodicea are the A and A' elements, Smyrna and Philadelphia are the B and B', and Pergamum, Thyatira, and Sardis correspond to C. This pattern draws attention to the dire need for repentance at Ephesus and Laodicea.

Looking at a map (see Chapter 2) may clarify an interesting geographical relationship among the cities: They're all linked by road to Ephesus, the capital of the province. Sir William Ramsay, a British archaeologist and New Testament scholar, suggested that the order of the messages corresponds to the imperial mail delivery route in the province of Asia.

Asking about the Audience

Audience is important. After all, when you have something to say, the details you reveal, the support you provide, and the language you use is likely to vary, depending on whether you're chatting with your boss, your great aunt, or the buddies you've known since the sandbox. So, for Revelation, the question remains: Who is the audience, and are they real or symbolic? Here's what scholars say.

Angels: Postmen or guardians?

The first question you may ask yourself when you read these passages to the seven churches is: Who are these angels that Jesus is referring to when he addresses each letter "to the angel of the church in *x*"?

You probably haven't seen any of these creatures hanging around your church. The question is complicated by the fact that the Greek word *angelos* (translated "angel") conveys the idea of a messenger or one sent, but it also has several nuances. Scholars have offered four main explanations. An angel may be

>> **The deliverer of the message:** If this is John's meaning, perhaps he's referring to the person who delivered the letter — the postman, so to speak. However, the problem with this explanation is that the angel is the *recipient* of the message, not the deliverer. Furthermore, the word *angel* occurs 67 times in the book and, in every other instance outside chapters 2–3, it refers to an angelic being of some kind.

>> **A pastor of the church:** A second explanation is that the *angelos* is the pastor of the church. The basic problem with this suggestion is that nowhere in the New Testament, or Christian literature outside the New Testament, does the word *angel* refer to a pastor, bishop, or any other human officeholder in the church.

>> **The spiritual attitude of the church:** Some scholars tweak the translation by saying the angel typifies the "spirit" or "attitude" of the church in question. This seems like a tweak that twists the meaning!

>> **A guardian angel:** The best explanation may be to take John at face value. But is this credible? Do churches have guardian angels? As strange as it may sound, that may just be what John intends. After all, in a few passages, the Bible does speak about angels who assume the role of guardians (Matthew 4:6, 4:11, 18:10, 26:53; Luke 15:10; Acts 5:19, 12:7–15, 27:23), and Paul alludes to angels concerned about proper decorum at Christian worship services (1 Corinthians 11:10).

In John's mind, like that of other New Testament writers, angels appear to be personal agents who watch over and protect the communities of the faithful. Because they're assigned to individual congregations, Jesus addresses them directly, even though they're spiritual representatives rather than visible participants in the life of the churches. This form of address strengthens Christian conviction that divine resources are indeed at their disposal.

THE CHURCHES AS ERAS OF CHURCH HISTORY

Many dispensationalists believe that the churches represent seven different eras of church history. For example, here's one possible scheme:

- Ephesus represents the first Christian century.

- Smyrna represents the era of persecution in the second and third centuries.

- Pergamum represents the age of Constantine, when Christianity became the religion of the Roman Empire.

- Thyatira is the Middle Ages.

- Sardis is the Protestant Reformation.

- Philadelphia is the period of the modern missionary movement.

- Laodicea represents the church of the End Times, which has abandoned its former beliefs and principles.

As intriguing as this may be, it oversimplifies church history, which is much more complex and nuanced.

The seven churches: Real or symbolic?

Many people look at the structure and pattern of these messages and wonder whether they're messages to seven real churches or whether this is simply a literary device that John uses to address Christians in general. What's more, given the symbolic nature of the number seven (it represents perfection or completeness), many speculate that its usage is a clear tip-off that these letters aren't really addressed to seven actual churches.

Because each church is to read the messages sent to the other churches, the intended audience is at least greater than any one congregation. What's more, the province of Asia contained other churches besides the seven John selected (see, for example, Colossians 4:13). In a very real sense, then, these seven churches represent a much larger constituency.

VIRTUES AND VICES OF LIFE IN THE CITIES

The following table summarizes the moral and spiritual condition of the seven churches. This chart is selective and representative. It doesn't simply document the various strengths and weaknesses of each church. Rather, it highlights a particular vice and its corresponding virtue. The point is to draw attention to the virtues that, according to Revelation, should always characterize Christian congregations.

At Ephesus, for example, the vice is a spirit of contentiousness; what's needed is an infusion of love. The church at Smyrna needs to hear the admonition to exercise courage. It's not as though they had none; they'd been quite courageous to this point. But they did need a reminder not to let fear grip their hearts and thereby undermine their courage.

Church	Vice	Virtue
Ephesus	Contentiousness	Love
Smyrna	Fear	Courage
Pergamum	Doctrinal compromise	Orthodoxy (correct belief)
Thyatira	Moral compromise	Orthopraxy (correct behavior)
Sardis	Overconfidence	Vigilance
Philadelphia	Lack of strength	Endurance
Laodicea	Indifference	Zeal

Still, each message includes too many historical details *specific to that church* for a symbolic view to be persuasive. My look at each church in the sections that follow underscores this point.

Good reasons exist for viewing the seven churches as actual churches of the first century, which are typical of churches throughout Christian church history. In short, they're both actual and representative. You can probably find a Smyrna, Philadelphia, and Laodicea, for example, just about any time or era you choose. In fact, you may even catch a glimpse of your own church in one of these snapshots!

Getting to Know the Seven Churches Up Close and Personal

A quick read of Revelation 2–3 reveals that all is not well among the house churches of Asia. Although you see a few indications of random violence directed at members of these churches, for the most part, the pressure is more subtle. More than a few Christians are succumbing and lapsing into their pre-Christian lifestyles and vices. It's worth noting what you don't read: nothing about state-sponsored persecution — yet. As you move into the central section of the book, however, a quite different scenario emerges. In other words, Jesus addresses these seven churches and challenges them to be faithful for a very good reason: The evil empire — Rome — is about to strike back!

REMEMBER

The second and third centuries witnessed widespread persecution and martyrdom of Christians who refused to participate in the state religion. This involved venerating the gods of Rome and even some of the deceased Roman emperors, such as Augustus. Christian refusal was considered treason — a crime deserving capital punishment in the view of most Roman citizens. The book of Revelation, written at the end of the first century, is almost a dress rehearsal for what's coming. Keep this in mind as you read the rest of the story in the later chapters of Revelation.

So, what was it like to live as a Christian at the end of the first Christian century in the Roman province of Asia? To help you enter imaginatively into their world, I first provide a brief snapshot of each city in which these believers lived and then reconstruct, as best I can, the spiritual condition in the house churches located within them. Bear in mind that early Christians met for worship in private homes.

TECHNICAL STUFF

Probably several houses hosted worship services in each city. Romans 16, for example, mentions "the church in their house" (Romans 16:5) and "the saints who are with them" (Romans 16:15). The oldest known building for Christian worship was discovered at Dura Europa (in modern-day Syria) and dates to circa 232 CE.

ACTS, ARTEMIS, AND THE SILVER INDUSTRY

The book of Acts indicates that Ephesus supported a thriving industry that specialized in making silver figurines of Artemis (the photo shows an image of this fertility goddess). Archeological work at Ephesus confirms the New Testament account. Undoubtedly, women who wanted to get pregnant wore some of these figurines around the neck as a lucky charm.

The Apostle Paul narrowly escaped disaster when disgruntled silversmiths, led by a man named Demetrius, sought to discredit and expel him from the city following his successful evangelistic campaign. Apparently, because of Paul's preaching, many converts abandoned their devotion to Artemis, so much so that business fell off and the silversmiths found their livelihood threatened (Acts 19:23–27). This led to a huge riot staged in the great theater. Today, tourists can sit in this magnificent 24,000-capacity theater and look out across the remains of the Arcadian way, a colonnaded street leading, in Paul's day, from the theater to the commercial harbor on the shoreline.

Vanni/Art Resource, NY

Ephesus: Down on love (2:1–7)

Though not the capital, Ephesus was nonetheless the largest and most important city in the province. It even boasted the title *supreme metropolis of Asia.* In fact, the Asian proconsul (Roman official who served as the governor of a province) resided in Ephesus and maintained government offices there.

Ephesus, the city

Ephesus was a splendid Greco-Roman city boasting a population of at least a quarter million. Its geographic location was ideal, beautifully nestled between two mountains close to the Aegean Sea's shoreline. The city was adorned with public and commercial buildings, fountains, gymnasiums, bath houses, stadiums, the-aters, and especially temples. Ephesus was also a commercial powerhouse and transportation hub. If all roads led to Rome, Ephesus was a major intersection on the way.

TECHNICAL STUFF

Besides its location where the Cayster River empties into the Aegean Sea, Ephesus is positioned at the western end of a great road linking western Asia to the Anato-lian interior and the Near East. Roman milestones on this ancient road calculate the distance using Ephesus as the point of origin. The city is also on a north-south road following the coastline of Asia Minor by way of Smyrna and Pergamum, all the way to Troas (the area around the city of Troy) and the Dardanelles (a strate-gically important strait). The products of the rich Anatolian lands flowed to the harbor and roads of Ephesus and from there to the larger Mediterranean world.

The crown jewel of Ephesus was the Temple of Artemis, one of the seven wonders of the ancient world. This magnificent structure measured 420 feet long by 240 feet wide, supporting a roof 60 feet high that was upheld by 117 imposing col-umns. Within the temple, open to the sky, stood a huge statue of Artemis (Diana is the Roman equivalent). Originally the Greek goddess of wild nature, she morphed into a fertility goddess at Ephesus.

The church at Ephesus

Based on what Jesus says to the church of Ephesus (Rev. 2:1–7), their spiritual fervor doesn't match the grandeur of their city.

Believers at Ephesus are doing some things right. Jesus commends them for their hard work and especially their vigilance against false Apostles. Ephesus was a hotbed of false teaching even in the early days following Paul's founding of the church. Paul, in fact, worried and warned about this problem while on his way to Jerusalem during his third missionary journey. He requested the Ephesian elders to come down to the beach and meet with him before he sailed on to the east. In a memorable scene, he predicts future trouble: "I know that after I have gone, savage wolves will come in among you, not sparing the flock. Some even from your own group will come distorting the truth in order to entice the disciples to follow them. Therefore be alert [. . .]" (Acts 20:29–31). Paul was right in his warning. Five years or so later, when Paul writes to his young assistant Timothy who is ministering in Ephesus, a major concern is dealing with false teachers who are upsetting the faith of many (1 Timothy 1:3–11; 4:1–9; 6:3–10).

Although Jesus commends the church for examining and rejecting the false teachers, he points to a scourge in their midst: Perhaps as an outgrowth of their zeal to defend the truth, an unloving attitude permeates the Ephesian church. Jesus says, "You have abandoned the love you had at first" (Rev. 2:4). The people have failed to remember the exhortation of their founding father, the Apostle Paul: "But speaking the truth in love, we must grow up in every way into him who is the head, into Christ" (Ephesians 4:15).

According to the Bible, their lack of love is inconsistent with the truth of Christianity and is deadly. After all, John says, "Whoever does not love abides in death" (1 John 3:14). Jesus, however, knows what the solution is: Love must first be directed to him because he's the source of all love. Genuine love for God always overflows as love for others (Philippians 1:9; 1 Thessalonians 3:12). The remedy is immediate repentance. For those who choose to repent, Jesus offers glorious promise — permission to enter paradise.

Smyrna: Faithful under fire (2:8–11)

Smyrna lies 40 miles to the north of Ephesus, just south of where the Hermus River empties into the Aegean Sea. Possessing a well-protected harbor, the city of Smyrna also sits at the western end of a trade route joining the major inland route across Anatolia to the east. Apollonius of Tyana, writing at about the same time as John, describes Smyrna as "the most beautiful of all cities under the sun."

Smyrna, the city

A disaster defined the city of Smyrna. In 600 BCE, Alyattes, king of Lydia (a powerful state in Western Asia), destroyed Smyrna. After the city lay in ruins for centuries, Lysimachus, one of Alexander the Great's generals and successors, resurrected the city in 290 BCE. Once again, Smyrna, with its choice location, became a thriving Greek city with all the trappings. Today, the modern city of Izmir, one of the largest cities in Turkey (3.5 million), stands on the same site. The description of Jesus in Revelation 2:8 as the one "who was dead and came to life" may subtly allude to Smyrna's remarkable return to life.

NIXING THE NICOLAITANS

Jesus commends the Ephesians for hating the works of the Nicolaitans. But who in the world are they? Here's the short answer: I don't know for sure. Mentioned again by name in the message to the church of Pergamum (2:15), they're likely the evildoers and false Apostles referred to in Revelation 2:2. But even this doesn't explain much.

Irenaeus, an early church father of the second century, claims they go back to Nicolaus, a former *proselyte* (gentile convert to Judaism) and deacon in the Jerusalem church (Acts 6:5). Irenaeus says Nicolaus himself had taught that one must rigorously hit and strike the body to suppress evil desires. Some of his followers, however, radically altered this and held that what one did in the body made no difference whatsoever because the body had no influence on the spirit. This generally led to what believers viewed as an immoral and lewd lifestyle. Irenaeus's theory may be correct, but there's not enough evidence to come to any certain conclusions. What I can say with some confidence is that the Nicolaitans urged certain compromises with the prevailing culture, a stance that John roundly condemns.

Of more consequence for early Christians, Smyrna loyally supported Rome in her struggles to gain control of the Mediterranean Sea. In fact, the Smyrneans supplied significant naval support for the emerging Roman Empire. Therefore, when Smyrna petitioned Rome for the honor of building a temple to the emperor Augustus and his mother in 23 CE, the city received the privilege over 11 other candidates. And even though the Roman Senate never officially deified Tiberius Caesar, the Smyrneans built a temple in his honor. The construction and official support of these temples reveal a city with a culture that took great pride in the Imperial Cult and zealously insisted on its support from the citizenry. This allegiance to the state presented a major problem for Christians.

The church at Smyrna

Jesus commends but doesn't censure the church in Smyrna. The people are bravely hanging on despite severe affliction and persecution around them. He says sympathetically to the Smyrnean Christians, "I know your affliction and your poverty [. . .]" (Rev. 2:9). But in spite of this, ironically, Jesus calls them rich! Perhaps this echoes Jesus's beatitude: "Blessed are you who are poor, for yours is the kingdom of God" (Luke 6:20). Belonging to the kingdom of God rather than the kingdom of Caesar carries with it riches the world knows nothing about (1 Corinthians 3:21–23; Ephesians 1:7–22).

Imagine how difficult it must have been for the believers in Smyrna to withstand the constant pressure to participate in the *Imperial Cult* (veneration of the gods of

Rome and the deified Roman emperors). Charges of treason and lack of patriotism would be constant issues for them.

Given that religious, civic, and political life were so intertwined in the Greco-Roman world, I wonder how many Christians were expelled from their guild and treated as outcasts and untouchables. If, for example, your guild adopted the emperor as its patron deity, you'd be expected to participate in the sacrifices and suppers held in honor of the divine Caesar. Not participating would be interpreted as lack of loyalty and friendship. And the same would be true if your guild invoked some of the other Greek/Roman gods and goddesses (of which there were many!) as patron deities. Already in the 50s, the issue of eating meat sacrificed to idols was a major concern of Christian house churches (1 Corinthians 8–10). Ironically, one of the early slanders widely circulated about Christians accused them of being "haters of all mankind."

TECHNICAL STUFF

The Latin phrase for a religion that Rome recognized was *religio licita*. To be unsanctioned was *religio illicita*. During Paul's missionary journeys, he got out of several scrapes because Roman officials viewed early Christianity as one of the sects or parties of Judaism, a *religio licita* (see Acts 18:12–17). However, because of increasing tensions between Jews and the early Christian church, Christianity was downgraded to *religio illicita*.

Jesus forewarns the Smyrneans: Hunker down because you're about to undergo imprisonment. The duration he mentions, "ten days" (Rev. 2:10), probably means a relatively short period of time. No biblical or extra-biblical sources mention this imprisonment, but there's no reason to doubt its reality. As you read this passage, remember the time frame is at the end of the first century (likely 90–95 CE). It won't be long before large numbers of believers experience imprisonment, enslavement, torture, and death because of their refusal to participate in the imperial cult.

Pergamum: Compromising convictions (2:12–17)

Pergamum, 70 miles north of Smyrna, is an impressive city perched high atop a hill overlooking the Caicus River plain and the Bay of Lesbos in the distance. Pergamum, like Smyrna, sided with Rome against the surrounding Greek city-states in the struggle to dominate the region. For this, the empire amply rewarded Pergamum. In 133 BCE, when Attalus III bequeathed his kingdom to Rome, the city functioned as the official capital of the province of Asia. Today, the city of Bergama in Turkey preserves the ancient name.

Pergamum, the city

Pergamum, a bustling city of some 180,000 inhabitants in John's day, reached its zenith under Eumenes II (197–159 BCE). He transformed the city into an architectural and cultural center. Among its many showpieces was a library of 200,000 scrolls rivaling that of Alexandria, Egypt.

TECHNICAL STUFF

The English word *parchment* derives from a Greek word meaning "of Pergamum." As a substitute for papyrus, scribes used animal skins (leather) for writing documents.

One of the significant architectural monuments of Pergamum was the great altar to Zeus (see Figure 7-1), standing some 40 feet high and crowning the rocky summit of the *acropolis* (a high, fortified part of the city). This altar celebrated the victorious defense of Pergamum against the invading Gauls. Perhaps the comment "where Satan's throne is" (Rev. 2:13) refers to this temple.

FIGURE 7-1:
A reconstruction of the Temple of Zeus.

© Wolfgang Kaehler/Getty Images

Many other temples punctuated the city, the most notable dedicated to Dionysius, Athena, Demeter, and Orpheus. However, because of Pergamum's loyalty to Rome, pride of place went to the Imperial Cult. As early as 29 BCE, citizens of Pergamum venerated the genius of Rome and its emperor by burning incense before a statue of the divine Caesar. This, too, is a good candidate for "Satan's throne."

A thousand feet below, at the bottom of the acropolis, lay a complex dedicated to Asclepius, the god of healing. The Asclepium, or health spa, achieved a far-flung reputation as early as 350 BCE. Thousands of people, suffering from a spectrum of disorders, descended on the Asclepium in hopes of a cure. Remarkably, the complex featured individual rooms with the soothing sound of gently flowing water piped into each. Although superstition abounded, the concern and care of the attendants was a point of pride that the patients greatly appreciated.

Today, visitors can view the plaster casts of various body parts that pilgrims left in the sanctuary of Asclepius as testimonials to their healing. Physicians there administered a rather surprising array of medicinal treatments with apparent success. Worth noting in this regard is the fact that Galen, one of the founders of modern medicine, received his medical training at the Asclepium of Pergamum.

The church at Pergamum

Jesus begins by commending the church at Pergamum for their faithful endurance: "Yet you are holding fast to my name, and you did not deny your faith in me [. . .]" (2:13). Clearly, these believers are under intense pressure to participate in the various temple rituals, especially emperor worship, because this was such a point of pride for the city. According to Jesus's message, a believer named Antipas, about whom nothing else is known, lost his life for refusing to participate. He may have even been executed at the temple of Zeus or the temple dedicated to imperial Rome ("where Satan lives").

However, not everything is fine in Pergamum. Some professing Christians aren't prepared to make the supreme sacrifice that Antipas did. They ask questions like, "Can't we all just get along? If we don't believe it, why not just go through the motions and burn the incense?" Jesus calls this response "the teaching of Balaam" (Rev. 2:14).

So, who's Balaam? In Numbers 22–25, Balaam, a greedy false prophet, counsels Balak, the king of Moab, to derail Israel on her march to the Promised Land — by sexually enticing the Israelites to participate in idolatrous rituals, anticipating that God will punish Israel as a result! Balaam nearly succeeds in his diabolical scheme. Some 24,000 Israelites perish in a divine visitation (Numbers 25:9; 1 Corinthians 10:8). Jesus warns the Christians at Pergamum of a similar fate: "Repent then. If not, I will come to you soon and make war against them with the sword of my mouth" (Rev. 2:16).

REMEMBER

From Jesus's perspective, participation in idol sacrifices and the Imperial Cult amount to spiritual prostitution. Either Jesus is Lord or Caesar is Lord — it's a zero-sum game. Furthermore, orgies often accompanied pagan sacrifice, so physical prostitution was never far removed from spiritual prostitution.

The Balaamites probably believed that what's done in the body doesn't affect the spirit (the view of the Nicolaitans — see the "Nixing the Nicolaitans" sidebar). In their view, illicit sex was a non-issue, a personal decision of no consequence. Some believers in Pergamum were tempted to agree. To those wavering, Jesus issues a stern warning.

However, Jesus promises those in Pergamum who hold fast to their Christian faith many things in Revelation 2:17:

>> **Hidden manna:** This mysterious substance sustained the Israelites through-out their wilderness wanderings after Moses led them out of slavery in Egypt (Exodus 16). It's a symbol of eternal life in Judaism and probably functions the same way here.

>> **White stone:** In the Greco-Roman world, stones of various kinds served as tickets and admission passes. Here, the white stone admits the holder to paradise — far better than a Taylor Swift concert!

>> **A new name:** In the Old Testament, the giving of a name or the changing of one's name carries great significance (Genesis 17:5, 17:15, 32:27–30; Isaiah 56:2, 62:2). In this passage, the new name indicates a completely transformed nature. The fact that no one else knows it suggests that each believer has a unique destiny in eternity.

One final note about this message: The description of Jesus holding "the sharp two-edged sword" (2:12) may allude to the famous Roman short sword that often functioned as a symbol of capital punishment. The fact that Jesus, not Caesar, holds the sword speaks volumes about who really holds the power of life and death.

Thyatira: Dirty dancing with Jezebel (2:18–29)

Thyatira lay on the south bank of the Lycus River in a broad and fertile valley running north and south and connecting the Caicus and Hermus valleys. Today, the Turkish city Akhisar occupies the ancient site.

Thyatira, the city

Thyatira was founded by Seleucus I, one of Alexander the Great's successors. Because of its location guarding the eastern approaches to the great coastal cities like Smyrna and Pergamum, Thyatira was a frontier outpost. Lacking a great *acropolis* (high, fortified part of the city) like Pergamum, Thyatira depended on the determination of its citizens to defend itself against all aggressors. Appropriately, early coins from Thyatira depict the patron deity astride a horse wielding a great battle-axe. Perhaps Jesus's commendation of the church for its "patient endurance" (Rev. 2:19) is an instance where church and city are mirror images of each other.

Perhaps the most significant feature of Thyatira was its large number of trade guilds (akin to modern-day trade unions) including woolworkers, linen workers, garment makers, leather workers, tanners, potters, bakers, slave-dealers, and bronze-smiths. Each guild adopted a patron deity to bring luck and bless the business.

Christians in Thyatira encountered grave difficulties because of the integral connection between the various guilds and their patron deities. Inscriptional evidence (that is, formal inscriptions on statues, public buildings, tombs, and so forth) indicates that the guardian deity of Thyatira was the god *Tyrimnos*, identified with the sun-god Apollo. No doubt some of the trade guilds invoked this deity.

The church at Thyatira

Interestingly, the letter to Thyatira is the longest of the seven, and yet in many ways, the city itself was the least well-known and important of the seven.

The start of the letter designates Jesus as "the Son of God" (Rev. 2:18), which is significant because it's the only time the book of Revelation uses that title. It's probably not a coincidence that Tyrimnos (Apollo) and the emperor were both acclaimed as "sons of Zeus." By the reference to Jesus as the Son of God, the Thyatiran believers are reminded that there's only one Son of God, and he's Jesus, not Caesar. What's more, it may be more than mere coincidence that Jesus is also described as having feet "like burnished bronze," especially in a town known for its bronze-working guild. Clearly, the Jesus of Revelation trumps all the guild gods and goddesses.

According to the message of Jesus, the believers at Thyatira are doing some things right, and they receive high praise for four works:

>> **Love:** This crowning virtue heads the list.

>> **Faith:** Faith, another one of the three Christian virtues (the third is *hope* — see 1 Corinthians 13:13), is also alive and well at Thyatira.

>> **Service:** If the first two items are virtues, the next two are the practical outworking of these virtues. The term *service* can also be rendered as *ministry*.

>> **Patient endurance:** Surviving amid suffering and hard times is a prerequisite for belonging to a house church in Asia Minor. For the most part, this small congregation is withstanding the pressure and receives a passing grade.

On the other hand, Jesus has a complaint about their compromises. A formidable female prophetess advocates accommodation with idolatrous rituals, a problem that also plagues Ephesus and Pergamum. Their challenge is to survive as Christians in a hostile environment in which false religion and economics are intimately intertwined.

Jesus calls out a false prophetess named "Jezebel," a reference to the notorious queen of King Ahab in the Old Testament. The original Jezebel promoted the sexually immoral cult of Baal and Asherah and persecuted the true prophets of God (1 Kings 18–19; 2 Kings 9). Thyatira's Jezebel is more subtle — claiming to have received direct insight from God that allows her to encourage Christians to compromise by participating in sexually immoral idol worship. In Revelation, Jesus knows better and describes her insights as "the deep things of Satan" (2:24). In short, she claims that Christians can dance with the devil and not get hurt. In the movie *Batman* (1989) the Joker asks his victims a question before attacking them: "You ever dance with the devil in the pale moonlight?" Dancing with the devil is always a bad idea!

Jesus's warning to the churches of Thyatira is direct and unambiguous: Repent or else! Jezebel and her cohorts will get what they deserve. In place of a bed of sensual pleasure, they'll get a bed of affliction and death.

At the end of the message, Jesus promises the churches two things:

>> **Authority to rule:** Victorious believers will share in Jesus's rule over the world to come. However, believers may not coast into the kingdom; they must be steadfast to the very end.

>> **The morning star:** Jesus promises to give his faithful the "morning star." The morning star perhaps refers to the planet Venus figuratively applied to Jesus (see Revelation 22:16 and 2 Peter 1:19). But the precise background is unknown. Jewish rabbis interpreted Numbers 24:17 ("a star shall come out of Jacob, and a scepter shall rise out of Israel"), as referring to the Messiah so maybe the morning star alludes to this passage.

Because of widespread fascination over this "star's" appearance just before sunrise, Venus serves as a fitting metaphor — the messianic herald of a new world that's coming. Taken together, the two images of authority and morning star may be making the same point: Conquerors — meaning believers who endure to the end — have a vital share and role in the new world.

Sardis: Sleepwalkers in the city (3:1–6)

Located at the junction of routes into the interior of Turkey (30 miles to the south of Thyatira and about 50 miles east of Smyrna), Sardis was an important transportation and commercial hub. Though Sardis was once one of the most prosperous cities in the region, today the ancient site lies abandoned, about 5 miles west of the modern city of Salihi, Turkey.

Sardis, the city

Sardis had a nearly legendary past. Once the capital of the kingdom of Lydia, it became a center of fabulous wealth. Its last great king, Croesus (560–546 BCE), was so rich he became a byword: "as rich as Croesus!" Gold and silver coinage was first minted at Sardis, a fitting achievement in a truly golden age.

Sardis was geographically blessed with a grand acropolis: The stronghold of Sardis stood perched atop a steep ridge 1,500 feet above the plain, seemingly impregnable to all assaults. The key word is *seemingly.* The great citadel of Sardis fell to the Persians in 546 BCE.

After Alexander the Great's conquests, Sardis fell under the control of various Hellenistic regimes (*Hellenism* refers to the Greek culture that dominated the Mediterranean basin from the time of Alexander the Great [334 BCE] until well into the late Roman age). Believe it or not, during this era, the citadel of Sardis was seized again and under similar circumstances. In 218 BCE, Antiochus III captured the fortress because no guard was posted above the steep slopes!

The Hellenistic era ended when Attalus III bequeathed Pergamum to Rome in 133 BCE. Sardis became an administrative center in the Roman province of Asia. But never again did the city regain the prominence it once held. In fact, in a competition to build a second temple to Rome's Imperial Cult in 26 CE, Sardis vainly vied for the honor based on its storied past. At this point, the city seems to have had a reputation but no real clout.

The remains of Sardis are impressive. At the foot of the acropolis of Sardis stands a great temple dedicated to Artemis, in imitation of the one at Ephesus. Archaeologists have also uncovered a gymnasium complex featuring a marble court area.

A strong Jewish community inhabited Sardis. Modern visitors to the site marvel at the remains of a beautiful synagogue — about the length of a football field — dating to the third or fourth century. Because Sardis was host to a thriving Jewish community from Hellenistic times, the city doubtless had a fine synagogue at the end of the first century CE as well.

The church at Sardis

In a sense, the church at Sardis is spiritually sleepwalking — appearing to be awake, but not fully aware of their circumstances — and they're heading for disaster! In his message, Jesus summons these believers from their spiritual slumber: "Wake up!" (3:2). There's still hope! The citadel hasn't fallen yet, and they can still stave off the enemy: "Strengthen what remains and is on the point of death." How? Three commands, barked out like military orders, point the way: Remember, obey, and repent. The book of Revelation leaves no doubt about what they're supposed to remember and obey: the word of God and the testimony of Jesus (1:2, 1:9, 6:9, 12:17, 19:10, 20:4).

The consequences of failure to respond immediately mirror the history of the city. Like previous successful assaults on the citadel of Sardis, Jesus will come "like a thief, and you will not know at what hour I will come to you" (3:3). In short, the local church at Sardis will cease to exist.

But all is not lost. A vigilant minority of people "have not soiled their clothes" (3:4). This vivid metaphor probably refers to compromise with the non-Christian environment. To them, Jesus holds out two glowing promises:

>> **White robes:** Worshipers in temples, whether Gentile or Jewish, were required to appear in clean clothes, typically in white linen. Christians are promised that they, too, will worship in the "New Jerusalem" and be dressed in white, a symbol of righteousness and moral purity.

>> **A place in the book of life:** The notion of a redeemed registry also occurs in the Old Testament (Exodus 32:32; Psalm 69:28; Daniel 12:1). Jesus promises the conquerors of Sardis — the believers who stick it out — that their names will not be removed from the registry of the New Jerusalem. On the contrary, Jesus himself will announce their names in the presence of God and his angels.

Philadelphia: Holding on 'til the end (3:7-13)

Philadelphia is best known today for the Liberty Bell, Rocky Balboa, and a great cheesesteak sandwich. But another Philadelphia, in the ancient world, resided on the Hermus River Valley at about 30 miles to the southeast of Sardis. Because it was situated at the junction of five roads leading to Mysia, Lydia, and Phrygia, it gained the title "gateway to the East." Besides being a frontier city, linking the interior of Anatolia (Asian Turkey) with the coastal cities (Smyrna was about 100 miles due west), Philadelphia was near an important vine-growing district, and it hosted textile and leather industries. The modern city of Alasehir lies near the same site.

Philadelphia, the city

Philadelphia, the "city of brotherly love," was so-named because of the affection Attalus II Philadelphus (159–138 BCE), the city's founder, felt for his elder brother Eumenes II, the noted king of Pergamum. Before becoming king himself, Attalus II served as a loyal general for Eumenes. In about 140 BCE, Attalus founded Philadelphia in honor of his brother, making it the youngest of the seven cities.

Attalus placed great hopes on this city. He viewed it as a launching pad from which Hellenism (Greek culture) might be spread into the barbarian interior of Anatolia. This was partially successful: The Lydian language finally ceased to be spoken by 19 CE, but Phrygian culture itself quite outlived Hellenism.

Greeks and Romans typically viewed other peoples and tribes as substandard and primitive. They used the Latin word *barbarus* and the Greek word *barbaros* for such non-Latin and non-Greek speaking peoples. The Apostle Paul uses the Greek term for non-Greek speakers in Romans 1:14 and Colossians 3:11 but without snobbish, elitist overtones.

The hopes for the city received a jolting setback in 17 CE, when a devastating earthquake leveled the city. Philadelphia, lying close to a major geological fault line, seems to have suffered the brunt of the quake, and successive tremors furthered the damage. According to ancient historians, the danger of collapsing buildings and walls so terrified the populace that most citizens lived outside the city in temporary shelters during these harrowing times. But owing to generous imperial funding made possible by Tiberius Caesar (Luke 3:1), the city made a comeback. Unfortunately, tremors rocked the area for years afterward, making life somewhat chaotic. Despite this, the city persevered and prospered, a testament to their steadfastness.

A major temple in Philadelphia was dedicated to Dionysius, god of merrymaking and wine — not surprising, considering the reputation of the surrounding area for high-quality grapes. No archaeological evidence indicates the presence of the Imperial Cult in Philadelphia during the first century CE, though there was at the beginning of the third.

The church in Philadelphia

Philadelphia, like Smyrna, receives no condemnation or stern warning. What's striking is Jesus's frank acknowledgment of their tough circumstances and his exhortation to hold on at all costs. Like the city in which they lived, the Philadelphian Christians were remaining steadfast during suffering and hard times. The threat to the church lay not inside its walls but outside of them. In particular, the Jewish community apparently made life difficult.

Jesus identifies himself as the one "who has the key of David, who opens and no one will shut, who shuts and no one opens" (Rev. 3:7). The description probably refers to a passage in Isaiah 22:15–22, in which Shebna, head steward during the reign of king Hezekiah of Judah (716–686 BCE), is replaced by Eliakim. A *head steward* controls the keys giving access to the palace and its rooms. (Palace reliefs from Assyria depict officials having a large wooden key attached to the shoulder.) The point is this: Jesus, like Eliakim, now has the authority to admit or disbar individuals from his kingdom.

The relevance for the church at Philadelphia probably lies in a painful dispute between church and synagogue. Which community is the true Israel, and is Jesus of Nazareth the true Messiah? The Jewish leaders denied Christian claims and may have even excommunicated (officially excluded) Jewish Christians from the synagogue (see John 7:13, 9:22). For Jewish Christians, this was a bitter blow, cutting them off from their cultural heritage. But Jesus reassures them: "I [like Eliakim] have set before you an open door, which no one is able to shut" (3:7). They're indeed members of the true Israel, and the Jewish community at Philadelphia, like Shebna, will one day acknowledge this transfer of status and authority (3:9).

WARNING

The message of Jesus in Revelation 3:9 is harsh, so handle it with care. It refers to the Jewish synagogue as "a synagogue of Satan" and even denies their claim to be Jews (see also 2:9). Read this passage in the context of a debate among members of the same group. After all, Christianity is a daughter of Judaism. During Jesus's earthly ministry, especially in John's Gospel, Jesus and the religious leadership frequently clash. They challenge his authority; he condemns their unbelief. Because they reject his message and are abusive toward him, he says, "You are from your father the devil" (John 8:43). The Jewish leadership in Philadelphia reacts in a similar way and thus receives his censure. But it's quite another thing for modern Christians to take up this harsh rhetoric and apply it to the Jewish people, as was done in the Middle Ages and continues to be done by *anti-Semites* (those who are hostile toward Jews). Christians are taught to leave the matter of people's spiritual status and destiny to Jesus as they bear witness to the gospel. Jesus was not rebuking Jews because of their Jewishness but because of their refusal to accept him and his message.

Jesus offers another promise to this beleaguered congregation: "I will keep you from the hour of trial that is coming on the whole world to test the inhabitants of the earth" (Rev. 3:10). This probably refers to the so-called Great Tribulation of the End Times. (See Chapter 8 for a discussion of the relationship of the rapture to the tribulation.)

Conquerors may claim two promises from Jesus:

>> **Pillars in the Temple of God:** How fitting for believers who live in an earthquake-prone city whose pillars may collapse at any moment! This metaphor speaks of stability and strength. It also speaks poignantly to those cut off from the heritage of the Jewish temple that once stood in Jerusalem. (It had been destroyed in 70 CE.) They're now members in good standing of the greater temple of the Lord (Ephesians 2:19–22).

>> **New names:** As in Pergamum and Sardis (see the earlier sections on these cities), the notion of receiving a new name plays a prominent role in Philadelphia. But in Revelation 3:12, it's not just one new name, it's three:

- **Name of God:** Is this the sacred name *Yahweh?* Perhaps. At any rate, the new name emphasizes that believers are part of the family of God. They bear his name as sons and daughters.

- **Name of the New Jerusalem:** Twice in its checkered history, Philadelphia adopted a new name. More relevant for the church, however, is possession of the name of the New Jerusalem, certifying citizenship in the celestial city.

- **New name of the Lamb:** Whatever this name is, believers share a new status with the Lamb. He is, after all, "the firstborn within a large family" (Romans 8:29).

Each of the promises point to a new reality: Believers are all in the family, so to speak.

Laodicea: Don't drink the water! (3:14–22)

Laodicea is in the eastern end of the Lycus Valley, a tributary of the Maeander River. It lies about 40 miles to the southeast of Philadelphia and 100 miles due east of Ephesus on the coast. Antiochus II (261–246 BCE) founded the Hellenistic city in honor of his wife Laodike. The ancient site is near the village of Eskihisar and the large, modern city of Denizli (population 800,000).

Laodicea, the city

Located on a plateau 100 feet above the river, Laodicea reached a pinnacle of prosperity during the Roman age. Like Thyatira, Sardis, and Philadelphia, Laodicea lay along the trade routes into the interior of Anatolia and onwards to Syria. It was, accordingly, a military outpost and commercial center. Among the city's assets was a high-quality black wool raised and carded in the region. The city was proud of its medical school and of a locally produced ointment ("Phrygian powder") reputed to cure eye ailments.

Laodicea was also a well-known banking center, with several wealthy citizens. The famous Cicero even cashed large bank drafts at Laodicea. Reflecting this wealth, the city minted its own coins and, following an earthquake in 60 CE, rebuilt itself, largely through private donations.

There were, of course, temples dedicated to various gods and goddesses, as witnessed by inscriptions on their coins. The most important deity in the region was Men Karou, a god connected with healing and whose temple lay 13 miles to the west of the city. Within the city itself were temples to Zeus and the divine Augustus, and nearby was a large marketplace where commodities were bought and sold.

TECHNICAL STUFF

Large-scale excavations began in the year 2000, so much of the ancient city of Laodicea remains to be discovered. Nevertheless, the ruins of two theaters, a *nymphaeum* (a Roman building featuring running water, fountains, flower gardens, and statues), an *odeum* (a small public building for music and poetry performances), a gymnasium, a stadium (380 yards long!), and other public buildings are clearly visible to visitors. Of special interest is a triple arch gateway dedicated to none other than the emperor Domitian.

Laodicea did have a downside: The water was lousy. Unlike Colossae, 10 miles to the east, where copious amounts of cool, refreshing water were readily available, Laodicea had to pipe water in from several miles away. By the time the water coursed its way through stone pipes to Laodicea, it was tepid. To make matters worse, it was full of foul-tasting mineral deposits.

The church at Laodicea

No other church is rebuked as severely — and no other church reflects more clearly the city in which they live — than the Christians of Laodicea.

The spiritual condition of this church is as unpalatable as the water its citizens must drink. More than a few sermons and commentaries miss the point here. Jesus is not saying that being spiritually lukewarm is worse than being spiritually cold. He's saying the Laodicean Christians are of *no spiritual benefit whatsoever*. Unlike the cool, refreshing water of Colossae or the hot, therapeutic, mineral waters of Hierapolis, six miles to the north, the "spiritual water" of Laodicea is worthless and nauseous. The NRSV translation, "I am about to spit you out of my mouth," is too tame (3:16). Something like "You make me want to throw up" better conveys Jesus's disgust with this dysfunctional congregation.

In addition, Jesus calls them "wretched, pitiable, poor, blind, and naked." What irony! Here's a city proud of its self-reliance, hard-earned wealth, world-famous medical school and ointment, and luxurious clothing. The church reflects a similar complacency. In short, they're oblivious to their spiritual need and completely lacking in zeal.

The remedy for Laodicea is heartfelt and immediate repentance. This is symbolically portrayed in terms of going to the marketplace and making three purchases. All three items speak of salvation through Jesus:

>> **Gold refined by fire:** What an appropriate metaphor for a city priding itself on its gold reserves! Pure gold speaks of genuine faith (1 Peter 1:7).

>> **White robes:** In place of the chic, black, wool garments, they need white robes, a symbol of the righteousness of Jesus freely grants to repentant sinners.

>> **Eye salve:** Once again, you can't miss the irony. These believers are spiritually blind, so Phrygian powder won't help a bit. Turning to Jesus in faith, however, restores spiritual sight to the blind (Luke 4:18).

In one of the most memorable metaphors in the entire book, Jesus stands outside the door of the Laodicean house church and knocks (Rev. 3:20). In other words, he puts the ball in their court: They can either open the door and allow him in or refuse him entrance. The problem at Laodicea is serious: Spiritual indifference threatens their spiritual life. Fling open the door, Jesus urges! Admit him and celebrate his supper (a reference to the Lord's Supper or Communion [Matthew 26; Mark 14; Luke 22] and the marriage supper of the Lamb [Rev. 19:6–9]). In short, they desperately need genuine conversion and discipleship.

The promise to the conquerors — there were *some* genuine believers at Laodicea ("I reprove and discipline those whom I love" [Rev. 3:19]) — is like that of Thyatira (see the earlier section on Thyatira). Conquerors sit on Jesus's throne and share in his reign (3:21). Here is some good news: The church at Laodicea did repent and continued to be a center for Christian witness for several centuries, hosting a famous church council in 363 CE.

IN THIS CHAPTER

» Surrounding the throne of God

» Scanning a sealed scroll: The mysterious book of destiny

» Revealing a supreme paradox: The Lion (of Judah) is a Lamb!

Chapter **8**

Peeking into the Throne Room (4:1–5:14)

O ne of the coolest things about the starship Enterprise in *Star Trek* — and there were a lot of cool things — was the capability of "beaming up" or "beaming down." So, if Captain Kirk was on the surface of an exotic planet or asteroid and the Enterprise was hovering in the vicinity, he simply issued the famous order, "Beam me up, Scotty," and presto! He dematerialized and vanished. The next thing you knew, he materialized back on the flight deck of the Enterprise. Now that's cool.

"Beaming up" isn't a new idea. In the first two centuries BCE and the first two centuries CE, Jewish and Christian writings, designated as *apocalyptic* (because they claim to reveal hidden secrets about the universe and the future), introduced new speculations to religious thought while also offering hope for those oppressed and persecuted. These works typically describe an ascent into the heavenly realms by a noteworthy figure from Jewish history and tradition. The climactic moment featured a visit to the throne room of God himself.

In this chapter, you discover that Revelation 4–5 has striking similarities to these apocalyptic accounts of visionary ascents — John has a "Beam me up" moment! But more importantly, as you peek into God's throne room, you dive into the meaning of John's vision and discern how it answers nagging questions for Christians: Who's in charge of all that happens in heaven and earth and what's going to happen? Chapters 4 and 5 of Revelation address these concerns and dispel anxiety about the outcome.

REMEMBER

TRYING TO DESCRIBE GOD: IT AIN'T EASY!

The Bible consistently shies away from describing God in visual terms. Judaism prohibits any images to represent the deity. This edict goes all the way back to the days of Moses, when God tells the Israelites, "You shall not make for yourself an idol, whether in the form of anything that is in heaven above or that is on the earth beneath or that is in the waters under the earth" (Exodus 20:4).

In the Old Testament, whenever God appears to human beings, a brilliant light or fire indicates his presence, but the text never describes his personal appearance (Genesis 15:17; Exodus 3:2, 14:24, 19:18; 1 Kings 18:38). Sometimes an angel of God appears in bodily form and speaks on behalf of God (Joshua 5:13–15). To be sure, God reveals his glorious presence to people. For example, Moses and a group of leaders "see" God in Exodus 24: 9–10. The text, however, doesn't describe his personal appearance; it describes what's "under his feet" — namely, a translucent sapphire-colored pavement. The book of Numbers describes Moses's frequent face-to-face conversations with the Lord (Numbers 12:8) but not what form God takes. When the Lord commissions Isaiah to be a prophet, he "sees" the Lord seated on a throne (Isaiah 6:1–3). However, the prophet portrays the flowing robe and the seraphim who surround the throne, not the actual appearance of God.

Okay, so the Old Testament does dare to describe God using visual imagery. But the language in these cases is always metaphorical. In the book of Daniel, the prophet calls God "the Ancient of Days," whose clothing is "white as snow; the hair of his head [. . .] white like wool" (Daniel 7:9). In a vision of the mobile throne chariot, Ezekiel describes the glory of God as a "figure like that of a man." He also depicts this figure from the waist up as being "glowing metal," and from the waist down, "he looked like fire" (Ezekiel 1:26–27).

Please note that these passages from Isaiah, Daniel, and Ezekiel provide the background imagery for John's vision of the exalted Jesus in the throne room in Revelation 4:2–6 (see also Rev. 1:2–16; 20:11).

The New Testament is consistent with the Old Testament prohibition against representing God the Father in bodily form (John 1:18; 1 Timothy 6:16). However, because Jesus is the Son of God in the flesh (John 1:14; Romans 1:3; Colossians 1:19, 2:9; 1 John 1:1–2, 4:2), the New Testament writings break with their Jewish heritage by affirming that the glory of God is actually seen "in the face of Christ" (2 Corinthians 4:6; John 14:9). It's worth noting, however, that nowhere do the Gospels or other New Testament writings give a physical description of Jesus. Perhaps this striking absence underscores an important New Testament concept, which is highlighted in the book of Revelation: Jesus, though born an ethnic Jew (Galatians 4:4), is the redeemer of people "from every nation, from all tribes and peoples and languages" (Rev. 7:9; see also John 3:16).

Focusing on the "Someone" on the Throne (4:1–11)

As Revelation 4 begins, John describes his ascent through a heavenly portal: "After this I looked, and there in heaven a door stood open! And the first voice, which I had heard speaking to me like a trumpet, said, 'Come up here, and I will show you what must take place after this.'" Hmm, I wonder if J. K. Rowling borrowed this notion for her Harry Potter books. Remember that when students boarded the Hogwarts Express at King's Cross, they had to use a special gate, hidden from Muggles, gate 9¾ between gates 9 and 10. Just wondering.

This moment marks a pivotal shift in Revelation. From chapter 4 through chapter 21 — the sweeping account of history's ultimate climax — John's viewpoint shifts back and forth between the realms of heaven and earth. He experiences a sequence of visions, some unfolding amid the glories of heaven with others anchored in the reality of earth. Each of these scenes connects, in its own way, to the final and glorious victory of God's kingdom.

In this section, you follow John on a guided tour of the throne room. He first describes, in highly symbolic language, the one seated on the throne. Then, starting from the throne and moving outward, he depicts three different classes of beings who circle the throne.

Seeing who takes the seat

Immediately after John is transported through the door into heaven, his focus fixes on a throne: "At once I was in the spirit, and there in heaven stood a throne, with one seated on the throne! And the one seated there looks like jasper and carnelian, and around the throne is a rainbow that looks like an emerald" (Rev. 4:2). By the time John completes his tour of the throne room (Rev. 5:13), it's clear that everything in the universe revolves around this magnificent throne.

REMEMBER

A throne signifies rule, authority, and power. In theological terms, John's vision of the throne is all about the sovereignty of God, a central idea emphasized throughout the book of Revelation.

Reflecting his Jewish background, John resorts to traditional images and metaphors to describe the presence of God on his throne. Precious gemstones, a rainbow, thunder and lightning, and a crystal sea all serve to depict God's presence *but not his person*. The invisible God "shows himself" by means of a dazzling light show while his heavenly entourage surrounds him in worship.

Debating when believers go up, up, and away

This may seem like an odd place to bring it up, but some commentators (mostly dispensationalists) link John's visionary ascent into heaven with the rapture of the church. The *rapture* is the event when believers living at the time of the second advent are caught up to heaven. If you're familiar with the popular *Left Behind* series of books or movies, then you're familiar with the idea.

This interpretation of John's ascent to heaven sparks fierce debate. The question is this: *Does* John's ascent correspond to or represent the rapture of the church just before the end time judgments begin? According to dispensationalists it does, and they label this event as the pre-tribulation rapture of the church (usually abbreviated as pre-trib).

The *Tribulation* is usually identified as Daniel's 70th week (Daniel 9:20–27 — see Chapter 3), and it consists of the judgments depicted in Revelation 6–18 under the symbols of seven seals, seven trumpets, and seven bowls (see Chapters 9, 10, and 12 for details). There is no consensus on the precise timing of the rapture in relation to the period of Tribulation. Some hold that it happens before (pre-trib), some in the middle (mid-trib), and some after (post-trib) the Great Tribulation. Here is a summary of the key arguments for each view.

Making the great escape: The pre-trib rapture

Pre-trib teaching, widespread in evangelical circles, holds that before the Great Tribulation, Jesus will remove his people from the earth, sparing them from the judgments that fall on an unbelieving world. It's labeled the *pre-tribulation* view because Jesus returns for the church *prior* to the last 7-year period of earth history. Arguments in favor of this view include the following:

>> Pre-trib adherents believe that God wouldn't inflict such suffering and misery on his chosen people. Proponents appeal to texts such as 1 Thessalonians 5:9 for support: "For God did not appoint us to suffer wrath but to receive salvation through our Lord Jesus Christ." This argument carries the most weight among regular church members who are pre-tribbers.

>> The account of John's rapture (Rev. 4:1–2) immediately follows the messages to the seven churches (Rev. 2–3). Each message was addressed to the angel (or messenger) of that church. The angels seem to function as representatives of each church. This may suggest that John himself functions as a representative figure for the entire church in 4:1.

>> The word for *church* (*ecclesia* in Greek) drops out of the text after Revelation 3:22 and doesn't reappear until the very end of the book at 22:16. Thus, the

church isn't explicitly mentioned during the Tribulation (chapters 6–18). Pre-tribbers believe this silence suggests that the church is raptured before the Tribulation.

>> Because Jesus told his disciples his coming would be "like a thief" (Luke 12:39) and "no one knows the day nor the hour" (Matthew 24:36), the rapture can't follow any known or prophesied event. This leads to the *any moment* rapture view. The imminence of the rapture rules out any preliminary signs. Therefore, the rapture must take place before the predicted seals, trumpets, and bowls occur. Consequently, John's being caught up to heaven in Revelation 4:1 represents the rapture of the church because it can't be dated and it precedes the judgments that follow. This interpretation preserves the pre-trib insistence on the imminence of the rapture.

TECHNICAL STUFF

Several bestselling authors have promoted the pre-tribulation position over the years. In 1970, Hal Lindsey published a blockbuster book, *The Late Great Planet Earth*, incorporating the pre-trib rapture scheme. More recently (1995), Tim LaHaye (with Jerry Jenkins) burst on the scene with the immensely popular *Left Behind* series in both book and movie formats.

Staying till the end: The post-trib rapture

Those who hold to the *post-tribulation* (post-trib) view argue that Jesus won't return and the church won't be raptured until after the Tribulation. They offer the following arguments in support:

>> Post-tribbers agree that God won't inflict his wrath on members of the church. But that's different from saying he'll protect believers from the wrath of antichrist. The bowl judgments are all directed at the antichrist and his followers. Just like the Lord protected the Hebrews in Egypt from some of the plagues (Exodus 8:20–12:30), so God protects his people from the bowl judgments of the End Times. The exhortation to be faithful unto death in the face of the persecution by the antichrist is directed to the first Christian readers (Rev. 13:9–13). This sounds hollow if in fact no Christians experience such a persecution.

>> John's ascent closely resembles Jewish and Christian accounts of other ascents to heaven. In all these other cases, the individual doesn't represent a collective entity. A face-value reading of John's ascent to the throne room accords with the Apostle Paul's ascent to paradise in 2 Corinthians 12:2-4, which all agree was an entirely personal and solitary experience.

>> Although the word for *church* doesn't appear in Revelation 4:1–22:15, this doesn't mean the church is absent during this period. An argument from silence is rarely a persuasive argument. The adage "absence of evidence

doesn't mean evidence of absence" applies here. There are in fact references to those who "have washed their robes and made them white in the blood of the Lamb" (Rev. 7:14), to "those who keep the commandments of God and hold the testimony of Jesus" (Rev. 12:17), to the "saints" against whom the beast (antichrist) wages war (Rev. 13:7), and to those "who have been redeemed from humankind as first fruits for God and the Lamb" (Rev. 14:4; see also Rev. 16:15; 17:6). Apparently, multitudes put their trust in Jesus throughout the period of the Tribulation (Rev. 7:14–17). To call them "tribulation saints" without acknowledging that they, too, are part of the church seems arbitrary and unconvincing. In other words, if something looks like a duck, walks like a duck, and quacks like a duck, it probably is a duck!

>> The imminence of Jesus's coming hardly rules out precursors. Although Jesus specified that one can't know the *day* or *hour,* that's not the same thing as *month* or *year.* Paul seems to indicate that at least two things must first occur before the rapture; namely, a great *apostasy* (a falling away from faith and trust in Jesus) and the appearance of the man of lawlessness (in other words, the antichrist; 2 Thessalonians 2:1–12). An event that's imminent or impending may quite properly have precursors and yet not be precisely datable.

Clearing out at halftime: The mid-trib rapture

Those who hold to a mid-trib view believe the rapture occurs approximately 3.5 years into the 7-year Tribulation, usually identified with Daniel's 70th week (Daniel 9:20–27). As a compromise position, this view incorporates arguments from both the pre-trib and post-trib views. Distinctive arguments are as follows:

>> The last trumpet of 1 Corinthians 15:52 and 1 Thessalonians 4:16 could be identified with the seventh trumpet of Revelation 11:15–18. The seventh trumpet in Revelation occurs just after the halfway point of the final seven years. This is based on Revelation 11:3, in which 42 months and 1,260 days equal 3.5 years.

>> The two witnesses of Revelation 11, who are martyred in the middle of the Tribulation, may symbolize the church and thus mark the moment of the rapture of the church.

>> The seven seals and trumpets of Revelation 6–8 are not judgments; rather, they're the "beginning of the birth pangs" that Jesus refers to in the Olivet Discourse (Matthew 24:8 — see Chapter 3 for more on the Olivet Discourse).

>> God's wrath begins at Revelation 11:18, after the church is raptured to heaven.

HEAVEN ACCORDING TO ENOCH

An example of a visionary ascent features the patriarch Enoch who, according to the Bible, lived prior to the great flood of Noah. "Enoch walked with God; then he was no more, because God took him away" (Genesis 5:24). Enoch was the perfect candidate for an ascent to the throne room — after all, the Bible implies he was "translated" to heaven.

An anonymous Jewish writer, two centuries before Jesus, composed *The Book of the Watchers,* which narrates the celestial travels of Enoch. This book, now part of a larger composite work called *1 Enoch*, goes into considerable detail describing the throne room and its surroundings (*1 Enoch* 14:8–19:3). There are striking parallels to Revelation 4–5.

Minority positions on the rapture question

Some tweak the mid-trib view and espouse a *pre-wrath rapture,* occurring just before the bowl judgments of Revelation 15–16 are poured out on the antichrist and unbelievers.

Others maintain a *partial-tribulation view,* which agrees with the pre-trib position about timing but differs in one important qualification: Only believers who are walking in fellowship with Jesus are raptured before the Tribulation. Disobedient believers will be "left behind" with unbelievers and not resurrected or transformed until Jesus's second coming proper, the so-called "revelation of Christ" at the end of the Tribulation.

Concluding with a word of advice

Attempting a definitive position on the timing of the rapture is "much ado about nothing" (Shakespeare). The book of Revelation begins and ends with a prophecy and a promise that Jesus will return (Rev. 1:7, 22:20), and the church's creeds (statements of belief) proclaim the fact that Jesus will return but don't set a date for his coming. Debating the timing shouldn't be an occasion for contention or suspicion, and certainly not a litmus test for orthodoxy. Attention should be placed on spiritual preparedness and not holding the correct timetable for the rapture. Perhaps a *pan*-tribulation view is best — everything will pan out in the end!

Circling the throne

As Revelation 4 unfolds, John describes the heavenly court surrounding the throne (the three distinct groups are in italics):

"Around the throne are twenty-four thrones, and seated on the thrones are twenty-four elders, dressed in white robes, with golden crowns on their heads. Coming from the thrones are flashes of lightning, and rumblings and peals of thunder, and in front of the throne burn seven flaming torches, which are the seven spirits of God: and in front of the throne there is something like a sea of glass, like crystal. Around the throne, and on each side of the throne, are four living creatures, full of eyes in front and behind." (Rev. 4:4–6)

Thus, John's description of the heavenly court consists of three concentric circles:

>> Twenty-four elders sit on the outer perimeter, each sitting on his own throne.

>> A second circle, inside the elders, consists of seven blazing lamps, which John identifies as the "seven spirits of God."

>> Within the innermost circle, four living creatures stand before the throne.

In this section, I explore the occupants of these circles.

The twenty-four elders

John describes the twenty-four elders as wearing an interesting combination of priestly and royal attire — white garments and golden crowns. But who exactly are these twenty-four elders? On this point, there's considerable disagreement (what else is new!). The most popular theories are:

>> Glorified humans who represent the entire people of God, composed of both Jews and Gentiles

>> Glorified humans who represent only the New Testament church, composed of both Jews and Gentiles

>> Angels patterned after the twenty-four priestly orders of the Old Testament (1 Chronicles 24:6-19)

>> The twenty-four star-gods of the ancient Babylonian pantheon (a temple of the gods)

>> Angels who symbolize the twelve tribes of Israel and the twelve apostles

REFLECTIONS OF HEAVEN

The notion that an earthly sanctuary is a replica of a heavenly one goes back into ancient Near Eastern thought. For example, in a creation epic called *Enumah Elish* dating to the second millennium BCE, the sanctuary of the chief Babylonian god Marduk replicates a heavenly prototype.

Closer in time to the book of Revelation are the Dead Sea Scrolls, which comprise over 900 individual manuscripts, including the *Songs of the Sabbath Sacrifice*. These texts describe a celestial temple where angelic priests conduct intricate rituals and worship. The Qumran community, caretakers of these scrolls, believed that their own liturgical practices on earth echoed the worship performed by angels in heaven. This belief underscored their commitment to orderliness in worship, echoing the Apostle Paul's directive in 1 Corinthians 11:10 that everything during worship should be conducted "decently and in order."

The glorified-humans interpretation is popular in evangelical circles. But many scholars argue that the immediate context rules out the idea that the elders are glorified humans because the elders later speak of human beings in the third person): "You have made *them* to be a kingdom and priests serving our God, and *they* will reign on earth" (Rev. 5:10 [emphasis added]). This shows a clear distinction between the elders and human beings.

The suggestion that John draws from Babylonian mythology is highly improbable. While biblical authors sometimes incorporate imagery from ancient myths — and Revelation itself contains several such allusions — they do so only when these elements align with the core theological principles of Scripture. Furthermore, given John's deep familiarity with Hebrew Scriptures, it's unlikely he would choose to describe the heavenly throne room using motifs from pagan mythology.

Many scholars support the view that the twenty-four elders are angels. In Jewish tradition, the earthly tabernacle was modeled after a heavenly sanctuary where angelic beings worship God. Numerous Old Testament passages reflect this idea, such as Exodus 25:9, 25:40, 26:30; Isaiah 6:1–5; and Ezekiel 40–48. Within this scriptural context, it makes sense to interpret the twenty-four elders as an angelic choir offering praise to God in his celestial sanctuary.

The seven spirits

John describes the seven spirits as "seven flaming torches" (Revelation 4:5), though their true nature is still debated. In Scripture, fire and radiant light often signify God's presence, suggesting that these spirits might either represent God directly or serve in his immediate company. Many scholars, however, continue to explore their precise identity and have put forward several possible explanations:

» Some scholars detect a symbolic significance in the number seven — the number of completeness and perfection — and identify them as the sevenfold activity of the Holy Spirit as enumerated in Isaiah 11:2.

» Others are content simply to identify them as an angelic order like the seraphim and cherubim.

» A final group considers the seven spirits to be the seven archangels mentioned in Jewish apocalyptic traditions.

FLIGHTS OF FANCY AND THE FOUR LIVING CREATURES

The description of the four living creatures has spawned far-fetched interpretations over the years. For example, Irenaeus, bishop of Lyons (130–200 CE), thought each creature was one of the four Gospels in the New Testament. A few modern interpreters still see this as a viable option. For example, one widely used commentary suggests the following identification:

- **The lion is the Gospel of Matthew.** A lion is a regal figure, and Matthew presents Jesus as the King of the Jews.

- **The ox is the Gospel of Mark.** An ox is a humble, servant figure, and Mark portrays Jesus as the servant of the Lord.

- **The man is the Gospel of Luke.** The man matches Luke's depiction of the humanity of Jesus, the Son of Man.

- **The flying eagle is the Gospel of John.** The eagle describes John's soaring portrait of the divine Son of God.

John would likely have been astonished by these imaginative interpretations! The four living creatures stem from a well-established tradition in Jewish apocalyptic thought, which John shares and which has its roots in Daniel and Ezekiel. In both books, there's no indication that the creatures symbolize anything other than angelic beings.

The identification of the seven spirits as archangels aligns with the Jewish apocalyptic work *1 Enoch* 20:1–7, which lists their names as Michael, Gabriel, Suru'el (also known as Uriel or Phanuel), Raphael, Raguel, Saraqa'el, and Remiel. These seven angels are described as standing before God's throne (see *1 Enoch* 9:1, 40:9), a similar role assigned to the seven spirits in Revelation 8:2. Additional parallels appear in other Scriptures: For instance, Paul references an unnamed archangel in connection with the church's rapture (1 Thessalonians 4:16). Interestingly, both Gabriel and Michael — two prominent archangels named in *1 Enoch* — are also specifically mentioned in the Bible. Gabriel appears in passages such as Daniel 8:16 and 9:21 and Luke 1:19 and 1:26, while Michael is referenced in Daniel 10:13, 10:21, 12:1, Jude 9, and Revelation 12:7.

The four living creatures

The group of four living creatures is closest to the throne. Here is John's description of them:

"Around the throne, and on each side of the throne, are four living creatures, full of eyes in front and behind: the first living creature like a lion, the second living creature like an ox, the third living creature with a face like a human face, and the fourth living creature like a flying eagle. And the four living creatures, each of them with six wings, are full of eyes all around and inside. Day and night without ceasing they sing, 'Holy, holy, holy, the Lord God, the Almighty, who was and is and is to come.'" (Rev. 4:6–8)

This description seems drawn from two Old Testament prophets: Ezekiel's vision of the mobile throne chariot (Ezekiel 1 and 10) and the seraphim in the book of Isaiah (Isaiah 6:2–3) who constantly worship "the Lord God Almighty." Because Ezekiel 10 explicitly calls the living creatures *cherubim*, this name seems the best identification in Revelation 4 as well.

An ode to the one on the throne

As Revelation 4 concludes, the elders sing a hymn to the Lord God:

"The twenty-four elders fall before the one who is seated on the throne and worship the one who lives forever and ever; they cast their crowns before the throne, singing: 'You are worthy, our Lord and God, to receive glory and honor and power, for you created all things, and by your will they existed and were created.'" (Rev. 4:10–11)

The praise song in Revelation 4 underscores the central theme of the vision of the throne room: God is the blessed controller of all things. All creation owes its existence to God; therefore, let all creation bow before him and praise him for his glory, honor, and power.

TECHNICAL STUFF

It's exciting to think that John's original audience — the Christians of Asia Minor — may have sung this hymn in their worship services. Modern scholars have drawn attention to liturgical elements (prescribed forms of public worship) incorporated into the book of Revelation.

In the end, the message of Revelation 4 is clear: Believers need not fear what Caesar or any other worldly potentate may do to them. As Robert Browning said, "God's in his heaven — all's right with the world." Browning knew his Bible!

Singing Praise to the Lamb with Scroll-Opening Skills (5:1–14)

As chapter 5 opens, John's attention now turns to a sealed scroll in God's right hand, a scroll of immense importance: "Then I saw in the right hand of the one seated on the throne a scroll written on the inside and on the back, sealed with seven seals" (Rev. 5:1). In this section, I describe the heavenly scroll and the heavenly person who is qualified to open it. The angelic choirs extol his virtues and achievements.

Examining a mysterious scroll

What kind of document is the mysterious scroll in Revelation 5:1? In the first century, documents were in scroll not *codex* format (in other words a manuscript in book form). The codex, a Christian innovation, did not become widespread until the second century CE. Let's unroll the scroll!

Where there's a will, there's a way (to open it)

To read a scroll — made from papyrus, parchment, or vellum — it must first be unrolled, because it's typically kept rolled up when not in use. The scroll described in Revelation is no ordinary document; it's sealed with seven seals along its edge (see Figure 8-1 for an example). This detail signals that it holds significant, legal, importance — much like the sealed scrolls mentioned in Jeremiah 32:9–15. A last will and testament fit this pattern: The person making the will (a testator) would seal it, with witnesses verifying its authenticity. Only after their death could the seals be broken and the testament opened to reveal its contents.

FIGURE 8-1:
A papyrus scroll
with three seals.

If the scroll is a last will and testament, this throws light on the major purpose of the book of Revelation. A will is a legal document declaring how an individual wishes their estate to be allocated after death. To be valid, it must possess three kinds of information:

>> A list of the heirs

>> A description of the estate

>> A valid signature of the testator

So, what kind of information will be revealed after the scroll is unrolled? In Revelation 3:5, the risen Lord promises the overcomers at Sardis (one of the seven churches — see Chapter 7) their names will not be blotted out of "the book of life." John mentions a book of life at the great white throne judgment (Rev. 20:12). I think the mysterious scroll lists all the heirs, those who believe in Jesus. Immediately after the Last Judgment comes an extensive section describing the new earth and the New Jerusalem (Rev. 21:1–22:6) — the real estate and possessions bequeathed to the heirs. All this fits quite nicely with the notion that the sealed scroll is a will. But is there a valid signature? Yes. Revelation 22:20 closes with these words: "The one who testifies to these things says, 'Surely I am coming soon.' Amen, Come, Lord Jesus!" But his signature also appears on the foreheads of his redeemed people (Rev. 14:1; 22:4; see also 3:12). And none dare contest the signature (Romans 8:31–34)! Don't worry — it's an invisible ink, written with his own cleansing blood.

There is, of course, a distinctive twist. In this case, the one who made the will — Jesus, the Son of God — did in fact die; but he also came back to life and now personally bequeaths his vast estate to those who believe in him. Because believers are joint heirs (Romans 8:17; 1 Corinthians 3:22–23), they share an everlasting body (1 Corinthians 15) and an everlasting inheritance (Rev. 21–22).

Reading the book of destiny

Some things aren't neatly accounted for, suggesting that the scroll is more than a will. After the scroll is opened (Rev. 8:1), you discover that the scroll also includes divine judgments that are poured out on unbelievers before the heirs receive their inheritance (Rev. 8:2–18:24).

GOD'S COSMIC SURVEILLANCE

At one point in *Return of the Jedi* (Episode VI) of the Star Wars series, the Galactic Emperor, Sheev Palpatine, in his Death Star battle station, sits in the control room, surrounded by a battery of video monitors. He watches the unfolding events in various locations of the galaxy. On one monitor, he sees Han Solo and Princess Leia trying to gain access to the shield generator protecting the Death Star. Everything, it seems, is under his surveillance. But as you learn in the movie, not everything is under his control!

The Bible teaches that on an infinitely greater scale, the one on the throne is immediately and comprehensively aware of everything that happens in his universe. Psalm 139 celebrates this all-knowing, all-present, all-powerful God who cares deeply for his children. Unlike the evil emperor (and the Dark Lord), God has good intentions and purposes to save his people from sin. The believers in Asia Minor may rest assured: Their heavenly Father is aware of everything happening in their lives.

In addition to being a will, the scroll is a book of destiny. According to the Bible, what's recorded there must come to pass. This idea of a predetermined course of history is completely in character with apocalyptic thought. The sovereign God is not sitting on his throne, nervously wringing his hands and wondering what on earth is going to happen next. Rather, he's calmly surveying an unfolding story whose every twist and turn is within his knowledge and control. The scroll serves to remind first-century readers of a fundamental Christian conviction: God is the blessed controller of everything that happens.

Double-siding the scroll

The scroll has writing on both sides of the parchment. Ordinarily, one would write only on the side with the fibers running horizontally — the recto side — because the ink goes on more smoothly. This would be the inside of the scroll. The outside or opposite side — the verso — has the fibers running vertically. This means that as you write across the page, the pen must cross minute ridges of the vertically aligned fibers. The script may not always be as legible on the verso side, with occasional smudges or blots in the ink.

Still, if you needed more space, you could use the verso because parchment was a rare commodity. The significance of this little detail is considerable: The scroll contains so much information that both sides of the parchment must be used (a similar idea occurs in Ezekiel 2:10). The list of the heirs is a long one — many names are "written down in heaven." Revelation 7 confirms this idea as the multitude of the redeemed is so large that "no one could count" its number (Rev. 7:9).

Handling a crisis in the throne room

At this moment, a crisis occurs in John's vision (Rev. 5:2–4). An angel issues a challenge: "Who is worthy to break the seals and open the scroll?" To John's dismay and grief, no one steps forward, nor does he volunteer.

In a visionary trance, the seer's senses are heightened; he sees, hears, touches, and tastes more acutely. Emotions are intense. John weeps and sobs openly. Clearly, the scroll must be opened if its contents are to become actualized. This is a scroll of destiny containing the course of redemptive history and its completion. If no one opens and reads the scroll, the kingdom of God won't arrive at its destination. Think if you're traveling somewhere by plane — you need someone to land the plane! No wonder John weeps.

But not to fear! A worthy candidate is waiting in the wings. With a curt command to cease crying, the angel announces the lineage of the worthy one (Rev. 5:5). He is none other than the great Lion of Judah (Genesis 49:9 and Numbers 24:17) and the Root of David (Isaiah 4:2, 11:1). These dynastic titles, which refer to the royal house of David, are deeply rooted in Old Testament history. After the collapse of David's dynasty in 586 BCE, they were reinterpreted as references to the promised *Messiah* — who would overthrow Israel's enemies and regather the Jewish people in their ancestral homeland (Jeremiah 23:5, 33:15; Zechariah 3:8, 6:12). By the first century CE, many Jews maintained a hope for one of David's descendants who would rescue them from oppression. The New Testament attaches great importance to the fact that Jesus of Nazareth descends from the royal line of David (Matthew 1:1–17; Romans 1:3–4; 2 Timothy 2:8) and is addressed as the *Son of David* (Mark 10:41–52).

TECHNICAL STUFF

Varying messianic expectations coexisted within first-century Judaism. Among them was the hope of a Messiah from the house of David. A Jewish writing dating to the mid-first century BCE already gives expression to this hope (*Psalms of Solomon* 17:21–46). Similar sentiments appear in Jewish apocalyptic texts (4 Ezra 11–12; *Testament of Judah* 24:1–5; *Testament of Dan* 5:10–13; and *Florilegium* 1:10–13, 18–19). The New Testament Gospels also witness to this belief among the Jewish people of Palestine in the first century CE (Matthew 2:1–6; 17:10–12; 22:41–45).

Not your ordinary lamb

What John sees next is stunning, and I have to admit, a little bizarre: "Then I saw between the throne and the four living creatures and among the elders a Lamb standing as if it had been slaughtered, having seven horns and seven eyes, which are the seven spirits of God sent out into all the earth" (Rev. 5:6). Because apocalyptic literature uses metaphors and imagery as symbols, you're correct to assume there's a lot more to this lamb than meets the eye.

This lamb has been "slain," graphically indicated by its slit throat, the mandated way to slaughter an animal according to Jewish tradition (Exodus 12; Leviticus 1). But this lamb is very much alive! Miraculously, the lamb survived death and now reigns alongside the One on the throne.

Slain for sins

The background of the slain-lamb image lies in the Old Testament sacrificial system. In ancient Israel, Jews ate meat only after first offering it up in sacrifice to the God of Israel. In other words, the eating of meat (from the herd or flock — that is, a bull, male sheep, or goat) always took place in a ritual/ worship context. The worshiper brought a sacrificial animal that was blemish free, the best he possessed. After laying hands on the head of the animal, symbolizing a transfer of guilt, he slaughtered it.

The long-established method of killing the animal was by slitting the carotid artery of the neck, the most painless and humane way to do it. The blood was poured out at the base of the altar (blood wasn't eaten because it served as the cleansing agent whereby the guilt and stain of sin were removed and thus rendered anyone who touched or ingested it "unclean").

The book of Leviticus contains a handbook for priests on how to sacrifice animals and which animals were appropriate for the various occasions and offenses (Leviticus 1–16). If one sinned, the sacrificial ritual, accompanied by genuine repentance, restored the sinner to fellowship with God.

The New Testament is saturated with sacrificial imagery in its depiction of what Jesus did on the cross. By his death, says the Bible, he atones for the sins of the world (1 John 2:2) and reconciles sinners to God (2 Corinthians 5:16–21). Like the Old Testament sacrificial animals and the Passover Lamb, Jesus is without blemish. The New Testament applies this in a moral sense (Hebrews 2:10; 5:9; 7:28). By shedding his blood, he effectively removes the contagion of sin and averts God's righteous wrath against sinners.

Protecting the Israelites

Central to Israel's life and worship was the feast of Passover, celebrating Israel's liberation from slavery in Egypt. The tenth plague, the death of the firstborn, came upon all Egyptians who didn't recognize the God of Israel. The Israelites gained protection from the destroying angel by slaughtering a lamb and daubing its blood on the doorframes of their homes (Exodus 11–13). The plague "passed over" the Israelite homes. By means of the blood of a lamb, without blemish and a year-old male, the people of Israel were saved. The lamb was then roasted and eaten by the family members.

This ancient festival, the longest, continually observed religious festival known to history, provides part of the New Testament imagery that explains what Jesus did for humanity by dying on a cross (John 1:29).

The Lord's Supper (Holy Communion or the Eucharist) reenacts Jesus's death on the cross and powerfully reinforces what Jesus did to save his people. As Christians eat the bread and drink the wine, as in the ancient Passover meal, they celebrate their deliverance from the power of sin and death (Romans 3:21–26). And how can Christians be sure Jesus's death really accomplishes what the New Testament says it does? Because they're convinced that Jesus is alive and well at the right hand of the Father! Jan van Eck's painting (Figure 8-2) from the altarpiece at the Cathedral of Saint Bavon visually depicts the living, slain Lamb in glory.

FIGURE 8-2: Jan van Eyck's altarpiece, *Adoration of the Lamb,* in Ghent, Belgium.

Master of the universe

In Revelation, the Lamb stands in the center of the throne. Silence hangs over the throne room. The moment of truth has arrived. The Lamb takes the seven-sealed scroll from the right hand of the one seated on the throne (Rev. 5:7). The angelic singers immediately prostrate themselves and erupt in a hymn of praise to the Lamb (5:8–10).

Why is there so much rejoicing by the *heavenly hosts* (the angelic beings who surround the throne)? The description of the Lamb having "seven horns and seven eyes" offers a clue:

>> **Horns:** John doesn't decode the horns, but they're standard apocalyptic terminology for power. The seven horns speak of fullness and perfection of power. In other words, the Lamb possesses the kind of power associated with God himself — he's omnipotent, all-powerful.

>> **Eyes:** The seven eyes are explicitly identified as the seven spirits of God, possibly indicating that the Lamb has authority over the highest angelic beings. Angels function as his "eyes" and convey to him exhaustive knowledge. If, however, the seven spirits represent the Holy Spirit, then the Lamb possesses the Holy Spirit to the nth degree. With either interpretation, the Lamb is aware of everything that transpires on earth; he's omniscient, all-knowing.

Here's the bottom line: The Lamb is a divine being in his own right alongside the one on the throne. Already, in symbolic imagery, you see the outlines of a teaching that's later enshrined in the great creeds (statements of belief) of Christianity — namely, the doctrine of the *Trinity:* three persons (Father, Son, and Holy Spirit) in one God. John's vision of the throne room depicts a profound paradox: The Lamb is a God-man.

John's Gospel and Paul's letters chime in with complementary portraits of a pre-existent, divine being through whom all things were made and through whom all things are reconciled (John 1:1–14; 1 Corinthians 8:6; 2 Corinthians 5:19; Philippians 2:6–11; Colossians 1:15–20, 2:9; 1 Timothy 2:16).

The Lamb holds the seven-sealed scroll; he is master of the universe. He determines the course of history and its ultimate outcome. He has a set purpose and goal, namely, to create a new people and a new heavens and earth. In short, he intends to make "all things new" (Rev. 21:5).

The chapter concludes with a visual and auditory celebration of the sovereignty of the Lamb (Rev. 5:11–14). John now enlarges the circles around the throne (see "Circling the throne," earlier in this chapter). Beyond the elders, an enormous multitude of angelic beings form an even larger circle. John uses the highest number he can conceive of to convey the magnitude — "ten thousand times ten thousand." They join in the chorus of praise and adore the Lamb who is worthy of a sevenfold tribute — the number of perfection and completion.

Reflecting on John's Literary Prowess

The throne room scene is a literary tour de force. It demonstrates John's creative talent in which he employs visual and auditory imagery in powerful ways. And his amazing use of irony and paradox is masterful and reminds us of his Gospel. The following sections illustrate what I mean.

Getting caught up in the heavenly chorus

Imagine chapters 4 and 5 as a celestial concert. John first introduces you to the performers on stage who are arranged in concentric circles around the center piece, the throne of God. The audience and the performers revolve around the throne. The concert begins in the innermost ring when the four living creatures sing the Trisagion (thrice holy). In my mind they sing it in a holy hush that calms the soul and prepares the heart for what's next. The twenty-four elders then join them in singing a magnificent anthem "You are worthy." The volume is extremely loud. This is followed by the addition of an angelic choir so large it's beyond numbering and the combined choirs sing: "You are worthy." By now the volume exceeds the decibel scale! But we aren't finished yet — all creatures in heaven and earth now join in to sing a deafening doxology "to the one seated on the throne and to the Lamb" (Rev. 5:13). Can you hear it in your mind? The entire universe revolves and vibrates around the throne. As John zooms out, the volume rockets up. The performance is off the charts. A Taylor Swift concert doesn't even register in comparison with the magnitude and magnificence of this production!

Pinpointing John's paradox and irony

John demonstrates an artistry in the throne room scene that has no equal. He does this by creating a soaring expectation and then surprising readers with something so unexpectedly profound it reduces us to silence and tears.

REMEMBER

After the first two choral numbers, John describes the crisis in heaven when no one was found worthy to open the sealed scroll. Opening the scroll in no way compares to the legend of King Arthur and the magic sword Excalibur. Opening the scroll is not a test of physical strength, it's a test of moral and spiritual strength.

As John is bitterly weeping, one of the elders comes up to him and tells him not to weep. There is a person who is worthy. The elder's description of this conquering hero as "the Lion of the tribe of Judah" would ignite the hopes of people downtrodden and marginalized because of Imperial Rome and its blasphemous cult. Readers are set up to expect a ferocious lion leaping onto center stage and roaring like the famous MGM lion. But that isn't what happens. Instead, John offers one of the most powerful instances of irony and paradox in literature. The spotlight falls on a lamb, a Passover lamb who displays the sign of sacrifice — a slit throat.

The Lamb, however, is hardly a defenseless, weak creature you normally associate with lambs. This Lamb is equipped with divine attributes and power (having seven horns, seven eyes, and the seven spirits of God) making him more than a match for the fearsome red dragon you will meet later.

But here is the supreme irony of the book of Revelation. The Lamb, though possessing divine power by virtue of being God, achieves redemption for his people not by exercising brute force against his enemies but by an act of self-giving love, sacrificing his life for the sins of the world. What John portrays through images and symbols in Revelation 4, he conveys through proclamation in his Gospel: "For God so loved the world that he gave his only Son" (John 3:16). He also includes it in pastoral prose in his first epistle: "We know love in this, that he laid down his life for us — and we ought to lay down our lives for one another" (1 John 3:16).

John's paradox of self-giving love as the most powerful force in creation finds its counterpoint in John's Gospel. Without going into all the details, John delays the moment when Jesus's time arrives, and he reveals himself as the savior. The moment of revelation occurs at the least expected moment, not the resurrection as in the Synoptic Gospels, but the cross. "And I, when I am lifted up from the earth [in other words, crucified] will draw all people to myself" (John 12:32).

REMEMBER

In *Harry Potter and the Half-Blood Prince*, Dumbledore tells Harry that love is a powerful force Voldemort can't fathom. Furthermore, it's the secret of Harry's strength. J. K. Rowling has clearly read the Bible.

IN THIS CHAPTER

» **Understanding the seals in context**

» **Meeting the four horsemen of the Apocalypse**

» **Witnessing the martyrs**

» **Exploring the Day of the Lord**

» **Interpreting the meaning of the 144,000**

Chapter **9**

Breaking Seven Seals (6:1–8:1)

This chapter has nothing to do with those adorable whiskered aquatic mammals that bark, smack their flippers together, and balance beach balls on their noses. Although these seven seals do sort of bark, they also bite and are not at all cute. Like adhesive flaps on envelopes, they secure the contents of a special scroll.

The seven seals in Revelation 6:1–8:1 are like the master key to an office building — only with the correct key can you open the main door and the offices inside.

In this chapter, you'll gain insight into how the sixth seal opens the door for the dramatic events leading up to the triumphant return of Jesus to earth. You'll also explore how apocalyptic and prophetic texts from the Old Testament shape much of the vivid imagery embedded in the seals. The chapter wraps up by offering interpretations of the enigmatic 144,000 who are marked with God's seal on their foreheads.

Unsealing the Beginning of the End

In Revelation 5 (see Chapter 8), the Lamb emerges as the only being worthy to take the scroll, break its seals, and thereby reveal its contents (Rev. 5:5). In Revelation 6:1, the Lamb initiates the process by breaking the first seal — an act that triggers a series of events culminating in the Lamb's total triumph. John watches as one of the four living creatures summons four actors who play a role in the unfolding drama of redemption.

Exploring the relationship of the three series of sevens

The Old Testament prophets warned that before the kingdom of God triumphs, fearful judgments will devastate the earth. They refer to this time of intense suffering as the *Day of the Lord* (Isaiah 13, 34; Jeremiah 4–7; Ezekiel 7, 25; Amos 5:18–20; Zephaniah 1–3). Although John doesn't use that term, his prophecy surely incorporates the concept and organizes it into three series of seven judgments. The following sections explain how these judgments relate to each other.

TECHNICAL STUFF

The number of judgments in each series may derive from the curse upon Israel for covenant violations. In Leviticus 26, the Lord forewarns the Israelites, "And if in spite of this you will not obey me, I will continue to punish you sevenfold for your sins" (Leviticus 26:18); this warning repeats three more times in the same chapter (26:21; 26:24; 26:28). In apocalyptic writing, the number seven typically signifies that which is complete, finished, or perfect. For example, when the last series of seven bowls is about to be poured out, John comments, "For with them the wrath of God is ended" (Rev. 15:1).

Timing

In Revelation, the seven seals are the first of three sevens; the others are the seven trumpets (Rev. 8:6–11:19) and the seven bowls (Rev. 15, 16). A key for interpreting the central section of the book of Revelation is understanding how the three series of sevens relate to each other. Several options are possible:

>> **Concurrent:** The seals, trumpets, and bowls run parallel to each other and end at the same point in time.

>> **Successive:** The seals, trumpets, and bowls follow each other in chronological sequence. On this view, the three series are like an expandable telescope.

>> **Both:** The arrangement of the seals, trumpets, and bowls combines both successive and concurrent elements, ending at the same point.

The third option appears to make the most sense (but you're welcome to disagree!). John designates the sixth seal as the day of the wrath of God and the Lamb (6:16–17). The succeeding series of trumpet and bowl judgments elaborate on the sixth seal, with this exception: All three series terminate at the same point — the triumph of the kingdom of God. This interpretation means that trumpets 1 through 6 expand on the sixth seal, and bowls 1 through 6 cover much the same ground, though most likely they occur near the end of the sixth seal or Day of the Lord, just before Christ returns. The upshot is that much of Revelation 8–19 involves the unfolding of the sixth seal. Perhaps the best way to get a handle on this is to skim through the diagram in Figure 9-1.

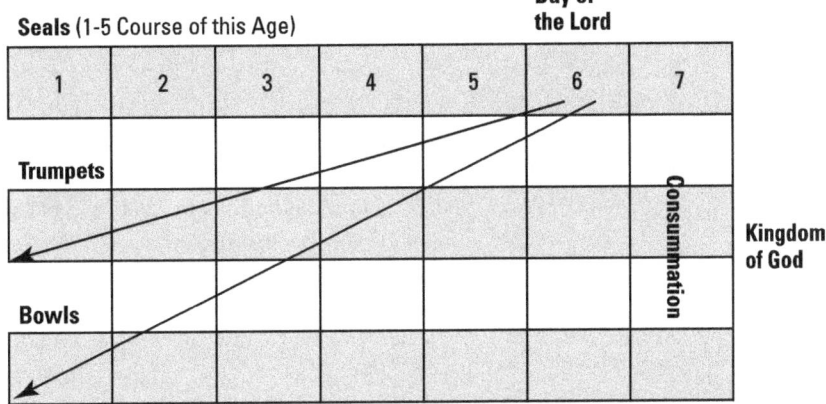

FIGURE 9-1: Possible timing of the seals, trumpets, and bowls.

WARNING

Given the obvious similarities between the trumpets and bowls, some scholars argue that both passages describe the same events. While the judgments in these series resemble each other, this doesn't mean they are identical. Instead, it's more plausible they present a progression — moving from a set of partial judgments to a final, much harsher round. John even calls the bowls "the seven last plagues" (15:1, emphasis added), highlighting that these events unfold in a particular order.

Scope

The content of the seals appears less intensive and extensive than that of the trumpets and bowls. The seals affect only a quarter of the earth: "They [Death and Hades] were given authority over a fourth of the earth, to kill with sword, famine, and pestilence, and by the wild animals of the earth" (6:8). By contrast, the trumpet judgments affect a third of the earth (8:7–12), and the bowl judgments are completely global. By then, poor ol' planet earth is maxed out!

Breaking the seals to gain access to the scroll

Visualize how you open a sealed scroll. Instead of a book containing a set of bound pages, think of a roll of papyrus (an early form of paper) several feet long. String tied around the scroll prevented it from unraveling. To this was added a clay seal impressed with the owner's signature. An intact seal guaranteed the authenticity of the document and provided evidence that no one had tampered with the contents. See Figure 9-2.

FIGURE 9-2:
A scroll with
seven seals
along the edge.

The scroll in Revelation 5–8 has seven such seals. To open the scroll, someone first must break all seven seals. More than a few interpreters go awry here by failing to realize this rather fundamental point: The seals are not the contents of the scroll! They're *preliminary events* that must happen before the contents can be read. The sealed scroll is a last will and testament (see Chapter 8) in which is written the names of the heirs and a description of their inheritance. Before the heirs receive their inheritance, certain events must first unfold.

Scoping out the seven seals

The seven seals in Revelation 6:1–8:1 fall into four categories:

>> **The first four seals:** Identified as horsemen on four differently colored horses, these seals depict terrestrial events.

>> **The fifth seal:** Though not depicted as a horse and rider, this seal is closely associated with the first four. It provides a heavenly perspective: a snapshot of Christian martyrs (killed because of their beliefs) beneath an altar, crying out for justice.

>> **The sixth seal:** This seal reveals a terrifying display of disturbances on the earth and in the heavens, including the sun's turning black, stars' falling to earth, and the moon's becoming red as blood.

>> **The seventh seal:** After a parenthetical section consisting of two explanatory visions, the last seal issues in silence in heaven, a quite unexpected result.

The arrangement of the seals significantly affects the overall interpretation of the section. The evils occurring during the first five seals generally result from human depravity (even famines have a human component in that they're often a byprod-uct of war). Injustice, inequality, prejudice, hate, greed, lust for power, and lack of self-control contribute to most human suffering during the present age. The fourth and sixth seals add so-called natural disasters to the mix. But when the Lamb breaks the seventh seal in Revelation 8:1 and the scroll can at last be opened and read, John delays explaining what happens. We describe the individual seals in detail later in this chapter.

Comparing notes with Jesus

The *synoptic Gospels* (Matthew, Mark, and Luke) provide a key to unlocking the meaning of the seals. In Revelation, everything under the first seven seals paral-lels a message Jesus gave to his disciples. This teaching — in which Jesus explains what will happen before the end of the world — is commonly known as the *Olivet Discourse,* named after the Mount of Olives (see Matthew 24:3–44; Mark 13:3–37; and Luke 21:7–36). Jesus predicts that catastrophic events such as war, famine, earthquakes, pestilence, and persecution will characterize the present age.

Table 9-1 shows how the seven seals parallel the teaching in which Jesus outlines the events leading up to and including his return to earth.

TABLE 9-1   Comparing the Olivet Discourse and the Seals

Event	Olivet Discourse (Matthew)	Seals (Revelation)
False Messiah(s)	24:4	6:1–2 First seal
Warfare and bloodshed	24:7	6:3–4 Second seal
Famine	24:7	6:5–6 Third seal
Earthquakes	24:7	6:7–8 Fourth seal
Martyrdom	24:9	6:9–11 Fifth seal
Cosmic disturbances	24:29	6:12–17 Sixth seal
Coming of the Son of Man	24:30–31	8:1 Seventh seal (implied but not stated)

WARNING

While Jesus sets forth a sequence of events in the Olivet Discourse, he cautions his listeners not to interpret these happenings as definitive signs of the end (Matthew 24:6). Instead, he frames them as "the beginning of birth pangs" (Matthew 24:8), echoing a period of tribulation familiar to Jewish apocalyptic thought, such as 1 *Enoch,* 2 *Esdras,* and the Babylonian Talmud. These works describe a time of intense suffering — the "woes of Messiah" — anticipated to precede the arrival of the Messiah.

It's essential to recognize that while early Christians saw these themes fulfilled in Jesus, the Jewish community rejected his messianic claims. Today, most Orthodox Jews continue to await the arrival of their Messiah, while many non-observant Jews have shifted their hopes from a personal redeemer to the vision of a messianic age: a future era marked by universal harmony and prosperity.

The First Four Seals: The Four Horsemen of the Apocalypse (6:1–8)

Galloping forth like figures from a Hogwarts School of Witchcraft and Wizardry dinner (Harry Potter) come four horses and their riders. Each one signifies disaster for the planet. The first five seals serve as preliminaries leading up to the earth-shaking events connected with the sixth seal.

Revelation portrays each of the first four seals as a differently colored horse with a rider. John borrows his imagery from the Old Testament:

>> In Zechariah 1:7–17, angelic horsemen patrol the earth and are mounted on red, sorrel (reddish brown), and white horses.

>> In Zechariah 6:1–8, the prophet has a vision of four chariots pulled by red, black, white, and dappled gray horses, respectively. The chariots (driven by angelic charioteers) are identified with the four winds of the earth, which patrol their respective regions.

>> Additionally, John may be drawing from Jeremiah's prophecy of four judgments (pestilence, sword, famine, and captivity) and four destroyers (sword, dogs, birds, and wild animals) of the sinful people of Jerusalem (Jeremiah 15:2–3).

>> Ezekiel likewise prophesied "four deadly acts of judgment, sword, famine, wild animals, and pestilence" against Jerusalem (Ezekiel 14:21).

In this section, I take a close look at John's four horsemen of the Apocalypse.

White horse and rider with a bow

The meaning of the first seal is debated and remains one of the more challenging passages in Revelation to decipher. In Revelation 6:2, John writes, "I looked, and there was a white horse! Its rider had a bow; a crown was given to him, and he came out conquering and to conquer." Interpreters generally fall into two camps regarding the identity of the rider on the white horse:

» **Jesus:** This view is linked to Revelation 19:11–16, in which Jesus is depicted riding a white horse in his triumphant return to earth.

» **The antichrist:** This view argues that because the other three horses represent negative, destructive forces, it's more consistent that all four share a common negative character.

So, which is it? Keep in mind that white horses don't always equate to the good guys in white hats. Generals of armies in the ancient world frequently rode white horses as a sign of prestige, not moral character. Furthermore, it seems inappropriate for an angelic being to summon Jesus to go forth; being summoned is more fitting for someone of lesser status and dignity. Also, the bow in the hand of the rider on the white horse doesn't seem appropriate for Jesus and deviates from the references in Revelation where Jesus has a sword issuing from his mouth (Rev. 1:16, 2:12, 2:16, 19:15). Bows in scriptural imagery frequently depict war and destruction (Jeremiah 6:23, 46:9, 49:35; Lamentations 2:4; Hosea 1:5, 1:7; Zechariah 9:10).

As we discussed in the earlier "Comparing notes with Jesus" section, the seven seals parallel Jesus's teaching on the End Times in the Olivet Discourse. There, the first thing Jesus warns his disciples about is false messiahs (Matthew 24:4–5). Many commentators, therefore, suggest that the first rider on the white horse is in fact the antichrist, the great imitator (see Chapter 11 for more on this bad boy).

In my view, the four horsemen represent conditions and circumstances characterizing human history from the first century until the present. Consequently, the rider is not *the* antichrist but *false messiahs* (supposed liberators of the Jews) who precede him. These pretenders were already active in the first century; for example, they appear in connection with the Jewish war against Rome in 66–74 CE. The Jewish historian Josephus describes several false messiahs leading up to the revolt. The early Christian communities were also troubled by false prophets. John, in his first epistle, says, "As you have heard that antichrist is coming, so now many antichrists have come" (1 John 2:18). Jewish false messiahs triggered revolutionary movements erupting in violence. Jewish Christians often suffered persecution from their fellow Jews because they didn't join or identify with these revolutionary movements.

Red horse and rider who removes peace

Opening the second seal (Rev. 6:3–4) reveals another rider and horse: "When he opened the second seal, I heard the second living creature call out, 'Come!' And out came another horse, bright red; its rider was permitted to take peace from the earth, so that people would slaughter one another; and he was given a great sword."

The bright red color of the second horse graphically represents blood. Bloodshed characterizes human history from the first century to the twenty-first. The Roman Empire went through a particularly violent era during the Jewish war of 66–73 CE and the power struggle following Nero's suicide in 68 CE. As many as a million casualties resulted from these conflicts. Though bloodshed was not so widespread during the reign of Domitian, numerous conflicts lay on the horizon. From then until now, the historical record documents a depressing recurrence of death and destruction owing to war. Fast forward to today, where TV and computer screens bombard you with images of violence, acts of terrorism, and oppression around the globe. No era in history has been untouched by violence and bloodshed, despite humanity's highest aspirations for peace.

Black horse and rider with a pair of scales

As the Lamb opens the third seal, a fearful specter rides forth. In Revelation 6:5–6, John writes, "When he opened the third seal, I heard the third living creature call out, 'Come!' I looked, and there was a black horse! Its rider held a pair of scales in his hand, and I heard what seemed to be a voice in the midst of the four living creatures saying, 'A quart of wheat for a day's pay, and three quarts of barley for a day's pay, but do not damage the olive oil and the wine!'"

This passage describes a time of famine where scarcity strikes hardest at the poor. While the wealthy still enjoy their luxuries, ordinary people struggle to afford even the necessities. Feeding a family for a day costs an entire day's wages — a staggering rate of inflation, twelve times the usual rate. Many are forced to survive on the less nutritious barley instead of wheat. This dramatic gap between the rich and the poor highlights a persistent reality throughout history: inequality and injustice.

Throughout the history of the Roman Empire, famines frequently ravaged the population (Acts 11:27–30). Even today, graphic images of starving children from war-torn regions regularly haunt our consciences. Never have greater numbers lived on the brink of starvation than in the twenty-first century. This illustrates our overriding point that the first five seals characterize human history from the first century to our own. Never have we had an era when famine was not a major concern for multitudes somewhere on the planet. The same goes for each of the five seals.

Pale green horse and Death and Hades

As the Lamb opens the fourth seal, the "Grim Reaper" rides out on his pale green mount: "When he opened the fourth seal, I heard the voice of the fourth living creature call out, 'Come!' I looked and there was a pale green horse! Its rider's name was Death, and Hades followed with him; they were given authority over a fourth of the earth, to kill with sword, famine, and pestilence, and by the wild animals of the earth" (Rev. 6:7–8).

Death and Hades are closely linked: Death is the moment at which physical life ceases; Hades is the continuing post-death existence of disembodied spirits. More specifically, *Hades* is the Greek term for the place of departed spirits, typically regarded as the *underworld.* The New Testament views Hades as a temporary place that's ultimately destroyed at the end of the world (Rev. 20:13–14).

This ghastly apparition speaks for itself. Pale green is chosen as the color of this horse to depict the appearance of a rotting corpse. Because of the red and black horses, death stalks the land.

Epidemics regularly decimated the Roman Empire. In fact, in Ephesus, plagues felled one-third of the population during the years 165–251 CE. And recall the devastating plagues of the Middle Ages, such as the Black Death of 1347–1351 that swept away one-third of all Europeans. Even in modern times, the great flu pandemic of 1918–1919 accounted for over 675,000 American deaths, far more than in WWI itself. Of course, we have recently passed through another pandemic with COVID-19 in which an estimated 7 million worldwide have died so far with more than 8,000 added daily. Who knows what other pandemics lurk in the dark world of viruses and microbes?

THE FOUR HORSEMEN OF NOTRE DAME

On October 18, 1924, Notre Dame football achieved a moment of immortality thanks to a *New York Herald-Tribune* sportswriter named Grantland Rice. Borrowing from the imagery of the Apocalypse, he filed a story following Notre Dame's 13–7 victory over an Army team at the Polo Grounds. Here is perhaps the most famous football story ever written in sports journalism:

"Outlined against a blue-gray October sky the Four Horsemen rode again. In dramatic lore they are known as famine, pestilence, destruction and death. These are only

(continued)

(continued)

aliases. Their real names are: Stuhldreher, Miller, Crowley and Layden. They formed the crest of the South Bend cyclone before which another fighting Army team was swept over the precipice at the Polo Grounds this afternoon as 55,000 spectators peered down upon the bewildering panorama spread out upon the green plain below."

George Stricker, a student sports publicist at Notre Dame, capitalized on this characterization. When the team arrived back at South Bend, he arranged with a local livery stable to have four horses available. The four players, quarterback Harry Stuhldreher, left halfback Jim Crowley, right halfback Don Miller, and fullback Elmer Layden, mounted up and posed in their uniforms. That picture appeared in the national press, and a legend was born.

© Bettmann/CORBIS

PUTTING TOGETHER THE WELCOMING PARTY

The return of Jesus is called the *Parousia*, a Greek term basically meaning an arrival, coming, or presence. For example, it can be used to refer to a royal visit to a Greco-Roman city. The visit of the emperor or a member of the royal family was a *parousia*. The city elected a delegation to meet the emperor and his entourage well outside the city limits and escort him back to the forum in the city center. Much to-do went into preparations, involving general sprucing up, minting of celebratory coins, civic speeches, public festivities, games, and so forth, to make a good impression.

The Apostle Paul skillfully adapts the Greco-Roman concept of a *parousia* to the return of Jesus. Jesus is the coming King of kings, and the welcoming delegation is believers who are taken up (*raptured*) to "meet the Lord in the air" (1 Thessalonians 4:17). Jesus's entourage includes believers who die before the Parousia. They won't miss out on the festivities; in fact, they have a front-row seat!

The Fifth Seal: The Blood of Martyrs (6:9–11)

Most people believe that the fifth seal, though standing apart from the four horsemen, is closely associated with them. John writes,

> *"When he opened the fifth seal, I saw under the altar the souls of those who had been slaughtered for the word of God and for the testimony they had given; they cried out with a loud voice, 'Sovereign Lord, holy and true, how long will it be before you judge and avenge our blood on the inhabitants of the earth?' They were each given a white robe and told to rest a little longer, until the number would be complete both of their fellow servants and of their brothers and sisters, who were soon to be killed as they themselves had been killed." (Rev. 6:9–11)*

The connection between this seal and the previous four is simply this: Martyrdom for one's faith, like war, famine, plague, and death on a massive scale, is a recurring historical phenomenon. Religious persecution has never totally disappeared. Based on John's vision, it's unlikely to end until the return of Jesus.

PERSECUTION THEN AND NOW

Ancient historians Tacitus, Suetonius, and Sulpicius Severus captured the gory details of the persecution of early Christians. These historians imply that Nero's actions were designed to deflect the outrage of the citizenry of Rome. In 64 CE, a devastating fire destroyed large portions of the city with a huge loss of life. A rumor circulated that Nero himself had set the fire, wanting to rebuild the city in a manner more suited to his taste. Needing a scapegoat, Nero fastened the blame on the Christians.

During the reign of Domitian (81–96 CE), there were periodic outbreaks of persecution, especially in cities of Asia, because Christians refused to burn incense to the divine Caesar. During the second and third centuries, extensive state-supported persecution swept over the empire, and thousands of believers perished.

Throughout the Middle Ages and into the Reformation and Counter-Reformation, violent episodes of persecution and martyrdom occurred. Christians in Asia Minor, where the seven churches were located, experienced several waves of conquest and persecution in the seventh and eighth centuries, eventually almost dying out entirely.

However, what many people don't realize is that never in history have there been as many martyrs as there are currently. In many areas of the world, various religious, political, psychological, and economic factors have created a hostile environment for those who follow the teachings of Jesus.

These martyrs, who've died because of their faith in Jesus, rest safely beneath the heavenly altar. In popular Jewish belief, the righteous dwell under God's throne until the day of resurrection. The "rest" promised to the martyrs (Rev. 6:11) speaks of more than mere physical refreshment; it conveys enjoyment of Jesus's presence and anticipation of his complete victory over evil.

As you explore the fifth seal, keep in mind that John wrote the book of Revelation at the end of the first century. But already in 64 CE, during a brief but bloody episode, Nero Caesar had put a great host of Christians to death. Multitudes died in the arena, torn to shreds by lions. Others were crucified, and some were burned alive at night to serve as torches for Nero's nightly dinner parties.

The Sixth Seal: The Day of the Lord Has Come! (6:12–17)

The events associated with the first five seals are sufferings that humans have encountered over the centuries. However, the description of the sixth seal in Revelation 6:12–17 places it in an entirely different category from the others. A great earthquake accompanied by unparalleled cosmic disturbances (such as falling stars!) indicates something off the charts.

Never in recorded history have such phenomena occurred. People in all walks of life cower in caves and cringe as terrible events unfold all around them. What's going on here? It's like creation returns to its original state of chaos (Genesis 1:2).

Like Old (Testament) times: Going back to the Day of the Lord

Crucial to understanding the sixth seal is the Old Testament notion of the *Day of the Lord*. In this regard, the prophetic books of the Old Testament are essential reading (see Chapter 3). The prophets paint a mural of the last days of earth's history, when the Lord God of Israel holds court and settles all accounts — Judgment Day. Metaphors depicting both its severity and its salvation collide, so get ready for some fire and brimstone.

Amos

The book of Amos is a striking example of doomsday imagery. In his writings, the prophet Amos tries to correct some common misconceptions. Israelites in Amos's day generally assumed the Day of the Lord would be a time of blessing and light. They believed this solely on the basis that they were Israelites, as if membership in their group brought automatic blessing as a privilege. They disregarded the inconvenient fact that willfully choosing to disobey God's directives would bring judgment — something they should've known based on the history of their people's interactions with God.

Amos, as God's mouthpiece, lets them know their wrong behavior has landed them in serious jeopardy. Just because they're the "children of Israel" doesn't mean they receive a free pass to God's kingdom. Amos graphically attacks their misconceptions. For example, he says that the Israelites are like a man who encounters a lion and bear and escapes both by fleeing to the safety of his home, only to be bitten by a deadly snake hiding in the wall (Amos 5:19). Thinking he's escaped disaster, he is suddenly stricken and dies. What a picture of bitter disappointment! As always, though, God offers an alternative: If the Israelites acknowledge their disobedience and conform to God's commands, then the Day of the Lord will be a day of light rather than a day of darkness (Amos 5:18–24).

Isaiah

Other prophets build on Amos's initial sketch of the Day of the Lord, none more graphically than Isaiah. Isaiah sketches a time of terror and trembling: "Enter the caves of the rocks and the holes of the ground, from the terror of the Lord, and from the glory of his majesty, when he rises to terrify the earth" (Isaiah 2:19).

Describing the cosmic disasters of the sixth seal, John clearly borrows Isaiah's imagery:

"See, the day of the Lord comes, cruel, with wrath and fierce anger, to make the earth a desolation, and to destroy its sinners from it. For the stars of the heavens and their constellations will not give their light; the sun will be dark at its rising, and the moon will not shed its light. [. . .] Therefore I will make the heavens tremble, and the earth will be shaken out of its place. [. . .]"
(Isaiah 13:9–10, 13:13)

In the same vein, Isaiah continues, "All the host of heaven shall rot away, and the skies roll up like a scroll. All their host shall wither like a leaf withering on a vine, or fruit withering on a fig tree" (Isaiah 34:4).

Compare Isaiah's description to the following events of Revelation 6:12–17:

>> The sun turns black, and the moon turns red.

>> The stars fall from the sky.

>> The sky disappears "like a scroll rolling itself up."

>> Islands and mountains are no longer in place.

In with the New (Testament): Looking to the Day of the Lamb

The expectation of divine intervention and vindication, as related in the Old Testament's Day of the Lord, became a standard feature of *Second Temple Judaism*, a term referring to Judaism during the period 517 BCE–70 CE. Here's how the New Testament relates Jesus to this day of judgment:

- In the Gospels, Jesus accepts this depiction and further elaborates on some of its features. The distinctive contribution of Jesus lies in his conviction that he, as the Son of Man, plays the pivotal role in the Day of the Lord.

- In John's Gospel, Jesus is quoted as saying, "The Father judges no one but has given all judgment to the Son" (John 5:22).

- The Apostle Paul simply expands the Old Testament expression and speaks of "the day of our Lord Jesus Christ" (1 Corinthians 1:8; Philippians 1:6, 1:10, 2:16; 1 Thessalonians 5:2).

TECHNICAL STUFF

SORTING OUT SECOND TEMPLE JUDAISM

First Temple Judaism refers to the form of Judaism that existed from the dedication of the First Temple in about 970 BCE until the Babylonians destroyed it in 586 BCE. It was rooted in the great covenant the Lord made with Israel at Mount Sinai (as recorded in Exodus 19–24).

Second Temple Judaism refers to the form of Judaism that existed from about 517 BCE, when the Second Temple was dedicated, up to its destruction by the Romans in 70 CE. It was characterized by the traditions of the First Temple, supplemented by the new traditions that arose as Jews interacted with their new Hellenistic (Greek) environment and their ongoing attempt to adapt the old laws to new settings.

During the Second Temple period, great controversy arose among the Jews. The various groups — known as Pharisees, Sadducees (as documented in the New Testament), Essenes (as depicted in some of the Dead Sea Scrolls), and others that scholars know about only by inference — arose during this era and had quite different understandings about what constituted genuine Judaism. Of course, the Jewish movement that eventually became known as Christianity also arose during Second Temple times and added another perspective.

Of the various Jewish groups, only the Pharisees and Christians survived the great war against Rome (66–74 CE). Pharisaism evolved into *Rabbinic Judaism*. This form of Judaism, shaped by the Mishnah and Talmud (authoritative interpretations of the biblical laws of the Old Testament), ended the age of diversity and ushered in a long period of uniformity until the period of the Enlightenment (eighteenth century CE). Judaism today is once again characterized by a great diversity of belief and even unbelief.

For John, this day clearly belongs to both the Lord and the Lamb. In Revelation 6:16–17, as the people flee to the mountains, they call to the rocks, "Fall on us and hide us from the face of the one seated on the throne and from the wrath of the Lamb; for the great day of *their* wrath has come, and who is able to stand?" Christians often call this time the *Great Tribulation,* a term that comes from Matthew 24:21 and Revelation 7:14 in the King James Version of the Bible.

Pausing for Effect (7:1–17)

As Revelation 7 begins, John hits the pause button. He feels the need to elaborate on an important point. As you read through the book of Revelation, several such pauses or interludes occur. These include the following:

>> Revelation 7:1–17

>> Revelation 10:1–11

>> Revelation 11:1–14

>> Revelation 12

>> Revelation 13

>> Revelation 14

John uses these moments of pause to draw attention to essential questions he believes must be addressed. At this point in Revelation 7, he interrupts the unfolding drama to respond to the profound concern raised by those witnessing the chaos: Is anyone able to withstand the day of God's and the Lamb's wrath (Rev. 6:17)? The answer, radiating with hope, is gradually revealed in the verses that follow.

Surveying the survivors

John identifies two groups of people who stand before the throne of God — "the 144,000" (Rev. 7:4) and a "great multitude" (Rev. 7:9). These individuals survive the Day of the Lord for one reason: because God seals and saves them. This salvation is a "God thing," not something they've achieved. As the Apostle Paul says, "For by grace you have been saved through faith, and this is not your own doing: it is the gift of God" (Ephesians 2:8). Seen in this light, the whole Bible is an overarching story of mercy showcasing how God rescues sinful people from otherwise inevitable judgment.

The imagery John uses to depict this salvation is striking. Four angels hold back the four winds of the earth, which represent destructive forces about to be unleashed on the world. But God intends to protect his chosen people just as he did long ago in Egypt (Exodus 8–12).

Another angel places God's seal on the foreheads of 144,000 people, identified as "the people of Israel" (Rev. 7:4). This feature of John's vision recalls a vision of the prophet Ezekiel in 592 BCE. Ezekiel saw six destroying angels about to wreak havoc on the inhabitants of Jerusalem because of their apostasy (abandoning belief in God) and rebellion. Before they're allowed to execute vengeance, however, another angelic being records the names of those who are truly repentant. These he seals with a mark on their foreheads. Only those with the mark escape the impending disaster (Ezekiel 9:1–11).

Suddenly, John sees another group he refers to as "a great multitude that no one could count, from every nation, from all tribes and peoples and languages, standing before the throne" (Rev. 7:9). An innumerable host experiences God's grace and joins the happy throng before the throne.

So, what's their story? One of the twenty-four elders asks John: "Who are these, robed in white, and where have they come from?" (Rev. 7:13). John doesn't know, but he knows the elder knows, so John asks the elder, who responds, "These are they who have come out of the great ordeal; they have washed their robes and made them white in the blood of the Lamb" (Rev. 7:14). In short, they're Christians who refused to deny their faith even at the cost of their lives.

REMEMBER

Consider the striking image here: garments are made white by being washed in blood. For Christians, such paradoxes lie at the very core of their faith. The Christian tradition is filled with these kinds of apparent contradictions — for example, the tension between God's sovereignty (his control over all things) and human freedom, or the balance between God being beyond the universe (transcendence) and at the same time intimately present within it (immanence). Similarly, Christians believe in salvation by faith yet also hold that actions matter in judgment. These paradoxes are not simply puzzles, but essential features of Christian teaching.

A regular feature of apocalyptic literature involves dialogue with a heavenly guide. The seer is either asked a question or asks a question. In this instance, John is asked a question he doesn't know and throws it back to the angel, who supplies the answer (Rev. 7:13–14, 17:6b–7; Ezekiel 37:3; Daniel 7:15–16; Zechariah 1:9, 1:19, 4:1–6).

Identifying the 144,000

John gives a roll call of the tribes of Israel, which results in a tally of 12,000 from each of the twelve tribes listed, for a grand total of 144,000. This amounts to twelve squared times 1,000. Considerable speculation and controversy surround the identity of the 144,000. Three major options present themselves.

All Christians

Some interpret the 144,000 as representing all Christians — in other words, this group is essentially the same as the vast multitude described later in Revelation 7:9–17, just seen from a different viewpoint. Interestingly, the tribal list in Revelation differs from the Old Testament: the tribes of Ephraim and Dan are left out, and each tribe is assigned the exact same, rounded number. Such details suggest that the figure is likely symbolic rather than a literal headcount.

In the New Testament, several passages view the church as a new Israel (Romans 2:28–29; Galatians 6:16). In other words, Gentiles and Jews who believe in Jesus make up a new people of God.

>> This may be reflected in the churches of Smyrna and Philadelphia, where you hear of "those who say that they are Jews but are not" (Rev. 2:9, 3:9). In other words, Christians believe they, not ethnic Jews, are the true Israel.

>> The group of 144,000 reappears in chapter 14, and Revelation 14:4 says, "They have been redeemed from humankind as first fruits for God and the Lamb." Proponents contend that this description suggests that the 144,000 — previously described as the tribes of Israel — symbolize the church because "from humankind" refers to Gentiles.

>> The Apostle Peter refers to Gentile believers as "exiles of the Dispersion" (1 Peter 1:1), an application of a Jewish expression to Christians. The same adaptation appears in the Letter of James, where Christians are stylized as "the twelve tribes in the Dispersion" (James 1:1).

Jewish Christians

The 144,000 may symbolize only Jewish Christians. The fact that the tribes of Israel are enumerated accords more naturally with the whole group being ethnic Jews who believe in Jesus. Paul speaks of a present remnant of Israel (including himself) who do believe, and he seems to predict that at the end of the age, a wholesale conversion of Jews will occur (Romans 11:26).

Proponents of this view point out that

>> People on earth give "glory to the God of heaven" in only one place in the book of Revelation (11:13), and these people appear to be Jews in Jerusalem.

>> Jesus promised his disciples that when he comes in his glory, they'll "sit on twelve thrones, judging the twelve tribes of Israel" (Matthew 19:28; Luke 22:30).

>> The Apostle Paul seems to envision a future conversion of Jews just prior to the Parousia, or second coming of Jesus (Romans 11:26–27).

Perhaps, say proponents, the last chapter of earth's history will include a remarkably dedicated group of Jewish Christians who bear witness to their faith in Jesus as the Messiah. Some interpreters also hold that the two witnesses of Revelation 11 represent Jewish Christians who minister in Jerusalem in connection with the End Times.

An elite group of Christians

The 144,000 may be an elite group of Christians who are especially devoted to Jesus and receive special status as a reward for their commitment. Most often, this group is equated with Christian martyrs. The number is symbolic because there have been many times this number of martyrs in virtually any period of church history you choose. But some religious groups view the number literally and teach that the 144,000 are a spiritually elite group of believers who enjoy exalted status in the final kingdom.

The biggest problem with this perspective is that the elitism implied in such a view clashes with the clear teaching on equality throughout the New Testament (Galatians 3:28–29; 1 Corinthians 12:13; Colossians 3:11). Moreover, attempts to take the number literally — exactly 144,000 people, not one more or less — ignores the non-literal conventions of apocalyptic writings.

Observing the multitude standing before the throne

Another throne room scene unfolds in Revelation 7:9–17. First, the multitude who have maintained faith in Jesus and who have come out of the great ordeal — commonly known as the *Tribulation* and linked to the Day of the Lord (see "The Sixth Seal: The Day of the Lord Has Come! [6:12–17]") — offer up a confession of faith: "Salvation belongs to our God who is seated on the throne, and to the Lamb!" (Rev. 7:10). This confession underscores the Bible's consistent teaching: God alone saves his people; they don't save themselves.

The angelic choir fills the heavens with a mighty sevenfold song of worship to God: praise, blessing, glory, wisdom, honor, power, and might. Consider that during the time John wrote the book of Revelation, people directed such attributes to Caesar. The angelic anthem makes it unmistakably clear: such attributes befit only one supreme being, namely the God revealed in Scripture.

Then, combining several Old Testament texts (Isaiah 49:10; Psalms 121:6, 23:1–2; Ezekiel 34:23–24; Isaiah 25:8), the section concludes by describing the blessings that await the multitude of the redeemed, those who have been faithful to Jesus. Like the angelic guardians of the throne, the redeemed surround and serenade the sovereign God. He, in turn, shelters them from the scorching sun. The imagery derives from the figure of an ancient Near Eastern monarch sitting on his throne under a canopy or awning. His subjects are likewise protected from the sun's rays by awnings or something similar, providing shade for the entire court area (see Figure 9-3).

REMEMBER

John is a master of irony and paradox. As Revelation 7 ends, it offers another striking example of paradox when the Lamb is also designated as the shepherd of the redeemed (Rev. 7:17). This picks up on John's Gospel, where Jesus is both "the Lamb of God who takes away the sin of the world" (John 1:29) and the "good shepherd [who] lays down his life for the sheep" (John 10:11). You can see similar examples of John's use of irony in Revelation 5:5–6, where the lion is a lamb.

FIGURE 9-3:
An Assyrian king
on his throne
with attendants.

The Seventh Seal: Silence in Heaven (8:1–5)

Revelation 8 begins with the opening of the seventh seal. When the Lamb opens it, there's silence in heaven for half an hour. But the drama and suspense quickly rebuild when "the seven angels who stand before God" (Rev. 8:2) receive seven trumpets. Something big is about to go down. Before you hit the fast forward button and hurry to find out what it is, pause and reflect on this delay. What does it signify? Angelic adoration ceases, and silence envelops the command center of the universe.

The significance of the pause is that with the opening of the seventh seal, the old order passes away. God's wrath against sin is spent, and judgment gives way to blessing, just like the prophets said it would (see Amos 9:11–15 and Isaiah 65:17–25). In other words, the future is now, and it's nothing short of a brand-new heaven and a brand-new earth (Rev. 21). John, however, deliberately delays a description of the grand finale. He has much more to say about the events leading up to the conclusion.

One of the hallmarks of John's literary technique, in addition to irony, is postponing the climactic moment of his narrative. He carries the reader along and sustains suspense for as long as possible. John skillfully does this in his Gospel where he narrates the ministry of Jesus by means of a literary device, namely "the hour of his glory," when referring to events related to Jesus's impending crucifixion. Throughout the Gospel of John, the writer repeatedly informs you that Jesus's hour has not yet come (John 2:4, 7:6, 7:8, 7:30, and 8:20). Finally, in Jerusalem, leading up to Passover, John quotes Jesus as saying, "The hour has come for the Son of Man to be glorified" (John 12:23). Ironically, the "hour of his glory" culminates in the death of Jesus on the cross, followed by his resurrection. Perhaps artist Salvador Dali comes closest to visually capturing this moment of glory (Figure 9-4).

FIGURE 9-4:
The Crucifixion of Christ, one of Salvador Dali's views of Jesus on the cross.

© Christie/Getty Images

Chapter **10**

Sounding Seven Trumpets (8:2–11:19)

To borrow a famous catchphrase from the 1970s series, *The Incredible Hulk*: "Don't make me angry. You wouldn't like me when I'm angry." In the dramatic unfolding of Revelation 8–11, it's as if God issues a similar warning. Here, the forces of evil are about to be hit with the initial blasts of divine judgment. But this is just the beginning — these first trumpet judgments merely pave the way for the even greater devastation of the bowl judgments (see Chapter 12), which will ultimately bring Satan's empire to ruin.

The trumpet judgments, cosmic blows that affect a third of the planet, are more extensive and devastating than the seals (see Chapter 9). The trumpet judgments, however, don't impact the people of God, only those still defying the rule of the warrior Lamb.

In this chapter, you explore God's judgment on evil in the world. As you do so, you see how the Old Testament helps you understand what's going on. The account of the plagues on Egypt (Exodus 7:14–10:23) provides a pattern for the trumpet judgments. Here, you also begin to understand why this is a fight to the finish between the two main characters of redemptive history, Christ and Satan. Both lay exclusive claim to the earth and its inhabitants. Only one will eventually triumph. And the triumph of the one means the demise of the other. (*Harry Potter and the Deathly Hallows* got this right, too — it's either Harry or Voldemort!)

AND IN THIS CORNER . . .

The fight began back in Genesis 3, when Satan (under the guise of a serpent) deceived Adam and Eve. Their disobedience resulted in expulsion from the Garden of Eden, and Satan usurped control over planet earth. The Apostle John, in his first epistle, doesn't mince words when he observes, "the whole world lies under the power of the evil one" (1 John 5:19). Even Jesus, during his earthly ministry, acknowledges Satan's present power and influence: "Now the ruler of this world will be driven out" (John 12:31). The Lord God, however, promises Eve that one of her descendants will crush the serpent's head — that is, deliver a mortal blow (Genesis 3:15).

According to the New Testament, that descendant is none other than Jesus of Nazareth. The Apostle Paul expresses this conviction when he writes to the believers at Rome, "The God of peace will shortly crush Satan under your feet" (Romans 16:20). The fight has turned out to be arduous and drawn-out, but the book of Revelation narrates the final blow — the knockout — in chapter 20. The trumpet judgments are the beginning of the end for the Dark Lord and his followers. The victor in this cosmic slugfest is never in doubt.

Previewing the Seven Trumpets

Revelation 8 begins with an introduction to the seven trumpets: "When the Lamb opened the seventh seal, there was silence in heaven for about half an hour. And I saw the seven angels who stand before God, and seven trumpets were given to them" (Rev. 8:1–2).

The trumpets herald the Day of the Lord, the Great Tribulation, the final era of earth history in which the Lamb decisively defeats the forces of evil. The seventh trumpet, like the seventh seal and seventh bowl, brings you to the grand finale, the triumph of the crucified Lamb and his kingdom.

These seven trumpets, like the seven seals (see Chapter 9), fall into four subgroups:

>> Trumpets 1–4 (Rev. 8:7–12), like the four horsemen (Rev. 6:2–8), form one distinct unit. For the most part, these judgments are directed at nature.

>> An eagle announces trumpets 5–7 and identifies them as the three "woes" (Rev. 8:13–11:19). Trumpets 5 and 6 are demonic in nature and are directed at rebellious human beings.

>> Trumpet 6 is followed by a delay and interlude highlighting specific aspects of the Day of the Lord (Rev. 10:1–11:14).

>> Trumpet 7, like the seventh seal, anticipates the triumph of the Lamb, only to be postponed by another delay and interlude (12:1–14:20).

Preceding the trumpets: Silence and prayer

Before the trumpets begin, Revelation 8:1 notes that heaven is silent for about half an hour (see Chapter 9). After an eerie pause, the proverbial calm before the storm, the heavenly sanctuary suddenly resumes its activity. The seven angels who stand before the throne of God prepare to sound their trumpets. This signifies that something big is about to happen. But before the trumpet blasts, a ritual unfolds as related in Revelation 8:3–4: "Another angel with a golden censer came and stood at the altar; he was given a great quantity of incense to offer with the prayers of all the saints on the golden altar that is before the throne."

Incense was a regular feature of non-Christian, Jewish, and Christian worship. The fragrant odor evoked in the worshiper a sense of the presence of the deity and was offered up as an expression of thanksgiving or intercession (requests on others' behalf). Jewish usage goes back to the Mosaic rituals of the Tabernacle and the subsequent first and second temples. Christianity later incorporated and adapted the Jewish practice for its liturgy. In this passage, John describes the incense drifting over the heavenly sanctuary as a sweet accompaniment to the prayers of believers.

The Bible teaches that the prayers of God's people facilitate God's will. Does prayer change things? Yes, it does! Scripture repeatedly affirms that it does (see Psalm 37:4–5; Isaiah 65:24; Matthew 7:7–8; Mark 11:22–24; Philippians 4:6; Hebrews 4:16; James 5:16), and Christian experience backs it up. These prayers at the golden altar aren't specified by content, but they probably include the prayers of the martyrs, mentioned in the fifth seal (see Chapter 9). In other words, the saints are crying out for vindication, a request about to be emphatically answered.

Making a stormy appearance

The incense container is hurled down upon the earth, signaling the beginning of the heavenly assault: "Then the angel took the censer and filled it with fire from the altar and threw it on the earth; and there were peals of thunder, rumblings, flashes of lightning, and an earthquake" (Rev. 8:5). These tempestuous events are signs that God is revealing his awesome power and presence.

To better understand this moment, you need to revisit one of the most dramatic theophanies (a theophany is an appearance of God) in the Old Testament. When the LORD descends on Mount Sinai, he is accompanied by terrifying terrestrial and celestial phenomena. Here's how Exodus 19:16, 19:18 describes it: "On the morning of the third day there was thunder and lightning, as well as a thick cloud on the mountain, and a blast of a trumpet so loud that all the people who were in the camp trembled. [. . .] Now Mount Sinai was wrapped in smoke [. . .] the whole mountain shook violently." The similarities of this passage to Revelation 8:5–6 are striking. God is about to reveal himself in the end like he did in the past to finish the salvation of his people. This is a really big deal!

The Lion of Judah is on the move! And whenever God displays his power on earth, there's a whole lot of fireworks and rockin' and rollin' going on (see 1 Kings 18:38)! Fire from the altar functions like a cosmic blowtorch to purify a contaminated world.

Paralleling the plagues of Egypt

The trumpet blasts echo the plagues that rained down on rebellious Pharaoh and his evil empire, built on the backs of Hebrew slaves (Exodus 7–12). Table 10-1 illustrates common features.

TABLE 10-1   **Comparing the Plagues of Egypt with the Trumpets**

Exodus	Revelation
First Plague: Water of the Nile River turns to blood (Exodus 7:20–25)	Second Trumpet: A third of the sea becomes blood (Rev. 8:8–9)
Fifth Plague: Livestock disease (Exodus 9:1–12)	First, Second, and Third Trumpets: A third of the trees and grass burn up; a third of living creatures in the sea die; many people die from the wormwood waters (Rev. 8:7, 8:10–11)
Seventh Plague: Hail and thunderstorm (Exodus 9:22–35)	First Trumpet: Hail and fire (Rev. 8:7)
Eighth Plague: Locusts (Exodus 10:1–20)	Fifth Trumpet: Locusts (Rev. 9:1–11)
Ninth Plague: Dense darkness (Exodus 10:21–29)	Fourth Trumpet: A third of all celestial light darkens (Rev. 8:12)

Although the plagues and trumpets don't align perfectly, and not every plague has a direct trumpet equivalent, the similarities between the events are striking and surely intentional. It seems that John incorporates imagery from the Egyptian plagues as he describes the trumpet judgments in his vision. Making these connections helps readers understand the theological purpose behind both sets of judgments. In Egypt, the plagues served as both a means to break Pharaoh's stubbornness and retribution for crimes against humanity — long before notions of international justice existed. The same is true of the trumpet judgments.

Pharaoh isn't a pawn in a predetermined power play; he has numerous opportunities to repent. According to Scripture, God graciously grants people the ability to choose. Though Pharaoh refuses, some Egyptians choose to believe in the God of Aabraham, Isaac, and Jacob and even cast their lot with the Hebrews.

Scripture shows that God does not take pleasure in punishing wrongdoers; on the contrary, he does not want "anyone to perish, but all to come to repentance" (2 Peter 3:9). Remember the criminal who, just before he died on a cross, repented and believed in Jesus (Luke 23:39-43). Thus, the trumpet judgments are more than acts of retribution — they function as warnings, urging people to turn back before it's too late. This mirrors the purpose of the plagues in Egypt, which were also remedial and not solely judicial.

WORSHIPING THE GOD OF LIGHT: ONE-GOD EGYPTIANS

Philo the Jew, a writer in the first century CE, interprets the "mixed crowd" who went up with the Israelites (Exodus 12:38) as proof that some Egyptians embraced *monotheism*, the belief in one god: "These were [. . .] those who, reverencing the divine favour shewn to the people, had come over to them, and such as were converted and brought to a wiser mind by the magnitude and the number of the successive punishments" (*On the Life of Moses* 1.147).

Pharaoh Akhenaton ruled Egypt after the time of Thutmose III and Rameses II — the two most likely candidates for the Pharaoh of the Exodus. Inexplicably, Akhenaton departed from a millennia-long, polytheistic tradition and affirmed a form of monotheism. Akhenaton spoke of Aton, the sun-god, as a unique, transcendent, and everlasting deity, remarkably like the biblical depiction of Yahweh (the special covenant name of the God of Israel). What prompted such a radical move? Could it have been a memory of the plagues on Egypt and the power struggle between Pharaoh and Yahweh, in which the gods of the Egyptians were exposed as impotent or even non-existent?

Admitting problems of interpretation

The trumpet judgments prompt two major questions: How should they be interpreted, and how do they square with the nature of God as depicted in scripture?

The character of the trumpets

Are the trumpets in Revelation meant to be understood as literal events or as metaphors? Interpreting them in a literal sense poses challenges, especially from a scientific standpoint — how, for instance, could exactly one-third of all celestial light be darkened? What must be borne in mind, however, is the presence of the supernatural sprinkled throughout Scripture. The God who spoke creation into existence by a mere word (Hebrews 11:3) also supernaturally intervened at certain key moments in redemptive history (especially the resurrection of Jesus). On the other hand, given the apocalyptic nature of Revelation, one needs to exercise caution as to the precise nature of the trumpet judgments. What remains unmistakable is the gravity with which God regards sin and resistance to divine authority.

The character of God

That leads to another question. How can a loving God inflict wide-scale suffering, even on his rebellious human creation? Is God sadistic? Does God get off the hook simply by saying these people deserve what they get? This is, of course, a long-standing theological problem that extends beyond the pages of Revelation. The technical name for this issue is *theodicy* — that is, justifying God's actions and attitudes.

I don't pretend to have an airtight answer. I can, however, point to the unwavering teaching of Scripture: God is holy, just, righteous, gracious, loving, and merciful (Exodus 34:6–7). He is also omnipotent (all powerful) and sovereign (exercises full control). The scriptural witness is seconded by the unwavering testimony of God's people through the ages: God is good, and God is great. Blessed be the name of the Lord (Job 1:21).

TIP

When approaching any passage in the Bible, it's essential to consider it within the broader context of Scripture as a whole. Strive to set aside personal assumptions rather than projecting them onto the text. Ask yourself whether your understanding aligns with reality and fits the overall biblical teaching. For practical advice on interpreting Scripture thoughtfully, see Chapter 17.

Honing old horns

Trumpets played an important role in biblical history as well as in the Roman world of the first century:

>> **Direction:** In the Old Testament, the Lord instructs Moses to make two silver trumpets (Numbers 10). These trumpets serve as directional and inspirational devices. For example, during the wilderness wanderings, the children of Israel assemble, pack up, and move out when they hear a distinctive blast from the trumpets. They stop and set up camp when they hear a different call (Numbers 10:3–8).

>> **Military commands and morale:** During war, the trumpets indicate attack, retreat, and so forth. The sound of the trumpets also constantly reminds Israel that the Lord fights on their behalf (Numbers 10:9).

>> **Dates:** The blowing of trumpets heralds various appointed festivals, the beginning of months, and the new year (Numbers 10:10, 29:1; Leviticus 23:24).

>> **Royal crownings:** Trumpets sound at the coronation of Israelite kings (1 Kings 1:34, 1:39; 2 Kings 9:13).

Perhaps the most famous episode involving trumpets is at the battle of Jericho during the invasion of Canaan, the Promised Land (Joshua 6). Seven priests with seven trumpets blowing continuously lead the army of Israel around the city for seven days. On the seventh day, after circling the city seven times, blowing the trumpets continuously, the priests blow one final blast as the people shout to the Lord — and the walls of Jericho collapse. The parallel to the trumpet judgments of Revelation seems unmistakable. Like Jericho, the evil empire is going down.

Like the Israelites, the Roman army used trumpets as a tactical device during battle. Legionnaires performed certain maneuvers at the sound of trumpets. One of the keys to Roman success was the well-coordinated movements of the various military units. Perhaps this feature of mighty Rome also lies behind John's vision. The angelic legions are being deployed against the inhabitants of earth.

The single, most important fact for understanding the trumpet judgments is this: They're *eschatological trumpets*. That's a fancy way of saying that they herald the day of God's wrath against sin. This theme is reflected in the Old Testament, in several apocalyptic works of roughly the same period as the book of Revelation, and in apocalyptic passages in Paul's epistles (1 Corinthians 15:52; 1 Thessalonians 4:16).

The First Four Trumpets: Fire, Blood, and Hail

Revelation 8:7–12 describes the sounding of the first four trumpets:

"The first angel blew his trumpet, and there came hail and fire, mixed with blood, and they were hurled to the earth; and a third of the earth was burned up, and a third of the trees were burned up, and all green grass was burned up. The second angel blew his trumpet, and something like a great mountain, burning with fire, was thrown into the sea. A third of the sea became blood, a third of the living creatures in the sea died, and a third of the ships were destroyed. The third angel blew his trumpet, and a great star fell from heaven, blazing like a torch, and it fell on a third of the rivers and on the springs of water. The name of the star is Wormwood. A third of the waters became wormwood, and many died from the water, because it was made bitter. The fourth angel blew his trumpet, and a third of the sun was struck, and a third of the moon, and a third of the stars, so that a third of their light was darkened; a third of the day was kept from shining, and likewise the night."

These first four trumpets focus directly on the planet earth. The Old Testament prophets speak of the dire consequences of sin on the environment and predict environmental repercussions for failure to keep covenant with God (Isaiah 24:4–13; Hosea 4:3). Because of massive noncompliance on the part of humanity, it's now zero hour, and earth reels under a heavenly bombardment.

Trumpet 1: Plague on the land

"Hail and fire, mixed with blood" descend upon earth when the first angel blows his trumpet (Rev. 8:7). This seemingly incongruous mixture may describe, in graphic imagery, violent thunderstorms in which lightning and hail result in huge loss of life. Whatever its nature, the results are devastating.

TIP

Don't insist on a literal understanding of the fraction one-third. Fractions like one-third are a regular feature of apocalyptic imagery (see Zechariah 13:8–9; Ezekiel 5:1–2).

The takeaway point is this: Vegetation of all kinds is completely wiped out in large portions of the earth. If the third and fourth seals depict the ravages of famine during world history (Rev. 6:5–8 — see Chapter 9), this first trumpet results in famine on an unprecedented scale at the *end of* world history. Wealth is of little help now. Obviously, both domesticated and wild animals perish in vast numbers.

The consequences are unimaginable. Human beings realize, too late, how dependent they are on the plant and animal kingdoms.

Trumpet 2: Plague on the high seas

When the second angel blows his trumpet, "Something like a great mountain, burning with fire, was thrown into the sea" (Rev. 8:8). One perspective is that this refers to an asteroid or comet slamming into the earth. After all, such things have occurred in earth's history with devastating consequences. Alternatively, is it a reference to volcanic activity in the Mediterranean? In 79 CE, Mount Vesuvius erupted and buried the inhabitants of Pompeii and Herculaneum alive. As many as 10,000 people died in that disaster.

This imagery is typical of that found in other Jewish apocalyptic writings. John's vision, then, in keeping with apocalyptic imagery, depicts a planetary disaster involving a large portion of the oceans. The "sea" as the location for the impact of this asteroid-like object probably reflects the fact that the Roman Empire was essentially the land areas surrounding the Mediterranean Basin. This was, for all practical purposes, the extent of the known world at that time. The implication, then, is that this is a truly worldwide disaster. The impact is staggering, and the fallout, in terms of ecology, economics, and human life, is incalculable.

Trumpet 3: Plague on fresh water

Compounding an already desperate situation, much of the freshwater sources of the planet are suddenly rendered toxic when the third angel blows his trumpet. As Revelation 8:10–11 says, "A great star fell from heaven, blazing like a torch, and it fell on a third of the rivers and on the springs of water. The name of the star is Wormwood."

A literal reading suggests something like an asteroid or comet. The problem here is the name given to the star. *Wormwood* — a type of bitter, poisonous herb (Jeremiah 9:15, 23:15) — makes it sound like a person whose name personifies what happens, as in C. S. Lewis's *Screwtape Letters* in which Screwtape is a senior demon who writes advice to a junior demon named Wormwood. Furthermore, in Jewish apocalyptic literature, stars are frequently associated with angelic or demonic beings. Following this tack suggests an angelic being who in some way degrades vast tracts of freshwater sources. The result is sobering: "Many died from the water" (8:11).

Some modern commentators, endorsing a literal interpretation of Revelation, draw attention to the increasing danger posed to world peace by inadequate drinking water. They entertain various scenarios involving international conflicts over the availability of drinkable water and cite this section of Revelation as support. Modern crises may well foreshadow the third trumpet judgment, but nothing like it has occurred in human history.

Trumpet 4: Plague on sources of light

The fourth trumpet involves something inexplicable in terms of known laws of physics. The light output from heavenly bodies diminishes one-third. Even worse, during a third of normal daylight hours and nighttime, total darkness reigns. This recalls the ninth plague of darkness upon Egypt (Exodus 10:21–22). The impact of such a reduction in light would be catastrophic. Besides the psychological effects (paralyzing fear and biological clocks completely out of synch), the consequences for earth's living creatures (death of plant life and animals that feed on it) are mind-boggling. The bottom line is this: Panic paralyzes the planet.

In the Old Testament, judgment is depicted in terms of darkness. The Old Testament prophet Amos likens the Day of the Lord to a day of darkness (Amos 5:18). The prophet Joel chimes in with a similar conviction: "a day of darkness and gloom, a day of clouds and thick darkness!" (Joel 2:2). Jesus also predicts that "the sun will be darkened, and the moon will not give its light" (Mark 13:24).

Yet darkness signals more than just a loss of light — it hints at something even more sinister. In biblical tradition, darkness often represents the presence of demonic forces. The calamity of the fourth trumpet sets the stage for even graver events, foreshadowing the fifth trumpet's terrifying vision of a demonic invasion. Before these forces are unleashed, the world is plunged into deep darkness. The Apostle John, attentive to such symbolism, makes a similar point in his Gospel: When Satan enters Judas during the Last Supper, John remarks forebodingly, "And it was night" (John 13:30).

Wailing the Woes of the Last Three Trumpets

At the end of Revelation 8, John hits the pause button, saying, "Then I looked, and I heard an eagle crying with a loud voice as it flew in mid-heaven, 'Woe, woe, woe to the inhabitants of the earth, at the blasts of the other trumpets that the three angels are about to blow!'" (Rev. 8:13). These "woes" are named appropriately: They're aimed directly at human beings.

The dark side now enters the arena: demonic invasion. No, the Martians aren't coming, nor are UFOs with strange-looking creatures — the situation's a lot worse than that. Demons from the bottomless pit are about to be unleashed on the Earth. Who you gonna call? Ghostbusters won't be any help this time!

Trumpet 5: Demonic locust plague

In Revelation 9:1–3, an angel blows the fifth trumpet. John sees a star fall from heaven to earth, and it receives a key to the bottomless pit (in some English translations, rendered "Abyss"). The fallen star then opens a shaft, allowing smoke and locusts to escape and envelop the earth (Rev. 9:1–3).

No, the star is not a "twinkle, twinkle, little star" gone rogue. Instead, in keeping with standard apocalyptic imagery, the star is probably an angel, just as Revelation 1:20 and 2–3 identify seven stars as the angels of the seven churches of Asia. The bottomless pit or abyss is another standard apocalyptic expression representing the underworld, a prison for demonic spirits.

Meeting the swarm

As for the locusts, these are nasty creatures (Rev. 9:4–11). The imagery is related to the prophecy of Joel in the Old Testament. Joel envisions locusts descending upon the land of Judah in massive numbers. At first, he seems to be describing the dreaded locust swarms that periodically infest the Middle East (Joel 1:1–7). But then his prophecy takes a bizarre turn and describes locust-like creatures that do the Lord's bidding and inflict terrible pain and suffering on humans. These are no ordinary locusts; they are demonic mutants (Joel 2:1–11).

TECHNICAL STUFF

The ancient Near East was subject to periodic locust infestations. Locusts occasionally experience a tremendous population explosion and form massive swarms. They then go in search of vegetation. The ancients were helpless in the face of such a plague. Today, aerial and satellite surveillance pinpoint such swarms, and pesticides head off potential disasters. The last major locust invasion in Israel occurred in 1916 and was featured in the *National Geographic* of that year.

John borrows Joel's imagery to describe an End Times plague by locust-like creatures. But they are hardly your typical, garden-variety locusts — they prefer humans to vegetation! These demonic locusts are permitted to torture those who lack the seal of God but are forbidden to kill them. The suffering is so intense that those stung attempt to commit suicide but are unable to.

John's demonic locusts defy description. They're likened to powerful war horses having human faces (reminiscent of Ringwraiths from *The Lord of the Rings*). They wear crowns like kings and princes, and they have long, flowing hair like women and bare teeth like lions. Covered in scale armor, they possess a scorpion-like tail with a stinger that inflicts intense agony (Rev. 9:7–10). The imagery combines to create a truly terrifying specter.

If there's a bright spot in this ghastly portrayal, it's this: The assault is limited to five months, the lifespan of ordinary locusts. The fact that God limits the duration points to the remedial intent of the judgment: Rebellious sinners still have an opportunity to repent and switch allegiance to the Lord of light (Rev. 1:16). It also illustrates how God permits evil to carry out his own purposes. This is reminiscent of Isaiah 10:5–11, in which the Lord allows the cruel empire of Assyria to punish rebellious Israel and Judah. Later, the Lord punishes Assyria for its arrogance and excessive cruelty.

Debating demonic invasions

Is such a thing conceivable? Theological assumptions play an important role in answering this question. If you believe that demons are real and that demonic possession is possible, then this scenario isn't bizarre. Jesus, the Apostles, and the church fathers believed in the reality of both demonic influence and possession (see Mark 1:32, 3:15, 7:26–30; 1 Corinthians 10:20–21).

Joel 2:1–11, along with Exodus 10:1–20 (the eighth plague against Egypt) and possibly Genesis 6:1–4, serves as the backdrop for the text in Revelation 9:1–11. A destroying angel leads the assault: "They have as king over them the angel of the bottomless pit" (Rev. 9:11). John gives him a descriptive name: the double name of Abaddon (Hebrew for *Destruction*) and Apollyon (Greek meaning *Destroyer*). The Destroyer orders his horde of demons from the bottomless pit to assault the earth.

THE GREAT FLOOD AND THE FIRST WAVE OF INVASIONS

One school of thought is that Revelation 9:1–11 refers to a second great demonic invasion of earth. Supporters of this theory believe the first invasion occurred before the flood of Noah and was the reason for the destruction of all living things. In this perspective, the "sons of God" of Genesis 6:1–4 refer to fallen angels or demons who cohabitate with human beings. The result is a monstrous hybrid, the *Nephilim* (Genesis 6:4). In this scenario, the Lord intervenes with a cosmic judgment and initiates a new beginning (Genesis 7–8). Both demonic invasions occur prior to cosmic destructions: The world that was (the pre-flood world) perished by water; the post-flood world perishes by fire (2 Peter 2:4–10; 3:1–13). It bears repeating: The sealed saints are spared this demonic assault (Rev. 9:4). The Dark Lord can't cause any of the Lamb's followers to defect and join the dark side (John 10:28–29). Like Luke Skywalker, they remain true to their convictions.

Trumpet 6: Demonic cavalry

A divine command kicks off the sixth trumpet and second woe: "Release the four angels who are bound at the great river Euphrates" (Rev. 9:14). In Jewish and Christian apocalyptic tradition, angels perform various regulatory functions in connection with the cosmos. Evil angels are also depicted as bound or restricted to certain locations, sometimes in subterranean caverns, sometimes in a watery abyss. The four angels of Revelation 9:14 appear to fall into this latter category, only in this case, they're bound somewhere at the Euphrates River. This great river, because of its fame and importance, is often simply referred to as "the river" or "the great river" in the Old Testament.

The Tigris-Euphrates River Valley is significant because it was one of the two great "cradles of civilization" in the ancient Near East (the other being the Nile River Valley). It was also the eastern border of the Roman Empire. To the east lay the threatening kingdom of the Parthians, today the area of eastern Iraq and western Iran.

Perhaps the action of released angels, which isn't explicitly described here, is related to the sixth bowl, in which the Euphrates River dries up, allowing the kings of the east to invade the Holy Land (Rev. 16:12–16) (see Chapter 12 for details on the bowls). But for now, the four angels unleash an even more ghastly demonic invasion, resulting in the torture and death of one-third of the world's population (Rev. 9:15).

In keeping with apocalyptic traditions, the exact hour, day, month, and year of this conflict is predetermined, but only God knows when that is (see Daniel 12:7, 11–12). Jesus tells his disciples that the exact day and hour of his coming is also known only by the Father; not even he nor the angels know the exact date (Mark 13:32).

TECHNICAL STUFF

The fact that Jesus seems not to know the exact date of his return has prompted more than a little theological controversy. How can he truly be divine if he's limited in knowledge? The traditional response has been to say that during his earthly ministry, Jesus voluntarily laid aside certain divine attributes such as omniscience. Now, in his exalted state at the right hand of God the Father, he fully exercises all his divine attributes and knows exactly the day and hour of his return.

Commentators differ considerably on the occasion and combatants in the slaughter following the sixth trumpet (see Chapter 4 to discover the four basic approaches to the book of Revelation):

>> **Idealists:** Idealists speak about world conflict as a regular part of human history.

>> **Historicists:** Historicists have championed several warmonger candidates, running the gamut from Genghis Khan to T. E. Lawrence (of Arabia).

>> **Preterists:** Preterists most often suggest a Parthian invasion. Parthia, a kingdom lying east of the Euphrates River and stretching across Iran, was the eastern frontier of the Roman Empire. The Parthians were a feared opponent, having more than once bloodied the eastern legions. John pictures this vast army as cavalry, and the Parthians were famous for their swift horses.

>> **Futurists:** Futurists of an earlier generation expected a literal cavalry, 200 million strong, to descend on Israel during the Tribulation. More recently, many have identified China as the invader. This invasion will supposedly force the antichrist to intervene in the Middle East.

Many modern futurists take the references to sulfur, fire, and smoke — and the enormous casualty rate — as evidence of thermonuclear weapons. In fact, some authors find allusions to a whole host of modern weapon systems, including attack helicopters and chemical and biological weapons!

Overall, many commentators argue in favor of a literal demonic army because the description exceeds anything known to human experience. Horses with lion-like heads and death-dealing mouths and tails, the latter having heads like serpents, probably indicate you're dealing with something supernatural. This connects the army with the fifth trumpet, the locusts, which most interpreters identify as demons.

TECHNICAL STUFF

Greek mythology includes a bizarre monster called Chimera (the name means *she-goat*). Chimera is a three-part creature, being like a lion in front, a snake behind, and a fire-breathing she-goat in the middle. Perhaps John's vision adapts this mythological imagery.

Whether these creatures are literal or figurative, the havoc they wreak is real. Yet despite these demonic judgments, the survivors "did not repent of their murders or their sorceries or their fornication or their thefts" (Rev. 9:21).

Trumpet 7: Not just yet

The seventh — and last — trumpet, like the seventh seal (see Chapter 9), is delayed. Before moving on to the seventh and final trumpet, John describes two more intervening visions. Why the delay? In part because there's still more to relate concerning certain aspects of the End Times, and in part because when the last trumpet sounds it's over. Well, almost . . .

The First Interlude: The Angel and the Little Scroll

Like a commercial that comes right before you hear whether a contestant is going to win on a TV game show, an interlude appears at the beginning of Revelation 10 — it's time for a word from our sponsor. Destruction, judgment, and chaos are momentarily set aside to, among other things, announce no more delays!

But the more significant role of this vision of the angel and the little scroll is that of a re-commissioning. John is divinely directed to continue his role as prophet to the nations. He, like Ezekiel the prophet, a watchman on the wall, must warn them of impending disaster.

Looking at a mighty angel

Emerging from the heavens in brilliant sunlight, an angel takes center stage:

"And I saw another mighty angel coming down from heaven, wrapped in a cloud, with a rainbow over his head; his face was like the sun, and his legs like pillars of fire. He held a little scroll open in his hand. Setting his right foot on the sea and his left foot on the land, he gave a great shout, like a lion roaring. And when he shouted, the seven thunders sounded. And when the seven thunders had sounded, I was about to write, but I heard a voice from heaven saying, 'Seal up what the seven thunders have said, and do not write it down.' Then the angel whom I saw standing on the sea and the land raised his right hand to heaven and swore by him who lives forever and ever, who created heaven and what is in it, the earth and what is in it, and the sea and what is in it: 'There will be no more delay, but in the days when the seventh angel is to blow his trumpet, the mystery of God will be fulfilled, as he announced to his servants the prophets.'" (Rev. 10:1–7)

Notice that John now appears to be viewing the action from the earth. Prior to this — after he was taken into the heavenly throne room (Rev. 4:1) — his vantage point was from heaven looking down on the earth. This alternation between heavenly and earthly perspectives is typical of apocalyptic literature, in which the seer moves easily between these two vantage points. This provides the reader with behind-the-scenes information and thus a more comprehensive picture of what's really going on than is accessible to outsiders.

At this point, John describes the descent of a powerful angelic figure to the earth as though he's looking upward. Perhaps it's fitting that he's on earth for this portion of the vision, because he's now re-commissioned to proclaim the

End Time judgments. Like the prophets who preceded him, he ministers to his fellow humans.

ID-ing the angel

But who is this mighty angel referred to in Revelation 10:1? Is it Jesus? An archangel? Or neither? Well, it's most likely either Jesus or an archangel. Here are the arguments for each:

>> **Jesus:** Because the description of the mighty angel in Revelation 10 includes items sometimes associated with deity, some commentators conclude that the angel is Jesus. For example,

- "Wrapped in a cloud" describes God in Psalm 104:3.

- "With a rainbow over his head" reminds readers of the rainbow above the throne in Revelation 4:3.

- "His face was like the sun" recalls Revelation 1:16, where the risen Jesus is so described.

- "His legs like pillars of fire" is like Revelation 1:15, where Jesus's feet are "like burnished bronze, refined as in a furnace."

This, at first glance, is rather convincing. The problem, however, is that nowhere else in the book of Revelation is Jesus referred to as an angel. Furthermore, it seems inappropriate that the Lord of all creation should take an oath to God as the mighty angel does in Revelation 10:6. Also, there's no biblical support for the notion that humans become angels in heaven; they're only said to be *like* them in a few specific ways (see Matthew 22:30).

>> **An archangel:** Most likely, the mighty angel belongs to one of the classes of angels mentioned in the Bible and in Jewish literature. Archangels are very powerful and perform critically important roles in redemptive history. In Jewish tradition, the archangel Uriel is associated with light and the luminaries, and he carries out several important divine missions. You can also make a good case for Gabriel, who comes to Daniel's assistance and explains the meaning of a vision (Daniel 8:15–16). Gabriel is also the messenger who informs Zechariah and Mary of their key roles in the births of John the Baptist and Jesus (Luke 1:11–20, 1:26–38).

Keeping secret things

When the mighty angel straddles the planet and shouts, seven thunders resound, apparently with an intelligible message. As John is about to record the message, a divine voice restrains him: "Seal up what the seven thunders have said, and do not write it down" (10:4). Such a prohibition is another standard feature of apocalyptic literature:

- » Daniel is instructed not to let the contents of his prophecy be known to his generation (Daniel 7:28; 8:26; 12:4, 9).

- » The Apostle Paul is forbidden to disclose the details of his visit to the throne room (2 Corinthians 12:4–7).

- » In John's Gospel, Jesus cries out, "Father, glorify your name" (John 12:28). In response, "A voice came from heaven." Some who are present that day think "it was thunder." Others said, "an angel has spoken to him" (John 12:29). But none of them really understands what was said and what it means. In this instance, only for believers is the veil of secrecy removed. But even in the case of believers, some things remain hidden and secret, beyond comprehension. Such is the case here in Revelation 10:4. As Deuteronomy 29:29 says, "The secret things belong to the Lord our God."

While the message of the seven thunders in Revelation 10 remains sealed, one thing is crystal clear: The end is imminent. When the seventh trumpet sounds, "the mystery of God will be fulfilled" (Rev. 10:7).

Tasting a bittersweet book

John is summoned to take a small scroll from the hand of the mighty angel:

"Then the voice that I had heard from heaven spoke to me again, saying, 'Go, take the scroll that is open in the hand of the angel who is standing on the sea and on the land.' So I went to the angel and told him to give me the little scroll; and he said to me, 'Take it, and eat; it will be bitter to your stomach, but sweet as honey in your mouth.' So I took the little scroll from the hand of the angel and ate it; it was sweet as honey in my mouth, but when I had eaten it, my stomach was made bitter. Then they said to me, 'You must prophesy again about many peoples and nations and languages and kings.'" (Rev. 10:8–11)

Visualizing this scene isn't easy. Imagine a gigantic angel straddling the continents and seas and John apparently zooming upward and asking for the scroll.

Similar to what happens with the Old Testament prophet Ezekiel (Ezekiel 2:10–3:3), John is told to eat the scroll. He's warned that at first it will taste sweet, but then it'll turn bitter in the stomach. The text itself gives no explanation for this upset stomach. Perhaps it refers to how God's word is sweet if it's believed, but if ignored, it becomes a bitter word of judgment. The fact that the prophet ingests the scroll implies that the message itself becomes a part of the prophet's life. Being a true messenger of God involves living out its message, and sometimes that message is harsh and bitter. Judgment is hard to digest.

The Second Interlude: Two Star Witnesses in Jerusalem

In Revelation 11, a second interlude (which is also the second of the three woes) further delays the blowing of the seventh trumpet. John is transported to the streets of Jerusalem to witness a remarkable example of street preaching. Two Jews-for-Jesus make a big splash in the Holy City! In fact, they get the attention of the ultimate bad boy himself, the antichrist. Here are a few of the highlights of this second interlude (see Rev. 11:1–11):

>> John is told to measure the Temple.

>> John is told about two witnesses who appear and prophesy for 1,260 days.

- Fire comes from their mouths to kill any attackers.

- They can stop rain and turn rivers into blood.

- They can release any manner of plague anywhere on the earth.

>> John is told about a beast from a bottomless pit that comes and kills the two witnesses.

- The people of the world celebrate the deaths of the witnesses.

- After three and a half days, the two witnesses return to life and are raptured to heaven.

>> John is informed about an earthquake that destroys one-tenth of the city.

- 7,000 people die.

- The survivors give praise to God.

In a mere 11 verses, you see an incredible story with multiple plot twists, populated by fantastic creatures and people with superpowers! Revelation may be complex, but it's not a boring book of the Bible!

Measuring the Temple

Remember how the three ghosts of Charles Dickens's *A Christmas Carol* transported Ebenezer Scrooge through past, present, and future scenes? Scrooge could see and hear all the people around him, but they couldn't see him. That's sort of what happens to John in Revelation 1:1–11.

He has been transported to Jerusalem sometime in the future, where he visits the Temple and sees all that takes place. But before the two witnesses show up,

John is told to take a special measuring stick and measure the Temple of God and the great altar in front of it, as well as count the worshipers. This, of course, prompts several questions.

What is this temple?

Bear in mind that at the time John wrote this vision, the second Jerusalem temple had already lain in ruins for over 20 years (unless you opt for an early dating, in the 60s CE, for the book of Revelation — see Chapter 2 for details). Readers must either imagine a third temple or use a symbolic interpretation. If you opt for a literal understanding, this lands you right in the middle of a highly controversial, politically charged issue! Will there be a third temple? And if so, what happens to the famous Dome of the Rock, the third most holy site in Islam, built over the site of the original temple? God alone knows.

The New Testament includes one other place that some people interpret as a reference to a third Jewish temple: Paul's passage describing the coming of the antichrist, whom he calls "the lawless one" (2 Thessalonians 2:3–12). There, Paul says, "He [the antichrist] takes his seat in the *temple of God*, declaring himself to be God" (2 Thessalonians 2:4). But there's considerable disagreement about what Paul means, and in other places, he says that believers themselves are the temple of God (1 Corinthians 3:16, 6:19). Ultimately, it's an open question.

Why do measurements even have to be taken?

The background of John's action in measuring the Temple recalls a similar task undertaken by two Old Testament prophets, Zechariah and Ezekiel.

In Zechariah 2:1–5, the prophet observes an angelic surveyor taking a measuring line to determine the dimensions of a restored and rebuilt Jerusalem. Jerusalem had been burned to the ground by Nebuchadnezzar's army in 586 BCE. Living in the era of return and restoration, before the rebuilding of the walls by Nehemiah (444 BCE), Zechariah is informed by his angelic guide that the city will swell and sprawl beyond its historic boundaries.

Ezekiel assumes a rebuilt Jerusalem, but more importantly, given his priestly perspective, focuses on a blueprint for a greatly enlarged temple replacing Solomon's structure (Ezekiel 40–48). His detailed measurements make up the bulk of this section of his book. An angelic being does the actual measuring with a 6-cubit-long reed (just over 10 feet long); Ezekiel writes down the measurements.

John echoes these prophetic accounts for his own purpose. The point seems to be a divine promise of protection for the people of God. That which God measures for restoration is safe from all alarms. This protective measure chimes in with Revelation 7, where John describes the sealing of God's people prior to the trumpet judgments (see Chapter 9).

Deciphering who or what the witnesses are

Who are these two witnesses of Revelation 11? This is the question everyone wants an answer to! From my experience, this section is one of the most difficult chapters to interpret in a book already notorious for its degree of difficulty.

A survey of commentaries reveals a dizzying array of candidates for the two witnesses. At least commentators agree that the number two is significant: This was the minimum number of required witnesses to sustain a charge in a court case (Deuteronomy 19:15). Beyond that, unanimity disappears. Here are some of the leading options:

>> **Zerubbabel and Joshua the high priest:** Revelation 11:4 identifies the two witnesses as "the two olive trees and the two lampstands that stand before the Lord of the earth." This phrasing comes from Zechariah 4:3–14, where it refers to the two leaders of the post-exile Jewish restoration movement at the end of the sixth and beginning of the fifth centuries BCE. (This was a movement among dispersed Jews to return to their ancient homeland and rebuild a Jewish colony). However, it's more likely that John simply borrows the imagery and applies it to some other individuals or group.

>> **The Law and the Prophets (Scripture):** In the first century, the Old Testament Scriptures were often referred to as "the Law and the Prophets" (see Matthew 5:17; John 10:34; Romans 3:31). Although the Scriptures serve as a witness to the truth, this hardly seems appropriate to the context of Revelation 11. The two witnesses, after all, are martyred and raised to life again!

>> **Peter and Paul:** Advocates of an early dating for the book of Revelation (preterists) are more likely to suggest this option because both Apostles were martyred at about the same time during the latter part of the reign of Nero Caesar (64–68 CE). Highly problematic for this view, however, is the obvious fact that neither Apostle was brought back to life.

>> **Israel and the Church:** This option capitalizes on the fact that both Israel and the Church (Christians) have a mission as witnesses to the nations (Isaiah 42:6–7, 49:6; Acts 1:8). Although martyrdom has often befallen Israel and the Church in their respective histories, and you can speak metaphorically of a "resurrection" for both in their ongoing mission, you must ignore the details of Revelation 11 rather wholesale on such a view.

- **>> Enoch and Elijah:** These two are selected because both were raptured (taken up) to heaven and did not experience death (Genesis 5:24; 2 Kings 2:11). Because Hebrews 9:27 says, "It is appointed for mortals to die once," some expositors hold that these two prophets are required to return and experience death like all mortals before being resurrected and raptured again.

- **>> Moses and Elijah:** The context of Revelation 11 fits these two better than any previously mentioned. For example, take Revelation 11:5: "And if anyone wants to harm them, fire pours from their mouth and consumes their foes" corresponds to an episode in the life of Elijah (2 Kings 1:9–12), as does Revelation 11:6: "They have authority to shut the sky, so that no rain may fall during the days of their prophesying" (1 Kings 18). The last half of Revelation 11:6 says, "They have authority over the waters to turn them into blood and to strike the earth with every kind of plague, as often as they desire," recalling Moses and the plagues on Egypt (Exodus 7–12).

  But is it credible to hold that these two individuals return to earth and carry out a witnessing ministry in Jerusalem? You can't rule this out. After all, according to the Gospels, Moses and Elijah appeared with Jesus to Peter, James, and John on the mount of Transfiguration (Matthew 17:1–8; Mark 9:2–8; Luke 9:28–36). Still, that appearance is hardly the same thing as the ministry described in Revelation 11. It's also true that the prophet Malachi spoke of Elijah's coming before "the great and terrible day of the Lord," in a context mentioning Moses (Malachi 4:4–5). In fact, there was an expectation among the Jewish people that Elijah would return and announce the coming of Messiah (see Matthew 17:10). To this day, observant Jews leave a special chair empty during the Passover ritual, giving tangible expression to the hope that Elijah will return and announce the coming of Messiah.

  On the other hand, Jesus seems to identify John the Baptist as coming in the spirit and power of Elijah and, in that sense, he was Elijah (Matthew 11:14, 17:11). This seems to tip the scales against the notion that Moses and Elijah return for one more mission.

I opt for a literal interpretation in which two individuals powerfully witness to the gospel in Jerusalem during the first 3.5 years of the Great Tribulation. Whereas many take a symbolic view of the "great city," I suggest that Jerusalem will indeed be the scene of this remarkable ministry. My reasoning is that John's prophecy accords with Old Testament prophecy placing Jerusalem right in the thick of things during the tumultuous Day of the Lord (see Zechariah 12–14). But, as is true with other parts of Revelation, no one knows the specific answer until it happens. You could say that John has written the ultimate cliffhanger!

A rising beast, raptured witnesses, and a deadly earthquake

The ministry of the two witnesses of Revelation 11 is cut short by "the beast that comes up from the bottomless pit" (Rev. 11:7). Interpreters agree that the beast is the antichrist. The abrupt introduction of a key figure in apocalyptic literature is not unprecedented. Fortunately, John lingers later with another interlude (Rev. 12–13), adding more details to the portrait of this bad boy.

At this point, John is content to inform the readers briefly about a power encounter in Jerusalem. The two witnesses seem invincible. A divine aura protects them from enemies (11:5), and they possess unprecedented power over nature (11:6). Who can stand up to them? The answer is a bit frightening. Satan, the Dark Lord, conjures up a person who can not only take them on but defeat them. Arising from the bottomless pit, this satanically energized person kills the two witnesses and leaves their bodies exposed as an act of humiliation and intimidation. None dare oppose the beast from the bottomless pit without mortal consequences! But apparently, most earth-dwellers are quite happy with the outcome: Global celebrations over the demise of the two prophets take place.

Does the Dark Lord get the last word? No. After 3.5 days, the bodies of the two witnesses are raised and raptured (taken up) to heaven in plain view of eyewitnesses. In fact, their rapture is a command performance in response to God's command: "Come up here!" (11:12). This is followed by a most unsettling phenomenon for the inhabitants of Jerusalem: A devastating earthquake occurs, leveling a tenth of the city and resulting in 7,000 deaths.

The response of the survivors is instructive. This is the only time in the sequence of seal, trumpet, and bowl judgments that indicates a positive reaction. Though filled with terror at what had happened, John says they "gave glory to the God of heaven" (11:13). This is in stark contrast to the reactions to prior judgments, where the people cursed God. This is also the conclusion of the second woe mentioned in Revelation 8:13.

CALCULATING WITH PROPHETIC YEARS

John's vision in Revelation 11 draws heavily upon the book of Daniel. Two time periods signal this: "forty-two months" and "one thousand two hundred sixty days" (Rev. 11:2–3; see Daniel 7:25, 9:27, 12:7, 12:11–12). The book of Daniel equates these time periods with "three- and one-half years."

John takes over a chronological scheme in the book of Daniel and incorporates it into his framework for the Great Tribulation or Day of the Lord. Daniel contains a prophecy of a succession of world powers (symbolized by various predatory beasts) leading to the eventual arrival and triumph of God's kingdom (Daniel 7). In this sequence, the seer discovers that a particularly evil king reigns during the fourth kingdom "for a time, two times, and half a time" (Daniel 7:25). In the context of the book (see Daniel 4:16, 36), a "time" equals one year.

Furthermore, Daniel reinterprets Jeremiah's prophecy that after 70 years elapsed, Jews would return to their ancestral homeland (Jeremiah 25:11–12). Daniel transposes the 70 years into 70 weeks of years, in which a "week" equals seven years. This, then, amounts to 490 years (70 × 7). Daniel sees that when the 490 years finally elapse, transgression, sin, and iniquity are put to an end and everlasting righteousness arrives (9:24). His primary focus, however, is on the seventh week of seven years. Apparently, this "week" is divided equally into two segments of 3.5 years. During the second segment, an evil person commits outrage and abomination in Jerusalem. John apparently accepts this framework for his description of the last "week" of the prophetic calendar. Like Daniel, John paints a portrait of an evil person who commits blasphemy and persecutes God's people for 3.5 years.

In other words, the Tribulation is calculated to last one prophetic week — that is, seven years, in keeping with Daniel's chronology. Putting this all together, John pictures a scenario in Jerusalem in which two witnesses proclaim the gospel for 3.5 years before being martyred — the midpoint of the final 7 years of earth.

Beginning of the End: The Seventh Trumpet

In Revelation 11:15, the seventh trumpet blast sounds, the last of the three woes mentioned in 8:13. The angelic choir again raises an anthem of praise. The keynote of fulfillment resounds in the heavens: "The kingdom of the world has become the kingdom of our Lord and of his Messiah" (Rev. 11:15). Seemingly, everything's ready for the grand celebration! The twenty-four elders intone the significance of this moment: "You have taken your great power and begun to reign" (Rev. 11:17).

As the great doors of the heavenly sanctuary open, John catches a glimpse of the ark of the covenant (Rev. 11:19). In both the Mosaic tabernacle and the first and second temples, the ark resided in a special room called the *holy of holies*, whose dimensions formed a perfect cube. Accompanying this disclosure are features regularly associated with a theophany, or appearance of God: lightning, thunder, earthquake, and hail (see Exodus 19:16–19; Psalm 18:7–15).

REMEMBER

Not to be confused with Noah's gigantic animal-filled boat, the ark of the covenant was the central piece of furniture in the tabernacle, cloistered in a cubical room (15 × 15 × 15 feet; see Exodus 25:10-22). The *tabernacle,* where the priests offered worship to God, was actually a very elaborate tent (Exodus 26). The tabernacle was disassembled and reassembled over and over during the 40 years that the Children of Israel wandered in the desert after leaving Egypt.

The ark (see Figure 10-1) was made according to the pattern God showed Moses on the mountain. In construction, it's essentially an acacia wood chest with a lid, covered in pure gold (see Figure 10-2). On the lid of the chest are two golden cherubim, angelic figures, facing each other with outstretched wings that touch above the ark. Inside are the book of the covenant, containing the Ten Commandments (Exodus 24:12), a golden bowl of manna (Exodus 16:32–34), and later, Aaron's staff (Numbers 17:2–10). The ark functions as Yahweh's footstool (1 Chronicles 28:2; Psalm 99:5), and a bright luminescence hovers over it.

FIGURE 10-1:
One artist's rendering of the Ark of the Covenant.

The Jewish Museum, NY/Art Resource, NY

TECHNICAL STUFF

So, where is the Ark? What happened to it is a mystery. Most scholars think the Babylonian king Nebuchadnezzar destroyed or melted it down in 586 BCE. Jewish tradition offers three different explanations:

>> The priests hid it beneath the temple.

>> The prophet Jeremiah hid it on Mount Nebo (in modern-day Jordan).

>> God's angels transferred it to heaven.

According to the first two versions, it remains hidden to this day. The Ethiopian Church claims the ark has resided in their holy city of Aksum for centuries, but this is not accepted outside their tradition. More recently, two pseudo-archeologists, Ron Wyatt and Tom Crotser, claim to have discovered and photographed it, but these claims are rejected by leading archeologists and historians. The mystery surrounding the disappearance of the ark makes for an entertaining movie — but you can be sure it's not stowed somewhere in a warehouse in Washington, D.C. (*Indiana Jones and the Raiders of the Lost Ark*)!

The appearance of the ark in Revelation 11:19 functions as a symbol of God's faithfulness to his covenant promises. The people of God need a strong reminder of this because they're about to experience the wrath of the antichrist.

Chapter **11**

A Woman, a Dragon, Two Beasts, and More! (12:1–14:20)

The climactic battle in the long struggle between good and evil commences, and the church is put on full alert. Revelation 12–14 describes some of the darkest days of church history. But it also resonates with hope because ultimate victory rests with those who follow the Lamb.

Revelation 13, the middle section, is rock bottom for the people of God. The forces of darkness and evil close in for the kill. Satan's antichrist crushes all resistance. But suddenly, just when all seems lost, in chapter 14, the Lamb counterattacks with devastating effect. The evil empire completely collapses. All this is crammed into three chapters!

In this chapter, you explore the topic of the antichrist and the secret formula for the Fellowship of the Lamb's ultimate victory over the Dark Lord.

Heavenly Drama: The Dragon Falls; the Woman Is Saved (12:1–17)

A skilled writer, John borrows imagery from the Old Testament and various pre-Christian sources and weaves them into a new tapestry displaying distinctly Christian themes. The finished work is a magnificent mini-drama about cosmic redemption.

The unfolding drama centers on the age-old conflict between Christ and Satan. The plot features a child of destiny, Jesus, who comes to planet earth to rule over all the nations. Satan (under the guise of a hideous red dragon) resists this invasion and tries to kill the infant Jesus. Failing in this, he unleashes his venom against the historic people from whom Jesus descended (the Jewish people) and those who profess allegiance to him (the church). The warfare that rages in this conflict is truly cosmic in scope involving both the celestial and the terrestrial realms. After the last battle, a new heaven and a new earth appear from the smoke of this cosmic clash (Rev. 21–22).

In composing his mini-drama, John incorporates imagery and concepts drawn from pre-Christian mythology and legend as window dressing. These borrowings are part of the shared traditions common to the Greco-Roman world to which John's audience belonged. By employing them, John adds vividness and luster to the basic storyline. C. S. Lewis does much the same in his Narnia books. The essential Christian message is dressed up in the language of myth and fable. Neither John nor Lewis is implying belief in the window dressing; they are creatively retelling the familiar gospel story.

John sets up his dramatic vignette by depicting the leading characters under the guise of "portents." Portents or signs signify something of great importance for understanding redemptive history. In the following discussion, I offer my take on the identity and meaning of these portents.

Meeting the cast of characters

John's mini-drama involves three leading characters; two others appear in minor roles. Each of these figures appearing on stage conveys important realities about redemptive history and thus are described as "portents" (or omens). Because John and his first-century audience share a common cultural heritage that is foreign to current culture, the imagery and symbolism require decoding.

Pregnant woman clothed with the sun

The first character to appear on the stage is "a woman clothed with the sun, with the moon under her feet, and on her head a crown of twelve stars" (Rev. 12:1). She speaks no intelligible lines but cries out in pain as she gives birth (Rev. 12:2).

As is common in apocalyptic literature, John depicts characters in the guise of symbols. A good example is an apocalyptic passage from a Jewish book called *1 Enoch*, dating to a period before the beginning of Christianity. It retells the story of Israel using animals like cows, sheep, bulls, and rams as symbols for the leading characters (*1 Enoch* 83–90). For this reason, modern scholars name this section as the "Animal Apocalypse." If one knows the story of Israel in the Bible, the various symbols are easily decoded.

Matters are not so cut and dried in Revelation 12 — considerable disagreement arises about the meaning of the woman. Here are four differing perspectives:

>> **The people of God:** Many scholars identify the woman as the people of God — Israel of the old covenant and the church of the new covenant. One reason for this connection lies in Genesis 37:9–11, which shares common features. In a dream, the 17-year-old Joseph sees the sun, moon, and eleven stars bowing down to him. His father Jacob, whose name was changed to Israel (Genesis 32:28), interprets this to mean that he and Rachel, Joseph's mother, will bow down and acknowledge Joseph's authority.

>> In John's adaptation of this vision, the twelve stars stand for the twelve tribes of Israel (Jacob's 12 sons became the 12 tribes of Israel, as narrated in Genesis 29 through Exodus 1). Furthermore, in several poetic passages prophets personify Israel as a woman (Jeremiah 2–3; Ezekiel 23; Hosea 1–3) and, especially significant for this passage, as a woman in childbirth (Isaiah 26:17–18, 66:7; Micah 4:10, 5:3).

>> **A Christianized version of ancient mythology:** From ancient Babylon comes a creation myth in which Marduk, the national god of Babylon, defeats the seven-headed, primeval dragon Tiamat (whose Old Testament equivalent is Leviathan [Job 3, 41; Psalms 74, 104; Isaiah 27]). From Egypt comes a myth in which Set-Typhon, a red dragon, pursues Isis, a mother-goddess, only to be killed later with fire by her son Horus. Greek mythology provides a closer parallel in the story of the pregnant goddess Leto. She is pursued by the dragon Python but escapes to the island of Ortygia.

>> Because his original readers were aware of these mythological traditions, John may have borrowed the imagery. His finished product, however, is thoroughly Christianized, as seen in this line: "But they have conquered him by the blood of the Lamb" (12:11).

>> **Domitia, the mother of God:** An intriguing possibility relates to the emperor Domitian. In the year 83 CE, Domitian's 10-year-old son died. In his grief, Domitian proclaimed his deceased son a god and his mother, Domitia, the mother of God. Coins from this period give expression to Domitian's fantasy. One coin, for example, displays Domitia enthroned, holding a scepter and wearing a diadem (a crown). The inscription reads "Mother of the Divine Caesar." Another coin depicts the child playing with the seven stars and sitting above the heavens. Still another coin shows Domitia on one side and the moon and six planets on the other (see Figure 11-1). On this view, John counters imperial ideology by portraying the true Lord of heaven and ruler of all the kings of the earth.

>> **Virgin Mary:** The prevailing view during the medieval era and continued in conservative Roman Catholic circles interprets the woman as the Virgin Mary. The correspondence between the imagery and the storyline is obvious. Whether this is what John intended, however, is debatable. For the reasons stated above in support of the first possibility, most Catholic scholars today agree that the woman symbolizes God's people of both the Old and New Testaments. One could, however, combine both views, in which case the Virgin Mary typifies the true people of God.

FIGURE 11-1:
A rendering of a
Domitia coin.

Alicia South.

Red dragon with seven heads and a bad attitude

There's no disagreement about the red dragon. You can hardly miss the symbolism. The "great red dragon, with seven heads and ten horns, and seven diadems on his heads" is a dead ringer for Satan. John dispels all doubt by decoding this big, bad dragon in Revelation 12:9 — "The great dragon was thrown down, that ancient serpent, who is called the Devil and Satan, the deceiver of the whole world" — and later in Revelation 20:2.

Male child with iron scepter

The identity of the male child in Rev. 12:5 seems an obvious reference to Jesus. Jesus is the one who will "rule all the nations with a rod of iron." The *rod* is a *scepter*, a symbol of power and royalty. John's opening salutation describes Jesus as "the ruler of the kings of the earth" (1:5), and to the conquerors at Thyatira Jesus promises, "I will give authority over the nations; to rule them with an iron rod" (2:26–27). And, says John, when Jesus finally returns, "he will rule them [the nations] with a rod of iron" (19:15). All this is based on Psalm 2:8–9, a Psalm given a messianic interpretation by some Jews well before the time of Jesus (see the sidebar, "Document 4Q174") and taken over and applied to Jesus by early Christians (Hebrews 1:2).

DOCUMENT 4Q174

In 1947, a shepherd was herding his flock near Qumran, a site near the northwestern corner of the Dead Sea. As the story goes, the shepherd thought a sheep had wandered into one of the dozens of caves in the area. He tossed a rock into one, hoping to scare the sheep out. Instead of hearing a bleating sheep, he heard breaking pottery. Going into the cave, he discovered seven clay jars holding seven ancient scrolls. The year was 1947, and it initiated the discovery of hundreds of documents in more than a dozen caves; these documents are known as the Dead Sea Scrolls.

One of those documents provides evidence that some Jews interpreted Psalm 2 in terms of the Messiah. The reference appears in a sectarian, Essene, document, called *Midrash on the Last Days* and is given the designation 4Q174. The Essenes were a sectarian group who broke away from the more influential and dominant party in first-century Judaism, the Pharisees. A *midrash* is an interpretation or paraphrase of a biblical text. The text quotes Psalm 2:1 and then offers this comment: "The meaning is that the nations shall set themselves and conspire vainly against the chosen of Israel [a title for the Jewish Messiah] in the Last Days. That will be the time of persecution that is to come upon the House of Judah, to the end of sealing up the wicked in the consuming fire and destroying all the children of Belial [another name for Satan]. Then shall be left behind a remnant of chosen ones, the predestined."

So, what does 4Q174 mean? Here's the key to break the code! The number 4 means this document was found in cave four (there were 11 in all), and the Q means it was found at Qumran, a site along the northwestern shore of the Dead Sea. The number 174 is an inventory number given by the researchers who studied the various documents. The total number of manuscripts found in these caves is thought to be between 800 and 900. The settlement was inhabited by an ascetic group of Jews called the Essenes.

(continued)

They rejected both the Sadducees and Pharisees as incorrect interpreters of the law of Moses and withdrew into the Judean desert to await the coming of two Messiahs — one from the line of David and the other from the priestly line of Zadok. They expected and wrote about a decisive battle between their community, styled the "sons of light" against evildoers labeled as "sons of darkness" (which included the Sadducees and Pharisees!) in the End Times.

Michael the mighty archangel

Revelation 12 speaks of Michael the archangel (Rev. 12:7), a leading actor in Jewish and Christian apocalyptic writing. He is typically the defender of Israel (Daniel 12:1) and the leader of God's angelic army (Daniel 10:13, 10:21; Jude 9). In the Dead Sea Scrolls, he appears ten times and functions as the great protector of God's people and as one who administers judgment upon the wicked forces allied against the true Israel (in other words, the Essenes). He also conveys heavenly mysteries and explains their meaning to a visionary like Enoch (See 1 *Enoch* 9:1; 10:11; 20:5; 24:6). He may be the unnamed archangel the Apostle Paul has in mind when he describes what will happen at Jesus's second coming (1 Thessalonians 4:16).

WITH THE WINGS OF AN EAGLE

Does Revelation 12:14 refer to an eagle or just its wings? If it is an eagle, could this be the same eagle that announces the three woes back in Revelation 8:13? If so, the eagle symbolizes an angelic being.

Or perhaps John depicts a powerful king or kingdom under the figure of an eagle. A passage in Ezekiel may shed light. In Ezekiel 17, the prophet gives an allegory involving two powerful eagles. The first stands for the Babylonian monarch, Nebuchadnezzar. The second is Pharaoh Psammetichus II of Egypt. Judah sought, unsuccessfully, to resist Nebuchadnezzar by forming an alliance with Psammetichus (Jeremiah 37:5).

It's also worth noting that Roman legions placed an eagle on top of their standards. John's first readers may have at once thought of Rome. Some well-known prophecy enthusiasts see a reference to the United States of America symbolized by the American bald eagle!

More likely, the wings recall the imagery of Exodus 19:4 ("I bore you on eagles' wings") and represent God's protection over the faithful remnant of the End Times. This protection may, of course, involve angelic agency under the symbol of a great eagle.

Unpacking the plot and viewing the action

Now that I've listed the leading characters appearing onstage, let's watch as the drama unfolds. It consists of three acts arranged in a logical, if not chronological sequence. The first act is necessary to understand what happens in the second, and the second act is essential for grasping what happens in the climactic third act. The bottom line is this: You learn why the dragon is so filled with rage. Despite his best efforts, he can't thwart the kingdom of the child destined to rule the nations. He can cause carnage, but he can't control planet earth.

Act one: The great escape

Act one opens with an immediate, life-threatening danger: a woman in the throes of childbirth confronted by a red dragon intent on devouring her newborn! The dragon is backed up by fallen angels (or demons): "His tail swept down a third of the stars of heaven and threw them to earth" (Rev. 12:4). This is terrifying! Reminds me of the Death Eaters in the Harry Potter series!

REMEMBER

Amazingly, the child escapes. All you're told is that he is "snatched away and taken to God and to his throne" (Rev. 12:5). As mentioned above, most commentators understand this as a reference to Jesus. A few, however, question whether a Christian writer would tell the story of Jesus in such a compressed way, omitting the cross and resurrection. Moving from birth to ascension leaves out incredibly important parts! But let's remember, John doesn't need "to give the whole ball of wax" because his audience already knows the story.

For example, the original recipients of Revelation were aware of the Gospel of Matthew, which provides a fuller account of the birth of Jesus. According to Matthew, eastern astrologers (magi or wise men) arrive in Jerusalem (Matthew 2:1–12). They're convinced from observations of a certain "star" that the promised Messiah will be born in Judea. Unfortunately, they go straight to the man in charge, the paranoid and cruel Herod the Great, and ask where the child is. Herod pretends eagerness to show homage to this royal heir to the throne. Having asked his religious experts where the Messiah was prophesied to be born and learning it was Bethlehem (Micah 5:2), Herod dismissed the magi with instructions to report back when they find the child. Herod's intention, of course, is to murder the infant, a potential threat to his throne.

Providentially, God steps in to save Jesus's life. God oversees the course of history down to the smallest details. In this instance, by a dream, the wise men are warned not to return to Herod. By another dream, an angel alerts Jesus's father Joseph to the mortal danger, and he flees to Egypt with his family just in the nick of time. When Herod realizes he's been outwitted, he orders a massacre of all males two years old or younger in the village of Bethlehem, adding to an already long list of atrocities.

John's vision summarizes the same event but from "behind the scenes." In other words, behind all the plotting of a paranoid Herod, the devil is at work. John's vision unmasks the ultimate culprit. Satan works through people who fully embrace evil to achieve their own evil ends. One thinks of the tragic story of the scholar Faust, who sold his soul to the devil in exchange for earthly pleasures and regaining his youth.

Act two: A cosmic slugfest

Act two quickly ensues in Revelation 12:7–12. Satan (appearing as a red dragon and later as a serpent) has been foiled. An all-out heavenly war erupts between the good angels under the command of Michael and the evil angels led by the dragon (Satan). This cosmic slugfest results in the expulsion of Satan and his evil cronies. They're consigned to the earth. This seems to be a case of good news/bad news. The good news is Satan can't hang out in heaven anymore; the bad news is planet earth becomes his new base of operations.

In this mini-drama, the last chapter of earth history is characterized by a cosmic power struggle. In John's vision, a loud voice from heaven spells out what this means: "Rejoice then, you heavens and those who dwell in them! But woe to the earth and the sea, for the devil has come down to you with great wrath, because he knows that his time is short!" (Rev. 12:12). A desperate devil digs in for "the last battle." If he can't win, he's going to take down as many as he can with him.

In short, Satan suffers two stunning setbacks in act two: Michael and the angels oust him from the heavenly court, and the saints on earth withstand his assaults. How do believers, so much weaker in every way, manage to overcome this powerful adversary? John provides the answer in a classic paradox: "They have conquered him by the blood of the Lamb and by the word of their testimony" (Rev. 12:11). In other words, they trust, not in retaliation, but in redemption, the death of the Lamb on their behalf. And they remain faithful to him even if it costs them their life (12:11b).

Act three: Satan on a leash

Act three returns the woman to center stage. The dragon directs his rage at the woman who gave birth. But Satan is on a leash; he doesn't have unlimited power. God protects the woman — the people of God (see the earlier "Meeting the cast of characters" section) — from Satan's attacks. This is the message John wants the church of his day to hear — a message relevant for the church in the last days.

REMEMBER

From the New Testament perspective, "the last days" began at Pentecost (Acts 2:17–21; Hebrews 1:2) and continue until the Parousia (the second coming of Jesus). In other words, we're in "the last days now"! But the last days climax with "the last days" of the Great Tribulation, and that's what the sixth seal, the seven trumpets, and seven bowls describe.

Revelation 12:12–16 envisions an extraordinary rescue operation. It's as if Peter Pan sprinkled pixie dust on the woman because she can fly! She flies to a wilderness retreat, "where she is nourished for a time, and times, and half a time" (3.5 years or 42 months or 1,260 days). Frustrated, the dragon tries to drown her with a flood of water issuing from his mouth. But the earth comes to the woman's rescue and swallows up the river, once again foiling the dragon's murderous plan. Admittedly, this is a difficult passage, and interpreters differ over its interpretation:

>> **Mostly Literal view:** The woman is the Jewish people of the End Times. They come under satanic attack led by the antichrist (the beast of Rev. 11:7 and Rev. 13). God providentially rescues them (perhaps by planes?) and transports them to a sanctuary in the Negev (a wilderness area of southern Israel).

One expositor of an earlier generation, Dr. Louis Talbot, believed the rose-red city of Petra (in modern-day Jordan) would serve as a haven during the great Tribulation. Following up on his conviction, he arranged to have gospel pamphlets printed and stashed in Petra in anticipation of that time! I've visited Petra several times and nary a scrap of these tracts have survived, nor have any of the Jordanian tour guides even heard about this!

Tim LaHaye, in his novel *Desecration: Antichrist Takes the Throne* (the ninth book in his *Left Behind* series), interprets the woman as "tribulation saints" — that is, individuals, both Jewish and Gentile, who are not believers when the rapture occurs but come to faith in Jesus during the Great Tribulation. They're part of a resistance movement dubbed "the Tribulation Force." LaHaye sketches a scenario in which a million believers, including many Israelis, escape the antichrist's wrath by also fleeing to Petra. This planned escape is called "Operation Eagle," based on Revelation 12:14.

>> **Symbolic view:** Those holding a symbolic view explore imagery drawn from Scripture. They believe this passage resonates with echoes of the story of the Exodus from Egypt. For example, notice the following items:

● Just like the red dragon who pursues the woman, so Pharaoh pursued the Israelites when they left Egypt (Exodus 14:8). In fact, Pharaoh's crown was capped by the Uraeus, a cobra poised to strike!

● The reference to the two wings of an eagle recalls the words of the Lord in Exodus 19:4: ". . . I bore you on eagles' wings and brought you to myself."

- Perhaps readers hear an echo of Pharaoh's charge to drown Hebrew male babies (Exodus 1:22) when the serpent pours forth water like a river to drown the woman.

- The opening of the earth to swallow up the water may allude to the episode in the wilderness when the rebellious house of Korah was swallowed up by the earth (Numbers 16:31–33).

REMEMBER

The imagery points to God's providential protection for his people during the great Tribulation. This doesn't mean they're spared the wrath of the antichrist. Rather, it means the antichrist can huff and puff as much as he wants, but he won't be able to blow the house down. Those who believe in Jesus will appear victorious whether by life or death. After all, Jesus himself promised that "the gates of Hades will not prevail against it [the church]" (Matthew 16:18).

Two Beasty Boys Join the Dragon to Make Their Mark (13:1–18)

As Revelation 13 begins, John describes how the dragon (Satan) conjures up two demonic henchmen who set out to deceive the world and destroy the Fellowship of the Lamb. In this section, you are introduced to members of an unholy trinity who try to control planet earth. Through counterfeit miracles, the beast from the sea (antichrist) secures economic and political control over the world. The beast from the earth, the antichrist's minister of propaganda, false prophet, and priest, installs an idolatrous religion requiring worship of the dragon and the beast. A worldwide identification scheme is implemented: the infamous number of the beast, 666. Only those bearing the number and taking part in this demonic cult can buy or sell. The Fellowship of the Lamb teeters on the brink of extermination.

Monster mash: The antichrist, beast of the sea

In ancient mythology and in the Hebrew Bible, the sea often is an unruly force echoing the chaos that existed prior to the creation of the earth (Genesis 1:2). One version of a creation story from Babylon, called *Enuma Elish*, speaks of the primeval sea waters as a great dragon called Tiamat. In this epic myth, Tiamat and Marduk (see Figure 11-2), the young, powerful god of Babylon, engage in hand-to-hand combat. Psalm 74:13–14 borrows the imagery of this primeval duel but changes the names: It's not Marduk but Yahweh who overcomes the chaos monster Leviathan (Hebrew equivalent of Tiamat). Just before this trial by arms, Tiamat spawns a massive army of dragons. (If you're a *Lord of the Rings* fan, think Sauron and his Orcs.) In keeping with that imagery, the dragon of Revelation now conjures up the ultimate chaos monster: "a beast rising up out of the sea, having ten horns and seven heads; and on its horns were ten diadems, and on its heads were blasphemous names" (Rev. 13:1). This monster shows up again in Revelation 16:13 and chapters 17–18.

FIGURE 11-2: The ancient dragon Tiamat and the Babylonian god Marduk.

John's description of the beast adapts imagery from the book of Daniel. The beast from the sea is a composite beast displaying features of a leopard, bear, and lion. Daniel uses these three animals to depict a sequence of four world empires that precede the final kingdom of God (Daniel 7). Many conservative scholars understand the sequence accordingly:

1. The lion is Babylon under the authority of Nebuchadnezzar.

2. The bear is the large and powerful kingdom of Persia launched by Cyrus the Great.

3. The leopard is the lightning-fast conquests of the Macedonian Greeks under Alexander the Great.

4. The nondescript beast who supplants all earlier kingdoms is either Rome or the final kingdom of the antichrist.

5. The little horn with human-like eyes and arrogant mouth is either Antiochus IV Epiphanes (215–163 BCE) or the antichrist. Some interpreters see this as a case of typology. Typology is a way of linking persons, events, or institutions from one biblical era to a later one. Thus the type foreshadows its antitype or fulfillment. Typology assumes a correspondence or pattern that unfolds within salvation history. In this case, the nondescript beast (Rome) foreshadows the kingdom of the antichrist. In Daniel 7, the "little horn" refers to Antiochus IV and foreshadows the final antichrist of the End Times.

In John's vision, the beast from the sea is so terrifying and hideous he incorporates all the evils of the wicked world empires preceding him. The most alarming fact about this beast is his source of power and authority: The dragon energizes the beast and authorizes him to act on his behalf. This is Satan's most cunning creature and harks back to the serpent in the garden of Eden who "was craftier than any other wild animal that the LORD God had made" (Genesis 3:1). Of course, we're not talking about a physical beast, like Godzilla walking around and terrorizing the earth. He's a human being, no doubt possessing charm and charisma, who cobbles together an immense, international, economic and political coalition. John's description, however, unmasks and exposes his real character and intentions.

The dragon cons the world into believing the beast is invincible. Receiving an apparently mortal blow to one of his heads, the beast recovers. It seems to be a miracle. In fact, it's a parody of the resurrection of Jesus. The world is amazed and responds with worship and adulation directed to both the dragon and his protégé: "They worshiped the dragon . . . saying, 'Who is like the beast, and who can fight against it?'" (Rev. 13:4). The answer seems to be *no one*.

A reign of terror ensues. This is the TV series *Stranger Things* on Steroids! The antichrist seizes power and authority over the planet. For the first time since the Tower of Babel (Gen. 11:1–9), a one-world government arises. God is ridiculed and debunked in the new regime. The antichrist claims he is God. This must be the same event the Apostle Paul describes in 2 Thessalonians 2:4: "He opposes and exalts himself above every so-called god or object of worship, so that he takes his seat in the temple of God, declaring himself to be God." For 42 months (3.5 years) the antichrist holds the reins of power and makes war against the saints (13:7). Believers nonetheless steadfastly refuse to worship the beast or receive his mysterious mark. John inserts a word of admonition and exhortation, noting the pointlessness of mounting violent resistance (Rev. 13:9–10). The exhortation has special relevance for believers in the first century confronting the blasphemous claims of the Imperial Cult. But it also has relevance for succeeding generations who must likewise resist false ideologies that supplant God. One thinks of Christians like Dietrich Bonhoeffer who resisted Nazi ideology during WWII at the cost of his life. The primary reference, however, is for that last generation of

Christians who are called upon to resist the onslaught of the antichrist. Believers must neither defect nor despair. God has foreseen everything. The saints must do the one thing in their power left to do: They must continue to be faithful to the Lamb even if it costs them their lives. As John says in Revelation 13:10, "Here is a call for the endurance and faith of the saints."

Head of PR: The false prophet, beast from inner earth

In Revelation 13, the dragon (also known as Satan) conjures up a second beast, this time from the depths of the earth, which has two horns like a lamb and speaks like a dragon (Rev. 13:11). Like most of the beasties and critters encountered in Revelation, this beast is not a literal monster; he's a false prophet promoting the antichrist.

TIP

Ancient and apocalyptic mythologies speak of two primeval monsters: a sea monster called Tiamat or Leviathan and a land monster, sometimes called Behemoth (1 Enoch 60:7–10; Isaiah 27:1; Job 20:15). John may draw upon these two primeval monsters in his portrayal of the antichrist and his false prophet.

Here's a profile of the antichrist's right-hand man:

>> **He has two horns like a lamb.** This implies an attempt to appear like the Lamb of God. In apocalyptic literature, animals with horns, like sheep and goats, are regularly used as symbols of strength and power (See Daniel 8). He is a sickening imitation of Christ.

>> **He speaks like a dragon.** This isn't Parseltongue, a rare magical language spoken by Harry Potter enabling him to communicate with snakes or some other mythical language only dragons understand. He speaks like a dragon because he speaks for the great red dragon, whom Jesus calls "a liar and the father of lies" (John 8:44).

Designated as a false prophet (Rev. 16:13; 19:20; 20:10), the beast from inner earth serves as the minister of propaganda for the antichrist's regime. One is reminded of Joseph Goebbels, Adolf Hitler's Minister for Public Enlightenment and Propaganda. The false prophet of Revelation, however, even performs miraculous signs like a modern Moses or Elijah and deceives a credulous world. Hmm. Wonder if the news media will broadcast this live!

The false prophet sets up a blasphemous cult featuring a speaking image of the beast. All must worship the beast; the penalty for disobedience is death. There's no escape for members of the Fellowship of the Lamb. A worldwide registration system comes online, the notorious "mark of the beast."

It's all a charade, the greatest hoax ever perpetrated. The father of lies counterfeits the Christian doctrine of the Holy Trinity (one God coexisting as Father, Son, and Holy Spirit) with his own, twisted version, the unholy trinity (see Figure 11-3). Multitudes fall for it.

TECHNICAL STUFF

In 41 CE (a mere eleven years after Jesus's death) Emperor Caligula decreed that his statue be set up and worshiped in the Jerusalem temple. The outraged Jewish community prepared to resist his decree to the death. Fortunately, he was assassinated before the command was carried out. At the time Revelation was written, worship of the divine Domitian was mandatory in some Asian cities, and at least one Christian, Antipas, suffered martyrdom for disobeying (Rev. 2:13). The Imperial Cult is probably the lens through which John portrays the false prophet's cult of the antichrist (for more on emperor worship in Ancient Rome, see Chapter 2).

Beastly markings: 666

Perhaps no single feature of the book of Revelation has fascinated readers more than the mark of the beast and its mysterious number, 666. The false prophet institutes a registration system whereby followers of the sea beast receive a number stamped on either their right hand or forehead. Without this number, no one can buy or sell. Survival literally depends on having this number, which is "the name of the beast or the number of its name."

So, what is this mysterious number and whom does it stand for? John throws out a challenge: "This calls for wisdom: let anyone with understanding calculate the number of the beast" (Rev. 13:18). Should you get your calculator and go at it? Some have, but the results are pretty wacky! Like a Gordian Knot, the problem of perpetual motion, or Colonel Sanders' secret blend of 11 herbs and spices, the number of the beast remains an enigma code. Here's a sampling of proposed solutions.

Nero Caesar

The early church Father Irenaeus, in the second century CE, mentions that people were already suggesting candidates for the role of antichrist. One was at the top of the list — and for good reason. Nero Caesar's brief but bloody persecution of Christians in the aftermath of the fire in Rome (64 CE) qualified him because Revelation 17:6 describes a woman (closely identified with the beast) as "drunk with the blood of the saints and the blood of the witnesses to Jesus."

A rumor that became a legend circulated to the effect that Nero either had not died (the official report said he committed suicide), or that he died but would come back from the dead. Supposedly he was alive and well in Parthia (Rome's bitter rival in the east) and would soon return and wreak vengeance on Rome. This became known as the *Nero redivivus* legend. Many modern scholars' conjecture John had this in mind when he penned this section, even if he only borrowed the legend to depict an eschatological (End Times) figure.

Here's where the story gets interesting and somewhat involved. If one takes the name of Nero Caesar, converts it into Hebrew letters, and then takes the numeral value of the letters according to their order in the alphabet, the sum is 666. This kind of calculation is part of a system of interpretation called *gematria* and was popular not only in Jewish circles but in Roman culture as well. Examples of *gematria* can be seen on the walls of the Roman city Pompeii (buried in volcanic ash when Mount Vesuvius erupted on August 24, 79 CE).

Irenaeus, however, warns his readers not to engage in idle speculation. The number can be known only when the antichrist arrives on the scene. For now, he notes, only God knows what the number means and who the antichrist is. Yet, despite Irenaeus's warning, scholars have tried their hand at breaking the code, with astonishingly different, and so far, incorrect results!

The pope

The Reformers, locked in an often-violent struggle over control for the hearts and minds of European Christians, readily found ammunition for their apologetic canons by pillorying the pope as the antichrist. The primary source for this identification comes later in Revelation 17–18. The mention of the seven mountains (Rev. 17:9) seemed to point to Rome, the center of papal power. The mention of being clothed in purple and scarlet, gold and jewels, along with a golden cup of abominations, thought to be an allusion to the doctrine of *transubstantiation*, the Roman Catholic teaching that the bread and wine of the Eucharist actually becomes the body, blood, and divinity of Christ when consecrated by the priest, seemed quite sufficient for the Reformers to erase all doubt: The pope was indeed the antichrist.

The number 666 was accordingly viewed as symbolic of the evil papal system. Because six falls short of perfection (seven), it is suitable as the number for fallen humanity. Thrice six simply intensifies the evil of this wicked person and that person's government. The first edition of the Church of England's *Westminster Confession of Faith* (1646) says, "There is no other Head of the Church, but the Lord Jesus Christ; Nor can the Pope of Rome, in any sense be head thereof: but is that Antichrist, that Man of sin and Son of Perdition, that exalteth himself, in the Church, against Christ, and all that is called God" (Chapter XXV, VI). This section of the book has long since been removed. Today, only a tiny minority of commentators hold this view.

Napoleon Bonaparte

During the upheavals of the late eighteenth and early nineteenth centuries, some commentators and preachers identified Napoleon Bonaparte, the Corsican corporal, as the antichrist. His return from exile in Elba (the wound that seemed mortal, Rev. 13:3) and mobilization of another army (Rev. 16:14–16) seemed to unfold according to the script. Then came Waterloo, exile in St. Helena, and death — but no return to life. Another candidate faded from memory.

Assorted modern dictators and tyrants

In more recent times, a few Bible teachers and preachers went into print claiming that Adolf Hitler and Benito Mussolini were the antichrist and false prophet. In fact, if one added Japan's emperor Hirohito to the equation, you had the three, self-designated Axis powers, an unholy trinity from the perspective of the Allies! To be sure, the Axis perpetrated enough heinous crimes to merit the dubious distinction, but their war crimes fell far short of fulfilling John's prophecy. Joseph Stalin, Mao Tse-tung, Pol Pot, Saddam Hussein, and Osama Bin Laden, among others, also merit dishonorable mention in the "Hall of Shame." But none of them displayed the unprecedented degree of cunning and cruelty as Revelation's antichrist.

World-renowned leaders

I mention the following people because they illustrate only too well the need for Irenaeus's warning about speculation. A few Bible prophecy buffs, following the old theory that the antichrist is a Jew, latched onto one of the most charismatic and enigmatic political figures of the twentieth century, Henry Kissinger, Secretary of State under President Richard Nixon. More than a little whiff of anti-Semitism can be detected in this supposed identification. Still others pointed to Mikhail Gorbachev, whose only real "credential" — besides the fact that he was the General Secretary of the Communist Party and President of the Soviet Union (some believe that Communism is a tool of Satan and will eventually be controlled by the antichrist) — was a rather prominent birthmark on his forehead!

Buildings, phone numbers, and computer codes

Speculation still runs rampant about the number 666. Bar codes and microchips provide a field day for 666 sleuths! The Internet abounds with theories, and new sightings regularly surface. A prominent building in New York City bears the address 666; rumors persist that it serves as the future office for the antichrist. When a new computer system came online in Europe with the code name 666, the prophecy experts were all over it! And when a telephone company assigned the area code 666 to a part of the Bible Belt in Kentucky, the uproar was sufficient to have it changed! One "expert" saw that Ronald Wilson Reagan's full name has six letters in each name; to top it off, when he left Washington, the number of his new address was originally 666. He had it changed to 668. So, what's in a number? Apparently, a lot!

The PIN of the antichrist

Most scholars in the premillennial tradition (Jesus returns to the earth and reigns 1,000 years before the final judgment and the new heavens and earth) believe the beast from the sea stands for an actual person who heads up an evil empire. They further suggest that 666 functions not as a personal identification number (PIN) but an index of depravity. Only during the Great Tribulation will his identity come to light.

Many historical figures and regimes have embodied some of the features of the antichrist (despotic cruelty and oppression for example), but none come close to matching the scale of deception, depravity, and destruction depicted in Revelation 13. The fictional realm of film and literature abounds with antichrist figures. Does the antichrist exist somewhere on earth right now? Only time will tell! How's that for a non-answer to the mystery of 666?

The Lamb and the 144,000 (14:1–5)

Revelation 14 opens with an image that gives comfort to all God's people: The Lamb is standing on Mount Zion with his redeemed. By sharing a short celebration that includes thunder, harps, and a new song, John assures believers that ultimate victory belongs to the Lamb.

The 144,000 (the number is symbolic) first mentioned in Revelation 7 (see Chapter 9) reappear in John's vision — this time on Mount Zion, with the Lamb, around the throne of God. Etched on their foreheads, as opposed to 666, is the name of the Lamb and the Father speaking to the character and status of those who bear it. These are children of God. None of them has the dreaded mark of the beast. They've resisted the most intense pressure and persecution imaginable. Their unswerving loyalty and commitment are expressed in the following biblical imagery:

>> **Virgins, or those who kept themselves pure:** This description draws attention to spiritual fidelity and chastity. In the Old Testament, Israelites often turned away from God and worshipped other gods, committing spiritual adultery. In the New Testament, believers are warned about mixed loyalties

(Matthew 6:14; James 1:8; 1 John 2:15, 5:21). In this context, the redeemed are called virgins (some translations are more descriptive, indicating they avoided sexual relations) because they acknowledge and confess that only Jesus is Lord: "These follow the Lamb wherever he goes" (Rev. 14:4). True believers in Jesus are, figuratively, the pure bride of Jesus.

In the first century CE, Christians had to make a choice: Is Caesar Lord or is Jesus Lord? In 64 CE, Christians who chose Jesus ended up as macabre entertainment, serving as torches for Nero's evening dinner parties and food for lions in the arena. According to Revelation, the end time generation will have to make a similar choice: Is the antichrist Lord or is the Lamb Lord? The redeemed choose the Lamb and celebrate their choice by singing a song of redemption that only they can sing.

>> **First fruits:** In the Old Testament, Israelites were commanded to bring a portion of the early harvest of the land to the temple of God as an act of thanksgiving and gratitude for the full harvest to follow (Leviticus 19:23–25, 23:9–21; Deuteronomy 26:1–11). The first-fruit offerings also supported the priestly and Levitical families who ministered at the tabernacle as specified in Numbers 3–4. Metaphorically, the expression refers to that which is first (Jeremiah 2:3) and that which belongs solely to the Lord. In the New Testament, believers are referred to as first fruits (James 1:18; 2 Thessalonians 2:13; Romans 8:23).

>> **Blameless:** The 144,000 reflect their status as followers devoted completely to the Lamb by their virtue. Transparent integrity characterizes these redeemed. John probably alludes to a prophetic text in Zephaniah 3:13: ". . . the remnant of Israel; they shall do no wrong and utter no lies, nor shall a deceitful tongue be found in their mouths." The stark contrast to the deceit and deception of the antichrist and the false prophet is palpable.

This vision of the Lamb on Mount Zion surrounded by 144,000 bearing his name differs dramatically from the earlier section. By the time chapter 13 concludes, one wonders how the Fellowship of the Lamb can possibly survive such an onslaught. Yet here they are singing a new song in the presence of the Lamb! The bottom line is this: Faith in the Lamb triumphs over demonic deception, economic deprivation, and brutal violence. John says in prose in his first epistle what he here depicts in imagery: "And this is the victory that conquers the world, our faith. Who is it that conquers the world but the one who believes that Jesus is the Son of God?" (1 John 5:4).

Three Angels with Three Messages (14:6–13)

Have you ever seen a production of *Peter Pan* or a play featuring actors who fly (by means of invisible wires)? What John witnesses is much better. Three wireless angels appear in mid-air, each with a special message, delivered with a wireless, cosmic microphone! These announcements anticipate and summarize the last series of seven judgments, the seven bowls of God's wrath. These bowls, when finally poured out, finish off the antichrist's kingdom headquartered in Babylon the great (14:8). All those who follow the beast suffer the same fate: They must drink the wine of God's wrath. This entails a fiery punishment whose smoke "goes up forever and ever" (Rev. 14:11).

Proclaiming an eternal gospel

Revelation 14:6–7: "Then I saw another angel flying in mid-heaven, with an eternal gospel to proclaim to those who live on the earth — to every nation and tribe and language and people. He said in a loud voice, 'Fear God and give him glory, for the hour of his judgment has come; and worship him who made heaven and earth, the sea and the springs of water.'"

The message spoken by the angel addresses a fundamental sin, failure to acknowledge God as creator and source of everything good. This primal offense (see Genesis 3) replicates itself in every human heart and leads to your alienation from God and your neighbors. The Apostle Paul is making the same point in Romans when he says: ". . . for though they knew God, they did not honor him as God or give thanks to him, but they became futile in their thinking, and their senseless minds were darkened. Claiming to be wise, they became fools; and they exchanged the glory of the immortal God for images resembling a mortal human being or birds or four-footed animals or reptiles" (Romans 1:21–23).

Proclaiming the fall of Babylon

A second angel announces the imminent collapse of Babylon: "Then another angel, a second, followed, saying, 'Fallen, fallen is Babylon the great! She has made all nations drink of the wine of the wrath of her fornication'" (Rev. 14:8). That doesn't sound like a very appealing vintage! In Chapter 12, I go into more detail as to the identity of Babylon. But for now, all you need to know is that Babylon is not necessarily a literal city but symbolizes a powerful political entity. Here's a sampling of the leading views on what this angelic message means (for more on general ways to read Revelation, see Chapter 4).

- **Literal approach:** People adhering to a strictly literal approach insist that ancient Babylon (which is in Iraq) will rise from the desert sands and become the global capital of the antichrist's evil empire. Back in the 1990s, when Saddam Hussein began restoration work on the ancient site of Babylon, prophecy buffs were buzzing. Their first enthusiasm has cooled considering more recent events, but some continue to teach that ancient Babylon will literally be rebuilt.

- **Symbolic approach:** Those holding a symbolic approach argue that Babylon is more likely a code name for Rome. An apocalyptic work contemporaneous with the book of Revelation (4 Ezra 3:1) uses Babylon as a symbolic name for Rome. Almost certainly, the Apostle Peter does the same when he concludes his first epistle: "Your sister church in Babylon, chosen together with you, sends you greetings" (1 Peter 5:13). In short, John encourages believers by predicting the demise of imperial Rome under the symbol of Babylon.

- **Futurist approach:** A moderately futuristic approach understands John to be using first-century imperial Rome as the lens through which to focus on the ultimate power center of the antichrist. John borrows prophetic language from the Old Testament prophet Isaiah that predicts the fall of historic Babylon for destroying Jerusalem and the First Temple in 586 BCE (Isaiah 21:9). John applies this prophecy to first-century CE Rome. God will judge Rome, the new Babylon, for destroying Jerusalem and the Second Temple in 70 CE. Likewise, God will destroy Babylon the great, the capital of antichrist's empire. The location of this Babylon the great, however, like the identity of the antichrist, will only be revealed at the end.

Proclaiming a warning with assurance

All who accept the mark of the beast are destined to experience God's wrath. There's simply no way to soften this. The third angel delivers a somber warning: "Those who worship the beast and its image, and receive a mark on their foreheads or on their hands, they will also drink the wine of God's wrath, poured unmixed into the cup of his anger, and they will be tormented with fire and sulfur in the presence of the holy angels and in the presence of the Lamb. And the smoke of their torment goes up for ever and ever. There is no rest day or night for those who worship the beast and its image and for anyone who receives the mark of its name" (Rev. 14:9–11).

This punishment's imagery comes from the Old Testament, featuring undiluted wine, fire, and sulfur — far from appealing and certain to cause heartburn. The first metaphor stresses the potency of God's judgment (Jeremiah 25:15–16, 51:7), and the second recalls the devastation of Sodom and Gomorrah (Genesis 19:24).

What is especially difficult is the seemingly unending nature of the judgment: "And the smoke of their torment goes up forever and ever" (Rev. 14:11). I look more closely at this judgment in Chapter 13.

That's the bad news; now the good news. The angel ends with a word of exhortation to the faithful, encouraging them to "hold fast to the faith of Jesus" (Rev. 13:9–10). A voice from heaven concludes with a benediction: "Blessed are the dead who from now on die in the Lord" (14:13). Whose voice is this? Most likely it's the voice of Jesus who is seconded by the Spirit with a resounding, Yes!

REMEMBER

Revelation 14:13 is the second of seven beatitudes or benedictions ("Blessed are") interspersed throughout the book of Revelation. The others are in Revelation 1:3, 16:15, 19:9, 20:6, and 22:7, 14.

Harvesting Wheat and the Grapes of Wrath (14:14–20)

A two-part, multi-layered, harvest-themed vision caps off Revelation 14:

>> In the first harvest, an angel tells someone sitting on a cloud and holding a sickle to reap the harvest of the earth.

>> In the second harvest, another angel tells a different angel holding a sickle to harvest grapes, which are then thrown into a winepress and trampled.

Are these two scenes positive or negative images? Or is one positive and the other negative? Most commentators agree that the grape harvest is a picture of divine judgment. Considerable disagreement, however, involves the meaning of the wheat harvest.

Reaping the earth

In agrarian cultures, harvest time typically denotes a joyous time of thanksgiving. In this passage, however, what is harvested is not corn, wheat, or any kind of grain. Human beings are reaped. Consequently, some interpreters understand the reaping imagery as the ingathering (or rapture) of the church. This view is strengthened by the fact that the one sitting on the white cloud who does the reaping is said to look like "the Son of Man," which is another title for Jesus.

John borrows the imagery for both the wheat and the grape harvests from the Old Testament prophet Joel. In Joel 3:13, in a context of impending divine judgment on the nations, the prophet says, "Put in the sickle, for the harvest is ripe. Go in, tread, for the wine press is full. The vats overflow, for their wickedness is great." The last line casts a quite different perspective on *both* the first and second harvests. From this perspective, both stand for divine judgment. John's vintage scene is introduced by describing an angel who performs the action: "And he too had a sharp sickle" (Rev. 14:17). This seems to link closely the two sickles, and clearly, the second conveys a negative image. Therefore, many commentators conclude that both harvests, in this context, depict God's end-time judgment on an unbelieving world.

On the other hand, Jesus's parable of the sower (Mark 4) may point in a different direction. In the parable, some "hear the word and accept it and bear fruit, thirty and sixty and a hundredfold" (Mark 4:20). Even closer in thought is the parable in which a farmer sows a field with seeds. Afterward, it sprouts and yields ripe grain. The farmer "goes in with his sickle, because the harvest has come" (Mark 4:29). But even closer yet is John's narrative of the Samaritan woman in his Gospel. Jesus says to his disciples, "But I tell you, look around you and see how the fields are ripe for harvesting. The reaper is already receiving wages and is gathering fruit for eternal life, so that sower and reaper may rejoice together" (John 4:35–36). Not surprisingly, then, some expositors take a positive view of the first harvesting of the earth.

Treading the grapes (of wrath)

The second harvesting involves gathering and then squeezing the juice from the grapes by treading on them. The grape vintage is typically another joyous occasion in biblical times. The entire family takes part in singing and games while crushing the grapes barefoot in the wine press. (The toe jam adds flavor!)

In some passages, however, treading grapes serves as a terrifying metaphor of God's judgment. In fact, John borrows the imagery from Isaiah 63:1–6. There, in a startling word picture, the prophet describes the Lord's coming upon the land of Judah bedecked in garments that are stained crimson. When asked why his royal robes are red, he replies, "I have trodden the wine press alone . . . I trod them in my anger and trampled them in my wrath; their juice spattered on my garments, and stained all my robes. For the day of vengeance was in my heart, and the year for my redeeming work had come. I trampled down peoples in my anger, I crushed them in my wrath, and I poured out their lifeblood on the earth." Most likely, the image of squeezing out the juice, like blood, vividly depicts God's wrath poured out on unbelievers during the Great Tribulation. I am inclined to the view that both harvests depict divine judgment.

TECHNICAL STUFF

Julia Ward Howe's "The Battle Hymn of the Republic" and John Steinbeck's novel *The Grapes of Wrath* both echo Isaiah 63:1–6.

Battle-spilled blood as high as a bridle

Chapter 14 ends with a grisly one-sentence depiction of death: "Blood flowed from the wine press, as high as a horse's bridle, for a distance of about two hundred miles" (Rev. 14:20). This is another dramatic image that most commentators don't take literally. Several accounts of ancient battles employ hyperbole to impress upon the reader the enormity of the loss of life. Josephus in his epic *The Jewish War* is a prime example. He says a million people died in the siege of Jerusalem! Similar exaggeration appears in Jewish accounts of the fall of Bar Kochba's fortress at Betar to the Romans in 135 CE. The Jerusalem Talmud says the blood from Betar flowed all the way to the Mediterranean. Despite John's hyperbole, don't minimize his main point — namely, the immense loss of life.

TECHNICAL STUFF

Simon Bar Kochba was the leader of the second revolt against Rome [132–135 CE] and publicly acclaimed Messiah by Rabbi Akiva. Bar Kochba's given name was Bar Kosiba. But Akiva changed it to Bar Kokhba, meaning "son of the star" in keeping with a messianic interpretation of Numbers 24:17: ". . .a star (*Kochav* in Hebrew) shall come out of Jacob, and a scepter shall come out of Israel." Simon was killed in the Roman assault on Betar and Akiva was executed for his part in fomenting the rebellion.

TIP

Notice that the wine press is trodden "outside the city" (Rev. 14:20). What city? Does John mean Babylon the great, whose collapse he fully describes in Revelation 18? Or does he mean Jerusalem, where the two witnesses ministered? I think he means Babylon the great, a code name for Rome and the lens through which John projects the ultimate imperial city of the antichrist.

Chapter **12**

Seven Angels, Seven Bowls, and a Final Smackdown (15:1–18:24)

The book of Revelation can seem like endless rounds of a heavyweight, world championship boxing match, with an added dash of extreme fighting and tag-team wrestling — many more combatants in the ring than two pugilists. And some of the characters are way weirder than any that show up on WWE Friday Night SmackDown! But in this match-up, the result is "fixed": The Lamb will win by a knockout. How can we know this? Because he who sits on the throne has determined the outcome and revealed (unveiled) the winner in the book of Revelation and a host of prophecies in the Scriptures. The people of God need constant reminding that the outcome of the match was never in doubt. Babylon and the beasties are going down for the count. So, if you're hanging on the ropes, hang on!

This chapter explores the final outpouring of God's wrath on rebellious humanity, spurred on by the unholy trinity: the dragon, the beast, and the false prophet (see Chapter 11). The imagery and metaphors draw heavily from the Old Testament story of the plagues on Egypt and judgment oracles found in the Hebrew prophets. The driving metaphor is that of bowls filled with God's wrath. Like a highly toxic liquid, these bowl judgments affect the entire planet rendering it uninhabitable.

In this section of Revelation, John also tantalizes the reader with more clues to the identity of both the beast and Babylon. Then, in the longest chapter in the book of Revelation (chapter 18), he composes a dirge (song of mourning) over the collapse of Babylon the great. Ironically, the saints are encouraged to join in and rejoice over Babylon's demise. Ladies and gentlemen, take your seats — the bell is about to sound on the final round.

A Preamble to God's Final Wrath (15:1–8)

Revelation 15:1–8 prepares readers for the final onslaught of God's wrath. The action unfolds in the form of a heavenly liturgy, or worship service. John first glimpses the faithful martyrs worshiping God around a sea of glass (15:2–4).

Seven angels solemnly emerge from the heavenly Temple (15:5–6). One of the four living creatures invests the seven angels with seven golden bowls containing the wrath of God (15:7). They prepare to pour out the contents, just like priests in the Jerusalem Temple regularly poured out drink offerings on the great bronze altar standing in front of the temple (1 Kings 7:50; 2 Kings 12:13). In the book of Revelation, however, the bowls are poured out on the earth, not the altar. The bowls function as a purification ritual. Fittingly, the scene concludes with the heavenly Temple filled with God's glory. None may enter its precincts until the purification is complete. The theological point, conveyed by means of priestly and liturgy imagery, is this: God's ultimate intention is to render his creation holy — that is, completely set apart for his worship and service.

TECHNICAL STUFF

The original Greek wording translates as "the sanctuary of the tent," which implies that the earthly Tabernacle was designed as a copy based on the heavenly one (see Hebrews 8:2; 9:11; cf. Exodus 25:9, 40; 26:30; 27:8).

Preparing for the end

As Revelation 15 opens, John views the proceedings from heaven. The first time John's perspective shifts to heaven occurs in Revelation 4, when he is raptured (caught up) to the heavenly throne room. This remains his vantage point until

Revelation 10–11, in which John is apparently back on earth. But Revelation 12 once again describes the action from a heavenly perspective, followed immediately by Revelation 13, in which John is back on the ground witnessing the rise of the beast and false prophet. Revelation 14 presents another visit to heaven, where he remains in Revelation 15.

TIP

Alternation between heavenly and earthly perspectives is characteristic of apocalyptic writings. Note that the book of Exodus, chapters 19–40, reveals Moses making several ascents and descents of Mount Sinai during the narrative. Perhaps this fundamental event, the Sinai theophany (appearance of God), establishing the children of Israel as the Lord's chosen people, served as a model for later visionary experiences during the Second Temple period (517 BCE–135 CE). In other words, the various recipients of visionary experiences (Enoch, Ezra, Baruch, and so on), like Moses, alternate between being in God's presence and being on earth among their fellow human beings.

For only the second time in Revelation, John describes a portent, or omen (the first mention of a portent is in Revelation 12, with the woman and the red dragon; see Chapter 11). Now, John sees seven angels who will unleash the seven final plagues. This is an omen of imminent destruction. That's the bad news.

If we can even speak of the good news, it's this: "With them the wrath of God is ended" (Rev. 15:1), meaning after the bowls are empty, it's all over.

Fulfilling two covenants

John sees what appears to be a sea of glass mixed with fire (Rev. 15:2). He also mentions the sea of glass in Revelation 4:6, indicating that it's situated directly in front of the throne of God.

By the Roman era, glass-making techniques were such that translucent glass vessels were readily available. John seems to describe glass having a highly polished glaze. John's reference to "glass mixed with fire" may describe the reflection and refraction of light coming from the throne of God.

Surrounding this surreal sea are the saints who remain steadfast in their commitment to the Lamb. They sing a song named after two key players in redemptive history: Moses and the Lamb. Moses represents the old covenant made at Mount Sinai with Israel (now embodied in the Old Testament), and the Lamb represents the new covenant made at Mount Calvary between Jesus and all who believe in him as Savior and Lord (now embodied in the New Testament).

UNDERSTANDING THE TWO COVENANTS

A *covenant* is a mutual arrangement and agreement defining a relationship between two parties. In the Bible, God enters a special relationship with certain individuals, such as Abraham (Genesis 15:18) and David (2 Samuel 7), and with a particular people, namely, Israel (Exodus 24). A covenant specifies certain obligations imposed upon the covenant partners.

The covenant between the Lord and Israel, made at Mount Sinai, was mediated by Moses (Exodus 24). It called for Israel's faithful observance of the moral and ritual commandments recorded in Exodus, Leviticus, Numbers, and Deuteronomy. For his part, the Lord promised to be their God and to bless and preserve them as a nation. Israel repeatedly broke this covenant and placed its continuance in jeopardy (Hosea 1–2).

Nonetheless, the prophets foresaw a new covenant being enacted between the Lord and Israel. The new covenant would be superior to the old one because the Lord would write it on Israel's heart so that Israel would faithfully carry out its obligations (Jeremiah 31:31–34; Ezekiel 34:25, 34:30–31, 36:25–27).

According to the New Testament, Jesus establishes this new covenant by his death, which atones for sin (Luke 22:14–20; 1 Corinthians 11:23–26). By the Holy Spirit, there's now a faithful obedience on the part of the new people of God, the new Israel (Galatians 6:16), composed of both believing Jews and Gentiles (Romans 3:21–26, 8:1–4).

REMEMBER

Both the old and new covenants share a common view of atonement: removal of the stain and guilt of sin requires shedding blood (see Hebrews 9:22). The blood of an innocent and blameless victim serves as the cleansing agent in both covenants.

Especially relevant for the study of Revelation is the borrowing of Passover imagery from the old covenant:

>> The old covenant festival of Passover features a Lamb whose blood is smeared on the lintel (top of the doorframe) and doorposts of Hebrew homes so that the destroying angel benignly passes over, sparing the lives of the inhabitants (Exodus 12:7). The ritual also reminds Israel of the Lord's promise to lead them into the Promised Land (Exodus 13:3–10). In the book of Revelation, believers in Jesus are spared the bowl judgments containing the wrath of God (7:1–17, 14:9–10, 15:2).

>> The new covenant features the ultimate fulfillment of this Old Testament ritual in Jesus, who is "the Lamb of God who takes away the sin of the world!" (John 1:29). It's more than coincidence that the primary image for Jesus in the

book of Revelation is that of "a Lamb standing as if it had been slaughtered" (Rev. 5:6). At a critical point in the action, the Lamb stands on Mount Zion with the redeemed (Rev. 14:1). Like the Lamb, the redeemed are now described as "blameless" (14:5). In the Apostle Paul's words, Jesus "rescues us from the wrath that is coming" (1 Thessalonians 1:10). This promise sustains believers through the ordeals described in Revelation (Rev. 14:12–13). The Promised Land of the old covenant becomes the New Jerusalem of the new covenant (Rev. 21–22).

The short anthem that the victors sing in Revelation 15:3–4 echoes the words of the Song of Moses in Exodus 15:1–18 and Deuteronomy 32, capturing this essential message: The holy God deserves all worship and glory. The anthem is in fact a mosaic of Old Testament texts skillfully pieced together. Not to be missed in this song is the clear implication that Jesus is the true King of the earth and the Lord God Almighty himself.

Clearing out of the Temple

A sobering scene ensues in Revelation 15:5. The portals of the heavenly sanctuary, here called "the temple of the tent of witness," open ominously. Seven angels proceed from the sanctuary. These may be the seven archangels, or seraphs (Isaiah 6:2–3, 6:6), or cherubim (Ezekiel 10:3–4). They're robed like officiating priests — white linen and golden sashes. The priestly garb draws attention to an important aspect of the heavenly throne room: continuous worship offered up by the "Angels of the Presence." The book of Hebrews, also manifesting apocalyptic features, describes angels as "spirits in the divine service" (Hebrews 1:14).

GIVING GOD SOME ALONE TIME

Two times in the history of Israel, the glory of the Lord prevents human beings from ministering in the sanctuary. After Moses finishes building and dedicating the tabernacle (narrated in Exodus 36–40), the text says, "Moses was not able to enter the tent of meeting because the cloud settled upon it, and the glory of the Lord filled the Tabernacle" (Exodus 40:35). Likewise, after Solomon builds and dedicates the First Temple, the text says, "And when the priests came out of the holy place, a cloud filled the house of the Lord, so that the priests could not stand to minister because of the cloud; for the glory of the Lord filled the house of the Lord" (1 Kings 8:10–11).

(continued)

(continued)

Two major prophets, Isaiah and Ezekiel, experience visions in which they see the heavenly sanctuary filled with smoke, symbolizing God's presence (Isaiah 6:4; Ezekiel 10:3–4). God's presence is simply overwhelming.

©CORBIS

One of the four living creatures, those angelic beings who stand closest to the throne of God (see Rev. 4:6), hands each angel a golden bowl full of the wrath of God. Immediately, God's glory, the *Shekinah* — a Hebrew word meaning *Divine Presence* — fills the Temple like thick smoke, and it's declared off-limits until the contents of the bowls are poured out and God's wrath is spent. God's reaction to human sin and rebellion is no light matter.

REMEMBER

Although the notion of God's wrath is not popular these days, Scripture insists that God's holiness and glory can't be upheld without reinstating his legitimate right to punish those who ultimately refuse and reject him as Lord. The point of this passage in Revelation 15 is to insist that God's judgment reveals his glory as surely as does his mercy (see Romans 2:4–11, 3:3–8).

Pouring Out the Seven Bowls (16:1–21)

In Revelation 16:1, a loud voice from the heavenly temple orders the pouring out of the bowls, the final series of divine judgments. Though the voice is not identified, ultimate authorization comes from God and the Lamb. In the verses that follow, seven angels pour out the contents of their bowls — the wrath of God.

In contrast to the seals and trumpets of Revelation 6–8 (see Chapters 9 and 10), the sequence of seven bowls has no distinct subdivisions, nor do any interludes separate the judgments. They're poured out without interruption. The only deviation from this flow of events occurs between the third and fourth bowl, during which an angel adds a brief commentary on the judgment, justifying God's action (Rev. 16:5–7).

Interpreting the bowls: Four views

Interpreters understand the bowl judgments in rather different ways. You may distinguish between four main views, corresponding to the four major approaches to the book. Following is a brief overview (for a more detailed discussion of these approaches, see Chapter 4):

>> **Preterist:** Preterists (those who interpret the book of Revelation solely from the perspective of the first century) try to connect these bowls with various historical events or features known to John's first readers. For example, the sixth bowl, the drying up of the Euphrates to prepare for the kings from the east, is often linked to the Parthian threat (this kingdom lay just to the east of the Euphrates and was hostile toward the Roman Empire). A legend that Nero would return to life and lead a Parthian invasion of Rome circulated widely during the latter part of the first century. Preterists don't agree, however, on the interpretation of the other bowls.

>> **Historicist:** Historicists (those who interpret the book of Revelation as if it depicts Christian history from the first century to the second coming of Jesus) diverge even more than preterists on the particulars. The reason is obvious: There's much more to consider and therefore so many more possibilities!

Typically, historicists find most of their "connections" in the Middle Ages and Reformation. The bowl judgments were often related to the religious wars that swept Europe in the sixteenth and seventeenth centuries.

Protestant historicist commentators, from the Reformation period through the nineteenth century, often identified the great whore, mystery Babylon, as the Roman Catholic Church and the papacy — a view rightly rejected by most Protestants today. A major criticism of historicism is its nearly complete omission of church history outside Europe. Western bias is apparent.

>> **Idealist:** Idealists aren't committed to discovering possible historical connections behind the bowls, because they view the book of Revelation as anessentially symbolic book depicting the ongoing struggle between good and evil. The various symbols are simply stock images drawn from Jewish apocalyptic literature. On this understanding, the message of the book is applicable to any time and place and not rooted in the historical circumstances of the first or any other century.

The problem here is the reductive nature of the approach. On a face value reading, the book proclaims more than timeless principles; it announces the victory of the Lamb *in real history*.

>> **Futurist:** Futurists hold that Revelation 4 (John's being taken up to heaven) signals a transition from John's day in the first century to the events of the Day of the Lord — that is, the Great Tribulation — the end of the age. On this understanding, the bowl judgments occur just prior to the Second Coming of Jesus. Futurists generally agree on the overall interpretation of the seven bowls, but when it comes to specifics, there's a wide range of opinion.

Most modern interpreters recognize an element of truth in each approach. The decisive question is whether the book of Revelation describes historical events or depicts principles and ideals. I think it's both-and, not either-or. Without denying that timeless principles are present, I think a moderate futurism makes the best sense of the text. That is, the book begins at the end of the first century in chapters 1–3 and concludes with the return of Jesus in chapters 19–20 and the inauguration of the new heavens and earth in chapters 21–22. But from chapter 4 onward, the focus is on the last brief period leading up to Jesus's return, the so-called Great Tribulation. The book of Revelation itself suggests that this period lasts seven years.

In our understanding of the relationship among the three series of sevens, the trumpets and bowls fall within the general time of the sixth seal, unleashing the Great Tribulation, which corresponds to the Old Testament Day of the Lord (see Chapter 9). This constitutes the final period of earth history, in which the Lamb decisively intervenes and judges human rebellion and wickedness. The number seven applied to the seals, trumpets, and bowls fittingly sums up the notion of completion and finality.

Checking out the bowls' contents

The plagues that come from the bowls, like the trumpets, are reminiscent of the plagues on Egypt. The most notable difference is the scale and intensity of these bowl judgments; they're simply off the Richter scale of seismic judgments and are truly global in their impact. In rapid succession, the contents of the seven bowls rain down on the evil empire and obliterate all resistance.

Bowl 1: Foul and painful sores erupt

The first angel pours his bowl of sores on the earth. This plague, reminiscent of the sixth plague of boils in Egypt (Exodus 9:10–11), affects only those who bear the mark of the beast (Rev. 13:16–17; see Chapter 11).

Bowls 2 and 3: The sea and fresh water turn to blood

The second angel pours his bowl into the sea. This time, the entire sea turns to blood, and all life in it perishes. The third angel pours his bowl into the fresh waters, and they, too, turn to blood. Notice that bowls two and three correspond to the first plague on Egypt, which turned the Nile River to blood (Exodus 7:19–21).

At this point comes a momentary interruption in the sequence of judgments. The angel of the waters justifies God's actions in Revelation 16:5–7:

"'You are just, O Holy One, who are and were, for you have judged these things; because they shed the blood of saints and prophets, you have given them blood to drink. It is what they deserve!' And I heard the altar respond, 'Yes, O Lord God, the Almighty, your judgments are true and just!'"

The principle invoked is deeply rooted in the Old Testament notion of justice: The punishment should fit the crime. This is known as *lex talionis,* the law of retaliation — the well-known eye-for-an-eye, tooth-for-a-tooth principle (Exodus 21:23–25).

Bowl 4: The sun scorches the earth

The fourth angel pours his bowl on the sun, causing it to increase in heat, which scorches the earth. Talk about global warming! Like a solar blowtorch, the sun bears down on earth's inhabitants with deadly intensity.

TECHNICAL
STUFF

The highest recorded temperature on earth to date is 136 degrees Fahrenheit on September 13, 1922, at El Azizia, Libya. The highest in the United States is 134 degrees Fahrenheit on July 10, 1922, at Death Valley, California. No doubt this plague far exceeds those temperatures.

How do the inhabitants of earth react to this "act of God," as so-called natural phenomena are sometimes referred to by insurance companies? They curse God and refuse to repent.

What about believers in Jesus? Aren't they affected as well? Remember that the trumpet and bowl judgments recall the Egyptian plagues, and the Hebrews weren't affected by all the plagues (Exodus 8:22, 9:6, 9:26, 10:23, 11:7).

Presumably, that's also the case with the bowl judgments of Revelation.

God seals and protects his people against his wrath.

PAYING UP FOR SIN

TECHNICAL
STUFF

In first-century Roman culture, people commonly used libation (pouring) vessels in religious rituals honoring the gods. Drink offerings were poured out to the gods on an altar. But Revelation's source for the bowl imagery probably stems from Old Testament rituals connected with Tabernacle and Temple. Golden bowls were used to catch the blood of sacrificial animals, which was then literally thrown against the base of the altar, where fire totally consumed it (Exodus 24:6; Leviticus 1:5, 3:2, 7:2).

There's a profound theological connection between expiation (making amends or reparation for wrongdoing and guilt) and retribution (punishment for wrongdoing). God's holiness, like a refining fire, totally consumes the blood offered as an atonement on the altar. In the fulfillment of this Old Testament ritual, Jesus offers his blood as the atoning sacrifice. The book of Revelation makes this point repeatedly (1:5, 5:6, 12:11, 19:13), and it runs like a scarlet thread throughout the entire New Testament (see Romans 6:10; Hebrews 7:27).

However, if sinful human beings refuse God's offer of atonement through blood shed on their behalf, the Bible says they face "a fearful prospect of judgment" (Hebrews 10:26) because "God is a consuming fire" (Hebrews 12:29). Clearly, according to the Bible, that same divine holiness consumes the unrepentant sinner (Rev. 20:14–15, 21:8). The bowls in Revelation serve a different purpose: They're vessels not of expiation but of punishment.

Bowl 5: Darkness falls

The fifth angel pours his bowl onto the throne of the beast. The very epicenter of the beast's empire is stricken with total darkness. This is no rolling blackout. In fact, the darkness is so complete it's palpable.

TURNING SEAS AND RIVERS INTO DRY LAND

The Euphrates River allows easy access to the Holy Land for an invasion force coming from the east. Twice in the Old Testament a body of water dries up permitting passage:

- During the Exodus from Egypt, the Red Sea parts and the Israelites escape certain retribution and recapture by Pharaoh and his crack chariot corps (Exodus 14).

- In the days of Joshua, the Israelites must cross the Jordan River in order to attack Jericho, the eastern gateway to Canaan, the Promised Land. The Jordan, however, is in flood stage, and the Israelites lack any means of negotiating the flood plain. The God of Israel stops the flow upriver, allowing the army of Israel to cross and initiate their invasion (Joshua 3–4).

A vision of the prophet Isaiah recorded in Isaiah 11 describes what the Lord God of Israel is going to do "on that day," a synonym for the Day of the Lord or Great Tribulation. Among those items detailed is a two fold drying up of bodies of water playing prominent roles in redemptive history:

- **The Red Sea:** In short, Isaiah envisions a new exodus. As in days of old, so in the future, says the prophet — God enables his people to escape bondage and make their way through the desert to the Promised Land. You can find this motif of a new exodus in several New Testament texts (such as Colossians 1:13).

- **The Euphrates River:** Remarkably, Isaiah also says that the Lord "will wave his hand over the River [that is, the Euphrates] with his scorching wind; and will split it into seven channels, and make a way to cross on foot; so there shall be a highway from Assyria for the remnant that is left of his people, as there was for Israel when they came up from the land of Egypt" (Isaiah 11:15–16).

This blackness only exacerbates the previous plagues and ratchets up the misery index to nearly unbearable levels. Although some commentators prefer to interpret the darkness symbolically, many see no need to depart from a more-or-less literal reading because the previous four bowls appear to be physical realities. Once again, the plague has no effect — the inhabitants curse God and refuse to repent.

Bowl 6: Kings arm for Armageddon

The sixth bowl, in Revelation 16:12, has striking similarities to the sixth trumpet (Rev. 9:14). In both cases, the Euphrates River figures prominently in the action, and demonic activity stirs up a final and decisive showdown between the dragon and the Lamb. The sixth bowl dries up the Euphrates, apparently allowing the army of an eastern coalition to cross easily.

The sixth bowl, however, doesn't relate to a return to the Holy Land (Promised Land) by the Jewish people; it involves an invading force sweeping in from the east and finding a potential barrier suddenly removed. Presumably, these forces have a hostile intent toward the Land of Israel.

Some interpreters think that this military incursion prompts the beast (see Chapter 11) to intervene and stave off the attack. The beast then proceeds to invade the Holy Land himself and proclaim himself God in the Jerusalem Temple. This perspective is based upon a futuristic interpretation of Daniel 11:40–45 and Ezekiel 38–39, along with Paul's comments about "the lawless one" in 2 Thessalonians 2:1–12.

TECHNICAL STUFF

BATTLEGROUND: YOU SAY MEGIDDO, I SAY ARMAGEDDON

The term *Harmagedon* (NRSV) or *Armageddon* (most English versions) refers to the ancient site of Megiddo, a strategic city guarding the main north-south route from Egypt to Syria. This road, later called the Via Maris ("Way of the Sea"), passes through a low ridge of hills into the fertile Jezreel Valley. Hebrew kings from Solomon onward fortified the site because it serves as a choke point controlling traffic and commerce along this important artery. Whoever controls Megiddo controls much of Canaan, the Promised Land.

As early as the sixteenth century, Pharaoh Thutmose III fought a battle against a Canaanite coalition at this site. Megiddo figures in the famous battle between the Canaanites and Israel in the days of Deborah, the prophetess and judge (Judges 4–5). The Assyrians and later the Babylonians assaulted and conquered Megiddo in their brutal conquests of the kingdoms of Israel and Judah. Even Napoleon Bonaparte won a convincing victory at Megiddo, and General Allenby, during World War I, defeated the Ottoman Turks there as well.

The sixth bowl describes the last battle, the location of which has become a house-hold word: Armageddon. The unholy trinity — the dragon, beast, and false prophet — send forth demonic emissaries to mobilize the forces of the earth against the Lamb. The demonic spirits look like frogs and are reminiscent of the second Egyptian plague of frogs (Exodus 8:1–6). The demons are successful in their war propaganda. A massive army assembles at a site laden with memories of former battles: Megiddo in the Jezreel Valley of Israel (see the sidebar "Battleground: You say Megiddo; I say Armageddon.").

Many scholars prefer to view the reference here in Revelation symbolically, seeing Megiddo as an assembly point for the coalition forces allied with the beast but not the site for the final battle. But you can also make a case for a literal reading in which a battle takes place at this ancient location. It's worth noting that the Old Testament prophets Joel and Zechariah located the main action of the Day of the Lord in the Holy Land, particularly in Jerusalem (Joel 3:1–21; Zechariah 12–14).

Bowl 7: An earthquake and hailstones shake things up

When the seventh angel pours his bowl into the air, John doesn't delay in describing what happens next (in contrast to the seals and trumpets in Revelation 6–8; see Chapters 9 and 10). An unprecedented earthquake convulses the planet, and a massive hailstorm pounds great Babylon and the entire planet with 100-pound hailstones! The devastation is complete, the evil empire collapses like a house of cards. Babylon splits into three parts, and all the cities of the world fall into ruins.

You may wonder how anyone could survive such an onslaught, but apparently many do. However, rather than call upon God for mercy and forgiveness, they curse him. John inserts another interlude in Revelation 17–18. In so doing, he provides an up-close-and-personal perspective on the mysterious Babylon, the great whore.

But First, a Word from Our End-Times Sponsor, the Lamb (16:15)

Tucked into the vision of the sixth bowl is a brief word of exhortation in Revelation 16:15: "See, I am coming like a thief! Blessed is the one who stays awake and is clothed, not going about naked and exposed to shame." In the style of the messages to the seven churches (see Chapter 7), John inscribes a word of prophecy from the Lamb himself. Though the Lamb isn't directly mentioned in

Revelation 16, you can be sure he's on the scene. The Lamb leads the charge against the evil empire and directs its destruction.

But this little word of prophecy isn't about the beast and his allies; it's intended only for believers. The message is this: Don't despair at what appears to be the success of the dragon, beast, and false prophet. Don't desert from the ranks of the Lamb and go over to the dark side. Remain steadfast and faithful to Jesus.

The imagery of the prophetic exhortation is like Jesus's teaching during his earthly ministry (for example, Matthew 24:42–44). The unexpected, open-ended timing of the return of Jesus requires constant vigilance.

In symbolic language, nakedness conveys being laid bare as a pretender and made accountable for unfaithfulness. Just as Adam and Eve, after their first act of disobedience in Genesis 3, suddenly realized their nakedness — signaling guilt and exposure to judgment — so, too, the Bible warns that anyone who abandons their allegiance to the Lamb will ultimately be revealed as fake. Psychologically, this means that all outward appearances are stripped away, leaving only the true self open to examination. Accordingly, the faithful are urged to persevere, because desertion under pressure leads only to exposure and shame.

This prophetic exhortation reminds readers of the purpose of Revelation: to maintain a firm, steadfast commitment to the gospel of Jesus. All counterfeits, whether they be the Imperial Cult of the first century or its end-times counterpart during the reign of the antichrist, must be rejected.

Exposing the Mystery of Babylon the Great (17:1–18)

Revelation 17–22 is a tale of two cities. No, I didn't borrow this from Dickens; he borrowed it from the Bible! The two cities, of course, are Babylon (Rome) and the New Jerusalem — not London and Paris as Dickens wrote about. The descriptions of these two biblical cities couldn't be more opposite. John devotes two chapters to Babylon and two chapters to the New Jerusalem. Babylon passes away; the New Jerusalem lasts forever. Another way of looking at this section portrays the two cities under the guise of two women: the great whore and the bride of the Lamb. The difference couldn't be more dramatic or pronounced.

Calling her names: Harlot on seven hills

In Revelation 17, John hits the rewind button. The seventh bowl in Revelation 16 ends with the utter collapse of Babylon. Now, he backs up and reviews the career of this wicked city, portraying it as a notorious prostitute. One of the seven angels in charge of the seven bowls becomes John's guide and conveys him down from the heavenly sanctuary to a wilderness area.

John's description of what he saw borrows imagery from Isaiah 21:1–17, a judgment oracle upon Babylon of the sixth century BCE. The setting of Isaiah's prophecy is southern Iraq and Kuwait, a desolate desert region brought vividly to television screens during two Gulf Wars. John applies Isaiah's prophecy to Imperial Rome, which in turn serves as the template for the ultimate God-defying empire of the antichrist.

An exposé of the great whore

John takes the reader behind the scenes and exposes political intrigues and treachery that eventually bring down Babylon. You gain an insider's view of the relationship between the beast and Babylon — what you might call a twisted version of *Beauty and the Beast!* In the end, the beast betrays "beautiful" Babylon and brings about her destruction.

John's description of Babylon resonates with echoes of Imperial Rome:

>> **"Seated on many waters":** The city of Rome and the empire of which it was the center controlled the waterways of the Mediterranean. In fact, by the end of the first century, the Mediterranean Sea was virtually a Roman lake. The imperial navy had numerous ports of call such as Syracuse (in Sicily), Corinth and Thessalonica (in Greece and Macedonia), Troas and Ephesus (in modern Turkey), Seleucia (in modern Syria), Alexandria (in modern Egypt), and Cyrene (in modern Libya), to name but a few. Rome plied the sea lanes to her commercial advantage, siphoning natural resources away from far-flung provinces and importing luxury items for the upper classes. Rome was the leading commercial emporium of the western world.

>> John calls Babylon "the mother of whores" (17:5) and describes her commercial activity as "fornication" because of its unjust and immoral nature. Literal prostitution was also a major cottage industry in the empire.

>> **"Sitting on a scarlet beast":** The fact that the empire sits on the beast points to the person who really wields the power. The emperor and the Imperial Cult (emperor worship) drive this vast political and mercantile enterprise. John's

description transcends a Roman emperor — though Nero Caesar certainly provides a chilling template — and embodies that ultimate dictator and tyrant, the antichrist.

>> **"Drunk with the blood":** The Roman Empire reveled in luxury and sensuality (17:4–5), all the while exhibiting extreme cruelty. Utter indifference to human need and dignity characterizes the moral climate. John draws special attention to the role of Rome in persecuting believers in Jesus. The image is appalling: "The woman was drunk with the blood of the saints and the blood of the witnesses to Jesus" (17:6).

In the book of Revelation, Babylon functions symbolically as the ultimate center of power for the antichrist. Freely borrowing language and imagery from Old Testament prophetic texts speaking of historic Babylon, John reapplies these to a first-century counterpart, the great city of Rome. Babylon and Rome are mirror images of each other — both dens of injustice and wonders to behold. They embody, in the words of a Clint Eastwood movie, "the good, the bad, and the ugly." In that respect, the original Babylon and Rome anticipate the appearance of that final Babylon: organized, rebellious humanity, oblivious to or pitted against the kingdom of the God and the Lamb.

ROME BY ANY OTHER NAME

Most New Testament scholars think Babylon is a code word for Rome. Just as Babylon, under Nebuchadnezzar II, destroyed Jerusalem and the First Temple and gloated over it, so Rome would play a similar role in the complete destruction of Jerusalem and the Second Temple.

In Jewish literature of the late first century, Rome is called Babylon (2 Esdras, 2 Baruch, and Sibylline Oracles), recalling its ancient role as nemesis and persecutor.

Even Peter concludes his first epistle (letter), written to primarily Gentile Christians in Asia Minor, by saying, "Your sister church in Babylon, chosen together with you, sends you greetings; and so does my son Mark" (1 Peter 5:13). Is Peter living at the ancient site of Great Babylon? Probably not. So why doesn't Peter just come right out with it and mention Rome by name? Well, the first epistle dates to just after the bloodbath that Nero initiated in 64 CE. Thousands of Christians perished. Peter is sensitive to the fact that another wave of persecution is possible. He doesn't want his letter to fall into the hands of government informers and be misconstrued as anti-government propaganda.

Unlocking the interpretation

John doesn't leave you to your own imagination for interpreting the passage about the whore of Babylon. An angelic informant reveals the key, and John records it in Revelation 17:7–18.

SEVEN HEADS

The scarlet beast's seven heads serve a twofold function: They're both seven hills and seven kings:

>> **Seven hills:** This piece of information points to Rome, long famous for its seven hills. The seven hills are Palatine, Capitol, Aventine, Caelian, Esquiline, Viminal, and Quirinal. References to these famous seven hills abound in the writings of historians and literary figures of the ancient world.

>> **Seven kings:** The seven heads represent seven kings. Interestingly, five of them have already died at the time of John's writing, one is currently in office, and the sixth is coming but has a noticeably short tenure.

An eighth king, says John, belongs to the seven and is none other than the beast from the bottomless pit — the one who was, is not, and is yet to come. In short, the eighth king is the antichrist, who appears to die and return to life. This correlates with the description of the beast in Revelation 13.

Some commentators argue that John is referring to the Roman emperors in this passage and claim that the eighth king was Domitian. After all, if you begin with Augustus Caesar, reckoned as the first emperor, the chronological sequence is as follows:

1. Augustus (27 BCE–14 CE)
2. Tiberius (14–37 CE)
3. Gaius [Caligula] (37–41 CE)
4. Claudius (41–54 CE)
5. Nero (54–68 CE)
6. Vespasian (69–79 CE)
7. Titus (79–81 CE)
8. Domitian (81–96 CE)

After Nero committed suicide in July of 68 CE, three men unsuccessfully laid claim to the title: Galba, Otho, and Vitellius. All three fell to assassins after short tenures. During this unstable period, Vespasian was leading five Roman legions against the Jewish rebels in Palestine (66–73 CE). When his legionnaires acclaimed him emperor, he quickly returned to Rome and seized power. This turbulent period was the so-called "year of the four emperors." Many scholars leave the three wannabes out of the reckoning because their stints were too short to qualify as emperors.

The problems fitting this historical sequence of emperors into John's scheme are considerable:

>> The only one on the list who fits nicely with John's scheme is number seven, Titus: "When he comes, he must remain only a little while." (Rev. 17:10). He reigned just over two years and then unexpectedly died of a fever (79–81 CE).

>> Julius Caesar, though the first to be called *imperator* (emperor), never officially assumed the title or office. If you do begin with him, this throws off the entire scheme in that Domitian now becomes the ninth.

>> Three claimants to the throne — Galba, Otho, and Vitellius — were considered legitimate emperors by the Jewish historian Josephus, as well as by a first-century work called the *Sibylline Oracles*. Including them makes Domitian the twelfth emperor.

>> John indicates that the king who is currently reigning is the sixth. According to the numbered sequence, the sixth king is Vespasian. Most scholars opt for the reign of Domitian as the time when Revelation was written, but for the sequence to fit John's scheme, Domitian needs to be the sixth king.

But should anyone even try to harmonize John's scheme with the list of Roman emperors? Given the symbolic nature of the number seven, this may only suggest the complete power and dominance of these kings. The beast is identified with these kings in that he, too, embodies absolute authority over his subjects. In that sense, he is one with them and thus the eighth.

Despite problems and uncertainties, John's essential point is clear: Imperial Rome, with its seriously flawed emperors, is mystery Babylon. But John may be using imperial Rome as the lens through which to portray that ultimate Babylon, the tool of the beast from the bottomless pit.

TEN HORNS

The beast's ten horns refer to a coalition of kings who ally themselves with him. In biblical thought, the horn of a bull, ram, or goat symbolizes strength and power.

In apocalyptic writings, an animal horn frequently represents powerful kings or generals (see, for example, Daniel 8). This alliance of ten kings was not yet in existence in John's day — that remains for a designated time called "one hour" (Rev. 17:12).

John draws his imagery from the book of Daniel, in which a fourth and final earthly kingdom, described as "terrifying and dreadful and exceedingly strong," is depicted as having ten horns (Daniel 7:7). Later in the same chapter, Daniel discovers that the ten horns represent ten kings who arise in connection with an insolent person who speaks against God and persecutes believers (Daniel 7:24–25). This dovetails with the career of the beast in Revelation 13, the antichrist. Ominously, John reveals that these ten kings will unite in battle against the Lamb. Yet, their joint effort fails, and victory goes to the Lamb.

WATERS

The waters represent a multinational, multiethnic empire. The beast forges his empire as a tool for achieving his own ambitions and, of course, those of the great dragon who energizes and spurs him on. This interpretive key points to imperial Rome as the template for the final evil empire.

The Roman Empire, at the end of the first century, was the largest and most diverse empire the world had ever known. Lest there be any lingering doubt or confusion in his readers' mind, John decodes the mystery woman: "The great city that rules over the kings of the earth" (Rev. 17:18). No other city but Rome fills the bill. End-Times Babylon exercises the same influence and sway as imperial Rome did in the first century.

The beast bites back

As the chapter ends, John mentions something that comes as a surprise: "And the ten horns that you saw, they and the beast will hate the whore; they will make her desolate and naked; they will devour her flesh and burn her up with fire. For God has put it into their hearts to carry out his purpose by agreeing to give their kingdom to the beast, until the words of God will be fulfilled."

Despite using Babylon to achieve his own ends, the beast and his allies (ten kings) harbor deep hatred for the imperial capital. They plot her complete destruction. The book of Revelation provides no rationale for this reversal. But I think we can surmise why they did it. They are ambitious politicians who loathe to share power and glory more than they have to. They covet the wealth and influence of Babylon the Great and want it all for themselves. As witnessed so many times in human history, covetousness is self-destructive.

In the end, however, it is God who decrees the destruction of mystery Babylon. Though quite oblivious to the sovereignty of God these despots do his bidding. The great city is burned up (19:3), a fate suffered by most ancient cities sacked by invading armies. But Babylon's burning is everlasting in duration, a sure indicator of divine, not human retribution.

Loveless in the Ruins: Celebrating Babylon's Fall (18:1–24)

Remember the nursery rhyme, "London bridge is falling down, falling down, falling down. London bridge is falling down, My fair lady"? The lyrics and fun games that go with this ditty derive from something quite grim. Historians trace it back to the medieval period when London Bridge suffered ruin multiple times by war, tornado, and fire. The "fair lady" may refer to the practice of burying a dead virgin in the foundation of a bridge to ensure its strength and longevity. Or she may be Queen Eleanor of Aquitaine, the mother of two kings of England, Richard the Lionhearted and John Lackland.

UNCOVERING THE REAL BABYLON

The story of Babylon begins in the book of Genesis, when the hero Nimrod founds a city named Babel (Genesis 10:10). The name means *gate of god,* already hinting at the city's self-claim to fame. At any rate, the city first appears in the historical record when Sharkalisharri (about 2250 BCE) mentions that he moved dirt from Babel to Agade, thereby transferring Babel's authority and sanctity to the new location.

During the second millennium BCE, the city of Babylon achieved new heights of prosperity under the guidance of Hammurabi (1792–1950 BCE), famous for his Code of Hammurabi, one of the earliest written law codes. He enlarged the city and extended its commercial ties.

The first millennium BCE found Babylon at the center of power struggles between the Assyrians (northern Iraq) and the more southerly tribes of Babylonia. Sargon II, king of Assyria and conqueror of Samaria (2 Kings 17:6), the northern kingdom of Israel's capital city, swept into Babylon in 710 BCE. Babylonia didn't regain independence until about 626 BCE.

The city came into its own under the leadership of the Babylonian superstar Nebuchadnezzar II (605–562 BCE). After claiming the throne in 605 BCE and defeating an Egyptian and Assyrian coalition at Carchemish, Nebuchadnezzar headed the most powerful military in the ancient Near East. Judea finally fell after foolishly rebelling against Nebuchadnezzar, provoking his destruction of Jerusalem and the temple in 586 BCE. He used Judean craftsmen and builders to enlarge and beautify Babylon. The massive Ishtar gates, hanging gardens of Babylon, soaring temples and ziggurats (towers), and waterways and palaces made it the most impressive city the world had yet seen. Hebrew prophets like Isaiah (Isaiah 13) and Jeremiah (Jeremiah 50–51), however, prophesied her fall because of cruelty to Judah.

And Babylon did fall — with no shots fired! Cyrus the Persian entered the city after diverting the Euphrates River that flowed right down its middle. By night, his soldiers simply walked up the now-empty riverbed right into the heart of the city. The city itself welcomed Cyrus as a liberator, and he assumed the title "King of Babylon" (539 BCE). For Jews, Babylon became a byword for all that's cruel and evil. Later, when Rome became master of the Mediterranean, Jews used Babylon as a code word for Rome. A famous Jewish oracle *(Sibylline Oracles)* gleefully prophesies the demise of this "new Babylon." As you can see in the book of Revelation, early Christians shared a similar sentiment regarding Rome.

Persian monarchs after Cyrus the Great, like Xerxes, neglected Babylon. This lasted until Alexander the Great swept across Asia Minor and into the heartland of the Persian Empire. After he defeated the Medes at Gaugamela, the city of Babylon welcomed him as a liberator (331 BCE). Alexander had great plans for the city, but he didn't live long enough to realize them. In the power struggles between Alexander's successors, Babylon fared poorly. Eventually, a new city, Seleucia, became the seat of government, and Babylon declined in importance. Though not totally abandoned, the city never regained its former glory. During New Testament times, a small town lay in the vicinity of the ancient site. Today, ancient Babylon is uninhabited; it remains, however, an important archaeological site.

Seen in this light, the nursery rhyme has two things in common with Revelation 18: Both recount a catastrophic collapse, and both feature a *femme fatale*. In Revelation 18, the spotlight falls on Queen Babylon, the great whore (17:1–2), who speaks in a soliloquy (a monologue), affording a window into her thoughts: "I rule as a queen; I am no widow, and I will never see grief" (Rev. 18:7). She revels in her seductive charm and power and considers herself invincible — a mistake powerful people often repeat.

The book of Daniel narrates a story (or fable) about Nebuchadnezzar II. While walking on the roof of his royal palace and surveying the great city of Babylon, he became inflated with his own self-importance and achievements: "Is this not magnificent Babylon, which I have built as a royal capital by my mighty power and for my glorious majesty?" Because of his overweening pride, God visits Nebuchadnezzar with a serious mental illness. Later, when he recovers, he makes an amazing confession: "I blessed the Most High, and praised and honored the one who lives forever. For his sovereignty is an everlasting sovereignty, and his kingdom endures from generation to generation" (Daniel 4:34). Before his fall from power, Saddam Hussein spent great sums to restore and reconstruct the ancient site of Babylon. He even erected gigantic statues of himself portrayed as Nebuchadnezzar! The statues were toppled and Saddam executed. Like these two dictators, Queen Babylon never gets the point and pays dearly for her arrogance.

Singing stinging sarcasm

A mighty angel announces the fall of Babylon the Great. This section is composed as a dirge, a lament sung at funerals:

> "Fallen, fallen is Babylon the great! It has become a dwelling-place of demons, a haunt of every foul spirit, a haunt of every foul bird, a haunt of every foul and hateful beast. For all the nations have drunk of the wine of the wrath of her fornication, and the kings of the earth have committed fornication with her, and the merchants of the earth have grown rich from the power of her luxury." (Rev. 18:2–3)

TECHNICAL STUFF

In popular imagination, undesirable creatures, whether animal or demonic, haunted the abandoned ruins of ancient cities. Isaiah 13:21–22 gives expression to these fears: "But wild animals will lie down there, and its houses will be full of howling creatures; there ostriches will live, and there goat-demons will dance. Hyenas will cry in its towers, and jackals in the pleasant palaces [. . .]" Travelers avoided such places, and frightening tales about the horrible things that happened there reinforced the stigma. Ghosts and ghouls hover in the rubble of formerly magnificent buildings. Such is the portrait of once-great Babylon in Revelation 18:2.

The reference to "the wine of the wrath of her fornication" is difficult to interpret. It combines two ideas:

>> Strong passion (the basic meaning of the Greek word *thumos*) aroused by the seductive power of Queen Babylon

>> God's wrath (divine punishment), which comes because of participating in the corrupt, immoral, and oppressive economic system of the great whore

This is a lament with a twist, however. It's a taunt song, a mocking dirge. That is, it celebrates the demise of a tyrant or wicked regime under the guise of a funeral lament. The wording of Revelation 18:2–3 draws on the language of Old Testament taunt songs (Isaiah 21:9; Jeremiah 50:39, 51:8). In fact, one of the most famous Old Testament taunt songs celebrates the death of a Babylonian dictator (Isaiah 14:3–21).

Revelation 18:3 serves to justify the treatment of Babylon. Why does she experience this fate? Using the language of the Old Testament prophets, John fastens on the damning sin of this vast political, economic, and military enterprise. The key word is *fornication.*

REMEMBER

To *fornicate* often means, in the Old Testament prophets, to break faith with the God of Israel and follow other so-called gods. This amounts to disloyalty, the fundamental sin of the Ten Commandments: "You shall have no other gods before me" (Exodus 20:3). Babylon the Great proclaims another god: the god of consumption, wealth, pleasure, and self-indulgence. Her motto is essentially *spend your way to happiness.* In short, the great sin of Babylon is to prefer creation to the Creator. In his letter to the Romans, the Apostle Paul provides an apt commentary on this section: "They exchanged the truth about God for a lie and worshiped and served the creature rather than the Creator, who is blessed forever! Amen" (Romans 1:25).

Fleeing the scene to safety

Revelation 18:4 warns believers to escape from Babylon and to have nothing to do with her (18:4). Drawing on language like that used by Jeremiah in the sixth century BCE (Jeremiah 51:45), John applies it to Rome, the Babylon of his day. Many scholars believe Rome serves as the template for End-Times Babylon, that final world empire utterly opposed to God and the Lamb.

John warns believers not to become enmeshed in the attitudes and lifestyle of Queen Babylon. To do so is to betray the values of the Lamb and his kingdom. Christians during the first century constantly struggled with the difficulty of making a clean break from the idol-worshipping Greco-Roman culture in which they lived and worked. Several New Testament passages highlight the temptation to slide back into their previous lifestyle (see 2 Corinthians 6:14–18; Galatians 4:8–11; Ephesians 4:17–24, 5:6–14; 1 John 2:15–17).

Shedding no tears for the fallen

In Revelation 18:5–8, John justifies the harshness of the sentence on Queen Babylon. Babylon deserves what she gets. In fact, her sins "are heaped high as heaven" (a phrase drawn from Jeremiah 51:9). Because of her self-indulgence and refusal to acknowledge God, she receives a sentence twice as harsh as expected, "double for her deeds" (see Jeremiah 50:29; Isaiah 40:2).

Consider Queen Marie Antoinette before the French Revolution — unaware of the hardships just beyond the palace walls, she indulged in trivial pleasures and extravagant comforts. The French Republic executed her by guillotine (beheading).

Reeling from financial collapse: Goods gone bad

In Revelation 18:9–20, John describes what amounts to a first-century version of SkyMall magazine — a catalog featuring the wares and finery of the absolute best stores in Rome. This extensive list of goods, imported from the far-flung corners of the empire, illustrates the insatiable appetite of the rich and powerful upper crust of Roman society. But instead of a tale in which money buys happiness, the passage reads like a wake.

Lamenting market loss

Kings, merchants, shipmasters, seafarers, and sailors, standing at a safe distance, lament the demise of this mercantile marvel. The political leaders are the first to intone their regret and shock: "Alas, alas, the great city, Babylon the mighty city! For in one hour your judgment has come" (Rev. 18:10). They're stunned. Nobody saw this coming.

Next, the merchants of the earth express their distress and grief in weeping and wailing. No more sales! No more profits! They can't comprehend that their wealth is gone: "All your dainties and your splendor are lost to you, never to be found again!" (Rev. 18:14). When America experienced the Wall Street crash on "Black Tuesday," October 29, panic and despair hung over Wall Street like a pall. Several financiers even committed suicide.

The merchant marines next offer their condolences. The scope of destruction is beyond their comprehension. First-century Rome was like a magnet attracting an unending flow of goods arriving on a vast network of waterways. The volume of commerce created a huge transportation industry. Following Middle Eastern funeral customs, the mariners throw dust on their heads as a sign of extreme grief and sorrow (Rev. 18:19). They are stunned by the suddenness of the disaster: "For in one hour she has been laid waste" (Rev. 18:19).

Ill-gotten gains

The bottom line is that with the fall of Babylon, the movers and shakers lose control of their economic and political empire. But before you feel sorry for them, look more closely at how they acquired such wealth and how they spent it. The lions' share of the imports were extracted unfairly from subject peoples; furthermore, the items listed in Revelation 18:1–13 are luxury items. The vast majority of citizens and non-citizens of the empire could never afford them, anyway. Here's what the Roman socio-economic pyramid looked like:

» **Slaves:** Anywhere from one-third to one-half of the population of imperial Rome were slaves. Not to be overlooked in this catalog of goods are the last two items: "slaves — and human lives." Slave trafficking was a common evil in the economic fabric of the empire (Rev. 18:13).

» **Freedmen:** These were individuals who were either born free or were able to work themselves out of slavery. Most of these folks, who made up a large segment of Roman society, were craftsmen and day laborers who did the grunt work for the empire.

» **Nobility and upper-class families:** This relatively small minority controlled the wealth and resources of the empire.

In reality, only a small proportion of society directly benefited from this immense wealth. To be sure, the wealthy and powerful often acted as benefactors and provided public works and programs for the masses. But this was little more than a bread crumb, and it didn't significantly lower the misery index for the average citizen, freedman or slave.

According to John, this system is fundamentally immoral. The good news of Revelation is that it will be dismantled and replaced. The book of Revelation envisions a vastly superior world to come. The other woman in the story, Queen Jerusalem, the beautiful bride of the Lamb, offers a truly "Great Society."

Ding-dong! The witch is dead!

One segment of society doesn't lament the demise of Queen Babylon. The people of God, designated as "saints and apostles and prophets" (Rev. 18:20), say goodbye and good riddance to this "mother of whores." It's a day of rejoicing. The setting for this portion assumes a courtroom. Queen Babylon is in the dock. She is arraigned for a wide array of crimes and offenses, not the least of which is the murder of countless saints (Rev. 17:6, 18:24). The verdict comes down from God, the supreme judge. Babylon is guilty as charged and sentenced to extinction (Rev. 18:20).

The imagery describing Babylon's end is striking. A mighty angel tosses a huge millstone into the sea and gives voice to this dramatic symbolic action: "With such violence Babylon the great city will be thrown down and will be found no more" (Rev. 18:21). (If this seems to conflict with the earlier image of destruction by fire, remember that this is poetry, not prose — strict logic need not apply.) The point is clear enough: Babylon sinks to the bottom of the sea, a fitting end to a city and system conjured up from the depths of the sea.

John probably borrows his imagery from Jeremiah's prophecy against the Babylon of Nebuchadnezzar's day in the sixth century BC: "When you finish reading this scroll, tie a stone to it, and throw it into the middle of the Euphrates, and say, 'Thus shall Babylon sink, to rise no more, because of the disasters that I am bringing on her'" (Jeremiah 51:63–64).

The dirge that accompanies the symbolic action opens another window into the life and times of first-century Rome. The reader glimpses musicians, artisans, and merchants, along with bridegrooms and brides. The language draws heavily from two Old Testament passages:

>> **Jeremiah 25:10:** The first, ironically, is a prophecy directed against Judah and Jerusalem, predicting that Nebuchadnezzar of Babylon will most certainly destroy the land. John, however, reverses the recipient of destruction: Babylon, not Jerusalem, falls this time.

>> **Ezekiel 26:13:** The Ezekiel passage is a judgment oracle uttered against the city of Tyre (located in modern Lebanon just to the north of Israel). Once again, Nebuchadnezzar is the agent of retribution against this ancient city, notorious for its greed and corruption. John simply borrows the imagery of destruction to make his point: No music, no creativity, no business and commerce, no joys and pleasures of life animate great Babylon; instead, she sits silent and solitary in the darkness at the bottom of the sea, never to seduce again.

IN THIS CHAPTER

» Rejoicing in God's justice and dressing up for a wedding

» Seeing a shocking supper

» Entering the Millennium

» Binding and loosing Satan

» Standing at the great white throne

Chapter **13**

Coming of the Kingdom (19:1–20:15)

The focal point of Revelation 19 is the long-awaited return of the King. Revelation 19 also juxtaposes two suppers and sketches more details about the battle of Armageddon and the Lamb's stunning triumph over Satan.

Next, Revelation 20 features a golden age, an idyllic time, in which the Lamb and the Fellowship of the Lamb reign on earth for a Millennium, 1,000 years. However, the exact meaning of the Millennium has generated considerable debate over the centuries. In this chapter, I sort out the different views.

Finally, I explore another mystery in Revelation 20. Satan, the ancient archenemy and antagonist, is bound at the beginning of the Millennium. Inexplicably, at its conclusion, he's released from prison. True to form, he sets about doing what he's always done: deceiving people and stirring up rebellion. He enlists another army more powerful than even the beast and the ten kings could muster in Revelation 19. They assault the very center of the Lamb's kingdom, the beloved city. The response to this attack is devastating and decisive: Fire devours the satanic army and Satan is cast into a lake of fire.

After the smoke clears, the scene shifts, and a majestic white throne comes into view, marking the moment of final judgment — often known as Doomsday.

Ultimately, two destinies await: entry into the New Jerusalem or consignment to the lake of fire.

In this chapter, you explore these decisive and epic events and delve deeper into the theological perplexities surrounding the Millennium and hell.

Returning as Promised (19:1–21)

In Revelation 19, five angelic anthems or acclamations herald the imminent return of the rightful king, King Jesus. Each one provides additional commentary on the demise of Babylon the Great and the defeat of the beast and false prophet. Four different titles for the Lamb appear in this section, each adding luster to his character and status.

This part of Revelation essentially describes what happens to the beast, the false prophet, and their vast army of ten kings. A sharp sword issuing from the mouth of him who is called "Faithful and True" and "the Word of God" destroys the allied forces. As for the beast and false prophet, they're captured alive and consigned to the lake of fire. Believers, on the other hand, are invited to the marriage supper of the Lamb and his bride.

Having a roaring good time

A massive heavenly choir leads off the celebration with a *doxology*. The anthem begins with a rousing "Hallelujah!" This keynote captures the mood of the heavenly courts.

The choir voices the appropriateness for thanksgiving and praise. In short, God acts in accord with his faithfulness and justice (Rev. 19:2). He upholds his promises, and his character never changes. Because this is so, the great whore receives her just "reward." She, by contrast, reveals her true character as unfaithful. Not only does she break faith with God, she also viciously persecutes his covenant partners, the people of God.

A second hallelujah rings out, declaring the duration of her punishment: "forever and ever" (Rev. 19:3). This raises some hard theological questions, which I explore in the section titled "Struggling to understand hell," later in this chapter.

ANOTHER WORD FOR BOOYAH!

Hallelujah! Christians the world over, who otherwise may not know Hebrew from Hindi, regularly sing, chant, pray, shout, or whisper this Hebrew word. Meaning literally *praise the Lord*, it resonates with deep spiritual and emotional overtones.

By the time you get to Revelation 19, you see that the people of God are shouting *Hallelujah!* all over the place in the wake of the Lamb's total victory over the unholy trinity (dragon, beast, and false prophet) and their allies.

The 24 elders and the four living creatures prostrate themselves before God's throne and add their voices to the heavenly liturgy: "Amen. Hallelujah!" (Rev. 19:4). The word *amen* comes from Hebrew, and it conveys the notion of that which is firm, established, and true. The angelic beings closest to God's throne thus affirm and agree with God's judgment.

Next, an unidentified voice "from the throne," perhaps one of the four living creatures, sings a solo part: "Praise our God, all you his servants, and all who fear him, small and great" (Rev. 19:5).

The angelic choir responds, antiphonally (singing in alternating parts) and in unison. The sound is overwhelming. Like waves crashing against a rocky shoreline during a thunderstorm, the concluding anthem resounds through the heavenly sanctuary. Two events are the subject of the lyrics:

>> **The Lord reigns:** All resistance crumbles. The ringleaders of the Dark Lord's kingdom are incarcerated. The fulfillment of the Lord's Prayer is a reality: "Your kingdom come. Your will be done, on earth as it is in heaven" (Matthew 6:10).

>> **The saints prepare for a wedding:** The imagery is striking but not unique; it draws upon a rich tradition in which Old Testament Israel is compared to a bride and God (Yahweh) is her husband (Isaiah 54:6–8; Jeremiah 2:1–3; Ezekiel 16:8–14; and Hosea 2:14–23). John now applies it to the Lamb (the groom) and the church (the bride), as he also does in his Gospel (John 3:29). The bride dresses in white as a symbol of purity.

Avoiding angel worship

In Revelation 19:9–10, John writes,

"And the angel said to me, 'Write this: Blessed are those who are invited to the marriage supper of the Lamb.' And he said to me, 'These are true words of God.' Then I fell down at his feet to worship him, but he said to me, 'You must not do that! I am a fellow-servant with you and your comrades who hold the testimony of Jesus. Worship God! For the testimony of Jesus is the spirit of prophecy.'"

The authenticity of the invitation is certified: "These are true words of God." No need to check with Sotheby's auction house on the genuineness of this invitation! This is the fourth of seven beatitudes or blessings John records in his book. (See Rev. 1:3; 14:13; 16:15; 19:9; 20:6; 22:7; 22:14.)

Once again, the prophet John interacts with his heavenly guide by prostrating himself (bowing down) to worship the angel. For this he is sharply rebuked: "You must not do that!" (Rev. 19:10). This episode serves as a warning to congregations in Asia against the veneration of angels. Paul's letters to the Colossians and Ephesians (both in the province of Asia) and the anonymous letter to the Hebrews suggest that venerating angels and boasting about visionary ascents to the heavenly throne room to participate in angelic worship were potential sources of error and false pride (Colossians 2:18; Ephesians 1:20–23; and Hebrews 1:4). The corrective is clear: "Worship God! For the testimony of Jesus is the spirit of prophecy" (19:10). This affirmation links the Old and New Testaments. In short, Jesus is the central biblical figure of redemptive history, as is said at the outset of the book of Revelation (Rev. 1:2; see also John 1:1–3, 1:14; 1 John 1:1–3).

YOU CAN'T CRASH THIS WEDDING

Jesus uses the metaphor of a wedding banquet in his ministry. In Matthew's Gospel, a parable about a king who prepares a lavish wedding banquet for his son only to be humiliated by the invited guests' refusal to come, highlights the spiritual blindness of the religious leadership of his day (Matthew 22:2-10).

Jesus takes the parable further by sketching a scenario in which a person shows up at the wedding banquet without the proper attire. The point is clear: One must be an invited guest to attend — no wedding crashers allowed! (Matthew 22:11-12). The point of Revelation 19:9 is the same: Only those belonging to the Fellowship of the Lamb, the true bride of Christ enjoy the blessing of this grand occasion.

Making a grand entrance

In Revelation 19:11, John writes, "I saw heaven opened, and there was a white horse!" For only the second time in the book, the heavens open. In the first instance, he ascended to the heavenly throne room to observe "what is to take place after this" (1:19). This time, there isn't an ascent but a dramatic descent: King Jesus comes down on a white horse, followed by the armies of heaven. These two heavenly portal openings frame the narrative action in chapters 4–20.

Figuring out who's on this white horse

The appearance of the white horse in Revelation 19:11 recalls the first seal in Revelation 6:2, where another figure rides a white horse. Some scholars suggest that the rider in chapter 6 stands for Jesus himself, symbolizing the spread of the gospel.

While both figures ride white horses, this doesn't mean they are on the same side. Some scholars argue that the rider in Revelation 6 stands for the spirit of the antichrist — already active at the end of the first century — spreading deception and falsehood (see 1 John 2:18–25). If so, these two white horse riders bookend Revelation 6–20 with a striking contrast: the final rider, Jesus, arrives to decisively overcome all opposition. Not only is he worthy, but he also has no rival.

Getting four names for one rider

Four names identify the rider on the white horse. Of course, John's readers already know who he is. These names speak to the character and qualifications of King Jesus. Each name highlights certain attributes or characteristics qualifying him to be the redeemer and rightful ruler of humanity:

- » **"Faithful and True":** The faithfulness of Jesus is a keynote in the book of Revelation. He is "the faithful witness" (Rev. 1:5, 3:14). Since there's no falsehood in him, he stands in splendid contrast to the dragon and his demons, who specialize in deceit and lies.

- » **Name known only to the rider:** This title reminds the reader that because Jesus is God, there are dimensions of his being and person that are inaccessible to mere mortals.

- » **"The Word of God":** This title connects the book of Revelation with the Gospel of John and is one of the indicators of common authorship. John doesn't elaborate on the pre-existence and creative activity of Jesus in Revelation as he does in his Gospel (John 1:1–5). But he does allude to it.

Jesus strikes with a sword from his mouth. This figure of speech means that he simply speaks a word of command, and it is so (see Genesis 1:3, 6; Psalm 33:6; Mark 4:39–41).

>> **"King of kings and Lord of lords":** This title answers a central question posed in the book of Revelation: Who's in charge? The repetition in the title (King of kings) reflects a characteristic of the Hebrew language: using repetition to emphasize something superlative or unique. Even though John writes in Greek, you can still, detect here and there the influence of the Aramaic-Hebrew language on his Greek. In short, Jesus is a king and a lord without peer. The title appears in a prominent location — on the rider's flowing robe and along their upper leg, where a warrior's sword would customarily rest. It's possible that even the sword itself is inscribed with this powerful title.

The robe has another distinctive mark: It's dipped in blood (Rev. 19:13). Does this refer to Jesus's sacrificial death, or is the image that of a warrior whose garment is stained with the blood of fallen enemies? Perhaps both images are intended; both ideas are rooted in biblical imagery (see Rev. 1:5, 5:6, 5:12, 7:14, and 12:11 for the sacrificial nuance, and Isaiah 42:13, 63:3–6; Habakkuk 3:11–14; and Zephaniah 3:17 for the conquering hero metaphor).

Taking multiple, descriptive names is a traditional practice among monarchs, both ancient and modern. At their coronation, leaders often assume throne names, which become part of the royal ideology. For example, Isaiah 9:6 lists four throne names of the prophesied Messiah: "Wonderful Counselor, Mighty God, Everlasting Father, Prince of Peace." Each name is a fitting description of the messianic King.

KNOWING GOD'S NAME

Throughout the ancient Near East, people believed that knowing a god's name could grant special favor or power. In contrast, the Bible teaches that knowing God's name draws a person into a deeper relationship and fellowship with the divine, but not as a magical formula (see Exodus 33:12, 18–19; John 17:6). Scripture makes clear that knowing God's name doesn't give humans control over God; rather, God's name controls all creatures and creation (Genesis 32:29; Exodus 3:13–15; Judges 13:17–18; Acts 19:13–16; Philippians 2:9–11).

TECHNICAL STUFF

While readers of the King James Version (KJV) of the Bible might see five names listed in Isaiah 9:6, this is due to a comma placed after "Wonderful," which separates it from "Counselor" as if they were distinct titles. George Frideric Handel used this translation in the libretto of the "Hallelujah Chorus," the grand and glorious finale of the oratorio *The Messiah*. Modern English versions, however, rightly give it as "Wonderful Counselor." Jewish scribes known as the Masoretes added punctuation and vowel marks to the Hebrew text around 700 CE and understood the passage as consisting of four titles, each made up of two words. This approach creates a balanced series of royal names, emphasizing the grandeur and significance of the Messiah's character.

Picking the bones clean and taking prisoners

John rewinds the tape of the last days' events as Revelation 19 concludes. He wants to show the battle scene at Armageddon one last time. The vision features another invitation to a banquet called "the great supper of God" (Rev. 19:17). But what a contrast to the marriage supper of the Lamb! If the former is glorious — a white-robe-only affair — this one is gory, a macabre feast of decaying flesh. An angel summons scavenger birds, like vultures, to the scene of the battle, a cosmic cleanup crew! So ends the army recruited by the beast and false prophet. One thinks of Matthew Brady photographs taken in the aftermath of Civil War battles that so shocked the American public — bloated, blackened, stiff corpses littered across the fields.

The spotlight now turns to the ringleaders themselves. What fate befalls the beast and the false prophet? They are swiftly seized and, without ceremony or trial, cast alive into the lake of fire burning with sulfur, as described in Revelation 19:20. But how is their army vanquished so suddenly? With just a word from the rider on the white horse — a sword proceeding from his mouth — his foes are slain in an instant. The same divine word that once summoned the universe into being (Genesis 1; Colossians 1:15; John 1:1–3) now pronounces their demise. No weapon of human invention could ever rival such overwhelming power.

Dawning of the Millennial Age (20:1–6)

Revelation 20:1–6 pictures an unprecedented moment in human history. The arch deceiver, Satan, who also bears four descriptive throne titles (note the irony!), is unmasked and incarcerated. Here are his aliases:

>> **Dragon:** This descriptive title, indebted to an ancient Near Eastern myth in which a chaos monster threatens to destroy the created order, depicts Satan as a dragon. As such, Satan is the archetypal chaos monster.

>> **Serpent:** This title may also reflect ancient Near Eastern mythology in which a snake tricks humanity and prevents their obtaining immortality. But even more relevant is the account of the serpent's deception of the first human couple in Genesis 3. Revelation 20:3 explicitly says why Satan is consigned to the bottomless pit: "so that he would deceive the nations no more."

>> **Devil:** The Greek word *diabolos*, translated as "Devil," means "one who slanders." Characteristic of the Devil's tactics are his slanderous accusations brought against God and his people (see Job 1–2; Revelation 12:10).

>> **Satan:** The basic meaning of this word is "adversary." That pretty much sums up Satan's *modus operandi*: He resists, obstructs, and subverts all attempts to realize God's kingdom on earth. He is the "mother of all adversaries."

With the Devil imprisoned, the reign of the Lamb begins. Jesus resurrects the faithful martyrs, granting them authority to rule alongside him for 1,000 years — a period marked by a unique blessing for all who share in this era (Revelation 20:6). This passage highlights both the defeat of the dragon and the triumph of the resurrected saints.

Seizing the dragon

Checkmate! The Devil has no moves left on the cosmic chessboard. An unidentified but obviously powerful angel, "holding in his hand the key to the bottomless pit and a great chain," drags the Devil off to prison. In the pit, he no longer practices his trade: deceiving the nations. Revelation says the length of his sentence twice: 1,000 years (20:2, 20:3). But then comes the ominous statement: "After that he must be let out for a little while" (Rev. 20:3). One last act in Satan's infamous career must be played out.

Reigning with the Lamb

A new administration takes charge. John sees thrones and sitting upon those thrones were individuals entrusted with authority to dispense justice. Though John doesn't name them, they're clearly followers of the Lamb. In the Gospels, Jesus promises his disciples that they'll occupy positions of leadership and judgment when his kingdom fully arrives: "Truly I tell you, at the renewal of all things, when the Son of Man is seated on the throne of his glory, you who have followed me will also sit on twelve thrones, judging the twelve tribes of Israel" (Matthew 19:28; see also Luke 22:29–30, and compare 1 Corinthians 6:2–3 for Paul's contribution to the subject).

John's attention fastens on one group of Jesus's followers: those who pay the ultimate price for their commitment to the Lamb. John sees the souls of the Christian martyrs who were beheaded by the beast. Earlier, during the fifth seal, John saw "the souls of those who had been slaughtered for the word of God and for the testimony they had given" (Rev. 6:9). They were under the altar, and they cried out for justice. The day of reckoning for evil doers has come and so has the day of reward for righteousness.

These souls are suddenly embodied — that is, they receive new, physical bodies, just like Jesus did in his resurrection: "They came to life and reigned with Christ a thousand years" (Rev. 20:4). This event is called "the first resurrection" (Rev. 20:5), and constitutes the fifth of seven blessings enumerated in the book. To experience resurrection places one beyond death; immortality is now an inherent and irreversible attribute. Added to this unending life is the privilege of serving as a priest of God and Jesus. These believer-priests, seated on thrones, reign with Jesus throughout the millennial era — that is, the period of 1,000 years (Rev. 20:6).

Notice the brief editorial comment concerning the fate of nonbelievers who die before Jesus's millennial reign. They, too, experience a resurrection of sorts, but its nature is drastically different from that of the saints; it receives a fuller discussion later in Revelation 20 (see "Termination of Death and Hades," later in this chapter).

Perhaps no single passage in the book of Revelation captures readers' imaginations more than the description of a 1,000-year reign of Jesus on earth, as described in the opening verses of Revelation 20. Hopes for a millennial golden age have stirred the hearts and minds of reformers, politicians, theologians, and poets for generations. Popular media resonate with millennial aspirations under varied figures and images. The question continually resurfaces: Will there truly be a prolonged period of peace and prosperity? Is a golden age in our future? I examine some of these issues in detail at the end of this chapter.

Letting Satan Loose (20:7–10)

Surprisingly, after 1,000 years of lockup, Satan gets paroled! Why does God allow this fiend to go free?

Perhaps the point is to prove once and for all how deeply sin affects the human heart. Even though Jesus himself personally reigns over the earth during the Millennium and Satan is unable to incite rebellion, as soon as Satan is released, he finds willing accomplices. Perhaps the prophet Jeremiah gives the best possible explanation: "The heart is devious above all else; it is perverse — who can understand it?" (Jeremiah 17:9). Scripture also assures us that "all things work together for good for those who love God, who are called according to his purpose" (Romans 8:28). In ways beyond human understanding, Satan's release is woven into God's grand plan.

Reverting to form

Satan, as portrayed in the Bible, is incorrigible. Many theologians think redemption is provided for human beings only, not angels, and Satan himself is a fallen angel (see Job 1:6–12; Ezekiel 28:11–16; Luke 10:18).

In the Bible, angels, like humans, are free moral agents who can decide for or against God. Maybe when Satan leads the primeval angelic rebellion (see 2 Peter 2:4; Jude 4), those who side with him are confirmed in wickedness (this idea appears, for example, in the Jewish apocalyptic work 1 Enoch 15–16). Perhaps this is so because of the enormity of their offense considering their exalted privilege and position. In the case of angels, God seems to require perfect obedience. Satan and his minions opted out and are now, by nature, utterly opposed to God and all that is good.

At any rate, once released from his prison, Satan wastes no time. He at once sets about duping the crowning achievement of God's creation, human beings. It's shocking how easily he carries out his aim. He's an expert in deception with a vast repertoire. Added to that, he knows humans — the children of Adam and Eve — better than they know themselves.

Googling Gog

More mysterious figures enter the fray: Satan goes to the *four corners of the earth* (an expression meaning the entire planet) to summon Gog and Magog to battle. Who are they?

Finding other biblical references

The name Gog appears in three separate texts: 1 Chronicles 5:4, Ezekiel 38–39 (ten times), and Revelation 20:8:

>> In 1 Chronicles 5:4, Gog is a son of Joel of the tribe of Reuben. Obviously, he's not under consideration in Revelation 20.

>> Ezekiel 38:2 mentions a Gog, "the chief prince of Meshech and Tubal." This text is doubtless the background of John's thought. In Ezekiel 38–39, *Magog* is a region to the extreme north of the land of Israel (Ezekiel 38:6). Gog of Magog, lured by the Lord, leads a coalition invasion force against Israel. In Ezekiel's vision, the Lord destroys this vast army on the mountains of Israel.

The name Magog occurs five times: Genesis 10:2; 1 Chronicles 1:5; Ezekiel 38:2, 39:6; and Revelation 20:8. According to Genesis and 1 Chronicles, *Magog* is one of the sons of Japheth, the ancestor of non-Semitic, Euro-Asian peoples.

Discerning what John meant

While Magog was historically a people who lived far north of Israel, it's unlikely that John's intent in Revelation was to be precise about geography or politics. Instead, he uses these names to illustrate a sinister alliance — one that includes nations from the farthest reaches of the earth, all united in opposition to the Lamb. Scholars generally agree that Gog and Magog, often referenced as a kind of end-times "axis of evil," are symbolic rather than literal entities. This interpretation was also widely held among Jewish rabbis, who saw these names as expressions of collective opposition rather than specific peoples.

The *aim* of this G&M coalition, however, is far from symbolic. Once again, Satan orders a frontal assault, this time on the city of Jerusalem, the abode of the redeemed. They attack the rider on the white horse and his army (Rev. 19:19), but G&M are stopped dead in their tracks — but not cold in their tracks. "And fire came down from heaven and consumed them" (Rev. 20:9). Talk about blunt force and trauma! The battle is short and, thankfully, the last.

No sympathy for the devil. His sentence is swift and severe. He joins his minions, the beast and false prophet, in the lake of fire and sulfur (Rev. 20:10). From his first appearance in the Bible in the Garden of Eden (Genesis 3), Satan has consistently sought to frustrate the purposes of God. He's responsible for an incalculable amount of suffering, and his punishment corresponds to his crimes: "tormented day and night forever and ever." The curtain comes down on the final act of his cursed career.

COMING FROM RUSSIA WITHOUT LOVE?

Dispensational students of Bible prophecy claim that Gog is a symbolic name for the leader of Russia and that Magog is an ancient tribal name for that region. They claim that because Russia is far to the north of Israel, this fits geographically. Furthermore, they claim that Meschech and Tubal (Ezekiel 38:2) are equated with the Russian cities Moscow and Tobolsk.

Going a step further, they suggest that *Gog* should not be translated as "chief prince" in Ezekiel 38:2 but as "Rosh." (The Hebrew word *Rosh* usually means "head, leader, commander," and so forth.) They take it as a proper name and appeal to the fact that one of the leading tribes in Russian history is the *Rus*. From this, they infer that Russia invades the land of Israel in the End Times. A difference of opinion surfaces, however, as to the timing of this invasion. Some place it before the Millennium, at the battle of Armageddon (Revelation 9:13–19; 16:12–17), while others follow the order of Ezekiel 38–39 and place it, like Revelation 20:7–10, after the Millennium.

Most scholars are wary of equating ancient biblical names for various tribal, ethnic groups with modern nation-states. Understanding the genre of the book of Revelation is crucial: John employs these ancient tribal names symbolically to depict a final coalition of peoples opposed to the kingdom of Jesus. Beyond that, readers (and preachers!) should exercise caution about making bold predictions involving contemporary nations and states.

Standing at the Great White Throne (20:11–15)

An awe-inspiring vision unfolds in the last third of Revelation 20. A great white throne sits in center stage and dominates the scene, speaking of authority and sovereignty. John doesn't have to say who sits on the throne — that point is uncontested: God the Father and the Lamb preside over this divine courtroom.

The New Testament attributes Judgment Day to both the Father and the Son (see John 5:22; 2 Corinthians 5:10; Romans 14:10; and 2 Timothy 4:1). The white throne judgment differs from other divine judgments in history:

>> Adam and Eve's expulsion from the Garden of Eden (Genesis 3:22–24)

>> Cain's banishment for murdering his brother Abel (Genesis 4:12)

>> The flood in the days of Noah, destroying the entire earth because of human and demonic wickedness (Genesis 7:11–24)

>> The destruction of Pharaoh's empire for infanticide and forced slavery (Exodus 7:14–12:36)

>> The extermination of the Canaanites for their extreme depravity and cruelty (Joshua 1–12)

JUDGING ART

Many artists and writers have labored to recreate the moment of final judgment in Revelation 20:11–15. Michelangelo finished his fresco rendition of "The Last Judgment" in the Sistine Chapel after four tortuous years (1541 CE). Dante Alighieri's literary masterpiece, *The Divine Comedy*, graphically depicts hell in the first *cantica* (section) called "Inferno." And Mozart's opera *Don Giovanni* ("the most perfect opera ever written," according to theologian Søren Kierkegaard) gives a dramatic and musical interpretation when the notorious seducer descends into the fires of hell. These artists were all indebted to John's description of Doomsday in Revelation 20. The scene is unsettling. Standing before God to be judged is indeed cause for concern!

These historical judgments pale in comparison to the final righting of wrongs and vindication of the righteous. According to the Bible, all human beings must give an account for their deeds before God (Romans 14:10–12; 2 Corinthians 5:10; 2 Timothy 4:1; 1 Peter 4:5). For that reason, this scene is properly called the *Last Judgment*.

John's vision shares some features with Daniel's earlier vision of the Last Judgment: "As I watched, thrones were set in place and an Ancient One took his throne. [. . .] The court sat in judgment, and the books were opened" (Daniel 7:9–10). As an afterthought, John mentions that earth and heaven flee from the presence of the one on the throne (Rev. 20:11). John returns to this startling idea in Revelation 21:1. The issue at center stage in this paragraph is the final judgment.

In this section, I explain who is judged, the standard and basis for judgment, and the two diametrically opposed outcomes.

Judgment by the books

The judgment process appears to involve two books. To be more precise, Revelation speaks of a collection of books and a single, very likely large book (20:12). Scholars hold three main views on the relationship between the two:

>> **Only the names of the redeemed are listed in the book of life, and only nonbelievers are listed in the books of deeds.** This view, however, runs contrary to the teaching of Scripture that even believers will be judged based on their deeds (2 Corinthians 5:10; Romans 14:10).

>> **Only the names of the redeemed occur in *both* the books of deeds and the book of life.** On this understanding, the deeds of believers prove the presence of saving and sanctifying faith. Obviously, nonbelievers aren't listed in the book of life because their deeds testify against them. Simply put, genuine faith produces good works (James 2:14–26).

>> **Those whose names are missing from the citizen list, the book of life, may appeal to the books of deeds.** Perhaps, proponents argue, some may even be admitted to the heavenly city at this late hour, testifying to an implicit trust in God and his Messiah. The Apostle Paul is sometimes cited in support of this conjecture:

> *"When Gentiles who do not possess the law, do instinctively what the law requires, these, though not having the law, are a law to them-selves. They show that what the law requires is written down on their hearts, to which their own conscience also bears witness; and their conflicting thoughts will accuse or perhaps excuse them on the day when, according to my gospel, God, through Jesus Christ will judge the secret thoughts of all." (Romans 2:14–16)*

I leave this an open question. What's clear in both the Old and New Testaments, however, is that salvation is not based on works; salvation is by *grace* (unmerited favor from God) through faith. Furthermore, good works are the fruit of genuine faith (Ephesians 2:8–10), and believers are judged based on their works regarding reward or loss of reward in the New Jerusalem (1 Corinthians 3:10–15).

Auditing the books and interviewing the people before the throne

John says, "And I saw the dead, great and small, standing before the throne" (Rev. 20:12). The collection of books holds an account of all their works. This has to be one massive database!

On a premillennial understanding of Revelation, these dead include all the people who have ever lived and have *not* responded to God's offer of salvation — in other words, the great majority are nonbelievers. Premillennialists assume that believers prior to the Millennium have already been judged at Jesus's judgment seat and received their rewards for faithful service or suffered loss for failure to do so (see 1 Corinthians 3:10–15; 2 Corinthians 5:10; and Romans 14:10–12). But many people did survive the great tribulation and entered the millennial era. They and their descendants born during the Millennium must make a personal decision to trust Jesus as Savior. Presumably, many of them do and, presumably, they're included in this judgment scene. But obviously, many do not because Satan is able to deceive a great host at the end of the Millennium. On this reckoning, nonbelievers from the millennial age are also present.

On an amillennial approach to Revelation, things aren't so complicated. Everyone, believers and nonbelievers alike, are present at this final court session because no interim earthly kingdom precedes the eternal state.

SALVATION IN THE WORKS?

While the Bible makes it clear that good deeds by themselves do not guarantee entry into heaven, the issue often feels contentious. Many wonder: If someone leads an honorable and generous life, shouldn't that count for something? Traditional Christian teaching, based on the overall message of Scripture, teaches that good works are the natural outcome of faith in Jesus, not the ticket to eternal life. For generations, respected scholars have affirmed this perspective, grounding it in the breadth of biblical teaching.

(continued)

(continued)

- **No one is *saved* because of good works.** The reason is that even noble deeds can be carried out with impure or false motives; the human heart is deceitful (Jeremiah 17:9). The Apostle Paul's exposé in Romans 3:9–18 builds to this conclusion: "For no human being will be justified in his sight by deeds prescribed by the law, for through the law comes the knowledge of sin" (Romans 3:20). He then summarizes his argument with this indictment: "For there is no distinction, since all have sinned and fall short of the glory of God" (Romans 3:23). The verdict is certain: Innumerable offenses litter everyone's personal transcript.

- **If judgment is on the basis of works, the flip side is that salvation is by grace through faith in Jesus (Ephesians 2:8–9).** Those who truly come to Jesus recognize their shortcoming and cast themselves on the mercy of the court. The work of the Holy Spirit in the heart, what theologians call *regeneration* or the *new birth* (see John 3:3–10), is such that good deeds follow as a natural consequence. Indeed, good deeds are an outward indicator of an inner work of grace but are not sufficient to secure salvation (Galatians 5:6, 6:15; 1 Corinthians 7:19).

- **Salvation comes down to a relationship, not human effort (Galatians 2:15–16).** Those who trust in Jesus are reconciled to God and become part of his spiritual family; they enjoy the privileges of being his children (Galatians 4:6; Romans 5:1, 5:6–11, 8:12–17) and show the fruit of the Spirit in their lives (Galatians 5:16–26). In short, those with admirable deeds turn out to be those who are spiritually reborn and have their names in the book of life. At the end of the day, then, the two sets of books in Revelation are in harmony.

Searching in the book of life

The *book of life* is a listing of all the heirs of God and joint heirs of Jesus (see Romans 8:12–17). In a sense, Jesus is the sole heir of God; however, he willingly shares his inheritance with the redeemed. Believers thus become joint heirs with their elder brother. The sealed scroll in Revelation 5:1–10 seems to function like a last will and testament. A will specifies who is to inherit and what they inherit. At the great white throne, the moment of truth arrives, and everyone learns who the beneficiaries are.

Perhaps first, a search is made of the book of deeds. The life of the individual is, so to speak, an open book. The transcript speaks for itself. But the crucial question is this: Is a person's name also found in the book of life? A listing in the book of life certifies a genuine believer. According to Revelation 20:15, this is decisive: "And anyone whose name was not found written in the book of life was thrown into the lake of fire."

Termination of Death and Hades

Modern readers may wonder what happens to those who die at sea (I have a second great-grandfather who died at sea serving in the British royal navy). Furthermore, what about those whose bodies are cremated? Does this prevent any possibility of resurrection?

John's vision is in harmony with the biblical view that *everyone* experiences a bodily resurrection before the final judgment. The quality of the resurrection of the righteous, however, differs drastically from that of the unrighteous. The root of this conviction goes back to the Old Testament book of Daniel. There you read, "Many of those who sleep in the dust of the earth shall awake, some to everlasting life, and some to shame and everlasting contempt" (Daniel 12:2). Jesus reaffirms this teaching:

"Do not be astonished at this; for the hour is coming when all who are in the graves will hear his voice and will come out — those who have done good, to the resurrection of life, and those who have done evil, to the resurrection of condemnation." (John 5:28–29)

John personifies the realm of the deceased under the twin names of Death and Hades. *Hades* is a Greek term for the place and condition of those who experience the separation of body and spirit called death. Dramatically, John sees the realm of the dead virtually emptied out and poured into the lake of fire. He adds this editorial comment: "This is the second death, the lake of fire" (20:14). With this statement, John closes the book, so to speak, on redemptive history. His next series of visions usher the reader into a new earth and a New Jerusalem.

Sorting Out Two Theological Issues

In this section, I briefly discuss two difficult theological problems — namely, the nature of final punishment and the nature of the Millennium. Instead of arguing for a specific position, I try to describe objectively the various options.

Struggling to understand hell

Christians and non-Christians alike struggle with the idea of hell. What are you to make of the idea of eternal punishment for nonbelievers in the lake of fire? Is such a teaching compatible with the core doctrines of Christianity, especially the love and mercy of God for all human beings?

I make no claim to having the final word on this complex issue. Distinguished theologians have wrestled with these questions and concluded that clear-cut answers remain elusive. Here, I simply present a range of perspectives offered by respected Christian thinkers.

A traditional view: No rest for the wicked

Traditionally, hell is viewed as a condition of eternal, conscious torment. Most Christian theologians through the ages have held this view. However, many of these same theologians have jettisoned a strictly literal lake of fire without abandoning ship on the notion of some form of eternal punishment. They stress the essential nature of hell as exclusion from God's presence. Nonbelievers are cast out or excluded from the blessings and joy of God's presence, the source of all that's truly good. The torment experienced by the impenitent is primarily anguish and remorse.

A minority view: Being wiped out of existence

These concerns prompt some theologians to deeply question the idea that God would impose everlasting punishment. They ask probing questions such as:

>> How can eternal punishment be anything other than torture, and is such a fate consistent with the character of a loving, merciful God?

>> If God teaches forgiveness, why wouldn't God also forgive those who oppose him?

>> Doesn't the existence of an everlasting place of punishment mean that evil is never truly eliminated?

>> Isn't such a punishment far too severe in relation to the wrongdoing?

Considering these questions, they suggest that the lake of fire stands for *annihilation*. That is, nonbelievers cease to exist; they're not conscious and suffer no pain. A slight modification of this view agrees that there's a time of conscious torment for nonbelievers, but it's limited in duration. Afterward, they cease to exist. The philosophical and theological advantage for those holding the annihilation view is that it eliminates the continuing presence of evil in the universe.

A more radical view: Everyone's forgiven

A more radical solution to what some see as the most pressing problem of evil affirms that God eventually pardons and receives virtually everyone into fellowship with himself — except, perhaps, for the devil and his angels! This position is often labeled as *universalism*. A few Christian theologians have dared to champion this position. One of the most noteworthy was the brilliant scholar and churchman Origen (who died 254 CE). His view, however, was later condemned in 553 CE at the Fifth Ecumenical Council in Constantinople (an *ecumenical council* is a called meeting of representative leaders from the entire church having authority to define doctrine and practice for all Christians).

No simple answers

Many Christian scholars see aspects of annihilation and universalism as attractive, but they note weighty objections. The Scriptures treat the destiny of believers and nonbelievers as parallel outcomes. That is, believers are pictured as enjoying the New Jerusalem forever. Nonbelievers are pictured as being in the lake of fire forever. Does limiting the extent of one jeopardize the other?

Perhaps the fundamental problem is the limitation of human language to describe spiritual realities. Scripture employs a range of conventional, even contradictory, figures and expressions to describe hell (for example, fire and darkness). But as with any analogy, these shouldn't be pressed too far.

REMEMBER

It isn't fair to attribute the suffering of the unrepentant solely to God. According to the Bible, this outcome results from choices individuals freely make; each person ultimately becomes who they choose to be, and God honors that decision — even when it leads to tragic consequences. Scripture echoes with urgent warnings about the reality of final judgment, declaring that there is "a fearful prospect of judgment, and a fury of fire that will consume the adversaries" (Hebrews 10:27).

Mulling the meaning of the Millennium

Five times in six verses, John mentions a 1,000-year reign. But how are you to interpret this chronological notation? Symbols, figures, metaphors, and images abound in the book of Revelation. Is the Millennium simply another symbol for a spiritual reality? This question has generated heated debate in Christian circles for a long time. Perhaps the best way to go ahead is simply to lay out the respective viewpoints and their arguments.

Pessimistic premillennialism: A literal 1,000 years

The earliest well-known interpretation of the much-discussed millennial passage in Revelation 20:1–6 is called premillennialism. According to this view, Jesus will return to earth before the 1,000-year kingdom begins and will rule alongside his followers during this period. That's why the term "premillennial" is used: Christ's return precedes the Millennium. The main arguments in favor of premillennialism are outlined below:

>> It's based on a literal reading of the text and coheres with a similar reading of the Old Testament prophets, who proclaim a very this-worldly future kingdom in connection with the Day of the Lord (see, for example, Amos 9:11–15; Joel 3:18–21; Isaiah 2:1–4, 4:2–6; and Jeremiah 31:38–40).

>> The earliest church fathers who write on matters dealing with the End Times appear to be premillennialists. Among these are Papias, Irenaeus, Justin Martyr, Tertullian, and Victorinus. Although such an argument is hardly decisive, neither should it be dismissed. Papias and Justin Martyr are quite close to the apostolic age (when John wrote Revelation), and it's difficult to imagine they already misunderstood the nature of the 1,000 years.

>> The mention of resurrection, specifically designated as "the first resurrection," is most naturally understood as the resurrection of the body, not a spiritual resurrection. The physical nature of the resurrection seems to require a corresponding physical dimension to the 1,000-years reign — in other words, an earthly kingdom.

Premillennialism is typically not optimistic about converting the great majority of the world's population to the gospel. Premillennialists have always been in the forefront of world missions but have not imagined that their evangelistic efforts would ultimately lead to a truly Christian world. Rather, premillennialism holds that at the end of the age, the Dark Lord (Satan) and his evil emissaries succeed in deceiving a majority of people to accept the mark of the beast (see Matthew 24:10–14).

Some critics, especially postmillennialists, find fault with premillennialists for not having more confidence in the power of the gospel to convert unbelievers. Premillennialists respond that Jesus and the apostles never teach that most will accept the gospel. Jesus and the apostles do, however, command that the gospel be preached to all the nations of the world.

Premillennial dispensationalism: Two separate destinies

Dispensationalism is a highly influential variant of premillennialism (see the preceding section). The distinguishing feature of dispensationalism is the conviction that there are two separate peoples of God: Israel (the Jewish people) and the church (all Christian believers). The mission and destiny of these two peoples of God are quite distinct:

>> The ultimate destiny of the Jewish people is to be regathered in their historic homeland and restored as a nation. They're also to put their faith in Jesus of Nazareth as their promised Messiah. Dispensationalism believes that all the Old Testament prophecies about the restoration of Israel are fulfilled literally during the Millennium of Revelation 20. They hold that the literal fulfillment of the Old Testament–covenant promises to Abraham and his descendants is the primary purpose of the Millennium.

>> The church does not share in this future program but rather is raptured out of this world (taken up to heaven) prior to the Great Tribulation. For this reason, another *pre*-gets added to the mix! Dispensationalists are almost exclusively *pretribulationalists* — that is, they believe Jesus returns for the church prior to the "70th week" of Daniel, the Great Tribulation, the Day of the Lord. The church is a heavenly people and has a destiny different from Israel's, reigning with Jesus in the heavens, not on the earth in a literal Jerusalem. (See Chapters 3 and 9–12 for details on the Great Tribulation.)

The cornerstone of dispensationalist thought is their unwavering commitment to interpreting biblical prophecy as literally as possible. For those who favor this approach, it's almost inevitable to adopt a perspective closely aligned with dispensationalism.

Dispensationalists share, perhaps even accentuate, the premillennial pessimistic view that the gospel will not convert the whole world before Jesus returns.

Negative amillennialism: A long, spiritual reign

As the prefix suggests, *amillennialists* reject the notion of a Millennium. This is somewhat misleading. To be sure, they don't believe in an earthly, interim kingdom before the new heaven and new earth (Revelation 21). On the other hand, they do believe in a figurative Millennium, referring to the present gospel era, the reign of deceased saints with Jesus in heaven, or both. In this sense, they affirm a millennial age. The arguments for this approach may be summarized as follows:

>> Amillennialists cite the figurative use of threes, sevens and multiples of six, seven, and twelve throughout the book. Nowhere else in the Bible is a literal, 1,000-year reign of the Messiah over the earth mentioned. In the book of Revelation, where symbols abound and numbers carry a spiritual rather than a literal significance, the 1,000 years simply conveys the idea of a long period of time (on this particular point, many premillennialists agree!). Amillennialists view the 1,000-year reign in a spiritual, not an earthly, sense.

>> To amillennialists, the notion of an earthly, interim kingdom seems to be a backward step. The trajectory of Scripture, according to amillennialists, encourages people to see a movement from the earthly to the heavenly,

from types and shadows to fulfillment and reality, from the temporary to the eternal. Amillennialists definitely reject the dispensational type of premillennialism (see the preceding section) because it seems to undercut the unity of one people of God that's so important to the covenant concept found in the Bible. The distinction between Israel and the church is flatly rejected and often viewed as heretical! Old Testament Israel *is* the church, and the New Testament church *is* the new Israel — one people of God.

>> The reference in Revelation 20:4 to those who "came to life and reigned with Christ a thousand years" is interpreted as a spiritual resurrection. That is, it's really a figurative way of speaking about conversion, about being born again. Thus, the "first resurrection" of Revelation 20:5 is the entire era during which the gospel is preached until Jesus returns. Amillennialists understand the second resurrection to occur in Revelation 20:11–14, when Jesus returns and all the righteous and the wicked are resurrected and stand at the great white throne of judgment (see the earlier section "Standing at the Great White Throne [20:11–15]").

Amillennialists point out that this is certainly a cleaner, simpler position than the premillennialist stance, which involves two resurrections and two different judgments. The dispensational variant, they say, is even more convoluted, with two different "second comings" of Jesus: the pretribulational rapture *for the saints* before the Great Tribulation and the return (or revelation) of Jesus to the earth *with the saints* seven years later.

>> Amillennialists often call attention to a literary technique that John uses. Several times, he recaps the storyline or flow of the narrative. He backs up and looks in more detail at certain pivotal people or events. Amillennialists often insist that Revelation 20:1–6 is another instance of *recapitulation*. After describing Armageddon (Rev. 19:17–21), John backs up and surveys the entire gospel era prior to the last battle. In their view, then, Revelation 20 offers no support for a literal Millennium.

Optimistic postmillennialism: Jesus's fashionably late return

As the prefix suggests, *postmillennialism* holds that Jesus returns *after* the Millennium. Here's a summary of this position:

>> Postmillennialists do not typically insist on a literal 1,000 years; they believe the expression simply means an extended period.

>> In agreement with premillennialists and contrary to amillennialists, postmillennialists hold to an actual, earthly kingdom. In contrast to premillennialists, however, Jesus is not physically present on earth during this golden era. He is

present spiritually, and by the power of the Holy Spirit, the gospel transforms society so that Christianity dominates the world. For this reason, you can consider this view optimistic.

» Postmillennialists appeal to the transformative power of the gospel and suggest premillennialists and amillennialists lack sufficient confidence in God's ability to redeem humanity. Postmillennialists cite biblical texts in which believers are commissioned to tell the good news to the ends of the earth. If the world is the mission field, then God must intend to save the great majority of the world (see Matthew 28:19–20; Acts 1:8; and Romans 1:16). In their view this is confirmed by John's vision of "a great multitude that no one could count from every nation, from all tribes and peoples and languages, standing before the throne and before the Lamb, robed in white, with palm branches in their hands" (Rev. 7:9).

Postmillennialism is not a widely held view. Although its confidence in the power of the gospel is commendable, the Scriptural support is slim. Texts from Jesus and the Apostles strongly suggest that the world won't be Christianized, nor will a majority embrace the gospel (see Luke 18:8; Matthew 24:3–31; 2 Thessalonians 2:3–12; Revelation 13). The actual course of history in the 20th century and the beginning of the 21st century offers little encouragement that the gospel is transforming society. The overall misery index shows little sign of improvement.

The primary contenders in this debate are premillennialists and amillennialists. The relative merits and deficiencies of the arguments are difficult to assess, and the reader with no vested interest in the outcome may be forgiven for thinking it's much ado about nothing! None of the great ecumenical creeds (statements of belief) render a verdict on this question, so I won't either. What do you think?

Chapter **14**

Seeing the New Jerusalem and a Triumphant Church (21:1–22:6)

O ut with the old, in with the new. A new world now replaces the old! In fact, the Greek word that John uses (*kainos*) stresses a quality of newness that means *unused, unprecedented, unworn, uncommon.* Although the old world is destroyed, God doesn't leave it in ashes.

In this chapter, you walk through the glorious newness of Revelation 21–22. John first describes the new heaven and earth in Revelation 21:1–8. Then his attention zeroes in on the centerpiece of this new world order: the New Jerusalem. He takes readers on a virtual tour of the celestial city (so-called because its origin is in heaven), noting some of its features and landmarks along the way (Rev. 21:9–22:6).

Finally, I explore John's imagery, which provides a fitting conclusion not only to his book but to the entire Bible. In short, he portrays the New Jerusalem as a garden of Eden (22:1–5). John Milton, the seventeenth-century English poet, picks up on this theme in his epic poem, *Paradise Regain'd*: God's people return to the garden of Eden.

Exploring a New Creation (21:1–8)

In Revelation 20:11, John says "the earth and the heaven" flee from the presence of the one on the great white throne, and "no place was found for them." As Revelation 21 begins, John describes the nature of the new earth and the quality of life for believers. Although John says there's a new heaven, he focuses on a few features of the new earth. This section unpacks these new qualities.

TECHNICAL STUFF

UNDERSTANDING THE HEAVENS

For modern readers, the Bible may seem to be quaint and quite out-of-date when it comes to the natural order. This shouldn't be worrying. The Bible was written long before the scientific method of hypothesis and empirical observation, which was first developed in the seventeenth century. Remember that the Bible reports on the physical world in terms of simple observation, unaided by microscopes or telescopes. Only the part of creation visible to the naked eye appears In the creation account in Genesis 1.

From the perspective of the Bible and later Jewish and Christian tradition, heaven consists of three main divisions (the Hebrew word for heaven, *shamayim,* is plural in number, in keeping with its three primary meanings):

- The first heaven is the atmosphere above the earth in which the birds fly (Genesis 1:20), the winds blow, the clouds float, and from which rain and snow fall (Genesis 9:14; Judges 5:4; Isaiah 55:9–10). According to Genesis 1:6–8, God made a dome (rendered as "firmament," "expanse," or "vault" in other English translations) separating the waters of the sea from the waters above the dome or atmosphere (see also Psalm 148:4). Genesis 7:11 says this reservoir above the dome was a major source of the flood waters; the other source was subterranean waters upon which the dry land of the earth was supported by the "foundation" and "bases" of the earth (Job 38:4–6; Psalm 102:25; 104:5). Apocalyptic works like *1 Enoch* (chapters 72–82) devote much attention to how the wind, rain, snow, sleet, and hail fall upon the earth through windows in this atmospheric dome.

- The second heaven refers to the celestial heaven: the planets, sun, moon, and stars (Genesis 15:5; Matthew 24:29). This is the realm of outer space. *1 Enoch* (chapters 72–82) also goes into (dreary!) detail about how the sun, moon, and stars move across the second heaven and appear through various portals in the dome below. Their movements occur in a predetermined sequence, thus causing the daily, monthly, and yearly cycles of life.

- The third heaven is above the first two. There, God sits on his throne, surrounded by his angelic retinue. The Apostle Paul says God dwells "in unapproachable light" (1 Timothy 6:16). Paul, like John, was raptured to the third heaven in a vision (2 Corinthians 12:1–4). It's this third meaning most often in view in John's visions. Occasionally, however, John refers to heaven in the sense of meanings one or two (see 8:13, 14:6, and possibly 10:6).

Despite its nonscientific understanding, the biblical notion of multiple heavens adequately depicts God's relation to his creation. After all, even sophisticated astrophysicists still speak about beautiful "sunsets"! The Bible affirms that God "made heaven, the heaven of heavens, with all their host, the earth and all that is on it, the seas and all that is in them" (Nehemiah 9:6; see also Genesis 1:1; 14:19; Psalms 8, 19; John 1:1–3; Colossians 1:15–20). Not only did he make all things, but he also sustains all things. Furthermore, he intends to recreate all things for his own glory (2 Peter 3:13).

Scrapping the old world

John merely says that the first heaven and earth pass away without explaining how this happens. The Apostle Peter, on the other hand, provides a graphic description of the end, which is the culmination of the judgments poured out on the earth described earlier in Revelation 16:17–21 (see Chapters 10–13). Peter writes, "But the day of the Lord will come like a thief, and then the heavens will pass away with a loud noise, and the elements will be dissolved with fire, and the earth and everything that is done on it will be disclosed. [. . .] The heavens will be set ablaze and dissolved, and the elements will melt with fire" (2 Peter 3:10).

Some speculate that this kind of global wipe out results from a nuclear mishap or perhaps even from a gigantic meteor strike. This is unlikely. From his Jewish background, John knows that God spoke the original world into existence *ex nihilo* (out of nothing). In this regard, see Genesis 1, in which God creates simply by voicing a command (see also Hebrews 11:3). So, bringing the old world to an end and recreating a new world is no big deal!

Removing the sea

I wish John had spent more time describing the new creation! What he says is tantalizing, but it raises more questions than it answers. John says simply, "The sea was no more" (Rev. 21:1). What? Does the new earth really lack oceans, a feature distinguishing the present earth from all known planets and the home of a huge number of species?

Taken literally, the new earth radically differs from the old, increasing the amount of land available by almost two and a half times (because approximately 71 percent of the earth's surface is presently covered in water). If this is what John means, this suggests a very large number of God's people and a very spacious dwelling place (see John 14:2; Revelation 7:9).

On the other hand, apocalyptic writings often describe the sea in figurative terms. In some poetic passages in the Old Testament, the sea is likened to the primeval chaos — the earliest period of earth history — and speaks of that which is restless and unruly (see Genesis 1:2; Job 16:12; Psalms 74:13, 89:9, 107:23–29). John has already spoken of the sea as the source of the dragon's great counterfeit: the beast, or antichrist (Rev. 13:1). Perhaps, then, John's statement is a dramatic way of saying that nothing potentially threatening exists in the new creation.

Making a fresh start

Long before John's vision on Patmos, the Old Testament prophet Isaiah foresaw a new heaven and a new earth. As a matter of fact, the Apostle John borrows some of Isaiah's language and imagery. In a key passage, Isaiah speaks in the name of the Lord: "For I am about to create new heavens and a new earth; the former things shall not be remembered or come to mind" (Isaiah 65:17; see also 66:22–23).

Another key Isaiah text depicts a wonderfully transformed world order: "In days to come the mountain of the Lord's house shall be established as the highest of the mountains, and shall be raised above the hills" (Isaiah 2:1). Jerusalem becomes a magnet for world pilgrimage and worship. The nations cease their warfare, and the Lord arbitrates their disputes (Isaiah 2:3–4).

NOT JUST ANOTHER MAKEOVER?

You may wonder why God must make a new creation. Couldn't he simply fix up the old one? In fact, some theologians think renovation is precisely what God does. On this understanding, the dissolving of the elements that Peter mentions in 2 Peter 3:10 doesn't mean matter disappears; rather, matter is reconstituted or reconfigured. By the way, Peter isn't thinking of the modern periodic table when he refers to the elements. Rather, he assumes the ancient Greek notion, widely accepted in the Near East, that the world is made up of four fundamental "elements" — earth, fire, water, and air. At any rate, Peter's point is that the present world is seriously flawed.

The list of things gone wrong in the present world is deeply disturbing: war, ethnic cleansing, genocide, murder, theft, robbery, rape, injustice, dishonesty, pollution, waste, exploitation, greed, poverty, starvation, indifference, selfishness — and on and on. The Old Testament prophets were right: The created order suffers because of human sin (Isaiah 24:4–13).

The magnitude of evil is such that only a brand-new creation is proper for the redeemed people of God. The Apostle Paul personifies the created order and depicts it as longing to be set free from its bondage:

> *"For the creation waits with eager longing for the revealing of the children of God; for the creation was subjected to futility, not of its own will but by the will of the one who subjected it, in hope that the creation itself will be set free from its bondage to decay and will obtain the freedom of the glory of the children of God. We know that the whole creation has been groaning in labor pains until now. [. . .]" (Romans 8:20–22)*

Apocalyptic thought, clearly reflected in the New Testament and especially the book of Revelation, radiates with a long-term optimism: God restores the fallen world to a pristine state. In fact, he does better than that — he creates a perfect world.

Yet another passage from Isaiah describes the great descendant of the house of Jesse and his righteous reign over the earth. Remarkably, his reign transforms even the animal kingdom:

> *"The wolf shall live with the lamb, the leopard shall lie down with the kid, the calf and the lion and the fatling together, and a little child shall lead them. The cow and the bear shall graze, their young shall lie down together; and the lion shall eat straw like the ox. The nursing child shall play over the hole of the asp, and the weaned child shall put its hand on the adder's den. They shall not hurt or destroy on all my holy mountain; for the earth will be full of the knowledge of the Lord as the waters cover the sea." (Isaiah 11:6–9)*

Some interpret these passages to mean that, in the new creation, even the natural order — where predators prey on the weak — is completely transformed. Some even suggest that before humanity's fall, the animals in Eden lived in harmony, free from violence. In this restored world, that peaceful coexistence returns. However, others argue that Isaiah's words are metaphorical, painting a vivid picture of profound moral change among people rather than a literal change in the animal kingdom. Regardless of the interpretation, the message is clear: The new earth will be marked by an astonishing new existence.

Welcoming a city from the sky

Immediately after his cryptic statement "the sea was no more" (Rev. 21:1), John's attention is totally absorbed by a truly awesome scene. Like a spacecraft docking, the holy city, the New Jerusalem, descends upon planet earth (see Figure 14-1). John is quite explicit about this: It comes "down out of heaven from God" (Rev. 21:2). This rings a bell. In John's Gospel, Jesus reassures his distressed disciples that he is going away to prepare a place for them (John 14:3). That "place" is the New Jerusalem which John describes in Revelation 21. The significant thing to note in Revelation 21 is where the New Jerusalem finally docks. It neither hovers over nor orbits planet earth; it comes down to the new earth.

FIGURE 14-1:
The New Jerusalem descending, from the *Cloister Apocalypse,* an early fourteenth-century illustrated manuscript.

© The Cloisters Collection/The Metropolitan Museum of Art/Public Domain

In heaven or on earth?

A new earth with a New Jerusalem raises questions about where believers will end up. Will they be up in heaven, or will they take up residence down on the new earth? The New Testament is somewhat ambiguous on this point and so, not surprisingly, Christian theologians arrive at different positions:

>> Some hold that believers spend eternity in heaven with God, the Lamb, and the holy angels. Biblical support for this view comes primarily from the

Apostle Paul's letters. In two passages, he sketches a scenario in which, at death, the believer passes at once into the presence of Jesus in heaven:

> *"For we know that if the earthly tent we live in is destroyed [a meta-phorical expression for death], we have a building from God, a house not made with hands, eternal in the heavens. [. . .] We would rather be away from the body and at home with the Lord." (2 Corinthians 5:1–8)*

> *"[. . .] My desire is to depart and be with Christ, for that is far better. [. . .] But our citizenship is in heaven, and it is from there that we are expecting a Savior, the Lord Jesus Christ." (Philippians 1:23; 3:20)*

Many Christians believe that the eternal destiny of believers is to dwell in heaven forever, a perspective echoed in ancient Jewish writings like 2 Baruch. This vision is often expanded in popular imagination by the image of heavenly music, inspired by references to harps in Revelation (Rev. 14:2, 15:2). Popular culture delights in imagining the joys of this celestial concert.

» Others think believers spend eternity on a new earth. In this view, the passages cited from Paul's epistles refer not to the eternal state but to an intermediate state that gives way to an eternal reign with Jesus on a new earth, either at the second coming of Jesus (amillennialism) or after the millennium (premillennialism and postmillennialism). Evidence from Revelation in support of this is in the passage describing the fifth seal. There, disembodied souls of the martyrs are depicted under the heavenly altar and are very much conscious of what is going on (Rev. 6:9–11). Furthermore, this view is in keeping with Jewish apocalyptic writings like *Jubilees* and *4 Ezra,* in which a New Jerusalem descends from heaven and replaces the old Jerusalem.

I think the latter view better fits the overall teaching of Scripture. Paul argues in 1 Corinthians 15 that God intends to raise up believers in physical bodies; indeed, immeasurably improved versions (1 Corinthians 15:42–49)! It's hard to imagine why God bothers to bestow new bodies for a purely heavenly existence. Life on a new earth is more in line with the original creation mandate to rule over earth (Genesis 1:26–30) and the very this-worldly, material vision of the new heavens and new earth in Isaiah 65:17–25 and other Old Testament prophets (see Amos 9:13–15 and Jeremiah 31). In short, the popular view probably owes more to Plato, with his disdain for the material, than to the Bible. God doesn't create second-rate stuff (Genesis 1:31)!

Getting ready to see the bride

John uses what may seem like an odd image to describe the holy city as it descends, saying it's "prepared as a bride adorned for her husband" (Rev. 21:2). The original recipients of John's Revelation would've readily understood this description.

The Old Testament occasionally compares Israel to the bride of the Lord (see Isaiah 62:5; Jeremiah 3:1–13; Ezekiel 16:6–14). A marriage bond or covenant shares many similarities with the covenant the Lord made with Israel at Mount Sinai (Exodus 19 and 24); in both cases, mutual obligations must be fulfilled. One prophet, Hosea, who divorced his wife Gomer for unfaithfulness, uses his own crisis as a powerful metaphor to describe how Yahweh (the Lord) is also going to divorce Israel for her covenant unfaithfulness (Hosea 1–2). Thankfully, Hosea prophesies that, in the end, Yahweh takes Israel back and reconciles with her (Hosea 3).

GOD'S CITY

In the Bible, aspirations to form a society began shortly after the fall into sin and the consequent alienation from God (Genesis 3–11). To compensate for his rejection by his fellow humans, Cain built a city (Genesis 4:12–17). Following the great flood of Noah (Genesis 7–8), the descendants of Noah came together to build the great city of Babel (Genesis 11:4) as an act of defiance against God's command to disperse and replenish the earth (Genesis 9:1–7).

These early attempts to create community were followed by an endless succession of great cities: Nineveh, "that great city," (Jonah 1:2); Babylon, of which Nebuchadnezzar boasts, "Is this not magnificent Babylon, which I have built as a royal capital by my mighty power and for my glorious majesty?" (Daniel 4:30); Athens, the cradle of democracy and taproot of Western civilization; and Rome, boasting over 1 million inhabitants and the lens through which the Apostle John depicts mystery Babylon, the great whore. Today, the global community is dominated by sprawling metropolitan centers, the top 20 all exceeding 10 million people. A new word was coined to describe this modern phenomenon: the *megacity*. Human aspirations haven't changed all that much! Still, none of these attempts succeeded in building a truly great society.

The Bible refers to another city, a city that God is building. The letter to the Hebrews describes this city in these words:

> *"But you have come to Mount Zion and to the city of the living God, the heavenly Jerusalem, and to innumerable angels in festal gathering, and to the assembly of the firstborn who are enrolled in heaven, and to God the judge of all, and to the spirits of the righteous made perfect, and to Jesus, the mediator of a new covenant, and to the sprinkled blood that speaks a better word than the blood of Abel." (Hebrews 12:22–24)*

The Apostle Paul reminds his Gentile converts in Galatia that they belong "to the Jerusalem above; she is free, and she is our mother" (Galatians 4:26). He also alludes to this when writing to the Philippians: "But our citizenship is in heaven, and it is from there that we are expecting a Savior, the Lord Jesus Christ" (Philippians 3:20). In both texts, Paul views Jerusalem as a heavenly reality to which people belong, even though it hasn't yet descended to earth. He makes the same point in Colossians 3:3 without explicitly mentioning the heavenly Jerusalem: "[. . .] For you have died, and your life is hidden with Christ in God. When Christ who is your life is revealed, then you also will be revealed with him in glory."

The church father Augustine, in the fourth century, wrote a book entitled *City of God*, contrasting the human attempt to build community with God's great building project. Augustine's thesis is this: Christians don't truly belong to this world; they're part of the community of faith having its citizenship in heaven. This is the ultimate destination of believers, and this idea must shape values and behavior. John Bunyan, the Baptist minister imprisoned for being a non-conformist to the Church of England, also captured this vision in *The Pilgrim's Progress*. All these believers testified that God is creating a community of redeemed people who fully experience what it means to be part of a truly great society.

The New Testament likewise presents the spiritual relationship between the Lord and his redeemed people in marital terms (1 Corinthians 11:2). The most notable instance is in Paul's famous passage about Christian marriage in Ephesians 5:25–32, where the church is likened to the bride of Christ. To be the bride of Jesus, however, the church must dress the part — that is, reflect the requisite virtues worthy of Jesus's bride.

The Greek term translated as "adorned" is the root of the English word "cosmetics." Of course, in Revelation, John envisions a Jewish wedding in which the adorning of the bride is a very costly and elaborate affair. Much time is given over to the preparation of her appearance, apparel, and accessories. Her complexion must shine with a luster like marble. Her hair is braided and interwoven with jewels, gold, and pearls. She is decked with all the precious stones and gems that the family inherited from earlier generations and, if need be, borrowed from friends and neighbors. The bride leaves her father's house in all her finery, with a crown on her head and perfume wafting about her person.

John couldn't have chosen a better way to describe the splendor of the holy city. The prophet Isaiah depicts the Lord's bride in similar terms: "[The Lord] has clothed me with the garments of salvation [. . .] as a bride adorns herself with her jewels" (Isaiah 61:10). The Apostle Paul rhapsodizes on the church as the bride of

Jesus in these words: "[...] so as to present the church to himself [Jesus] in splendor, without a spot or wrinkle or anything of the kind — yes, so that she may be holy and without blemish" (Ephesians 5:27).

Moving in with God

In the new world order, God is continuously and intimately present — and that sort of closeness hasn't happened since God walked with Adam and Eve in the garden of Eden (and Jesus walked the earth). John says simply, "See, the home of God is among mortals. He will dwell with them; they will be his people and God himself will be with them" (Rev. 21:3). This encounter is sometimes called the *beatific vision* because of its utter bliss and blessedness. Rather than simply a physical location, this city is best understood as a vibrant community of people.

The progression in John's vision is significant. First, he says that the "home of God is among mortals." This contrasts with earlier phases of redemptive history, in which the degree of closeness was markedly less. After being kicked out of the garden of Eden, the first human couple no longer had daily visits with God "at the time of the evening breeze" (Genesis 3:8). Instead, during the primeval era (the early period of earth history, as recorded in Genesis 4–11) and the patriarchal era (the time of the founding fathers of the Israelites in the second millennium BCE, as recorded in Genesis 12–50), there were infrequent *theophanies,* appearances or manifestations of God through heavenly representatives or in dreams and visions.

But then, the Bible says, a child is born to a Jewish virgin in Bethlehem (around 6 or 5 BCE). He is a descendant of King David and is named Jesus, meaning "the Lord saves." John offers the theological meaning of this birth in his Gospel: "And the Word became flesh and lived among us, and we have seen his glory, the glory as of a father's own son, full of grace and truth" (John 1:14). Note that the Greek word translated as "lived" in John 1:14 is the same Greek word that's translated as "dwell" in Revelation 21:3. A very literal rendering of this Greek word would be he *tabernacled* among us. For John's original readers, the connection to the Old Testament tabernacle (the portable tent Moses erected in the Sinai desert to house the Ark of the Covenant, as recorded in Exodus 25–40) and this new temple is unmistakable. (See Chapter 10 for more on the Ark of the Covenant.)

Enjoying a new existence

John notes that life in the new world is radically different and supremely better than the old: no more crying, no more pain, and the water (better than bottled!) is free.

Relishing the end of suffering

Characteristics of life now are banished from the new earth and the New Jerusalem (Rev. 21:4):

>> **No more death:** For many, death is the ultimate human tragedy. Why must people be taken from their loved ones? Why can't people continue to live with the vitality and energy of youth? The author of the Old Testament book of Ecclesiastes claims, "All go to one place; all are from the dust, and all turn to dust again" (Ecclesiastes 3:20). But that's not the end of the story, says John: Death will be no more!

>> **No more mourning or crying:** Tears speak of the whole array of human suffering and tragedy. Grief, rejection, failure, disappointment, frustration, suffering, and persecution characterize life outside the Garden of Eden. Who knows how many tears have been shed during the long, dark night of human history? Once again, Ecclesiastes gives expression to the human condition: "Again, I saw all the oppressions that are practiced under the sun. Look, the tears of the oppressed — with no one to comfort them!" (Ecclesiastes 4:1). Thankfully, human responses to tragedy are no longer needed in the new world order.

>> **No more pain:** The word John uses for *pain* is typically used in Scripture to refer to hard, exhausting work. It's labor so strenuous it saps all one's strength. It's the kind of toil the Israelites experienced during their bondage in Egypt (Exodus 1:13–14).

But John may also mean that physical pain itself no longer exists. If so, this points to a radically different kind of existence after the resurrection. In the present, earthly bodies, pain is essential to long-term survival. Without it, people would be unaware of many life-threatening situations. But with immortal bodies (1 Corinthians 15:42–44), this is no longer an issue. The superiority of the spiritual body that the Apostle Paul describes sounds better with each passing year to those who are part of the AARP crowd!

Having a drink

John fastens on one fundamental human need that answers the question of death. In Revelation 21:6, the one on the throne says, "To the thirsty I will give water as a gift from the spring of the water of life." This metaphor has deep roots in the Old Testament and in the teaching of Jesus. Isaiah the prophet is the taproot of this idea. In a short hymn, the prophet portrays redeemed Israel in this word picture: "With joy you will draw water from the wells of salvation" (Isaiah 12:3). In a generally arid land, where water was often a matter of life and death (Isaiah 21:14), it's no surprise that water becomes a symbol of spiritual life.

In John's Gospel, Jesus tells a Samaritan woman he can give her "living water" (John 4:10). To her bewildered response, Jesus adds, "The water that I will give will become in them a spring of water gushing up to eternal life" (John 4:14). No wonder she jumps at the chance!

The supreme moment in which Jesus employs the symbol of water occurs during the festival of Booths in Jerusalem (John 7:1–43). This feast included a seven-day ritual in which the priest carried a golden pitcher of water from the Pool of Siloam up to the Temple. This was a reminder of the miraculous supply of water when the Israelites wandered in the wilderness (Exodus 17:1–5). Dramatically, on the last day of the festival, Jesus cries out to the assembled multitudes, "Let anyone who is thirsty come to me and let the one who believes in me drink. As the scripture has said, 'Out of the believer's heart shall flow rivers of living water'" (John 7:37–38). *Living water* symbolizes eternal life, and this is what John is referring to in Revelation 21:6. All inhabitants of the New Jerusalem have this inexhaustible resource.

Inheriting an eternal treasure

John declares, "Those who conquer will inherit these things, and I will be their God and they will be my children" (Rev. 21:7). "These things" affirms all the items previously mentioned: the banishment of all evil and the presence of all that's truly good. The ultimate heritage of believers is belonging to God's family (Romans 8:14–17).

But what becomes of those excluded from this inheritance? They are left with nothing good or beautiful, nothing true or pure — only what is evil. This stands as the ultimate human tragedy. See Chapter 13.

THE END-ALL, BE-ALL, FROM A TO Z

Three times, the book of Revelation uses the divine title "Alpha and Omega." In Revelation 1:8, it refers to God the Father. In Revelation 21:6 and 22:13, it refers to Jesus. And what does that mean?

Alpha is the first letter of the Greek alphabet, from which the English letter *a* is derived. *Omega* is the last of the 24 letters in the Greek alphabet. In English, when you want to speak of the entire range of possibilities, you can use the expression *from A to Z*. In Greek, that same idea is expressed as *alpha and omega*. The Bible says only God fits the bill. He alone is before and after all things and the source of all things (see 1 Corinthians 8:6). The implication is profound: All that God is, Jesus is. In short, this title affirms the full deity of Jesus Christ.

Taking a Virtual Tour of the New Jerusalem (21:9–27)

Time for a virtual tour of this new city! Most interpreters of the book of Revelation recognize that John's description, although it conveys spiritual realities, shouldn't be squeezed into a literal mold; symbolism and imagery abound. I don't mean to deny that John has a real city in mind; however, readers should be aware that he employs stock images from the apocalyptic thesaurus in order to depict certain features that are especially noteworthy, such as splendor, security, and sanctity.

An angel John has seen before takes him on a guided tour of the New Jerusalem, called "the bride, the wife of the Lamb" (Rev. 21:9). The contrast of Jerusalem (the Lamb's bride) with "Babylon the great, mother of whores and of earth's abominations" (17:5) is deliberate and stark. The two images symbolize two opposing societies. Their completely different stories dominate Revelation 17–22.

John is caught up by the Spirit to get a good look at the holy city. Following apocalyptic conventions (see Ezekiel 40:2; 1 Enoch 17:2), the seer is whisked off to a high mountain providing a spectacular viewpoint. From there, he watches as the holy city descends from heaven to the earth.

His first impression of the city is its glory, its sheer radiance. The city has a luminescence that overwhelms the senses; it's the ultimate "crystal cathedral"! Precious gems and costly jewels convey the splendor of the New Jerusalem.

Admiring the architecture: Walls, gates, and foundations

John examines the city, including its gates, foundations, and walls and records their height, number, names, measurements, and materials.

The city itself is surrounded by a massive wall built on twelve foundations and entered by twelve gates. The gates are named after each of the twelve tribes of Israel, and the foundations are named after the twelve Apostles. Taken together, the gates and foundations emphasize the continuity and unity of the people of God.

In the book of Exodus, twelve pillars were set up at the foot of Mount Sinai representing each of the tribes of Israel as part of the covenant ratification ceremony (24:4). In the wilderness, the tabernacle forms the center of the Israelite camp.

Arrayed around it in a specific order are the twelve tribes, three on each side (Numbers 2:1–34). A part of the land of Canaan is distributed to each tribe after the conquest (Joshua 13–17). The fact that there are twelve gates named after each of the twelve tribes of Israel conveys an unmistakable theological message: The Old Testament people of God from the twelve tribes of Israel are part of the New Jerusalem community, the Fellowship of the Lamb. Those who put their trust in the God of Israel will be there.

The twelve foundations are named in honor of the twelve Apostles of the Lamb — the appointed successors of Jesus and custodians of his gospel. Paul wrote that believers in Jesus are "built upon the foundation of the apostles and prophets, with Christ Jesus himself as the cornerstone. In him the whole structure is joined together and grows into a holy temple in the Lord [. . .]" (Ephesians 2:20–21).

Siege warfare often involved undermining the foundations of walls. City walls are only as strong as their foundations, so builders put enormous effort into constructing walls on solid bedrock. Thus, the twelve foundations memorialize the role of the Apostles in constructing an impregnable church against which "the gates of Hades will not prevail" (Matthew 16:18).

Considering dimensions and shape

The city is a massive cube with all streets intersecting at right angles. Its dimensions are 1,500 miles in length, width, and breadth. (This is the English equivalent of the Greek expression "twelve thousand *stadia*." The NRSV obscures the fact that another twelve actually occurs in the Greek text.) The thickness of the walls is 144 cubits (about 216 feet), which is 12 times 12.

The cube, composed of perfect squares, features prominently in biblical history. The Holy of Holies (inner sanctuary) of the Tabernacle constructed in the wilderness was a cube, about 15 feet in each dimension (Exodus 26). In Solomon's Temple, the holy of holies was also a cube (20 cubits, or 30 feet in each dimension). In Ezekiel's vision of a new Temple, the Holy of Holies was 34 feet per side (Ezekiel 41:3–4).

What's so radically different about John's vision is that *the entire city is a cube*. In theological terms, the city of God, which is also the bride of Jesus, is where God himself dwells with his people. The cubic nature of the New Jerusalem symbolically proclaims its perfection. What John portrays symbolically, Paul describes metaphorically by comparing believers to a "holy temple in the Lord" (Ephesians 2:21–22).

Scoping out the building materials

John's description of the city defies precise analysis. Although the wall is built of jasper, the city itself is composed of translucent gold. Added to that, each of the 12 foundations is adorned with 12 different precious stones, and the 12 gates consist of gigantic, single pearls. The streets, like the city, are "pure gold, transparent as glass" (21:21). John's language symbolizes spiritual realities.

In the Old Testament and Apocrypha, precious stones provide a standard recipe for depicting splendor and glory. Isaiah the prophet describes a restored Jerusalem in the following way: "I am about to set your stones in antimony, and lay your foundations with sapphires. I will make your pinnacles of rubies, your gates of jewels, and all your walls of precious stones" (Isaiah 54:11–12).

APOCRYPHA: NOW WHERE'D WE PUT THOSE BOOKS?

The *Apocrypha,* a word meaning "hidden or esoteric," refers to 14 books appearing in the Old Testament of Roman Catholic and Eastern Orthodox Bibles. The Roman Catholic Church recognizes eleven of them as canonical — that is, as inspired and authoritative. Protestants admit none of the fourteen into the canon of Scripture.

Palestinian Jewish rabbis didn't reckon these works as inspired Scripture, and thus, they don't appear in the Hebrew Bible. Protestants accept this determination as valid, though many (such as Martin Luther) acknowledge that the apocryphal works contain edifying material.

The prophet Ezekiel, in a funeral song over the fall of the king of Tyre, compares the deposed dictator to a cherub (an angelic being) in Paradise before his fall from grace. Consider the description of his splendor: "You were in Eden, the garden of God; every precious stone was your covering, carnelian, chrysolite, and moonstone, beryl, onyx, and jasper, sapphire, turquoise, and emerald; and worked in gold were your settings and your engravings" (Ezekiel 28:13).

In the apocryphal book of Tobit, dating to about the third century BCE, the anonymous author describes Jerusalem's future greatness and glory in these terms: "The gates of Jerusalem will be built with sapphire and emerald and all your walls with precious stones. The towers of Jerusalem will be built with gold, and their battlements with pure gold. The streets of Jerusalem will be paved with ruby and with the stones of Ophir" (Tobit 13:16).

One more piece of information fills out the picture. The twelve stones of the foundations seem modeled after the breastplate worn by the Israelite high priest (Exodus 28:15–20). After detailing the twelve different precious stones, the text concludes by saying, "There shall be 12 stones with names corresponding to the names of the sons of Israel; they shall be like signets, each engraved with its name, for the twelve tribes" (Exodus 18:21).

John's description of the holy city is especially indebted to the breastplate. The New Jerusalem is a priestly city, and all the people of God — the twelve tribes, the new Israel — are priests of God, precisely what Jesus intended for the Fellowship of the Lamb: "To him who loves us and freed us from our sins by his blood, and made us to be a kingdom, *priests serving his God and Father* [. . .]" (Rev. 1:5–6, italics added).

Recognizing what's not there

The New Jerusalem is defined as much by what isn't there as by what is. Revelation 21:22–22:5 details five items or groups of items that aren't present. When you add these five to the two that John has already mentioned, you arrive, not surprisingly, at the magic number seven: The city is the epitome of perfection! Here's the complete list:

>> No sea (21:1)

>> No death, mourning, crying, or pain (21:4)

>> No Temple (21:22)

>> No need of sun and moon (21:23)

>> No night (21:25)

>> Nothing unclean (21:27)

>> No curse (22:3)

The lack of a Temple is unexpected because the Jerusalem Temple was central to Jewish tradition. The Apostles Paul and Peter both use temple imagery to describe the present church (1 Corinthians 3:16–17, 6:19; 2 Corinthians 6:16; Ephesians 2:21; 1 Peter 2:5). The Old Testament prophet Ezekiel spends eight chapters describing and extolling the glories of a third temple he seems to envision on the site of the first and second temples (Ezekiel 40–48).

The first temple was built by Solomon, and it stood from about 970 BCE until it was destroyed by Nebuchadnezzar II in 586 BCE. The second temple was dedicated in 517 BCE and was greatly enlarged and enhanced by Herod the Great beginning in 20 BCE. The Romans destroyed the second temple in 70 CE, near the end of the first Jewish revolt against Rome, only some twenty years before John wrote the book of Revelation. In Jewish literature of this period, prayers for a new and glorious temple appear often.

Furthermore, in the book of Revelation, the conquerors in Philadelphia are promised, "I will make you a pillar in the temple of my God; you will never go out of it" (Rev. 3:21). And Revelation includes numerous references to a heavenly temple (7:15, 11:19, 14:15, 15:5–8, 16:1, 16:17); one would naturally assume a counterpart in the New Jerusalem. So, it comes as a surprise that the New Jerusalem lacks one. On the other hand, John's explanation makes perfect sense: There's no temple building because all that the temple stood for in the past is now realized by the very presence of God: "Its temple is the Lord God the Almighty and the Lamb" (21:22).

Item four lists another astonishing omission: no more sun or moon! The city is so suffused with glory it illuminates itself. The glory of God and the Lamb are a perpetual source of light (Daniel 12:3; 2 Thessalonians 1:10; Romans 8:30; 2 Corinthians 3:18).

The fifth remarkable omission is the absence of night. While scientists might puzzle over how a new earth could exist without darkness, John's explanation simply says, "The first things have passed away" (Rev. 21:4).

Coming Home to the Garden (22:1–6)

The culmination of the vision Jesus gave to John is like stepping back into the garden of Eden — only it's better than the original. The long, dark night of exile is over at last; cherubim no longer guard the garden's entrance with a flaming sword (Genesis 3:24). If you're a C.S. Lewis fan, you'll appreciate a comparison to Narnia; the white witch of the north is dead and gone, the snow melts, and springtime returns!

In this section, I revisit John's description of paradise. It features a crystal-clear river with life-giving properties; its banks are lined with twelve kinds of fruit dispensing healing for the nations. The single most important feature, however, are the two persons who made it possible. Planted squarely in the middle of the garden is the throne of God and the Lamb, surrounded by their willing and worshiping servants. The garden is off limits to all but the redeemed. And once again a reminder is given, "the Lord God will be their light" (Rev. 22:5).

Dipping into the river of life

In Revelation 22, the first feature pointed out is a river; and what a river it is! The river symbolizes spiritual life. No innate human need is more urgently felt and essential than water. The symbolism of this river is so special it requires further unpacking.

What's the source of this wondrous river, with its water as bright and clear as crystal? Right in the very center of the city stands the throne of God and of the Lamb from which flows this life-giving water. The theological point? God himself is source of life.

The origin of this word picture lies deep in the Old Testament Scriptures. In the book of Genesis, the narrator explains that "a river flows out of Eden to water the garden, and from there it divides and becomes four branches" (2:10). John's New Jerusalem incorporates features of the garden of Eden; in other words, biblical history comes full circle. Genesis 2–3 and Revelation 21–22 serve as bookends, framing redemptive history — or to change the analogy, they're like two massive towers of a bridge on opposite banks of a river, suspending the roadway between them. Apocalyptic thought often includes the hope of a return to a primordial garden.

John's description is most indebted to Ezekiel 47:1–12 (see also Joel 3:18). In this passage, Ezekiel describes a river that springs from beneath the threshold of a rebuilt temple in Jerusalem. It flows eastward "below the south end of the threshold of the temple, south of the altar" (Ezekiel 47:1). Particularly striking about Ezekiel's river is the rapid increase in volume and depth as it courses its way from the temple courtyard toward the Dead Sea. After the river exits the temple compound on the east side and flows 150 feet, it's ankle-deep (Ezekiel 47:3). Another 150 feet and the river is knee-deep (Ezekiel 47:4). And by the time it's gone a further 150 feet, the river is waist-deep (Ezekiel 47:4). Finally, 150 more feet brings Ezekiel to a place where the river is so deep it "could not be crossed" (Ezekiel 47:5).

No known river increases in volume so rapidly, but then, this is no ordinary river. It's a symbolic river that speaks of God's power to cleanse the guilt and pollution of sin, sin that affects not only individuals but the entire universe. In Ezekiel's vision, the water transforms the desert into an oasis, and the Dead Sea (so named because the salt content is so high that only the most highly adapted organisms live in it), called the *Salt Sea* in the Old Testament, is converted into a sweet-water lake teeming with fish and lined with trees along its shore. In fact, an abundance of fruit trees lines the channel of this life-giving river. Ezekiel notes that "their leaves will not wither nor their fruit fail. [. . .] Their fruit will be for food, and their leaves for healing" (Ezekiel 47:12; see also Psalm 1:3). John sketches the river of life in the New Jerusalem using Ezekiel's vision as template. (See the earlier section titled "Having a drink" for more details on the symbolism.)

Recovering the tree of life

John's description of the garden changes Ezekiel's many trees with fruit (Ezekiel 47:12) into one tree of life bearing twelve different kinds of fruit (another twelve!).

TECHNICAL STUFF

The idea of a tree of life is far from new. Echoes of this ancient symbol appear across various civilizations, long before John set it in his vision. In early Mesopotamian mythology, legends spoke of a magical tree bestowing life to those who found and tasted its fruit. Similarly, Chinese and Egyptian traditions feature stories and depictions of a tree linked to immortality. These recurring images reveal humanity's enduring desire to overcome mortality and the hope of discovering an elusive path to eternal life.

John is primarily indebted to the Hebrew story of the garden of Eden and its two, most important trees (Genesis 2:8–3:24). In the center of the garden is a tree that provides knowledge of good and evil. Its fruit is forbidden, not to be eaten or touched (Genesis 3:3). There's also the tree of life, which is accessible. After humanity's fall, Scripture records: "See, the man has become like one of us, knowing good and evil; and now, he might reach out and take also from the tree of life, and eat, and live forever" (Genesis 3:22). The phrase "one of us" is often interpreted as a reference to the Trinity, though some suggest it could refer to an angelic council. To prevent eternal separation from God — living forever in a state of alienation like the fallen angels — Adam and Eve are banished from Eden, and its entrance is closed off. Access to the tree of life is lost. This underscores the urgent need for redemption, and as Revelation emphasizes, only the Lamb's sacrificial death can bring restoration, a truth echoed throughout both the Old and New Testaments.

Against that backdrop, John's vision brings salvation history to a satisfying conclusion. The garden is once again open, and all citizens have full and equal access to the tree of life. And the Lord God resumes his daily walks with the crown of his creation! "They will see his face, and his name will be on their foreheads. [. . .] And they will reign forever and ever" (Rev. 22:4).

Chapter **15**

Promising to Return (22:6–21)

In the movie *The Terminator* (an End Times story), Arnold Schwarzenegger's character utters the famous phrase, "I'll be back." Jesus concludes the unveiling of himself and his salvation with an "I'll be back" promise," the central point of the closing verses of Revelation.

John reassures believers of Jesus's enduring promises: a return to earth, rewards for the faithful, the removal of all that is unrighteous, and a reign in a city aglow with divine light. Above all, the faithful are granted the greatest revelation ever, the beatific vision, beholding the face of God and the Lamb!

The portrait is finished, the puzzle completed, every piece in its proper place. Words can hardly capture the joy that fills the hearts of believers. How long will this blessed state last? For all eternity. Until then, the faithful must hold on and hold out, for the King is coming soon.

In this concluding section, John recaps the revelation given him by the risen Christ. You also hear the risen Christ personally issue one last invitation to partake of the living water. He also warns against tampering with the prophecy — this is no light matter!

Verifying the Source of the Message (22:6–8)

Most Christians generally accept that the Bible is a divine revelation. To examine the arguments for the authenticity and authority of the Bible goes beyond the scope of this book. However, what's striking is the unshakable conviction of biblical prophets, sages, psalmists, and apostles that God's word, Scripture, is *self-authenticating*. Listen to John's wording: "These words are trustworthy and true, for the Lord, the God of the spirits of the prophets, has sent his angel to show his servants what must soon take place" (Rev. 22:6).

According to John, God himself authenticates the message that comes from Jesus. The message is delivered by means of an angel, perhaps the same angel mentioned in a similar capacity in Revelation 1:1. John now adds his personal testimony: "I, John, am the one who heard and saw these things" (Rev. 22:8; John 19:36).

Getting to the End on Time (22:7)

When John records Jesus's words in Revelation 22:7 — "I am coming soon" — he brings forward a promise that has puzzled believers through the ages. With nearly two millennia having passed since Revelation was written, many wonder about the delay and question when this return will happen, if at all. For generations, the expectation has persisted, echoing a familiar question children ask their parents: "How much longer?"

The Old Testament prophets who spoke about the Day of the LORD (see Chapter 3) describe it as imminent, impending, right at the doorstep. For example, Isaiah, speaking in the name of God, proclaims, "For soon my salvation will come, and my deliverance be revealed" (Isaiah 56:1). Joel likewise says, "For the Day of the LORD is near" (Joel 1:15). Through Ezekiel, the Lord promises, "they [the exiled people of Israel] shall soon come home" (Ezekiel 36:8) and Zephaniah warns, "The great day of the LORD is near, near and hastening fast" (Zephaniah 1:14).

The New Testament adopts the same note of imminence about Jesus's second coming — the day of the Lord Jesus Christ (see Romans 13:12; James 5:8; 1 Peter 4:7; 1 John 2:18). At the very least, there's a consistency of expectation between both Testaments.

So what's the holdup? Perhaps, as many commentators point out, the real problem is one of perspective. From a human point of view, 2,000 years is incompatible with the notion of imminence. On the other hand, from God's eternal perspective, 2,000 years is a mere blip. As the psalmist says, "For a thousand years in [God's] sight are like yesterday when it is past" (Psalm 90:4).

REMEMBER

Consider this: About 2,000 years after God promised that Abraham's descendants would be as numerous as the stars in the sky and as the sand on the seashore (Genesis 15:5, 22:17), Jesus appeared on earth and launched his church (Galatians 4:4; Acts 1:8; 2:1–47). The Apostle Paul describes those who believe in Jesus as Abraham's spiritual children (Romans 4:1–25). The number of people who identify themselves as Christian was estimated at about 2.3 billion in 2020. It's now about 2,000 years since Jesus walked the earth and launched his church. I'm not making any predictions, just pointing out an interesting correlation. The world *may* be approaching the time of his coming. Be ready!

It's possible that John expected Jesus to return before he died. But John doesn't, nor does any other New Testament spokesperson, not even Jesus himself, predict *when* he returns (Matthew 24:36; 1 Thessalonians 5:1–11).

The sixth beatitude of Revelation — "Blessed is the one who keeps the words of the prophecy of this book" (22:7) — returns to the theme of the first blessing (Rev. 1:3) and emphasizes the importance of doing what is enjoined in the book. The first and sixth beatitudes, like bookends, frame the entire book of Revelation.

Knocking "Other" Worship (22:8–9)

Perhaps as an involuntary response to the overwhelming impact of all he heard and saw, John prostrates himself before the angelic messenger (22:8–9). And for a second time he is curtly reprimanded (see Rev. 19:10). The angel's rebuke sends a pointed message to the Christians in Asia Minor, and by extension, to all Christians in all times and places. Only God is to be worshipped — not angels, emperors, or anyone or anything else in all creation (Exodus 20:3).

Leaving the Scroll Unsealed (22:10–15)

Many refuse to join the Fellowship of the Lamb. They make their own bed and now must lie in it. The angel instructs John not to seal the scroll. Let its contents lie open for inspection and reflection. This stands in contrast to the book of Daniel (and standard apocalyptic literature), where Daniel is told several times to "seal up" his visions in a scroll because they refer "to many days from now" (Daniel

8:26; see also Daniel 12:4, 9). In the case of John's message, the time is short, and the churches must listen up right now.

In antiquity, scrolls were sealed and often stored in jars for safekeeping (see Chapter 8 for more on scrolls and seals). In Revelation, there's no need to reseal the scroll because the churches have immediate need of its message.

In this section, you see how John begins to draw out the practical implications of what he has seen in his visions. He spells out what is going to happen on the day of reckoning. Decisions must be made; one can't sit on the fence. You're either for or against the Lamb. The consequences of the two choices are mutually exclusive. Rest assured, no mistakes are made in the sorting-out process because the eternal God knows his own (2 Timothy 2:19) and dispenses perfect justice.

Making your own choices

Revelation 22:11 might sound callous: "Let the evildoer still do evil, and the filthy still be filthy, and the righteous still do right, and the holy still be holy." Doesn't God care what people do? Is he indifferent to whether they repent?

The verse has a proverbial ring to it. It seems to be saying that most people simply won't change their attitudes and commitments — they won't switch horses midstream! By this time, those who have decided against the kingdom have, like Pharaoh in the days of Moses, hardened their hearts against the truth and are unlikely to have a change of heart; on the other hand, those who have counted the cost and committed to the Fellowship of the Lamb are very unlikely to opt out — they stay the course to the end.

Looking to an eternal judge

Jesus says, "See, I am coming soon; my reward is with me, to repay according to everyone's work. I am the Alpha and the Omega, the first and the last, the beginning and the end" (Rev. 22:12–13). You hear from the Lamb himself.

The message is crisp and clear — everyone may expect to be treated with complete fairness and justice. Each receives precisely what their work merits. At first sight, this may sound contrary to the New Testament teaching that salvation is by grace through faith, not works (Ephesians 2:8–9). The resolution to this antinomy (an apparent contradiction) is this: Genuine faith produces good works (Ephesians 2:10; Galatians 5:6). Lack of good works points inevitably to lack of genuine faith (James 2:14–26). In the end, there's no real conflict.

How can the Lamb assume such responsibility? Here's the short answer: He's God. *Alpha* and *omega* are the first and last letters of the Greek alphabet, and together, they're one way of expressing the notion of eternity, an attribute only God possesses. The Lamb can be an impartial judge because he's not subject to the varying opinions of time and place about what constitutes justice and fairness. From everlasting to everlasting, he knows what's right and wrong, just and unjust.

Reaping reward

The final blessing of Revelation is now invoked, "Blessed are those who wash their robes, so that they will have the right to the tree of life and may enter the city by the gates. Outside are the dogs and sorcerers and fornicators and murderers and idolaters, and everyone who loves and practices falsehood" (Rev. 22:14–15). This text presents two starkly contrasting outcomes. The first is couched in language previously used to describe the New Jerusalem: a return to the Garden of Eden and access to the tree of life (see Rev. 22:1–3 and Chapter 14). The reward amounts to everlasting life and unending companionship with the Lamb and his lambs (the saints, see John 21:15).

Friends forever

Can a state of friendship really exist forever? The Bible says yes. On the way to the garden of Gethsemane, just before Jesus was arrested, the Gospel of John reports Jesus saying to his disciples, "I do not call you servants any longer, because the servant does not know what the master is doing; but I have called you friends, because I have made known to you everything that I have heard from my Father" (John 15:15). Then a bit later, in what's often called the *high priestly prayer,* Jesus requests, "Father, I desire that these also, whom you have given me, may be with me where I am, to see my glory, which you have given me because you loved me before the foundation of the world" (John 17:24). The duration of the relationship is clearly stated: "This is eternal life" (John 17:3). For believers in Jesus, this is not just a possibility; they "have the *right* to the tree of life" (Rev. 22:14, emphasis added). In the words of the old gospel hymn, "What a Friend We Have in Jesus."

Blood-washed robes, the ticket inside

What qualifies a person to be a friend of Jesus? A familiar metaphor reappears in Revelation 22:14: One's robes must be washed in the blood of the Lamb. As seen earlier (Revelation 5:9, 7:14, 12:11, 19:13), this figure of speech portrays a spiritual transformation. The notion of washing one's robes invokes the symbolism of baptism, a cleansing initiation ceremony.

Very early in the Christian church, a special ritual during baptism gave visible expression to this "washing of one's robes." The baptismal candidate came to the baptismal font and took off their outer garment. The candidate was clothed in a white robe after immersion in the water.

Figure 15-1 shows a delicate carving that features three objects: a lamb, a cross, and a dove. The Lamb has its muzzle inserted into the arm of the cross, reminding the viewer that the blood of Jesus the Lamb, voluntarily shed on a cross, is what washes away sins. The dove is a symbol of the Holy Spirit and has in its mouth a wreath of victory. The Lamb wins! Every time Christians celebrate the Lord's Supper, they "proclaim the Lord's death until he comes" (1 Corinthians 11:26).

FIGURE 15-1:
An artist's rendering of The Lamb of God (Agnus Dei) based on an early Christian sarcophagus.

Don't miss the seventh and final benediction of the book (Rev. 22:14)! In the opening greeting of Revelation there is a salutation to Jesus who "loves us and freed us from our sins by his blood" (1:5). Fittingly, the book concludes with a blessing upon the recipients of amazing grace. What is assumed in this blessing is made explicit in Revelation 7:14: "They have washed their robes *and made them white in the blood of the Lamb.*"

Facing punishment: The outsiders

Those who reject the Lamb forfeit entrance into the New Jerusalem. The ominous word *outside* says it all. As I discuss in Chapter 13, the teaching of final punishment is best expressed by the notion of exclusion.

You may wonder, however, who the dogs are in Revelation 22:15, especially if you have a pet dog. In the book of Deuteronomy, the Hebrew word for *dog* is translated as "male prostitute" (23:18). This is probably John's meaning here. Also, calling someone a dog was a common insult. It was a term Jews used to refer to Gentiles. Generally, however, it indicated anyone who was "unclean" by the standards of Jewish ritual purity laws (as found in the Old Testament books of Exodus, Leviticus, Numbers, and Deuteronomy and further expanded and elaborated on in the *Mishnah,* a compilation of rabbinic interpretations of these laws).

John doesn't give a complete listing of those excluded from God's presence. After mentioning behaviors widespread in Greco-Roman society — occult practices and magic, sexual immorality, murder, and idolatry — he inserts a generalizing description: "and everyone who loves and practices falsehood." In many ways, this comes right to the heart of the matter. Paul analyzes human rebellion in much the same way: "They [Gentiles] exchanged the truth about God for a lie and worshiped and served the creature rather than the Creator, who is blessed forever! Amen" (Romans 1:25).

Given that those labeled as sinners have already been consigned to the lake of fire (Rev. 20:15), how can they be described as "outside" the city? Most likely, John is employing familiar imagery to underscore his point: Unbelievers will not be present.

And Now, In Conclusion (22:16–21)

The concluding six verses of the book of Revelation accomplish four aims:

>> Authenticating the source of the message

>> Inviting the reader or listener to respond to the message

>> Warning against tampering with the message

>> Wrapping up the entire book

Jesus himself confirms John's message: "It is I, Jesus, who sent my angel to you with this testimony for the churches" (Rev. 22:16). The immediate audience is specified as "the churches." These churches were the seven churches of the Roman province of Asia and others in the same region (see Chapter 7). The early Christian church throughout the second and third centuries valued the book of Revelation and eventually, though not without a few dissenting voices, officially recognized its place in the canon of Scripture in the fourth century CE (see Chapter 1 for further discussion of this issue). Consequently, Revelation continues to proclaim, "the testimony of Jesus" and summon believers to undivided loyalty.

In this section, we draw attention to John's finishing flourishes. He wraps up with a sweeping invitation and a severe warning. Fittingly, John allows Jesus to have the last word.

Signing the message

By declaring, "I am the root and descendant of David, the bright morning star" (22:16), Jesus affirms his authority and authenticates the message of Revelation with a closing signature. He adds two more distinguished titles to the list already belonging to him (see Chapter 14). These names emphasize both his royal heritage and his radiant, divine identity.

Jesus, the Son of David

The title "root and descendent of David," firmly anchors Jesus's story in the larger story of Israel by reminding readers that he descends from one of the superstars of Hebrew history — David, son of Jesse, shepherd boy, slayer of Goliath, and sovereign over the united Kingdom of Israel. Both Matthew and Luke include a genealogy showing Jesus's lineage from the House of David (Matthew 1:1–18; Luke 3:23–38). Other Bible passages related to this title include the following:

>> "When your [David's] days are fulfilled and you lie down with your ancestors, I will raise up your offspring after you, who shall come forth from your body, and I will establish his kingdom. He shall build a house for my name, and I will establish the throne of his kingdom forever. [. . .] Your house and your kingdom shall be made sure forever before me; your throne shall be established forever." (2 Samuel 7:12–13, 16)

>> "For a child has been born for us, a son given to us; authority rests upon his shoulders; and he is named Wonderful Counselor, Mighty God, Everlasting Father, Prince of Peace. His authority shall grow continually, and there shall be endless peace for the throne of David and his kingdom. He will establish and uphold it with justice and with righteousness from this time onward and forevermore. The zeal of the Lord of hosts will do this." (Isaiah 9:6–7)

> ❯❯ "A shoot shall come out from the stump of Jesse, and a branch shall grow out of his roots. The spirit of the Lord shall rest on him, the spirit of wisdom and understanding, the spirit of counsel and might, the spirit of knowledge and the fear of the Lord. His delight shall be in the fear of the Lord. [. . .] On that day the root of Jesse shall stand as a signal to the peoples; the nations shall inquire of him, and his dwelling shall be glorious." (Isaiah 11:1–2, 10; see also Isaiah 55:3)

The prophets Jeremiah (Jeremiah 23:5–6, 30:9, 33:15, 21, 25–26), Ezekiel (Ezekiel 34:23–24, 37:24–25), Hosea (Hosea 3:5), and Zechariah (Zechariah 12:7–9) all add distinctive touches to an emerging portrait of David's Greater Son. Psalmists also join the prophetic chorus in heralding this descendant (Psalms 89:3–4, 89:19–37, 132:11–18).

The Apostle Paul clearly recognizes the portrait they painted. He announces the gospel of God as "promised beforehand through his prophets in the holy scriptures, the gospel concerning his Son, who was descended from David according to the flesh [. . .]" (Romans 1:1–3; see also 2 Timothy 2:8).

Jesus, the bright morning star

The derivation of the "bright morning star" in Revelation 22:16 is not as straightforward as that of the connection to David. Because of the brightness of the planet Venus seen in the morning skies, the Greeks identified Venus as Aphrodite (goddess of light, love, and beauty), and some commentators think John may have borrowed from this imagery.

Others, however, say it may refer to an Old Testament prophecy. In Numbers 23–24, the prophet Balaam utters four oracles about the future of Israel and its relationship to the surrounding countries. The fourth oracle includes the following passage: "I see him, but not now; I behold him, but not near — a star shall come out of Jacob, and a scepter shall arise out of Israel. . ." (Numbers 24:17). In its context, the prophecy alludes to David who descends from Judah, one of the twelve sons of Jacob. The scepter speaks of his royal power as the founder of the Davidic dynasty. Jewish apocalyptic texts, predating the time of Jesus, interpret Numbers 24:17 as a reference to the Messiah.

Among the church fathers, Numbers 24:17 was interpreted as a reference to Jesus as the promised Messiah. They simply follow in John's footsteps. Jesus's message to the church of Thyatira holds out this reward to those who keep the faith: "To the one who conquers I will also give the morning star" (Numbers 2:28). In short, the bright morning star is Jesus himself. The brightness of the morning star refers to Jesus's glorified state that consists of brilliant light (Matthew 17:2).

Invoking and inviting

Revelation 22:17 has two invocations (calls upon God) and two invitations (calls from God). Both sets involve the climax of redemptive history. Jesus appears to be the one speaking: "The Spirit and the bride say, 'Come.'"

The Spirit is the Holy Spirit, and the bride is the church, or the Fellowship of the Lamb. The command *come* is singular, and it refers to Jesus the bridegroom. The Holy Spirit and the church — the reclamation project of the Holy Spirit — are both eager to bring biblical history to its grand consummation. The bridegroom himself encourages his bride to pray for his soon arrival. This striking metaphor conveys the spiritual union between Jesus and his church, mediated by the Holy Spirit.

Jesus urges those who read his prophecy to embrace its central message and join in the invocation: "And let everyone who hears say, 'Come.'" This is a genuinely universal offer of salvation.

The two invocations are followed by two invitations: "And let everyone who is thirsty come. Let anyone who wishes take the water of life as a gift" (22:17). This recalls similar wording from the prophet Isaiah and from Jesus himself as recorded in John's Gospel:

> ≫ "Ho, everyone who thirsts, come to the waters; and you that have no money, come, buy and eat!" (Isaiah 55:1)

> ≫ "Let anyone who is thirsty come to me, and let the one who believes in me drink." (John 7:37; see John 4:13–14)

To "come and drink" symbolizes entering a personal relationship with God — one marked by obedience and trust. This echoes the Lord's invitation to Moses, Aaron, Nadab, Abihu, and the seventy elders to ascend Mount Sinai and share fellowship in His presence (see Exodus 24). It also mirrors Jesus's call during his ministry: "Come to me, all you who are weary and burdened, and I will give you rest . . . For my yoke is easy, and my burden is light" (Matthew 11:28–30). By responding to Jesus's invitation — accepting him as Savior and Lord — believers secure their place with him, both in the present and for all eternity.

Warning against tampering

One of the conventions of apocalyptic writing is a severe warning against additions and deletions (see 1 *Enoch* 108:6). John's apocalypse is no exception: "I warn everyone who hears the words of the prophecy of this book: if anyone adds to them, God will add to that person the plagues described in this book: if anyone takes away from the words of the book of this prophecy, God will take away that person's share in the tree of life and in the holy city, which are described in this book." (22:18–19)

John calls his book a prophecy (see 1:3) even though it also incorporates a few features of first-century letters and, of course, not a few features of apocalyptic literature (see Chapter 2).

Covenant documents (such as testaments, marriage contracts, and national treaties) also carried weighty sanctions against tampering. In the Old Testament, the Lord warns against additions and subtractions to the Sinai covenant (Deuteronomy 4:2; 12:32; see also Proverbs 30:5–6). Covenant documents possess binding authority and are not subject to being amended or altered at the whim and fancy of those charged with its observance and preservation.

John follows suit making it clear that any addition to or subtraction from his book will result in severe consequences: ". . . the plagues described in this book" and losing a "share in the tree of life and in the holy city" (Revelation 22:18–19). This is serious copyright protection!

Getting a final word from the Lamb

For the third time in Revelation 22, the Lamb promises, "I am coming soon." (22:7, 12, 20). Only this time, there's one small but significant addition: the word *surely*. This translates the little Greek word *nai*, which, in this context, indicates a solemn declaration. This is no idle prediction: The Lion of Judah and the Lamb of God *surely* is coming again.

The Apostle John attaches his enthusiastic agreement: "Amen. Come, Lord Jesus!" This affirmative cry from the heart captures the very wording of the earliest Christians who voiced this prayer in Aramaic the native language of Jesus and his Apostles. This little phrase also pops up (in Greek) in Paul's letter to the Corinthians (1 Corinthians 16:22). In Aramaic, it's two words that you may have seen or heard as one word: *Marana tha* ("Our Lord, Come!").

PS: Be blessed with grace!

Just as business letters often end with formal closings like "Sincerely yours" or "Respectfully yours," so too did letters from the first century. More personal correspondence might conclude with phrases reflecting the warm relationship between sender and recipient.

John's closing is a grace benediction: "The grace of the Lord Jesus be with all the saints. Amen" (Rev. 22:21; see also see Romans 16:20; 1 Corinthians 16:23; 2 Corinthians 13:13; Galatians 6:18; Ephesians 6:23; Philippians 4:23; 1 Thessalonians 5:28; and 2 Thessalonians 3:18).

The word *grace* captures the heart of what the gospel is about: the free, undeserved intervention of God's saving power. It's easy to lose sight of the message of grace in the book of Revelation, with its horrific plagues and terrifying lake of fire. But the overarching message of the book is this: Grace and mercy triumph over sin and death. The devil and his demons do not have the last word; the last word belongs to the Lamb.

4

The Part of Tens

Chapter **16**

Ten Common Questions about the End Times

Although the final book of the Bible is officially known as Revelation, it's easy to imagine giving it a more lighthearted name — something like The Book of Mysteries, John's Compilation of Confusing Visions, or Chronicles of a Fantastic Dream. However, Revelation doesn't have to remain shrouded in mystery; by unpacking its unique symbols and language, you can gain a clearer understanding of its true message.

This chapter sets out to answer ten often asked questions about the End Times, offering clarity and direction as you explore these complex topics. As you journey through each question, you'll also discover helpful pointers to other sections in the book for deeper study. For added insights into the various interpretive perspectives — futurist, preterist, historicist, and idealist remember to refer to Chapter 4.

What Does Eschatology Mean?

The word *eschatology* originates from two Greek words — *eschatos*, meaning "last," and *logos*, meaning "subject-matter or teaching." *Eschatology* is the study of last things that are prophesied in the Bible. These final events, primarily those recorded in Revelation 4–22, include the great tribulation, the return of Christ, the Millennium, the Last Judgment, Armageddon, and heaven and hell.

What Do the Seals, Trumpets, and Bowls Symbolize?

Reference: Revelation 6–16

The seals, trumpets, and bowls symbolize the three stages of a series of judgments foretold in Revelation. As Jesus opens the seven seals of a heavenly scroll, a first series of earth-rattling events begins to unfold (Rev. 6:1–8:1). A second series of more-severe judgments occurs when seven angels play trumpets (Rev. 8:7–11:15). Finally, seven bowls are poured out resulting in the final set of catastrophic, global judgments (Rev. 16:2–17).

Some scholars suggest that the seals, trumpets, and bowls unfold in a sequence — each group of events triggering the next. Others propose that they depict events that overlap or happen simultaneously.

Here's how the different schools of interpretation approach the judgments:

>> Futurists teach that the seals, trumpets, and bowls are key moments that happen either leading up to or during the great tribulation prior to Jesus's second coming. There's no agreement, however, on how they relate to one another.

>> Preterists interpret these events as having occurred during the destruction of Jerusalem in 70 CE.

>> Historicists interpret these judgments as fulfilled progressively throughout church history.

>> Idealists interpret the seals, trumpets, and bowls as symbols portraying the natural disasters and social evils that have always characterized human history.

See Chapters 9, 10, and 12 for more on the seals, trumpets, and bowls.

What's the Great Tribulation?

References: Matthew 24:21; Revelation 7:14

The *tribulation*, or *great tribulation*, is a short period of intense persecution of God's people living on the earth; it's the time during which the seal, trumpet, and bowl judgments of Revelation occur:

>> Futurists believe the great tribulation is a 7-year period preceding the return of Jesus. They usually divide it into two 3.5-year periods. The second half sees the rise of the antichrist and features an all-out assault on Christians.

>> Preterists believe that the great tribulation took place in the first century at the destruction of Jerusalem in 70 CE.

>> Historicists generally interpret the great tribulation not as a final, 7-year period of intense suffering, but as the persecutions and sufferings the church experienced throughout history. Here the agreement ends as historicists offer differing interpretations of how that played out in history. Many Protestants (especially in the Reformed tradition) see these sufferings culminating in the Reformation (16th century CE) and ultimately leading to the second coming.

>> Idealists hold that the prophecies in the book of Revelation are symbolic, not literal. This differs from the other approaches in that the seals, trumpets, and bowls are symbols that depict the continuous spiritual conflict between God and Satan, good and evil throughout history.

See Chapter 13 for details.

What's the Rapture?

References: 1 Thessalonians 4:13–18; Matthew 24:29–31, 24:40–41; 1 Corinthians 15:52

The Bible never actually uses the word *rapture* in the sense people use it in respect to Revelation — that is, a sudden, instantaneous taking up of all living believers into heaven. But the idea isn't without precedent. In biblical history, two men experienced a similar phenomenon: Enoch (Genesis 5:24) and Elijah (2 Kings 2:11). Paul presents this idea in 1 Thessalonians 4:17, where he states, "Then we who are alive, who are left, will be caught up in the clouds together with them to meet the Lord in the air; and so we will be with the Lord forever."

The End Times *rapture* is the theory that believers living in the End Times will be physically removed from the earth and transported directly to heaven. Futurists and premillennialists hold this view, and they have various theories concerning the timing of the rapture:

>> *Pretribulationists* (mostly dispensationalists, whom I discuss in Chapters 3, 4, and 13) hold that the rapture of the church will occur before the tribulation period begins (at Rev. 4:1). This is sometimes called the secret rapture of the church. According to this interpretation, people who are believers prior to the rapture will be spared from the terrible tribulation period. This is the perspective of the *Left Behind* series.

>> *Midtribulationists* hold that the rapture will occur midway through the 7-year great tribulation.

>> *Postribulationists* argue that the rapture occurs at the end of the tribulation, in conjunction with the second coming of Jesus. They hold that the church will be called upon to persevere during the tribulation period. Believers will not be protected from the wrath of the antichrist, but they will be protected from the wrath of God that falls on the antichrist and his kingdom of darkness (see 1 Thessalonians 5:9).

>> A final theory is that the rapture has already taken place in a figurative, spiritual sense. This is said to be what Paul means when he says, "So, if you have been raised with Christ, seek the things that are above, where Christ is seated at the right hand of God . . . for you have died, and your life is hidden with Christ in God. When Christ who is your life is revealed, then you also will be revealed with him in glory" (Colossians 3:1, 3–4).

Many Christians, including those in the Roman Catholic, Eastern Orthodox, and several Protestant traditions, do not embrace the literal rapture concept. This holds true even among believers who interpret Revelation in a literal manner. Those who reject the idea argue that the rapture isn't explicitly taught in Scripture, nor was it a doctrine of the early church.

See Chapter 8 for the lowdown on the various views of the rapture.

Who Are the Four Horsemen of the Apocalypse?

Reference: Revelation 6:1–7

The four horsemen of the Apocalypse are one of the most familiar images of Revelation and the end of the world. The horsemen are the ultimate bearers of bad news and implementers of nasty events; they're released when the Lamb, Jesus, opens the first four seals in Revelation 6. Here's the lineup:

>> The first horseman rides on a white horse. He holds a bow, wears a crown, and rides out as a conqueror bent on conquest.

>> The second horseman rides out on a fiery red horse. He carries a large sword and is given power to make war.

>> The third horseman rides on a black horse. He carries a pair of scales, denoting scarcity of food and goods.

>> The fourth horseman rides out on a pale horse. His rider is Death. The pale color of the horse is sickly, deathly, greenish color.

Granted authority over a quarter of the earth, these four riders wreak havoc through war, famine, disease, and natural catastrophes. While only the final horseman is named in Revelation, tradition refers to them collectively as Conquest, War, Famine, and Death.

Interpretations about the identity of the first equestrian vary widely. Some believe this figure signifies Jesus himself, triumphantly riding in victory; others see him as the embodiment of conquest, while still others interpret the rider as the antichrist. For preterist idealists, the four horsemen collectively symbolize God's supreme authority over evil. Additionally, some preterists suggest that first-century audiences might have recognized the first rider as a reference to the Parthians, historical adversaries of Rome known for charging into battle on white horses.

See Chapter 9 for more on the four horsemen.

Who Is the Antichrist?

References: 1 John 2:18, 22, 4:3; 2 John 7; Rev. 13:1–4; Daniel 7:7–8; 2 Thessalonians 2:3–4, 2:8–10

In connection with Revelation, the *antichrist* is the archenemy of Jesus and the ultimate false prophet. The antichrist appears as a powerful leader who will deceive the world and defy God. He receives his power directly from Satan.

Although often associated with the Revelation's tribulation period, the term *antichrist* never appears in Revelation itself. Instead, it shows up only a handful of times in the epistles of John to label anyone who tries to pervert the gospel (good news) of Jesus and lead God's people into false doctrines and beliefs. For example, in 2 John 1:7, John writes, "For many deceivers have gone out into the world, men who will not acknowledge the coming of Jesus Christ in the flesh; such a one is the deceiver and the antichrist."

Here are the four major interpretations of the antichrist:

>> Futurists believe that the beast from the sea, depicted in Revelation 13, is the antichrist. Others hold that the first rider (see the preceding section) is him.

>> Preterists often understand Nero as the antichrist, or beast.

>> Historicists often understood the antichrist as the Roman Pope.

>> Idealists don't identify the beast or antichrist with a single individual; rather, he symbolizes the evil socio-political systems of the world.

People often believe numerous other Scriptures point to the antichrist, including the fourth beast in Daniel 7, the false Christs that Jesus talks about in Matthew 24:5, 24:23–24, and the "man of lawlessness" that Paul discusses in 2 Thessalonians 2:3–4.

See Chapter 11 for the lowdown on the antichrist.

What's the Mark of the Beast (666)?

Reference: Revelation 13:16–18

Literal interpretations understand the *mark of the beast* as a way in which the false prophet controls the economic system. The mark is applied to a person's right hand or forehead and is required for purchasing or selling items. According to John, believers are strictly warned not to accept this mark, as doing so signifies allegiance to the beast and a rejection of God's commands (Revelation 14:9–12).

In Revelation 13:18, John identifies the mark as the number 666, which has sparked countless theories and interpretations. Many have tried to link this mysterious number to various names by matching it with letters of the alphabet, resulting in a wide range of possibilities — some serious, like Nero, the Pope, Hitler, and Ronald Reagan, and others more humorous or far-fetched. The speculation around 666 can sometimes reach absurd levels!

John describes 666 as "man's number." In biblical symbolism, the number seven often represents divine perfection, while six symbolizes humanity — falling short of perfection. This suggests that six stands for imperfection or even evil, and that 666 could represent a triple emphasis on imperfection, forming a kind of unholy trinity. It's certainly a thought-provoking concept.

Here are some major interpretations of the mark:

>> Futurists believe that the antichrist will use the mark of the beast during the tribulation to control the economic system of the world. Theories about how technology could play a part in the beast's plans range from computer-chip implants to fingerprint-scanning devices.

>> Preterists hold that the mark of the beast refers to the economic persecution that existed against Christians in the first century. Preterists often associate the beast with Nero.

>> Earlier generations of historicists believed that the mark of the beast was belonging to the Roman Catholic Church and worshipping in Latin.

>> Idealists teach that the mark of the beast is a figurative symbol of false religion.

If I could definitively explain what 666 means and exactly pinpoint who the antichrist is, this book would be a best seller! But I can't — and neither can anyone else.

If you'd like to know more, turn to Chapter 11.

What's the Significance of the Term Babylon?

References: Revelation 14:8, 16:19, 17:5, 18:2

In Revelation, *Babylon* symbolizes an organized entity that defies God. A first-century reader of John's Revelation would've clearly understood the evils of a symbolic Babylon. Ancient Babylon (a city found in contemporary Iraq) was a powerful empire in the Old Testament era, and it typified a powerful society that openly and aggressively defied the God of Israel. In the book of Revelation, Babylon represents a collective force or system that stands in opposition to God.

For readers in the first century, John's depiction of Babylon would immediately evoke recognition of its immoral nature. Historically, the ancient city of Babylon — located in what is now Iraq — was a formidable empire during Old Testament times, known for its strength and its blatant rebellion against the God of Israel.

Here are the futurist, preterist, historicist, and idealist takes on Babylon:

>> Futurists hold that Babylon symbolizes an actual city, country, or political system that will arise in the End Times; it emulates the idolatrous values of ancient Babylon. Others suggest that Babylon, at least in the first half of the Tribulation, refers to an apostate (God-defying) religious body, organized by the antichrist.

>> Preterists have mixed views about the symbol of Babylon. Some argue that it's a clear reference to Jerusalem; others believe it refers to Rome.

>> Classic historicism holds that Babylon symbolizes the Roman Catholic Church.

>> Idealism says that Babylon is a figurative description of human society organized against God and indifferent to the claims of Jesus.

See Chapter 12 for more on Babylon.

What's the Millennium?

Reference: Revelation 20:1–6

The *Millennium* is a 1,000-year period that John talks about in the first six verses of Revelation 20. He tells readers that at the start of this period, an angel binds Satan and throws him into the bottomless pit, preventing him from deceiving the nations. After that, Christ will reign with his people over the earth.

Here are three interpretations of the Millennium:

>> *Premillennialism* holds that John is referring to a literal 1,000-year reign on earth after Jesus returns.

>> *Amillennialism* believes the Millennium is a figurative term referring to the extended period between Jesus's birth and his return to earth. Instead of a literal reign of Jesus, this view teaches that he is now reigning in heaven and, spiritually, on earth through his church.

>> *Postmillennialism* teaches that the Millennium refers to the church age, the time between Pentecost (ca. 30 CE) and the return of Christ. This view says the Kingdom of God gradually extends over the entire world and displaces Satan's rule. Once this is complete, Christ returns to earth and inaugurates the new heaven and new earth.

See Chapter 13 for more details on the Millennium.

What's the Lake of Fire?

References: Revelation 19:20, 20:10, 20:14–15

The concept of the lake of fire is a difficult and often debated subject — many find it unsettling to consider the idea of being thrown into an actual lake of fire. However, the Bible presents the lake of fire as the final place for all evil, including Satan, the beast (antichrist), the false prophet, and those who choose to reject Jesus Christ as Lord. Additionally, Death and Hades are also cast into this fiery place, which John refers to as the "second death."

Some believe the lake of fire is not a literal burning lake but an image of never-ending mental and spiritual anguish; others understand it as being eternally separated from God and all that is good. A final group believes the lake of fire will consume those who enter, and they'll cease to exist (annihilationism).

See Chapter 13 for more on this topic.

Chapter **17**

Ten Tips for Interpreting Scripture and Prophecy

Most contemporary texts strive to communicate with the reader. When you pick up a novel by John Grisham, for instance, you rarely need to consult outside sources to grasp its meaning. Reading the daily news online doesn't usually prompt you to call a friend and dissect the journalist's words. Whether sharing stories, ideas, or information, modern authors strive, though not always successfully, to make their message easily understood.

However, in the case of ancient texts translated into English, the task is not always so straightforward. Even though your Bible is in your native language, you encounter several difficulties:

» **Translation:** The original languages — Hebrew, Aramaic, and Greek — are quite different in structure, grammar, and idioms from modern English. Therefore, translating is both an art and science; comprehension depends to a considerable extent on the expertise and skill of the translators.

» **Culture:** The worldview and presuppositions of ancient Middle Eastern cultures differ considerably from the 21st-century outlook. Actions performed and activities prohibited, while obvious to original readers, may seem quite opaque or even shocking to modern sensitivities. A continual pitfall is misinterpreting or misunderstanding certain passages.

> » **Writing style:** The types of literary styles used throughout Scripture add a further layer of complexity and nuance to the text. This is especially true with apocalyptic writings, such as Revelation.

Whenever you read Scripture, you need to bridge these linguistic, historical, and cultural gaps to gain a better (not necessarily a perfect!) understanding of the text. Here are ten rules to aid in the process.

Don't Depend on English Words for Sorting Out Hidden Meanings

In most Scripture, you can take ordinary words and figures of speech at face value; you don't need to discover hidden meanings beneath the text. A plain reading of the text usually gives you the best reading of the text. However, according to an allegorical approach, the apocalyptic nature of Revelation makes this book an exception to the rule. There is an element of truth in this observation, but it shouldn't be taken too far.

TIP

Look at the words in the Bible in light of the meaning of the original languages (Hebrew, Aramaic, or Greek). A good study Bible, Bible dictionary, concordance, and commentary (by a recognized scholar or team of scholars) are essential tools for diving into the original meanings of specific words. Online Bible studies and commentaries, such as StudyLight (www.studylight.org), BibleGateway (www.biblegateway.com), and Bible Hub (www.biblehub.com; an online platform for in-depth Bible study) are good places to start.

Keep Verses in Context

WARNING

When reading the Bible, it's important to recognize how individual words, sentences, and sections work together to communicate meaningful ideas. These expressions are always rooted in a specific historical and literary setting, from which key theological concepts appear. To interpret these ideas accurately, consider them within their immediate verse, then explore them in the broader context of the chapter, the book, and, ultimately, the whole of Scripture.

When reading the Bible, remember that individual passages are the raw material for broader theological ideas and themes. To interpret these accurately, always consider them within their immediate context — first in the verse, then the chapter, the book, and ultimately across the entire narrative of Scripture. This layered approach allows you to grasp the author's intent and the full meaning of the passage. If you ignore context, you may wind up with some pretty offbeat theology. Virtually all cults commit the fundamental error of building theology on isolated passages divorced from their canonical context (the whole Bible).

Look to Other Scripture as a Guide

Scripture sheds light on other portions of Scripture. So, when you're investigating the meaning of a given passage, compare it to related portions of Scripture. A good study Bible with copious cross references is indispensable. For example, as Chapter 3 discusses, Revelation contains imagery and symbols drawn from the Old Testament. To grasp a symbol's significance in Revelation, you should begin by looking at how the imagery functioned in prophetic books like Daniel, Ezekiel, Isaiah, and other prophets, as well as in poetry like the book of Psalms.

TIP

Many Bibles have cross-references in the margins and footnotes of the text. Use them!

Remember the Target Audience

Each part of Scripture was written for a particular audience in a particular time. The more you understand the historical setting and circumstances, the better you understand the author's message. (For info on John's world, see Chapter 2; Chapter 7 discusses Revelation's intended audience.) A good Bible commentary can provide invaluable background material by opening a window into the world of the first readers.

Look for the Original Meaning

The idea of *relativism* — the notion that truth and morality are not absolute but shaped by individual and societal values — can creep into the way you interpret Scripture. In other words, instead of looking at the author's *intended* meaning, you might fall into the trap of focusing on your preferred meaning.

TIP

To look at the original meaning of the author, you need to view a given passage from multiple angles. Here are suggested steps you can take:

>> **Look at what the text actually says.** Using tools mentioned above, discover what the original word was. Then turning to online tools like StudyLight (www.studylight.org) or a Greek/Hebrew dictionary, discover the range of possible meanings for a given biblical word. Compare these options with modern translations. Good commentaries should be trusted companions in sorting out likely meanings.

>> **Get a basic idea of the author's and the book's historical backdrop.** Try to gain an understanding of what would've been in the author's mind. To get this info, you can use online Bible resources. Many study Bibles also provide excellent help in this regard.

REMEMBER

Christians consider all Scripture to be inspired, written with an intended meaning from God. Therefore, when you read Scripture, your mission is to discover that meaning. The application of the message should flow out of its originally intended meaning and not be imposed upon that meaning.

Identify the Literary Style

The Bible has a variety of literary styles, including historical, expository, worship, poetry, prophecy, and apocalyptic. As you read, be aware of the style of text you're reading because that can affect interpretation. For instance

>> You can understand expository/explanatory messages, as in Paul's epistles, quite literally.

>> Poetry, as in Song of Solomon, has allusions, similes, and metaphors that require unpacking.

>> Apocalyptic literature, such as Revelation and Ezekiel, needs to be read with the understanding that the vivid imagery and metaphors are symbolic in nature.

>> You should read prophecy primarily as important messages from God to his people.

>> Read the Psalms as prayers to God full of personal experience expressed through poetic images and symbols.

>> Historical texts, as in Exodus, can be read as a chronicle or narrative of Israel's story in relation to the wider context of the ancient Middle Eastern history.

Therefore, as you consider the meaning of a particular passage, first identify its literary style. A Bible commentary or study Bible is a great resource for this information.

REMEMBER

Remember that figurative language has always been an essential part of human communication. Symbolism, metaphors, and figures of speech abound in Scripture and become second nature when immersed in its pages.

View Fulfilled Prophecy as a Prototype

Many prophecies, particularly those in the Old Testament, have already been fulfilled. For example, Daniel or Isaiah foretells a coming judgment on Israel, and years later, that judgment actually occurs. In fact, probably around one-half of the prophecies were fulfilled within the timeframe of the Bible itself. Use these prophecies as signposts to help you better understand how prophecy in Revelation may be fulfilled. For example, over 400 years before crucifixion was invented as a means of capital punishment, Zechariah (12:10) describes the Messiah's death in language that reflects crucifixion.

Don't Try to Pin Down Timelines for Fulfillment

Although people are always trying to do so, you'll never be able to figure out the exact timing or duration of the fulfillment of a prophecy. In the Old Testament, some prophecy was fulfilled shortly after being given by the prophet; others took hundreds of years to happen, and some still haven't been fulfilled.

TIP

A plain reading of Old Testament prophecy usually makes it possible to determine whether the prophet is talking about things happening in the past, the present, or the future.

Note that Biblical Prophecy Can Have Stages of Fulfillment

When people read prophetic messages, they generally assume its fulfillment occurs at a particular point in time. Although that's true in most instances, a good case can be made that some prophecies actually have multiple fulfillments. Joel

1:2–12 prophesies a devastating locust plague in the near future. That plague almost certainly was fulfilled in Joel's lifetime. But in 2:1–11, Joel foresees another locust plague, this time occurring during the imminent Day of the Lord and featuring an unprecedented locust plague. John adapts Joel's language and applies it to a demonic horde of locusts originating from the bottomless pit during the great tribulation (Revelation 9). The point is that Joel's locust plague had both a near and far fulfillment. The prophet Malachi said Elijah the prophet would come "before the great and terrible day of the Lord comes" (Malachi 4:5). Jesus said that John the Baptist fulfilled that prophecy (Matthew 11:13; 17:9–13). But John seems to place the final fulfillment during the days of the two witnesses as discussed in Revelation 11:6.

Consider that Some Biblical Prophecy Is Conditional

As you read prophecy in the Bible, keep in mind two types of prophetic messages: Some are conditional, dependent upon how God's people (and in the case of the Ninevites, pagans) respond to God's calls for repentance and obedience; other prophecies are unconditional and inevitable. Context usually reveals which type of prophecy you're reading.

Appendix

Glossary

allegorical interpretation: *See* idealism.

amillennialism: A system of Christian eschatology (End-Times teaching) that holds that the millennium depicted in Revelation 20 is not a literal 1,000-year reign of Jesus on earth. Instead, it symbolizes the current age of the church. Amillennialists believe the second coming of Jesus occurs at the end of the church age.

angel: A spiritual messenger of God used to carry out his purposes.

antichrist: During the tribulation, an evil world leader who opposes God and Jesus Christ (Rev. 13:1–10).

apocalypse: A term that sometimes refers to the book of Revelation or to the end of the world. It's derived from the Greek word *apokalupsis,* which means "an unveiling."

apocalyptic literature: A genre of writing that's characteristic of Second Temple Judaism (around 300 BCE to 200 CE) and the early Christian church. The apocalyptic style makes heavy use of vivid imagery and symbolism to portray End-Times events.

apostasy: A desertion or falling away from faith in Christ as savior and Lord.

Ark of the Covenant: The sacred chest in which ancient Israel kept the tablets holding the Ten Commandments.

Armageddon: A geographic or symbolic location at which the last battle between good and evil takes place (Rev. 16:16). The term comes from the Hebrew *har Megiddo,* "mountain of Megiddo" which refers to a site overlooking the Jezreel Valley in modern-day Israel, a strategic strong point and scene of many ancient battles.

Asia: A Roman province that encompassed much of what is now western Turkey. See below.

Asia Minor: The place where the continents of Europe and Asia meet. The Greeks called this region Anatolia from the word *anatolē* meaning, "sunrise or east" because it lay to the east of Greece. Asia minor consists of the western part of Turkey.

Augustine: One of the great fathers of the early Christian church who lived in North Africa from 354–430 CE.

Babylon: Originally an ancient city found in what is now Iraq. In Revelation, John uses Babylon as a code word for Rome which typifies an organized system that defies God in the End Times.

bowl judgments: The final, global judgments that occur when angels pour out seven bowls of God's wrath on rebellious human beings (Rev. 16:2–16:17).

beast of the earth: *See* false prophet.

beast of the sea: *See* antichrist.

book of life: A registry of believers recorded in heaven.

bride of the Lamb: A symbol that refers to the church.

chiliasm: The belief in a literal 1,000-year reign of Jesus on earth (Rev. 20). It's derived from the Greek word *chilias*, meaning 1,000.

Christ: *See* Messiah.

church age: The period of history that lasts from Jesus's ascent into heaven (following his resurrection) until his descent back to earth at the Second Coming.

covenant: A solemn agreement between God and his people in which God promises to take care of them and his people promise to fulfill certain moral and spiritual obligations.

diadem: A crown signifying a sovereign ruler.

dispensationalism: A system of belief, introduced by J.N. Darby of the Plymouth Brethren Church in 1830, that held that human history is divided into seven "dispensations" (eras) that are represented by the seven churches of Revelation 2–3. Dispensationalists hold that we are living near the end of the sixth dispensation and that the seventh period (the millennium) will be preceded by a secret rapture of the church and the great tribulation.

Dionysius: A bishop and later the pope of the influential church of Alexandria during the third century CE. He was one of the first church leaders to argue that John the Apostle did not write Revelation, believing instead that an obscure early church leader name John the Presbyter was the author.

Domitian: A Roman emperor from 81 to 96 CE and a persecutor of Christians throughout the empire.

doxology: A hymn that ascribes all glory and honor to God.

epistle: A book of the New Testament that's written in the form of a letter from an Apostle.

eschatology: A term that refers to the study of the last days. It comes from the Greek word *eschatos*, which means "last" or "extreme."

Ezekiel: An Old Testament prophet who lived in the 500s BCE, during the Babylonian exile. Ezekiel authored the book of Ezekiel, one of the most striking examples of apocalyptic literature in the Bible.

false prophet: An evil spiritual leader who teams up with the antichrist during the great tribulation to deceive people on earth (Rev. 13:11–17, 19:20).

final judgment: *See* Last Judgment.

First Temple: The Jewish Temple that King Solomon raised on Mount Moriah in Jerusalem in the tenth century BCE. It was destroyed by the Babylonian Army of Nebuchadnezzar in 586 BCE.

four horsemen of the apocalypse: Executioners of judgment that are released when the Lamb (Jesus) opens the first four seals in Revelation 6.

futurism: The interpretation of Revelation that holds that, starting with Revelation 4:1, John's prophecy chronicles literal events that will take place on earth sometime in the future. Many futurists are also dispensationalists.

Gabriel (archangel): An angel who serves as a chief messenger from God in the Bible. He appears to the prophet Daniel and to Mary, the mother of Jesus. Some people believe him to be the unnamed angel who blows his horn in Revelation 10.

Gentile: A person who is not Jewish.

Gospel: Literally meaning "good news," the gospel refers to the good news of redemption (being saved from the punishment of sin) that Jesus proclaimed in his life and teachings.

Gospel: One of the first four books of the New Testament: Matthew, Mark, Luke, and John.

grace: God's unmerited favor made possible by the death and resurrection of Jesus.

Great Tribulation: *See* Tribulation.

great white throne judgment: *See* Last Judgment.

Hades: In the New Testament, a term that refers to the temporary location for dead unbelievers between earthly death and Last Judgment (Rev. 20:11–14). In the Old Testament, *Sheol* is the Hebrew term referring to the same place.

heaven: A place where God lives and rules.

hell: The permanent place of punishment for the wicked.

historicism : Interprets the book of Revelation as a symbolic representation of church history from the first century up to the second coming of Christ. The historicist, therefore, sees Revelation as history in the making.

Holy of Holies: The inner sanctuary of the Tabernacle and the Jerusalem Temple in Jerusalem that only the High Priest could enter one time of the year — on Yom Kippur.

idealism: The interpretation of Revelation that holds that the book is a figurative description of the age-old battle between good and evil. The idealist, therefore, does not look for prophecy to be fulfilled in literal events but looks to discern spiritual principles behind the symbolism. Also known as *spiritualism* or *allegoricalism*.

Imperial Cult: During the Roman Empire, the Imperial Cult was the worship of the Roman emperor as a god.

inspiration (of Scripture): The orthodox belief of the church that holds that God guided the writing of the Scripture in such a way that authors, through their own unique personalities and writing styles, wrote God's revelation exactly in the manner in which God wanted the text to be written.

Isaiah: An Old Testament prophet whose ministry took place between 740–687 BCE. He is best known for writing the book of Isaiah.

Jeremiah: A prophet who, from 628–586 BCE, warned Jews of coming disaster and urged his people to turn back to God. He's author of the book of Jeremiah.

Joel: A minor prophet in the Old Testament and author of the book of Joel.

Johannine: Relating to the Apostle John.

lake of fire: The eternal state of unbelievers and Satan separated from God because of their evil and their rejection of Jesus (Rev. 19:20). It's associated with the *second death* in Revelation 20:14 and Revelation 21:8.

Last Judgment: The judgment in which everyone whose name isn't written in the book of life is cast into the lake of fire (Rev 20:12–15). Also known as the *great white throne judgment*.

mark of the beast (666): Literal interpreters of Revelation believe the mark of the beast is an actual number by which the antichrist controls the global economy. The mark itself is placed on a person's right hand or forehead, and it's essential in order to buy and sell goods (Rev. 13:16–18, 14:9–12).

Meggido: *See* Armageddon.

Messiah: A Hebrew title, literally meaning "the anointed one," that refers to the promised savior of ancient Israel. *Christ* is the Greek translation of Messiah.

Michael (archangel): An angel who is mentioned in Revelation 12:7 and is often considered to be the commander of the army of God.

midtribulation rapture: The belief that the rapture will occur in the middle of the tribulation (after 3.5 years).

Millennium: The period of time depicted in Revelation 20 in which Jesus reigns on earth for a 1,000 years. *Amillennialism* holds that this time period is symbolic, but *chiliasm* believes it to be a literal 1,000-year space-time event.

New Jerusalem: The new dwelling place for God's people after the Last Judgment.

Olivet Discourse: A sermon that Jesus gave on the Mount of Olives (found in the Matthew 24, Mark 13, and Luke 21); many scholars interpret it as prophecy concerning future events. It's also known as *Little Apocalypse*.

Parousia: *See* second coming.

Patmos: A small Greek island that John was exiled on when he scribed Revelation.

postmillennialism: The belief that the second coming of Jesus occurs after the Millennium.

post-tribulation rapture: The belief that the rapture will occur at the end of the 7-year tribulation period at or close to the second coming of Jesus.

premillennialism: The belief that all the events from Revelation 1–19 will occur before the millennium begins.

preterism: The interpretation of Revelation that holds that John's prophecy refers not to future events but to events that already took place back in the first century. From this perspective, Revelation is largely fulfilled prophecy.

pretribulation rapture: The belief that the rapture will occur before the 7-year tribulation begins.

Prophecy: A special message from God, often concerning future events that God promises will happen on earth and in heaven. More generally, it can also refer to the act of speaking the mind and counsel of God.

rapture: An event in which all believers on earth are suddenly transported to heaven to be with Jesus. Futurists believe the rapture to be a literal space-time event in the future, occurring just before, in the middle, or at the end of the Tribulation. The term itself comes from the Latin translation of 1 Thessalonians 4:16–17.

seal judgments: A first set of judgments that occurs on earth when the Lamb (Jesus) opens seven seals of a heavenly scroll (Rev. 6:1–8:1).

second coming: The time in history in which Jesus returns to the earth.

second death: Being physically and spiritually removed from the presence of God. Revelation refers to the second death in 2:11, 20:6, 20:14, and 21:8. *See also* lake of fire.

70th week of Daniel: This term refers to the Tribulation period, or the last seven-year period of the 70 weeks (490 years) that Daniel prophesies in Daniel 9:24–27. *See also* Tribulation.

666: *See* mark of the beast (666).

Spiritualism: *See* idealism.

Synoptic Gospels: A term referring to the first three books of the New Testament (Matthew, Mark, and Luke). These books are similar in sequence and structure, and they often use similar wording.

theophany: A visible manifestation of God.

Tribulation: The 7-year period of unprecedented evil that futurists believe will occur prior to the second coming of Jesus. During this period, Satan will exert his power on the earth through the antichrist, and God will unleash a series of judgments against the antichrist and his dark domain (Rev. 6–19). The period of great suffering that Jesus refers to in Matthew 24:21 is often equated with the last half of the tribulation period (sometimes known as the *great tribulation*). *See also* 70th week of Daniel.

trumpet judgments: A set of judgments more severe than the seal judgments that are carried out when seven angels play trumpets (Rev. 8:7–11:15).

Zechariah: A prophet from 520–518 BCE, a time in which Jews who returned from exile were seeking to rebuild the temple and re-establish a Jewish community in the ancient homeland. He is author of the book of Zechariah.

Index

A

Abaddon Apollyon (Destroyer), 194

Abraham (Old Testament figure), 112, 305

action, John's call to, 16

Acts, book of, 81

AD *(Anno Domini),* 3

Adam and Eve, 246, 301

"Adoration of the Lamb" (van Eyck), 157

Akhenaton (Egyptian Pharaoh), 187

Alexander the Great (Greek king), 219, 253

allegorical view, 62, 63. *See also* idealist view

alpha, 294, 306

alpha-omega, 294, 306

amillennialist view

   described, 324, 333

   at Millennium, 91, 279–280

   parallel events, 20

Amos, prophet and book of, 173–174, 192

angel(s). *See also* seven trumpets; twenty-four elders

   avoiding veneration of, 262, 305

   Babylon, fall of, 257–258

   choirs of, 260–261, 333

   defined, 333

   as free moral agents, 268

   New Jerusalem tour, 295–299

   the 144,000, identifying, 178

   preamble to God's final wrath, 234–238

   Satan as fallen, 268

   second coming, 260–262

   three angels with three messages, 227–229

Animal Apocalypse, 210–211

annihilation, 276

Anno Domini (AD), 3

Anointed One, Jesus as, 100

Antichrist, 1, 51, 53, 166–167, 218–219, 321–322

Antiochus Epiphanes (Greek king), 54

Antiochus IV Epiphanes (Greek king), 220

anti-papal interpretations, 64

Antipas (martyr), 30, 222

anti-Semites, 137

apocalypse, 2, 97–100, 333

Apocalypse, four horsemen of the, 88–90, 164–168, 320–321, 335

Apocalypse, Little (Olivet Discourse), 46, 54–57, 165–166, 336

apocalyptic imagery, 84, 162

apocalypticism, 97–98

apocalyptic literature, 38–39, 198, 330, 333

apocalyptic writing, 235, 312–313

Apocrypha, 2, 297

apostasy, 35, 146, 333

Apostles, 111, 295. *See also specific Apostles*

   appearance of God (physical), 142

   appearance of God (theophany), 185–186, 235, 292, 337

archangels

   Gabriel, 49, 50, 151, 335

   greetings from seven, 104

   and little scroll, seven trumpets, 198

   Michael, 151, 214, 216, 336

   Mighty angel, 92–93

architecture of New Jerusalem, 295–296

Ark of the Covenant, 205–207, 333

Armageddon (war in heaven), 1, 15, 243–245, 265, 333

Artemis (goddess), 124

Asia Minor, 24, 33, 35, 104, 333. *See also* seven churches, messages to

Athens, 290

Attalus III (Philadelphian king), 127, 134

attention, John's bid to get, 110

audience considerations

   Revelation, 38, 80, 309–310

   Scripture, 329

   seven churches, messages to, 11, 13, 86, 309

Augustine (church father, author), 63, 291, 333

Augustus (Roman emperor), 28, 249

B

Babel, 290
Babylon, 85, 86, 91
  Babylonian captivity, 46–47, 49
  city creation, 290
  compared to New Jerusalem, 295
  Daniel's 70 weeks prophecy, 47–54
  described, 323–324, 333
  escape from, 255
  fall of, 88, 227–228, 252–258
  the great harlot, 247–248, 257–258
  historical, 252
  on many waters, 247, 251
  market collapse, 256
  pregnant woman as, 211
  scarlet beast, 247–251
  as symbol, 88
  three angels proclaiming fall of, 227–228
Balaam (false prophet), 129, 311
barbarians, 135
Bar Kokhba (Jewish leader), 231
Baruch, book of, 100, 289
BC (before Christ), 3
BCE (before common era), 3
beasts. *See also* mark of the beast (666)
  of the earth, 47, 221
  of the sea, 218–219
  seven trumpet interlude, 200, 204
beatific vision, 292
beatitudes/benedictions/blessings, 102, 229, 262, 305, 313
before Christ (BC), 3
before common era (BCE), 3
Behemoth, 221
believers as priests, in doxology, 105–106
benedictions/blessings/beatitudes, 102, 229, 262, 313
Bible. *See also* New Testament; Old Testament; Scripture; *specific books of the Bible*
  citation conventions, 2
  King James Version (KJV), 265
  as reason to read Revelation, 10
  self-authenticating word of God, 304
  study, to aid in understanding, 328
  verses, 2, 328–329
BibleGateway (Web site), 328
biblical Christianity, 2–3, 330

biblical prophecy, 3
  audience considerations, 329
  compared to other Scripture, 329
  conditional prophecy, 332
  context for verses, 328–329
  cultural challenges, 327
  Daniel's 70 weeks prophecy, 49–54
  defined, 40
  fulfilled prophecy as prototype, 331–332
  Old Testament, 44–57
  Olivet Discourse, 54–57
  original meaning, 329–330
  as Revelation background, 42–44
  stages of fulfillment, 331–332
  style considerations, 327, 330–331
  timelines and fulfilled prophecy, 331
  translation challenges, 327
Black Death, 169
black horse, four horsemen of the Apocalypse, 90, 168
blessings/beatitudes/benedictions, 102, 229, 262, 313
blood
  fresh water into blood, 191, 241
  as high as a bridle, 231
  red horse, four horsemen of the Apocalypse, 90, 167
  robes washed in blood of Lamb, 177, 264, 307–308
  trumpet plague of, 190
  water into blood, seven bowls, 241
bodily resurrection, 109, 267, 275
Bonaparte, Napoleon (French emperor), 224, 244
book of life, 15, 153, 272–273, 334
books of Bible. *See specific books of the Bible*
books of deeds, 272–273
bow and white horse, four horsemen of the Apocalypse, 90, 166–167
bowl judgments, 333. *See also* seven bowls of wrath
bride of the Lamb, 246, 257, 334
bright morning star, Jesus as, 311
building materials, New Jerusalem, 297–298
Bunyan, John (author), 291

C

Caligula (Roman emperor), 28, 222, 249
canon, 108
Catholics, 2

historical text, as literary style, 330

historic Christianity, 2–3

historicist view

Antichrist, 322

Babylon, 324

defined, 62, 335

evaluating, 78–82

interpretation, 63–64, 71–72, 80–85

John's audience, 80–81

as literal or allegorical, 62, 63

mark of the beast (666), 323

overview, 71

pros and cons, 72

purpose of Revelation, 71–72

on seals, trumpets and bowls, 196, 239, 318

timeline, 67

on Tribulation, 319

Holy of Holies, 205–206, 296, 335

Holy Spirit, 104, 236

hope, as reason to read Revelation, 10

horns, of Lamb, 155, 158, 221–222

horsemen of the Apocalypse, 88–90, 164–168, 320–321, 335

Hosea, prophet and book of, 311

Hussein, Saddam (Iraqi president), 228

hymns, 105, 151, 236, 260–261, 334

I

idealist view

Antichrist, 322

Babylon, 324

defined, 62, 335

evaluating, 78–82

interpretation, 63–64, 76–78

John's audience, 80–81

as literal or allegorical, 62, 63

mark of the beast (666), 323

pros and cons, 77–78

on seals, trumpets, and bowls, 195, 228, 318

timeline, 67

on Tribulation, 319

immanence (omnipresence), 177

immediacy and timing, 80, 147, 162

imminence of second coming, 304–305

imperator, 250

Imperial Cult, 222, 335

imprimatur, 107

indirectly explained symbols, 87

infidelity, 289

initiating vision, 107

inspiration (of Scripture), 40, 335

interlude

seven bowls, 245

seven seals, 165, 176–181

seven trumpets, 197–199

interludes, 16–17

internal evidence of authorship, 23, 24

interpretation. See symbolism and interpretation

"in the Spirit" experiences of John, 17, 108

invisible-visible dualism, 99

invocations and invitations from Jesus, 312

Irenaeus (bishop of Lyons), 23, 150, 223

iron scepter, male child with, 213

Isaiah, prophet and book of

appearance of God (physical), 142

Babylon, fall of, 228, 247, 253

Day of the Lord, 243

described, 173–174, 336

End Times, 46

grape harvest, 230–231

Jesus's lineage, 310–311

on Messiah, 287

messianic prophecies, 46, 287

new heaven and earth, 286–287

Tabernacle, 237

Transfiguration, 111

24 elders, 149

Israel

Babylon captivity in Daniel, 49–54

Egypt, deliverance from, 43

Passover Lamb, 156

as tribe, 178

trumpets in, 189, 202

12 tribes of, 178, 295, 296

J

Jacob (Old Testament patriarch), 179

James, Apostle, 22, 111

Jenkins, Jerry (author), 145

Jeremiah, prophet and book of, 49, 166, 255, 258, 311

R

S

Sadducees, 175, 214

salvation, 177, 273–274, 306

Samuel 2, book of, 310

Sardis, church at
  message overview, 13
  promises to, 153
  seven stars and lampstands, 114
  virtues and vices in, 13

Sargon I (Assyrian king), 252

Satan, 15. *See also* mark of the beast (666); seven owls of wrath; seven trumpets
  Antichrist, 51, 53, 166–167, 218–221, 321
  defined, 266
  dualism, 98–100
  in Garden of Eden, 270, 271
  Millennial capture and release, 266–270
  red dragon and pregnant women, 16, 88, 93, 210–218

scales and black horse, four horsemen of the Apocalypse, 90, 168

scarlet beast of Babylon, 247–251

scepter, male child with, 213

Scripture. *See also* Bible
  audience considerations, 329
  compared to other Scripture, 329
  conditional prophecy, 332
  context for verses, 328–329
  cultural challenges, 327
  fulfilled prophecy, 331–332
  God's appearance in, 142
  Law and the Prophets, 202
  original meaning, 329–330
  style and translation considerations, 327, 330–331

scroll(s). *See also* seven seals
  as book of destiny, 153–154
  Dead Sea Scrolls, 149, 175
  eating, by John, 16
  as last will and testament, 152–153, 274
  left unsealed, 305–309
  little, and angel, seven trumpet interlude, 197–199
  as symbol, 88, 89

sea, 218, 241, 285–287

sea, beast of the, 218–221

sealed scroll, opening, 152–158

seal judgments, 14, 337

seals, 88, 89, 318. *See also* seven seals

seas, plague on, 184, 191

second coming
  Armageddon clean-up, 265
  avoiding angel veneration, 262
  defined, 337
  as "good news", 166
  Hallelujah, 260–261
  imminence of, 304–305
  John's announcement of, 108
  of Lamb, 313
  post-tribulation rapture, 145–146
  seventh seal, 165, 181–182
  white horse with armies of heaven, 260, 262–265

second death, 275, 325, 337

Second Esdras, book of, 100

second heaven, 284–285

second Temple, 174, 201, 235, 248, 299

self-authenticating word of God, 304

Sennacherib (Assyrian king), 265

Septuagint, 23

serpent, 212, 216, 266

Suetonius (historian), 172

seven, as number, 89, 162

seven angels and seven bowls, 234–238

seven archangels, 150

seven bowls of wrath, 14
  as apocalyptic imagery, 162
  bowl 1, plague of sores, 240
  bowl 2, sea water into blood, 241
  bowl 3, fresh water into blood, 241
  bowl 4, sun scorches the earth, 241
  bowl 5, darkness, 242–243
  bowl 6, battle at Megiddo, 243–245
  bowl 7, earthquake and hail, 235
  futurist view, 240
  historicist view, 239
  idealist view, 239–240
  post-tribulation rapture, 145–146
  preterist view, 239
  scope of, 163
  sixth seal, and Day of the Lord, 163
  as symbol, 88, 91, 318
  voice of divine judgment, 238

Trinitarian, 3

Trinity, 224

trumpet, role of, 189

trumpet judgment, 337. *See also* seven trumpets

12, New Jerusalem, 296–298

12 Apostles of the Lamb, 296

12 tribes of Israel, 178, 295, 296

24 elders

Hallelujah, 261

seventh trumpet, 205–206

as symbol, 88

throne room, 148–149, 151, 176

two witnesses, seven trumpets, 88, 200, 202–203

U

unexplained symbolism, 87

unity reinforcement through symbolism, 86

universalism, 277

V

van Eyck, Jan (artist), 157

verses, 328–329

verso of scroll, writing on, 154

Vespasian (Roman emperor), 28, 249

Virgin Mary, pregnant woman as, 212

virgins and virtue, and mark of the lamb, 225–226

visible-invisible dualism, 99

visions of John. *See specific topics*

Vitellius (Roman emperor), 28, 250

voice of divine judgment, 238

W

war in heaven (Armageddon), 243–245, 265, 333

water

Babylon on, 247, 251

flood and Noah, 56, 147, 194, 271, 290

fresh water into blood, 184, 191–192, 241

living water, 294

sea, 218, 285–287

Web sites for Bible commentary, 328–330

wedding, symbolic, 260–262, 290–292

Westminster Confession of Faith (Church of England), 223

white horse

four horsemen of the Apocalypse, 89, 166–167

second coming, 263–265

white robe, robes washed in blood of Lamb, 177, 216, 264, 307–308

white throne judgment, 271–275

whore of Babylon, 247–252

will, scroll as, 152–153, 274

wings of a great eagle, 88, 214

witnesses

Jesus as faithful witness, 105, 263

seven trumpet interlude, 88, 200, 202–203

temple of the tent of witness, 237

Wonderful Counselor, Jesus as, 265

Word of God, 263, 304

works and faith, 274

Wormwood (star), 191

worship, as literary style, 330

X

Xerxes (Persian king), 253

Y

year-day principle, historicist view, 72

Z

Zechariah, prophet and book of

apocalyptic imagery and literary style, 25, 98, 331

defined, 48–49, 337

End Times in Jerusalem, 245–246

four horsemen of the Apocalypse, 44, 166

Jesus's lineage, 311

measuring temple, 201

second coming, 108

Zerubbabel (witness), 202

Zeus, Temple of (Pergamum), 128

About the Author

Dr. Larry R. Helyer is Professor Emeritus of Biblical Studies at Taylor University in Upland, Indiana. He received his doctorate in Biblical Studies from Fuller Theological Seminary, Pasadena, California. He pastored Baptist churches in Portland, Oregon, and Sun Valley, California, before moving to the Midwest and teaching biblical studies at Taylor University for 30 years. He has taught a wide range of Bible courses covering both the Old and New Testaments and Jewish literature of the Second Temple. Larry lived in Israel for a year during his student days at Jerusalem University College and has been a Bible teacher for tours in Greece, Turkey, and Israel. He is author of *Yesterday, Today, and Forever: The Continuing Relevance of the Old Testament, Exploring Jewish Literature of the Second Temple Period: A Guide for New Testament Students, The Witness of Jesus, Paul and John, The Life and Witness of Peter, Mountaintop Theology, The Life and Witness of David, The Life and Witness of Jeremiah*, and *The Life and Witness of Ezekiel*. He has also authored numerous journal and dictionary articles on biblical and theological subjects and was the initial translator of Second Samuel for the *Holman Christian Standard Bible*.

The first edition of this volume was a significant contribution toward understanding one of the most challenging books in the NT and this edition is better yet. Dr. Helyer is very familiar with the current critical literature on Revelation and combines the humor in the title with an excellent introduction to one of the most controversial biblical books. The revised and reorganized content including new illustrations are most helpful as well as the new sections on the millennium and sharpening his updated views on the interpretation of Revelation. Helyer's new investigations add considerably to this new edition. Few scholars of Revelation come close to Helyer's careful and well-researched interpretation that is both available to lay-readers and biblical scholars alike. I recommend this new edition without reservation.

—LEE MARTIN MCDONALD, PHD, PRESIDENT EMERITUS AND PROFESSOR OF NEW TESTAMENT STUDIES AT ACADIA DIVINITY COLLEGE; DEAN OF THE FACULTY OF THEOLOGY AT ACADIA UNIVERSITY; AND PAST PRESIDENT OF INSTITUTE FOR BIBLICAL RESEARCH.

Dedication

This book is lovingly dedicated to Joyce, my cherished wife of sixty years. She has been my closest companion, exemplifies the qualities of a virtuous woman (Proverbs 31:10), and, like Abigail, is truly "intelligent and beautiful" (1 Samuel 25:3).

Author's Acknowledgments

I deeply appreciate the support I received from the Wiley Publishing team during this revision. Editorial Assistant, Shannon Kucaj, Senior Project Editor, Paul Levesque, and Associate Acquisitions Editor, Alicia Sparrow, all offered helpful guidance that greatly contributed to the completion of the project. I would like to extend special thanks to my outstanding Development Editor, Jennifer Connolly. Her knowledge of the Dummies format and her patient guidance helped me navigate each step of the process.

My literary agent, Matt Wagner, reached out to me regarding the possibility of producing a second edition. Thanks, Matt, for negotiating the contract and overseeing financial arrangements.

I would like to offer a heartfelt tribute to Richard Wagner, Matt's brother. Richard co-authored the first edition with me, and his influence remains deeply woven into this second edition. Though he is now "with Christ, which is better by far" (Philippians 1:23), his legacy endures. May his memory continue to be a source of blessing.

Lastly, I want to express gratitude to former teachers. Dr. David Allan Hubbard and Dr. Ralph P. Martin played pivotal roles in shaping my perspective on biblical studies. Their mentorship has had a lasting impact on my journey, and I cherish the hope of meeting them again in the New Jerusalem.

Publisher's Acknowledgments

Associate Acquisitions Editor: Alicia Sparrow

Development Editor: Jennifer Connolly

Copy Editor: Jennifer Connolly

Editorial Assistant: Shannon Kucaj

Managing Editor: Murari Mukundan

Production Editor: Bharaneedharan Murthy

Cover Image: © Tuul & Bruno Morandi/ Getty Images